GW00818420

PART 2

Paper 2.1

Information Systems

ACCA Textbook

Official Publisher

FOULKS LYNCH
PUBLICATIONS

British Library Cataloguing-in-Publication Data

A catalogue record for this book is available from the British Library.

Published by Foulks Lynch Ltd
4, The Griffin Centre
Staines Road
Feltham
Middlesex
TW14 0HS

ISBN 0 7483 6261 4

© Foulks Lynch Ltd, 2003

Printed and bound in Great Britain by Ashford Colour Press Ltd, Gosport.

Acknowledgements

We are grateful to the Association of Chartered Certified Accountants and the Chartered Institute of Management Accountants. The answers have been prepared by Foulks Lynch Ltd.

Contents

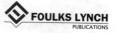

Introduction

This Textbook is the ACCA's official text for Paper 2.1 *Information Systems*, and is part of the ACCA's official series produced for students taking the ACCA examinations.

This new edition, updated for 2004 exams, has been produced with direct guidance from the examiner. It covers the syllabus and study guide in great detail, giving appropriate weighting to the various topics. Targeted very closely on the examination, this textbook is written in a way that will help you assimilate the information easily. Numerous practice questions and exam type questions at the end of each chapter reinforce your knowledge.

DEFINITION

- **Definitions.** The text defines key words and concepts, placing them in the margin, with a clear heading, as on the left. The purpose of including these definitions is to focus your attention on the point being covered.

KEY POINT

- **Key points**. In the margin you will see key points at regular intervals. The purpose of these is to summarise concisely the key material being covered.

ACTIVITY 1

- **Activities**. The text involves you in the learning process with a series of activities designed to catch your attention and make you concentrate and respond. The feedback to activities is at the end of each chapter.

SELF-TEST QUESTIONS

- **Self-test questions**. At the end of each chapter there is a series of self-test questions. The purpose of these is to help you revise some of the key elements of the chapter. All the answers to these questions can be found in the text.

EXAM-TYPE QUESTIONS

- **End of chapter questions**. At the end of each chapter we include examination-type questions. These will give you a very good idea of the sort of thing the examiner will ask and will test your understanding of what has been covered.

FOULKS LYNCH
PUBLICATIONS

Syllabus and study guide

Objectives of the study guide

This Study Guide is designed to help you plan your studies and to provide a more detailed interpretation of the Syllabus for ACCA's professional examinations. It contains both the Syllabus and a Study Guide for each paper, which you can follow when preparing for the examination.

The Syllabus outlines the content of the paper and how that content is examined. The Study Guide takes the Syllabus content and expands it into study sessions of similar length. These sessions indicate what the examiner expects of candidates for each part of the Syllabus, and therefore gives you guidance in the skills you are expected to demonstrate in the examinations.

Syllabus content

1 MANAGING INFORMATION SYSTEMS (IS)

a   Business strategy and IS/IT alignment.

b   Delivering information systems – organisational arrangements.

c   Delivering information systems – accounting issues.

d   Organising information systems – structural issues.

e   Feasibility study.

f   Project initiation.

g   Project planning.

h   Project monitoring and control.

i   Software support for project management.

2 DESIGNING INFORMATION SYSTEMS

a   The information systems development process.

b   Investigating and recording user requirements.

c   Documenting and modelling user requirements – processes.

d   Documenting and modelling user requirements – static structures.

e   Documenting and modelling user requirements – events.

f   External design.

g   Developing a solution to fulfil requirements.

h   Software package selection.

i   Software support for the systems development process.

3 EVALUATING INFORMATION SYSTEMS

a   Technical information systems requirements.

b   Legal compliance in information systems.

c   Implementing security and legal requirements.

d   Quality assurance in the management and development process.

e   Systems and user acceptance testing.

f   Implementation issues and implementation methods.

g   Post-implementation issues.

h   Change control in systems development and maintenance.

i   Relationship of management, development process and quality.

Excluded topics

Detailed systems design – file / database design, program design is an excluded topic. Computer hardware will not be explicitly examined.

Key areas of the syllabus

The syllabus has three key areas, managing information systems, designing information systems and evaluating information systems.

Study guide

PART 1: MANAGING INFORMATION SYSTEMS

Overall

This section provides the candidate with an insight into how information systems (IS) and information systems projects are organised and managed. The intention is to concentrate on the following areas.

- Information Systems strategy, organisation and financing
- Project Management

FOULKS LYNCH
PUBLICATIONS

1   Business strategy and IS/IT alignment   Chapter 1

- Explain an approach that an organisation may follow to formulate its strategic business objectives.

- Discuss how information systems may be used to assist in achieving these objectives.

- Identify current trends in information technology (IT) and the opportunities they offer to organisations.

- Distinguish between a business strategy and an information systems strategy.

- Identify responsibility for the ownership of the IS strategy.

2   Delivering information systems – organisational arrangements   Chapter 2

- Describe the traditional structure of a centralised Information Systems department and the roles and responsibilities of each function.

- Explain the principles of a decentralised Information. Systems function.

- Discuss the advantages and disadvantages of centralising or decentralising the Information Systems function.

- Explain the principles of outsourcing the Information Systems function.

- Describe the advantages and disadvantages of outsourcing the Information Systems function.

3   Delivering information systems – accounting issues   Chapter 3

- Briefly describe the types of cost incurred in delivering information systems.

- Describe how the costs of the Information Systems function may be distributed between customer departments.

- Explain the principles, benefits and drawbacks of cross-charging costs.

- Discuss the issues raised by establishing the Information Systems function as a cost or profit centre.

- Describe the advantages and disadvantages of establishing the Information Systems function as a separate company.

- Explain the problems of accounting for shared infrastructure costs.

4   Organising information systems – structural issues   Chapter 3

- Describe the typical hardware, software, data and communications infrastructures found within Information Systems functions.

- Discuss the meaning and need for a disaster recovery plan.

- Discuss the meaning and need for a risk management process.

- Describe the meaning and implications of legacy systems.

- Discuss the relationship of Information Systems with end-users and the implications of the expectations and skills of end-users.

5   Feasibility study   Chapter 4

- Explain the purpose and objectives of a feasibility study.

- Evaluate the technical, operational, social and economic feasibility of the proposed project.

- Describe and categorise the benefits and costs of the proposed project.

- Apply appropriate investment appraisal techniques to determine the economic feasibility of a project.

- Define the typical content and structure of a feasibility study report.

6   Project initiation   Chapter 5

- Define the content and structure of terms of reference.

- Describe the typical contents of a Project Quality Plan and explain the need for such a plan.

- Identify the roles and responsibilities of staff who will manage and participate in the project.

- Define in detail the role and responsibilities of the project manager.

- Explain the concept of a flat management structure and its application to project-based systems development.

7   Project planning   Chapter 6

- Assist in splitting the project into its main phases.

- Participate in the breakdown of work into lower-level tasks.

- Assist in the estimation of the time taken to complete these lower-level tasks.

- Define dependencies between lower-level tasks.

- Construct and interpret a project network.

- Construct and interpret a Gantt Chart.

8   Project monitoring and control   Chapter 6

- Describe methods of monitoring and reporting progress.

- Define the reasons for slippage and how to deal with slippage when it occurs.

- Discuss the reasons for changes during the project and the need for a project change procedure.

- Reflect the effects of progress, slippage and change requests on the project plan.

- Discuss the particular problems of planning and controlling Information Systems projects.

9   Software support for project management   Chapter 6

- Define the meaning of a project management software package and give a brief list of representative products.

- Describe a range of features and functions that a project management software package may provide.

– Explain the advantages of using a project management software package in the project management process.

PART 2: DESIGNING INFORMATION SYSTEMS

Overall

This section provides the candidate with an insight into how systems are defined and developed. The intention is to concentrate on the following areas.

- The definition and agreement of business requirements
- The external design of the system
- The selection of a software package solution

10 The information systems development process
Chapter 7

– Define the participants in the systems development process – managers, analysts, designers, programmers and testers.

– Describe the waterfall approach to systems development and identify its application in a representative systems development methodology.

– Describe the spiral approach to systems development and identify its application in a representative systems development methodology.

– Discuss the relative merits of the waterfall and spiral approaches, including an understanding of hybrid methodologies that include elements of both.

11 Investigating and recording user requirements
Chapter 8

– Define the tasks of planning, undertaking and documenting a user interview.

– Identify the potential role of background research, questionnaires and special purpose surveys in the definition of requirements.

– Describe the purpose, conduct and recording of a facilitated user workshop.

– Explain the potential use of prototyping in requirement's definition.

– Explain how requirements can be collected from current computerised information systems.

– Discuss the problems users have in defining, agreeing and prioritising requirements.

12 Documenting and modelling user requirements – processes
Chapter 9

– Describe the need for building a business process model of user requirements.

– Briefly describe different approaches to modelling the business process.

– Describe in detail the notation of one of these business process models.

– Construct a business process model of narrative user requirements using this notation.

– Explain the role of process models in the systems development process.

13 Documenting and modelling user requirements – static structures
Chapter 9

– Describe the need for building a business structure model of user requirements.

– Briefly describe different approaches to modelling the business structure.

– Describe in detail the notation of one of these business structure models.

– Construct a business structure model of narrative user requirements using this notation.

– Explain the role of structure models in the systems development process.

14 Documenting and modelling user requirements – events
Chapter 9

– Describe the need for building a business event model of user requirements.

– Briefly describe different approaches to modelling business events.

– Describe in detail the notation of one of these business event models.

– Construct a business event model of narrative user requirements using this notation.

– Explain the role of event models in the systems development process.

15 External design
Chapter 10

– Define the characteristics of a 'user-friendly' system.

– Describe the task of external design and distinguish it from internal design.

– Design effective output documents and reports.

– Select appropriate technology to support the output design.

– Design effective inputs.

– Select appropriate technology to support input design.

– Describe how the user interface may be structured for ease of use.

– Explain how prototyping may be used in defining an external design.

16 Developing a solution to fulfil requirements
Chapter 11

– Define the bespoke software approach to fulfilling the user's information systems requirements.

– Briefly describe the tasks of design, programming and testing required in developing a bespoke systems solution.

– Define the application software package approach to fulfilling the user's information systems requirements.

– Briefly describe the tasks of package selection, evaluation and testing required in selecting an appropriate application software package.

– Describe the relative merits of the bespoke systems development and application software package approaches to fulfilling an information systems requirement.

17 Software package selection   Chapter 11

– Describe the structure and contents of an Invitation to Tender (ITT).

– Describe how to identify software packages and their suppliers that may potentially fulfil the information systems requirements.

– Develop suitable procedures for distributing an ITT and dealing with subsequent enquiries and bids.

– Describe a process for evaluating the application software package, the supplier of that package and the bid received from the supplier.

– Describe risks of the application software package approach to systems development and how these might be reduced or removed.

18 Software support for the systems development process   Chapter 12

– Define a Computer Aided Software Engineering (CASE) tool and give a brief list of representative products.

– Describe a range of features and functions that a CASE tool may provide.

– Explain the advantages of using a CASE tool in the systems development process.

– Define a Fourth Generation Language and give a brief list of representative products.

– Describe a range of features and functions that a Fourth Generation Language may provide.

– Explain how a Fourth Generation Language contributes to the prototyping process.

PART 3: EVALUATING INFORMATION SYSTEMS

Overall

This section provides the candidate with an insight into how systems are implemented and evaluated. The intention is to concentrate on the following areas.

- The definition and agreement of non-business requirements

- The quality assurance of the solution

- The implementation and maintenance of the solution.

19 Technical information systems requirements   Chapter 13

– Define and record performance and volume requirements of information systems.

– Discuss the need for archiving, backup and restore, and other in 'house-keeping' functions.

– Explain the need for a software audit trail and define the content of such a trail.

– Examine the need to provide interfaces with other systems and discuss the implications of developing these interfaces.

– Establish requirements for data conversion and data creation.

20 Legal compliance in information systems   Chapter 14

– Describe the principles, terms and coverage typified by the UK Data Protection Act.

– Describe the principles, terms and coverage typified by the UK Computer Misuse Act.

– Explain the implications of software licences and copyright law in computer systems development.

– Discuss the legal implications of software supply with particular reference to ownership, liability and damages.

21 Implementing security and legal requirements   Chapter 14

– Describe methods to ensure the physical security of IT systems.

– Discuss the role, implementation and maintenance of a password system.

– Explain representative clerical and software controls that should assist in maintaining the integrity of a system.

– Describe the principles and application of encryption techniques.

– Discuss the implications of software viruses and malpractice.

– Discuss how the requirements of the UK Data Protection and UK Computer Misuse legislation may be implemented.

22 Quality assurance in the management and development process   Chapter 15

– Define the characteristics of a quality software product.

– Define the terms, quality management, quality assurance and quality control.

– Describe the V model and its application to quality assurance and testing.

– Explain the limitations of software testing.

– Participate in the quality assurance of deliverables in requirement specification using formal static testing methods.

– Explain the role of standards and, in particular, their application in quality assurance.

– Briefly describe the task of unit testing in bespoke systems development.

23 Systems and user acceptance testing   Chapter 15

– Define the scope of systems testing.

– Distinguish between dynamic and static testing.

The examination

Format of the examination

	Number of marks
Section A: 3 compulsory questions (20 marks each)	60
Section B: choice of 2 from 3 questions (20 marks each)	40
	100
Total time allowed: 3 hours	

Section A is based on a short narrative scenario.

Section B contains three independent questions, one question from each main area of the syllabus.

Additional information

The examination does not assume the use of any particular systems development methodology. Practical questions will be set in such a way that they can be answered by any published methodology. However, the following examples of models may be useful (see table below).

Syllabus heading	Example models
Documenting and modelling user requirements – processes	Data Flow Diagram Flowchart
Documenting and modelling user requirements – static structures	Entity relationship model. Object Class model
Documenting and modelling user requirements – events	Entity Life History State Transition Diagram

Examination tips

- Spend the first few minutes of the examination **reading the paper**.

- Where you have a **choice of questions**, decide which ones you will do.

- **Divide the time** you spend on questions in proportion to the marks on offer. One suggestion is to allocate 1½ minutes to each mark available, so a 10 mark question should be completed in 15 minutes.

- Unless you know exactly how to answer the question, spend some time **planning** your answer. Stick to the question and **tailor your answer** to what you are asked.

- **Fully explain** all your points but be **concise**. Set out all workings **clearly and neatly**, and state briefly what you are doing. Don't write out the question.

- If you do not understand what a question is asking, **state your assumptions**. Even if you do not answer precisely in the way the examiner hoped, you should be given some credit, if your assumptions are reasonable.

- If you **get completely stuck** with a question, leave space in your answer book and **return to it later.**

- Towards the end of the examination spend the last **five minutes** reading through your answers and **making any additions or corrections**.

- Before you finish, you must fill in the required information on the front of your answer booklet.

Answering the questions

- **Multiple-choice questions**: Read the questions carefully and work through any calculations required. If you don't know the answer, eliminate those options you know are incorrect and see if the answer becomes more obvious. Remember that only one answer to a multiple choice question can be right!

- **Objective test questions** might ask for numerical answers, but could also involve paragraphs of text which require you to fill in a number of missing blanks, or for you to write a definition of a word or phrase, or to enter a formula. Others may give a definition followed by a list of possible key words relating to that description.

- **Essay questions**: Make a quick plan in your answer book and under each main point list all the relevant facts you can think of. Then write out your answer developing each point fully. Your essay should have a clear structure; it should contain a brief introduction, a main section and a conclusion. Be concise. It is better to write a little about a lot of different points than a great deal about one or two points.

- **Case studies**: To write a good case study, first identify the area in which there is a problem, outline the main principles/theories you are going to use to answer the question, and then apply the principles/theories to the case. Include relevant points only and then reach a conclusion and, if asked for, recommendations. If you can, compare the facts to real-life examples – this may gain you additional marks in the exam.

- **Computations**: It is essential to include all your workings in your answers. Many computational questions require the use of a standard format: company profit and loss account, balance sheet and cash flow statement for example. Be sure you know these formats thoroughly before the examination and use the layouts that you see in the answers given in this book and in model answers. If you are asked to comment or make recommendations on a computation, you must do so. There are important marks to be gained here. Even if your computation contains mistakes, you may still gain marks if your reasoning is correct.

- **Reports, memos and other documents**: Some questions ask you to present your answer in the form of a report or a memo or other document. Use the correct format - there could be easy marks to gain here.

Study skills and revision guidance

This section aims to give guidance on how to study for your ACCA exams and to give ideas on how to improve your existing study techniques.

Preparing to study

Set your objectives

Before starting to study decide what you want to achieve – the type of pass you wish to obtain. This will decide the level of commitment and time you need to dedicate to your studies.

Devise a study plan

- Determine which times of the week you will study.

- Split these times into sessions of at least one hour for study of new material. Any shorter periods could be used for revision or practice.

- Put the times you plan to study onto a study plan for the weeks from now until the exam and set yourself targets for each period of study – in your sessions make sure you cover the course, course assignments and revision.

- If you are studying for more than one paper at a time, try to vary your subjects, this can help you to keep interested and see subjects as part of wider knowledge.

- When working through your course, compare your progress with your plan and, if necessary, re-plan your work (perhaps including extra sessions) or, if you are ahead, do some extra revision/practice questions.

Effective studying

Active reading

You are not expected to learn the text by rote, rather, you must understand what you are reading and be able to use it to pass the exam and develop good practice. A good technique to use is SQ3Rs – Survey, Question, Read, Recall, Review:

1 **Survey** the chapter – look at the headings and read the introduction, summary and objectives, so as to get an overview of what the chapter deals with.

2 **Question** – whilst undertaking the survey, ask yourself the questions that you hope the chapter will answer for you.

3 **Read** through the chapter thoroughly, answering the questions and making sure you can meet the objectives. Attempt the exercises and activities in the text, and work through all the examples.

4 **Recall** – at the end of each section and at the end of the chapter, try to recall the main ideas of the section/chapter without referring to the text. This is best done after a short break of a couple of minutes after the reading stage.

5 **Review** – check that your recall notes are correct.

You may also find it helpful to reread the chapter and try to see the topic(s) it deals with as a whole.

Note-taking

Taking notes is a useful way of learning, but do not simply copy out the text. The notes must:

- be in your own words
- be concise
- cover the key points
- be well-organised
- be modified as you study further chapters in this text or in related ones.

Trying to summarise a chapter without referring to the text can be a useful way of determining which areas you know and which you don't.

Three ways of taking notes:

- **summarise the key points** of a chapter.

- **make linear notes** – a list of headings, divided up with subheadings listing the key points. If you use linear notes, you can use different colours to highlight key points and keep topic areas together. Use plenty of space to make your notes easy to use.

- **try a diagrammatic form** – the most common of which is a mind-map. To make a mind-map, put the main heading in the centre of the paper and put a circle around it. Then draw short lines radiating from this to the main sub-headings, which again have circles around them. Then continue the process from the sub-headings to sub-sub-headings, advantages, disadvantages, etc.

Highlighting and underlining

You may find it useful to underline or highlight key points in your study text – but do be selective. You may also wish to make notes in the margins.

Revision

The best approach to revision is to revise the course as you work through it. Also try to leave four to six weeks before the exam for final revision. Make sure you cover the whole syllabus and pay special attention to those areas where your knowledge is weak. Here are some recommendations:

- **Read through the text and your notes again** and condense your notes into key phrases. It may help to put key revision points onto index cards to look at when you have a few minutes to spare.

- **Review any assignments** you have completed and look at where you lost marks – put more work into those areas where you were weak.

- **Practise exam standard questions** under timed conditions. If you are short of time, list the points that you would cover in your answer and then read the model answer, but do try and complete at least a few questions under exam conditions.

- Also **practise producing answer plans** and comparing them to the model answer.

- If you are stuck on a topic find somebody (a tutor) to explain it to you.

- **Read good newspapers and professional journals**, especially ACCA's *Student Accountant* – this can give you an advantage in the exam.

- Ensure you **know the structure of the exam** – how many questions and of what type you will be expected to answer. During your revision attempt all the different styles of questions you may be asked.

Chapter 1

BUSINESS STRATEGY

This first chapter in your studies of Information Systems investigates the need for information systems within organisations, and in particular how those systems are used to support the overall business strategy in organisations. The difference between a Business Strategy and an Information Strategy is also explained, and the links between these strategies are established.

Objectives

By the time you have finished this chapter you should be able to:

- explain an approach that an organisation may follow to formulate its strategic business objectives
- discuss how information systems may be used to assist in achieving these objectives
- identify current trends in information technology (IT) and the opportunities they offer to organisations
- distinguish between a business strategy and an information systems strategy
- identify responsibility for the ownership of the IS strategy.

K E Y   P O I N T

Objectives outline exactly what the organisation intends to do as well as provide a check on whether or not those objectives have been achieved.

1 Strategic business objectives

All organisations should have objectives. Objectives define what an organisation is trying to achieve, in the long term as well as the short term. Without objectives, an organisation will have no overall direction, and possibly even no purpose for its existence. However, providing objectives gives the focus for the organisation in terms of the things it must do in order to be a success.

There is a hierarchy of objectives. For companies, the prime objective should be to increase the wealth of its shareholders, possibly by seeking to grow long-term profits. For state-owned organisations such as schools and health authorities, the prime objectives are different and related to providing education and health services.

Below the main objective, there are subsidiary objectives. Subsidiary objectives are stepping stones on the way to achieving the main objective, and an organisation might have a variety of subsidiary objectives, such as objectives for marketing, objectives for product development, objectives for being at the leading edge of technological development, objectives for the development of employee skill, and so on. Organisations might also have a strategy for the information systems it would like to have and use.

1.1 Critical success factors

One method of quantifying objectives is to identify critical success factors or CSFs.

CSFs were developed by John Rockart (1970), at the Sloan School of Management at MIT. The idea of CSFs is that chief executives need to know what achievements are critically important for the strategic success of the organisation. By identifying CSFs and stating them clearly, senior managers can remain focussed on what really matters.

Critical success factors are defined as:

The limited number of areas in which results, if they are satisfactory, will ensure successful competitive performance for the business. They are the vital areas where 'things must go right' for the business to flourish.

There must be a clear and shared understanding of what the critical success factors of the business are, and a recognition throughout all levels of the organisation of what the overall business objectives are, and how each unit or department can contribute to satisfying these objectives. The management process itself must be integrated in the sense of sharing a common purpose and approach.

Generally, the corporate objectives are defined by thins such as increased profits, develop new products or diversify. Once they have been stated, the managers involved in strategy formulation will identify the critical success factors that must be achieved for the organisation to flourish.

1.2   Sources of CSFs

The sources of critical success factors can be wide ranging. It is useful to categorise the sources to understand the nature of CSFs. Rockart claims that there are four sources for them:

1   **The industry that the business is in** – each industry has CSF's that are relevant to any company within it. For example, the car industry must have as one of its CSFs 'compliance with pollution requirements regarding car exhaust gases'.

2   The company itself and its situation within the industry e.g., its competitive strategy and its geographic location. CSFs could be to develop new products, create new markets or to support the field sales force. Actions taken by a few large dominant companies in an industry will provide one or more CSF's for small companies in that industry.

3   **The environment** e.g., the economy, the political factors and consumer trends in the country or countries that the organisation operates in. An example used by Rockart is that, before 1973, virtually no chief executive in the USA would have stated 'energy supply availability' as a critical success factor. However, following the oil embargo many executives monitored this factor closely.

4   **Temporal organisational factors**, i.e. areas of company activity that are unusually causing concern because they need attention in the short term. Cases of too little or too much inventory might generate a CSF for a short time during recession.

Rockart identified two types of CSF.

- **monitoring**: keeping abreast of ongoing operations
- **building**: tracking progress of the change programs initiated by the executive.

Chief executives have both monitoring and building responsibilities and CSFs will reflect this. The CSFs will vary with the level in the hierarchy; the higher up the management triangle the more likely it is that CSFs will be of the building variety. For example, 'decentralise the organisation' and other programmes for change concerned with tracking the progress are building CSFs. 'Expand foreign sales' is a monitoring CSF that requires keeping abreast of the ongoing sales operations.

There may be more than one source of information that can be used. It will be up to the managers concerned to decide what information is required, how much it is required, the frequency of collection and the level of aggregation.

Examples of information that can be used to monitor some of the CSFs of a garden furniture manufacturer include:

CSF	Information needs
Achieve quoted delivery dates	• Production schedules
	• Inventory levels
Consistent performance to budget on major jobs	• Job cost budgeted/achieved
Market success	• Change in market share
Sound image in financial market	• Price/earnings ratio
Morale of employees to be high	• Turnover, absenteeism, sickness
	• Informal communication

1.3   Critical success factors and performance indicators

CSFs can be expressed in general terms. In addition to identifying CSFs, managers need to know how well or badly the organisation is performing, and whether its CSFs are being achieved or not.

For every CSF, there should be a known and reliable performance measure, or **key performance indicator**. Performance indicators are established as measured targets for achievement of CSFs, and so are used to monitor the actual success of each factor, providing information to management about performance calls for information to be supplied in a form that the executives and managers can use. We have already discussed the fact that not all the information needed will be available from existing or new information systems. If this is the case, new ways of acquiring the information will need to be evaluated.

The organisation will identify its CSFs by first determining its goals and objectives and then by setting performance indicators to check whether or not those CSFs have been achieved.

Goals are long-run, open-ended attributes or ends a person or organisation seeks, and are sufficient for the satisfaction of the organisation's mission.

Objectives are time-assigned targets derived from the goals, and are set in advance of strategy.

Performance Indicators (PI) are quantifiable measures used to check that critical success factors have been achieved.

Goals represent the aspiration of the organisation; the direction in which it will focus its effort. Objectives are measurable targets that an organisation sets to meet its goals. Each set of objectives will support one goal. There may be many or few objectives supporting one goal.

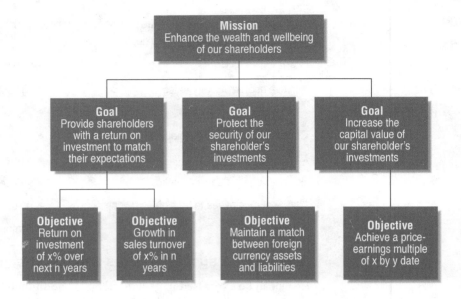

The goals, objectives, CSFs and information needs should be aggregated to eliminate overlap and to check that there are no obvious omissions. Once the objectives are identified, they can be used to determine which factors are critical for accomplishing the objective. Not all objectives are equally important. Management need to obtain a relative ranking to assign priorities; this can be carried out using techniques such as incidence scoring or pair wise comparison.

To feed back the results and obtain a consensus, all the managers involved in the strategy formulation should meet and confirm the understanding of the business strategy and its information needs to support that strategy. Any conflict between management and departments must be minimised.

The performance measure for the CSF is a characteristic of its associated objective. Knowing the units of measurement for each objective makes it easy to identify the information required.

After the critical factors have been determined, two or three prime measures for each factor are found. Some measures use hard, factual data and these are the easiest to identify. Other measures are softer, such as opinions, perceptions and hunches and take more analysis to uncover their appropriate source.

One of the major problems with strategy implementation in many organisations is a failure to translate declarations of strategic purpose into a practical statement of those factors, which are critical to achieving the targets, and the key tasks that will ensure success.

These issues can be addressed systematically:

The critical success factors for the specific strategy must be agreed and scrutinised to make sure that all the factors are genuinely necessary and the list is sufficient to underpin success.

The key tasks, which are essential to the delivery of each critical success factor, must be identified. These may relate to the organisation's value activities, be identified in the value chain, and include improvements in support activities or changes in linkages within the value system. For example, an office supply company with a critical success factor of customer care would underpin the CSF through the three key tasks of responding to enquiries, supplying accurate information and an efficient and quick breakdown and maintenance service. These tasks are dependent on the office supplies company's infrastructure, particularly the database of customer installations.

Allocate management responsibility for the key tasks identified. For the office supplies company, the area that could go wrong is the maintenance of the customer database. The responsibility for this is assigned to the maintenance department but there should be linkages established with both the sales and the software department to ensure accurate information.

1.4   CSF analysis

Analysing the CSFs allows managers to articulate their needs in terms of the information that is absolutely critical to them. The process can be illustrated as follows:

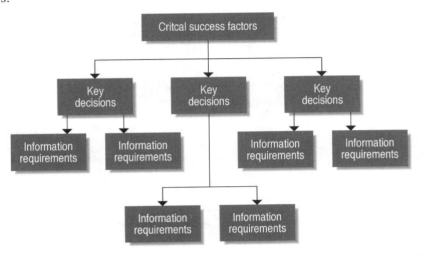

The relationship between the critical success factors, key decisions and information requirements is a process whereby the identification of the CSFs will allow the manager to identify the key decisions related to those CSFs and then the key decisions will give a bridge into the information requirements. The point is to structure and highlight the link between what must be done and why it is needed, either to support a key decision or because it forms a key performance indicator or because it would be a measure of situational control or situational effectiveness.

KEY POINT

CSFs provide a way of achieving a clear definition of the information that is needed, limiting the costly collection of more data than is necessary.

CSFs provide a way of achieving a clear definition of the information that is needed, limiting the costly collection of more data than is necessary. For example, the parts department of a large organisation may have a business strategy where the CSF is to minimise the length of time a part is kept in stock. One of the key decisions related to that CSF might be to decide what quantities must be ordered. The information requirements may be the level of demand by day/week/month.

Meeting the CSF ensures that the investment in stock is kept low and that parts are distributed quickly. IS supplies support for this e.g., a key report would compare part purchasing with part demand patterns to help managers anticipate order demand without overstocking, whilst at the same time help avoid shortages.

The lower down in the management structure one goes, the more difficult it becomes to express only a few things that must go right, especially for those management layers that focus on gathering and filtering data for other parts of the organisation. It could be that they have no CSFs and nothing they do is critical.

2 Information for decision making

2.1 Strategy and information systems

An **information system** is a combination or network of computer equipment and software and communications equipment and software that together carry out a function of processing and providing information.

Having considered and set the CSFs and PIs within an organisation, an information system must be developed to monitor the CSFs and provide the detailed information to ensure that the PIs can be measured and reported on.

The first part of setting up any information system will be determined by exactly what the CSFs and PIs within the organisation are, and then checking with the potential users of the information system exactly what information they will require. Taking this approach will ensure that any information system, when it is eventually implemented, will meet the needs of the organisation and the people using that system within the organisation.

Organisations use information systems for various reasons.

- Transaction processing. Systems are used to process transaction data in a routine manner. An example of a transactions processing system is a computerised accounting system. Another example of transaction processing is the processing of customer sales via the internet. 'Internet shopping' is developing rapidly as a major channel for selling certain types of goods.

- Providing routine management reports. Such systems are known as management information systems. An example is a system that provides budgetary control reports to management every month, by comparing actual results with a budget and reporting the differences or variances between actual and budget.

- Providing information to management to help them to analyse more complex problems and to make decisions in relation to them.

Having information systems that are capable of processing transactions or providing management information to a certain level or standard could be a CSF for the organisation.

2.2 Strategic information systems planning (SISP)

Strategic Information Systems Planning (SISP) is concerned with establishing a strategy for the information systems that an organisation will use. The importance of information systems can vary between different organisations, and for some it is much more important than others. It is important to remember that if an organisation uses information systems that are inferior to those used by its competitors, it might be putting itself at a competitive disadvantage that the competitors will exploit.

The stages in the SISP process are as follows.

Planning incorporates the tasks of:

- determining the project's objectives and scope. (Will it relate to the whole corporate entity or a given function? Will there be constraints imposed on interviewing senior executives?)

- obtaining project sponsorship (i.e. the backing of either a member of the board, or the chief executive)

- identifying persons to interview (avoiding interviewing those with similar responsibilities, where possible) from senior grades

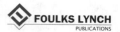

- establish the project plan.

- selecting project team members – including user management, senior specialists in computer systems, project administrator, perhaps external consultant(s)
- establishing the project plan – interviewing schedules and content, analysis stage, establishment of milestones, schedule of reporting (usually monthly) to inform executives.

Interviewing is a highly structured stage, every interviewee being interviewed twice (usually for two hours, then one hour), to discover:

- individual functions
- objectives (short, medium and long-term)
- factors needed for success
- information requirements.

The facts obtained can be recorded by data flow diagrams, resulting in a view of the organisation with its strengths, weaknesses, opportunities and threats.

From all this, methods of evaluating alternative strategies and implementation emerge, with facts which may be used for future comparisons. The prevailing management culture and values are identified so that the new strategy will not run counter to them. The number of interviews for any SISP project is unlikely to exceed 40 from the point-of-view of time taken to interview them.

Analysis. The conceptual information architecture consists of the data flow diagrams and the **data model**. The information requirements discovered by the interviews must be compared with the information actually currently provided, and any discrepancies carefully noted.

The current position is explained by referring to the **organisational model** in which the corporate body is described in terms of six categories:

- external environmental influences
- formal organisation arrangements
- personnel (and other tangible assets)
- technology utilised
- the organisational social system
- the dominant groupings.

This model exists in macro form for the complete corporate body, and in micro form (greater detail) for the IS department. It is utilised to create policies to achieve the corporate objectives. The fundamental components of corporate strategy are these policies and the objectives, plus the available corporate resources.

We have been looking at the 'ideal' SISP approach, which should be completed within six months. It may not be possible to follow through the stages we have been looking at and so a piecemeal approach (see earlier) has to be adopted; the above process is divided up into different components which can be carried out as independent activities and which do not overlap:

Information systems effectiveness review (ISER) – determining the current and future corporate objectives and reviewing the current and planned applications (to discover extent of support for the objectives).

Critical success factors (CSFs) – determining individual management objectives to select job-aspects vital to objective-attainment and deriving information necessary to achieve the objectives and to monitor the factors.

Organisational modelling (OM) – examining the six key corporate aspects (listed above) to determine strengths and weaknesses, and the opportunities and threats from external influences, thereby setting up the model to allow consideration of alternative strategies.

This takes much more time than a 'top-down' approach. It also tends to give the impression that all data elements are of equal significance in decision support. Generally the 'top-down' approach for SISPs is the most effective due to optimisation of resource allocation. At times however, this method may simply not be possible.

The SISP may well be initiated by the IS department (IS-driven) or by the users, perhaps the board of directors itself (user-driven). The driving force giving rise to the project governs the main purpose of the exercise and the SISP scope and approach.

3   Information resource management

3.1   The role of information as a resource

Having identified the CSFs and PIs and then the information required by staff within an organisation, detailed work can begin on setting up the information system itself. As the information system is established, it is useful to note that the information provided will vary in detail depending on the level of management that information is being provided to. Management information can be divided into three broad categories:

- operational information to meet the day-to-day needs of managers

- tactical information which is of a slightly longer-term nature

- strategic information which can be long-term in nature and focus.

Very crudely, we can say that operational information is for junior operational managers whereas strategic information is for senior managers. Tactical information is somewhere in the middle, and often associated with budgeting and budgetary control.

The **Gorry and Scott-Morton model** presents a detailed picture of information attributes and how they vary with the level of management hierarchy.

Characteristics of information	Management hierarchy		
	Operational	Tactical	Strategic
Source	Mainly internal		Mainly external
Scope	Narrow, well-defined		Very wide
Level of aggregation	Detailed		Aggregated
Time horizon	Historical		Future
Currency	Highly current		Quite old
Required accuracy	High		Quite low
Frequency of use	Very frequent		Infrequent

The system to deliver this information must also have attributes:

- **decision oriented** – the system must produce material in an appropriate way to enable informed decision-making

- **data processing** – although there will be a shift in focus, the system must still maintain DP checks, controls, etc, to ensure timeliness and efficient resource use.

- **data management** – the system should maintain the three Is of data storage – integrity, independence and integration
- **flexibility** – to avoid being stuck with outdated technology and solutions, the system should be sufficiently adaptable to the business' varied and changing needs, and individuals' varied behaviour
- **human computer interface** (HCI) – the system should capitalise on the best of humans and of machines to obtain the optimum mix of people's intuition and machine reliability, usability, and speed.

The commonest complaints levelled at management information systems are the lack of decision orientation and the lack of flexibility. The unsatisfactory systems are those that deny access to data necessary to take decisions.

3.2   Decision Support Systems (DSSs)

Information systems are designed to provide information to management. Information has no value unless it is put to use, and information is used by managers to make decisions.

Decisions can be categorised into three types:

- **Structured decisions** are routine decisions that are made according to a clear set of rules and procedures. Computer systems are often able to make structured decisions themselves, without the need for human intervention. Alternatively, computer systems might produce routine reports, and managers might use the information given in reports in a fairly standard and predictable way.

- **Unstructured decisions** are decisions where there are no clear rules, and the decision maker has to use judgement. The degree of uncertainty and risk could be very high. Information systems can help with an analysis of the factors in the decision, and can help managers to reach a more rational and well-informed decision, thereby improving the likelihood that the decisions taken are sensible. Information systems that assist managers with unstructured decisions (and semi-structured decisions) are called **decision support systems**.

- Many decisions are neither purely structured nor entirely unstructured, but area combination of elements of both. **Semi-structured decisions** are decisions that require a combination of applying decision rules and using qualitative judgement.

(**Note**. You might also come across the term '**expert systems**'. These are information systems to assist with decision making, where the process of analysing the problem calls for the application of logical reasoning rather than computational work. An expert system is a computer system that provides help for 'experts' in making an analysis and reaching a judgement. An example of an expert system is a medical computer system that can be used to analyse the symptoms of a patient's condition, to assist with reaching a medical diagnosis. Another example is a legal expert system that can be used by solicitors to analyse a case, and reach a view on how the case should be handled on behalf of the client.)

3.3   Databases in Decision Support Systems

A database is defined as a collection of structured data with minimum duplication, which is common to all users of the system but is independent of programs that use the data. The database can grow and change and is built up stage by stage within the organisation. It will actually comprise several databases, each providing the anticipated information for several logically related Management Information Systems (MIS) where the data can be accessed, retrieved and modified with reasonable flexibility.

The database must:

- avoid redundancy or duplication of data

- have the ability to be used by all applications (programs), and must therefore accept entirely new data formats and be open to major modifications, the data being independent of the programs

- accept that different applications have various uses for data (so all possible relationships between data items must be comprehended and available for access)

- adopt a universally acceptable approach for all applications in respect of data retrieval, insertion and changes.

The following diagram shows the place of databases in the Decision Support Systems.

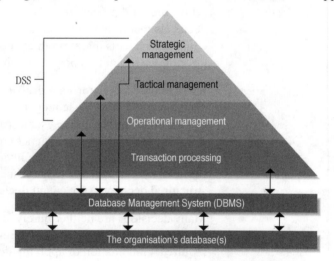

The database system provides a number of advantages:

- data is utilised for a wide range of reasons, but is only input to the database and stored once

- data is utilised in the knowledge that all departments concerned are using identical data; whereas if each department has its own data, it is possible that the facts and figures used may conflict with those of another user

- the database supports management requirements – especially at the strategic level, although all levels need access – and provides both routine and *ad hoc* reports.

What kind of data will be held in the database? The mix is likely to contain:

- transaction data in detail (resulting from processing through application programs)

- data needed by current and probable future programs.

4   IT, IS and IM

Having considered the reasons for the development of the objectives in an organisation and how those objectives give rise to information requirements, this next section investigates how an information system can be developed to meet those objectives and provide the appropriate information.

4.1   Information Technology

A coming together of data processing, communication technologies, office automation and production automation so that information technology (IT) describes any equipment concerned with the capture, storage, transmission or presentation of information.

The convergence of this technology has brought the separate disciplines into one management arena and paved the way for an integrated view that permits an organisational focus on the purpose of the whole rather than upon the technical difference of the parts.

4.2   Information Systems

Information systems (IS) refers to the provision and management of information to support the running of the organisation. The IT is the supporting hardware that provides the infrastructure to run the information systems.

IS refers to the part of the organisation related to information technology (IT), management information systems (MIS), decision support systems (DSS) And strategic management information systems (SMIS). MIS is a generic term used to describe information systems, although it can refer to provision of management information, normally at the tactical level of management. DSS are available at higher management levels to support decisions being made. Finally, the SMIS is available to strategic management to provide summarised information to assist their decision-making.

4.3   Information Management

The convergence of the individual technology disciplines demands coherent management responsibility for all aspects of information handling. Hence, whilst still requiring technical expertise that must be specific, the nature of information management (IM) has changed.

IM has become a complex activity and the issues and tasks involved are being defined by a number of organisational and technical changes. The key issues include:

- people focus, rather than concentrating on technological concerns
- cost effectiveness – management must be seen to be cost effective by way of demonstrable business value
- information dissemination – relinquishing inappropriate control mechanisms that reduce information use
- business process redesign or re-engineering – the real embodiment of technology-enabled change
- reporting relationships that position IS into the organisation and not at a distance.

The most significant change is that IS can no longer be viewed as a single homogenous area with a single, middle level manager responsible for it.

 FOULKS LYNCH
PUBLICATIONS

5   Strategy planning for information systems

Planning is an ongoing process that provides the framework that determines the implementation detail. Neither general strategy planning nor IS strategy planning are simple activities but most managers agree that they perform more effectively if they plan and stick to the objectives of that plan.

IS needs effective strategic planning as much as, or even more than, other functional areas do. The aim of planning is to get a clear view of the value to the organisation and without this, the allocation of resources is unlikely to match that value.

Planning and implementing a suitable IS strategy produces the organisational confidence that IS will cost-effectively deliver these strategic systems.

IS systems without planning may mean financial losses and additional hidden, and often greater, costs such as lowered staff morale, missed opportunities, continuous management fire-fighting and customer dissatisfaction. Planning helps an organisation identify its information needs and find new opportunities for using that information. It also defines the activities required to implement the chosen strategy.

5.1   Ownership of IS strategy

Senior managers recognise the need for information systems development to link to the business objectives and therefore take a major role in the planning stages. During the final stages of growth the planning of information systems takes on a strategic perspective with planning being carried out by teams consisting of senior management, users and information systems staff. They all have a stake in the final system.

5.2   IS strategy consistency

The organisation's IS strategy, and the plan that documents it, must be consistent with:

- the corporate plans
- the management view of the role of IS in the organisation; and
- the stage of maturity of use and management of IS.

Identifying an organisation's goals and objectives should lead to articulating an overall business or corporate strategy. This strategy then feeds down, through divisional or business unit strategies, into a number of functional strategies. One of these is the IS strategy, which feeds into a number of sub-strategies e.g., the IT strategy and the communications strategy. These, in turn, develop ever more detailed strategy elements.

Because the system of strategies has a hierarchy, it would be tempting to assume that strategic planning must be a top-down activity. However, this is not the case and the systems hierarchy should not imply a fixed sequence. Many organisations make a start at developing an IS strategy before articulating their business/corporate strategies, despite the fact that a lot of IS strategy development approaches depend upon the prior identification of corporate strategies. During experiments in IS strategic planning, IS often acts as the catalyst for generating and documenting the business strategy.

This system of strategies and its hierarchy is shown in the diagram below:

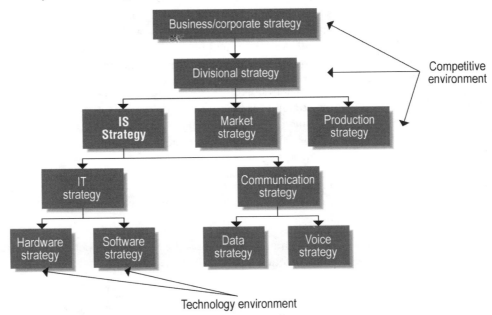

(Adapted from *Strategic Management and Information Systems* Robson, 1997, Pub Pitman)

The hierarchy helps to explain some of the problems of IS strategic planning.

An organisation is trying to connect the exploitation of IT, which is in itself complex, rapidly changing and often not well understood by managers, to development of business strategies where neither the principles not the methods are agreed. It is no wonder that managers find it difficult to develop IS strategies that support the business strategies.

5.3   Connection in systems

Traditionally, business management has focused on corporate planning, with little understanding of, or interest in, how IS could support and influence, its objectives. IS management has concentrated on technical issues, with little understanding of, or interest in corporate objectives. A sort of systems planning has always taken place but usually in the form of project planning with a concentration on getting the system done right, rather than getting the right system and being performed in isolation from mainstream business planning. This type of planning is practical at the systems level but leads to lost business opportunities and incompatible systems, data stores and architectures and often-unacceptable implementation lags.

By the 1980s there was a perception of information as a resource that should be managed to the advantage of the organisation, just like capital and manpower, and an appreciation of IS effectiveness issues i.e., the relationship between output and goals.

From the modern perspective of consumers of IS services, the key concern of IS strategy planning is that they are able to provide an estimate of the business demand and priorities for IS development and activities in order to get the best business value from IS resources and investments. By reconciling requirements they hope to avoid inappropriately duplicated or incompatible investments.

The overall objective is to regain control of information by the business, irrespective of the strategy for the technical delivery of it, and hence to be able to exploit the use of information to improve business performance. Whether this improved business performance can be said to equate to competitive advantage will be discussed in another chapter.

From the recent perspective of those destined to provide and manage IS services, the overriding objective must be to provide service levels and styles that are appropriate to the organisation's needs.

The diagram below shows the relationship between IT, IS and the corporate strategies, or connection in systems terms.

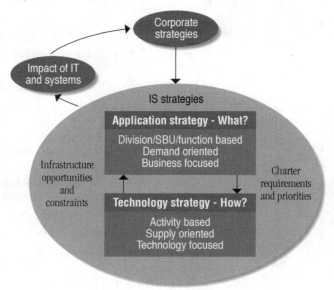

(Adapted from Integrating Information Systems into Business Strategies by Ward, *Long range planning* Vol 20, No 3 pp 19-20, 1987)

Information systems are concerned to reconcile and satisfy user requirements to identify, plan for and so manage the IS resources and technologies needed. They are concerned to fill the technical, probably advisory role in identifying and exploiting opportunities to use information to improve business performance.

5.4　The objectives of the IS strategic plan

Any resource must be managed. Some would say that information is not just a critical resource, but rather that it is the critical resource allowing the organisation to manage all others.

Strategy planning for IS arrived in the 1980s with the primary objectives of the planning effort broadening:

- to encompass the desire to improve communications with users;
- to increase the degree of top-management commitment; and
- to find more opportunities for improving the IS function and spot new, higher business pay-back MIS applications.

Like any planning, IS strategic planning is not a one-off activity. Ideally, it would be a continuous cycle synchronised with or, even better, embedded into the cycle of the corporate planning. Given that organisations address IS strategic planning in different ways, there are still common circumstances that require frequent revision to reflect technology changes. These include:

1   Major organisational changes e.g., the collective result of new owners, management, rationalisation programmes, restructuring exercises etc will mean that the new business will require different things from IS. If this is so, the primary objective of the IS strategy will be the definition of the new role for IS. Its scope will be uncertain but the emphasis will be to build on senior management commitment to the changing role of IS within the new organisation.

2   External competitive opportunities and threats. The symptoms of this kind of change are the emergence of new markets and/or commodities that may be created by IS or the competitive need for major cost factor changes and improved performance. This set of circumstances is likely to produce a plan where the objective is to move IS resources, in the widest sense of the term, into the new long-term commitments to high benefit or threat protection. This requires focusing effort and resources on those areas where the most good can be achieved. The emphasis of the objectives is to exploit IS strengths and the weaknesses of competitors by being entrepreneurial and developing new attitudes, skills and uses of IS in these new commitments.

3   Evolutionary change in IS maturity – probably the most frequent reason for re-assessing the IS strategy. The most obvious symptoms of this are the changing views on the required level of control over IS, or its budget allocation and/or the degree of dissatisfaction expressed by everyone. Unfortunately, as you will see later in the manual. Moving from one stage to another generates fears and anxieties. Under these circumstances, the IS objectives will be to get and keep senior management commitment and to demonstrate managed evolution. The next section explores the notion of stages of IS evolution, since modelling the stage is a valuable analysis tool.

6   Formulating an IT strategy

A plan for information technology should be co-ordinated with the IS strategy and the corporate strategy. The plan will show the direction of the systems effort and lay down the basis for later evaluation of its performance.

Many organisations agree that a plan is needed, but do not develop one. A frequent reason is that the three to five-year information systems planning horizon is not compatible with the planning horizon of the organisation. It is both possible and highly desirable to develop an information-processing plan even without a formal corporate plan.

A typical plan will describe the activities and resources required for the development of the new application of technology. One of the key tasks is to identify new application areas in order to gain strategic advantage.

6.1   Why is IT important?

IT is in effect the fusion of developments in both computing and telecommunications, including the use of fibre optics as cables and transmissions via satellites. The coming together of these two areas (the French have coined the word 'telematique') has begun to transform business communications and, indeed, the very pattern of our lives. A former Minister for Information Technology, pointed out: 'IT is the fastest developing area of industrial and business activity in the Western world. Its markets are huge, its applications multitudinous and its potential for efficiency immense.'

Not only are developments in IT of immense importance to those companies engaged in the industry, they also have considerable influence on all other businesses, who must therefore recognise the need for a clear information technology strategy. Perhaps the most fundamental concept in the development of such a strategy is the recognition that information is a valuable corporate resource.

The importance of information as a resource cannot be overstressed. As pointed out by Diebold: 'Information, which in essence is the analysis and synthesis of data, will unquestionably be one of the most vital of corporate resources. It will be structured into models for planning and decision- making. It will be integrated into product design and marketing methods. In other words, information will be recognised and treated as an asset.'

6.2   Elements of a strategy

The structure of the plan is:

1   **Executive summary** – a statement containing the main points of the scheme. The document should have a section on the *goals*, specific and general, of information processing in the organisation.

2   **Goals** – a general goal might be to provide a different customer service, whilst a specific goal could be to completely update the database enquiry system.

3   **Assumptions** – the plan will be based on certain assumptions about the organisation and the current business strategy. It is essential that this plan is linked to the organisation's strategic plan.

4   **Scenario** – sometimes it is helpful to draw up a scenario of the information-processing environment that will result from executing the plan.

5   **Application areas** – the plan should outline and set priorities for new application areas being planned and for those applications which are in the process of development. A report on their progress and status should be produced. For major new applications there should be a breakdown of costs and schedules. The plan should outline and set priorities for the application areas. A corporate steering committee containing high-level representation should set the priorities as this committee can make the trade-offs among functional areas.

6   **Operations** – the current systems will be continuing and the plan should identify the existing systems and the costs of maintaining them.

7   **Maintenance** – the plan should incorporate the budget for the maintenance of, and enhancements to, the existing system. The resources required for maintenance and enhancement of existing applications should also be planned if the operation of existing systems is to continue.

8   **Organisational structure** – the plan should describe the existing and future organisational structure for the technology, in terms of location, and human and financial resources.

9   **Impact of the plan** – management is interested in the impact of a plan on the organisation, particularly its financial impact.

10 **Implementation** – the plan should identify implementation risks and obstacles.

KEY POINT

Aspects to consider for an overall information technology strategy:

- key areas which benefit from IT
- costs
- performance criteria
- implications for existing work force.

6.3   Developing the strategy for information technology

When developing an overall information technology strategy the following aspects should be taken into consideration:

1   What are the key business areas that could benefit most from an investment in information technology, what form should the investment take and how could such strategically important units be encouraged to effectively use such technology?

2   How much would the system cost in terms of: software; hardware; management commitment and time; education and training; conversion; documentation; operational manning; and maintenance? The importance of lifetime application costs must be stressed. Most companies try to assess how much it will cost them to install an information technology function, but all too few measure the costs and benefits after implementation. Yet this is the area of greatest potential loss.

3   What criteria for performance should be set for information technology systems? The quality of an information technology application should be measured in two ways: the technical standard it achieves and the degree to which it meets the perceived and often changing needs of the user.

4   What are the implications for the existing work force. Have they the requisite skills? Can they be trained to use the systems? Will there be any redundancies?

KEY POINT

Use a database when need to:

- change applications frequently
- access data rapidly
- to reduce long lead times for systems
- shared data
- communicate across functions and departments
- improve quality of data
- avoid dedicated programming.

Whether such a strategy should be based on a database approach will depend on a number of factors. According to the US Department of Commerce a database approach is called for when:

- application needs are constantly changing, with considerable uncertainty as to the important data elements, expected update or processing functions, and expected volumes to be handled

- rapid access is frequently required to answer *ad hoc* questions

- there is a need to reduce long lead times and high development costs in developing new application systems

- many data elements must be shared by users throughout the organisation

- there is a need to communicate and relate data across functional and department boundaries

- there is a need to improve the quality and consistency of the database and to control access to that resource

- substantial dedicated programming assistance is not normally available.

6.4   Liaison between IT managers and users

Because the existing portfolio of IT applications will influence future policy, there should be an evaluation of the efficiency of current systems. The types of question that managers need to ask are about the satisfaction of the users and the reliability of the system.

KEY POINT

Benefits of bottom-up evaluation:

- users may suggest evolutionary add-ons
- can identify technical quality of current system
- can rate a system on: its business impact.

The evaluation is a bottom-up exercise, depending vitally on the contribution of the users. The benefits of the exercise are:

- users may suggest evolutionary add-ons to systems

- users and systems specialists can indicate the technical quality of the current system in terms of its reliability, ease of maintenance and cost efficiency;

- users can rate a system on: its business impact (how would we manage without it?); its ease of use and user-friendliness; and the frequency of its use, giving an indication of its importance and value.

6.5   Implementation of plans

The implementation of a plan requires:

- selection of an appropriate strategy
- management planning and control
- operational planning and control.

To clarify the distinction between strategic planning and management planning and control, it is useful to quote the definitions given by R.N. Anthony.

Strategic planning is the process of deciding on the objectives of the organisation, on changes in those objectives, on the resources used to attain the objectives, and on the policies that are used to govern the acquisition, use and disposition of the resources.

Management control is the process by which the managers ensure that resources are obtained and used effectively and efficiently in the accomplishment of the organisation's objectives.

In other words, strategic planning determines what is to be done and the general policies that will decide how it is done, while management planning and control is concerned with the detail of how resources are to be acquired. The Board of the organisation therefore own the IS strategy and make key decisions regarding its implementation and any changes that are required.

Operational plans are the short-term element of the company's overall plan. They are concerned with the day to day running of the company in the immediate future and usually cover a period of one year.

Operational planning and control can be defined as planning and controlling the effective and efficient performance of specific tasks. It therefore differs from management planning and control in focusing on one task at a time, whereas management planning and control focuses on resource requirements for the whole range of tasks.

Backwater is a company with an established base of IT applications. The finance department has a fully computerised accounting system. The marketing department has a customer-modelling package and the production department does not see the need for technology.

The Finance Director is in charge of IT and he is proposing a 12% increase in IT expenditure to upgrade systems in the relevant departments, based on last year.

Briefly comment on the weaknesses in the IT provision at Backwater, and any improvements you might make.

Feedback to this activity is at the end of the chapter.

7   Developments in information technology

As explained above, an organisation will always try and ensure that the IT strategy is driven by the organisation's objectives and information requirements. However, taking this perspective does not mean that new developments in information technology cannot be monitored or that new ideas cannot be brought to the attention of key decision makers. Knowing what IT solutions are possible in the real world is part of the IS strategy; the trick is to ensure that any new developments in IT are used to meet specific business needs, rather than the business implementing new IT systems because it seems like a good idea.

Here are just some developments in recent years.

Trading on the Internet

Trading on the Internet is already commonplace, with most major organisations having a web site and offering on-line purchasing of goods and services. Current jargon includes B2B (business to business) and B2C (business to consumer) trading with some web sites also offering C2C (consumer to consumer) trading in the form of auctions. Perhaps the main trend to watch in the next year or so is the development of large B2B sites, with large market places being developed to bring many customers and suppliers together. The co-operation between the major motor manufacturers in the USA in setting up a single trading site to purchase parts for their cars is an example of this trend.

Access to organisation databases

Access to organisation databases in the form of extranet and intranet links is another trend that is becoming more commonplace. Rather than provide information on request, organisations allow favoured customers to access their own databases direct through Internet connections. For example, the Dell organisation allows access to its fault and error databases on computers to major clients. Provision of information in this way will have an impact on the IT infrastructure needed to provide access, as well as ensuring that the overall organisation strategy is to allow this provision of information. The issue of payment for information may also arise if free access is provided where information was previously charged for.

Intranet

An Intranet is effectively a Web site, the access to which is restricted to internal users only. It is a network that is not available to the world outside of the Intranet. If the Intranet network is connected to the Internet, the Intranet will reside behind a firewall and, if it allows access from the Internet, could be an Extranet. The firewall helps to control access between the Intranet and Internet to permit access to the Intranet only by people who are members of the same company or organisation.

In its simplest form, an Intranet can be set-up on a networked PC without any PC having access via the Intranet network to the Internet. For example, consider an office with a few PCs and a few printers all networked together. The network would not be connected to the outside world. On one of the drives of one of the PCs there would be a directory of web pages that comprise the Intranet. Other PCs on the network could access this Intranet by pointing their browser (Netscape or Internet Explorer) to this directory. This would allow them to navigate around the Intranet in the same way as they would get around the Internet.

Intranets are commonly used for sharing knowledge, collaboration and general internal communication.

Extranet

An Extranet is very similar to an Intranet except that the users are either clients or suppliers. It is an Intranet that is partially accessible to authorised outsiders. The actual server (the computer that serves up the web pages) will reside behind a firewall. The firewall helps to control access between the Intranet and Internet permitting access to the Intranet only to people who are suitably authorised. The level of access can be set to different levels for individuals of groups of outside users. The access can be based on a username and password or an IP address (a unique set of numbers such as 209.33.27.100 that defines the computer that the user is on).

Broadband

Primarily networks have been designed for the transmission of text data. With the increasing use of audio and video presentations, video conferencing, and more general multimedia applications, Local Area Networks are required to support these non-text services. Broadband networks can accommodate the high transmission rates associated with data, speech and video.

Mobile computing

Mobile computing is becoming more and more common with laptop PCs having more power and communication capabilities. This should enable better client service to be given, particularly in situations where information would previously been obtained from databases held at head office. There is now the opportunity to copy those databases onto the laptop or provide on-line access from any telephone connection (or even via satellite and mobile telephone). A technician requiring a particular plan or drawing to mend faulty equipment can now obtain this via communication link rather than arrange for a fax to be sent.

Improved telecommunication structure

Improved telecommunication structure also allows work to take place at a location convenient to the employee rather than the employer. In other words, employees can work from home where particular jobs or tasks do not require formal meetings. The use of ISDN and, eventually, ASDL technology will continue to improve data transfer rates, making transfer of information and even video-conferencing from home quite feasible.

Look out for other new developments in the computing press and supplements to quality newspapers as you continue studying this topic.

ACTIVITY 2	Take 30 minutes to try and find out about new IT products and services that became available in the last month.

Feedback to this activity is at the end of the chapter.

Conclusion

This chapter has summarised the development of the objectives of an organisation; shown how the information to meet those objectives can be determined and explained that the Information Technology strategy is necessary to implement the appropriate hardware and software solution to provide that information. The information systems strategy therefore supports the overall business strategy of an organisation, rather than providing information for the sake of it.

SELF-TEST
QUESTIONS

Strategic business objectives

1   What is a critical success factor? (1.1)

2   What are the four sources of CSF's according to Rockart? (1.2)

3   Explain how CSF analysis helps managers determine their information requirements. (1.4)

Information for decision making

4   In overview, what does Strategic Information Systems Planning involve? (2.2)

Information resource management

5   Show how the characteristics of information change depending on the management level that information is being used by. (3.1)

Strategy planning for information systems

6   What must an organisations IS strategy be consistent with? (5.2)

7   Draw a diagram showing the relationship between IS, IT and the corporate strategies. (5.3)

Formulating an IT strategy

8   Define 'Information Technology'. (4)

9   What is 'Management Control'? (6.5)

EXAM-TYPE QUESTION

IS strategy

Many major organisations use formal strategies to identify development priorities for information systems (IS).

Required:

Discuss the reason for this.   **(10 marks)**

FEEDBACK TO ACTIVITY 1

There is no strategy for information technology at Backwater. The Finance Director is still treating it as a cost, rather than a way of achieving competitive advantage. The only strategy that exists is directed to enhancing its existing base, which seems to be mainly in the Finance Director's domain, rather than areas where it may prove to be of strategic value and help the company gain strategic advantage.

A revised approach may be to check what IT is actually being used for in the organisation, and then to determine what other areas (such as developing competitive advantage) are available and necessary. The possibility of integrating the systems in the different departments within the organisation can also be considered to improve information sharing. Finally, while the FD may enjoy being in charge of the IT function, the appointment of a full time IS director may help in improving the IT systems, and allow the FD to focus on the organisation's finances.

FEEDBACK TO ACTIVITY 2

There are various sources of information to assist you in your search. The internet is probably the most easily-accessible source.

On the Internet check out search engines such as www.google.com or www.yahoo.com and enter key words or phrases into a search. With a bit of trial and error, you should come across some interesting sites to visit.

In your bookstore, you could look out for PC related magazines such as PCPRO and Computer Weekly. Both of these products provide reviews of current technology as well as examples of how that technology is being used in practice.

Chapter 2
DELIVERING INFORMATION SYSTEMS: 1

This is the first of two chapters investigating how organisations provide information to their employees or third parties. This chapter examines the different structures that can be used by the Information Systems function and the benefits or otherwise of outsourcing that function to a specialist company.

Objectives

By the time you have finished this chapter you should be able to:

- describe the traditional structure of a centralised Information Systems department and the roles and responsibilities of each function

- explain the principles of a decentralised Information Systems function

- discuss the advantages and disadvantages of centralising or decentralising the Information Systems function

- explain the principles of outsourcing the Information Systems function

- describe the advantages and disadvantages of outsourcing the Information Systems function.

1   Information systems department

The Information Systems department within an organisation will have various tasks and responsibilities in relation to the information systems within that organisation. These tasks and responsibilities will tend to be pervasive to the whole organisation, like other service departments such as finance, rather than focusing on one or two small areas.

The main functions of the department, as shown in the diagram below:

Information System Department

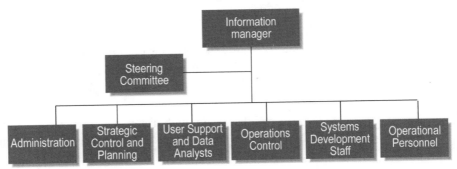

FOULKS LYNCH
PUBLICATIONS

1.1   Information systems manager / director

The IS department will be under the control of the information systems manager or director, who will normally occupy a position on the Board or similar executive decision making body in the organisation.

In his book *Introducing information systems management,* Malcolm Peltu, describes the skills that the IT director should possess. These are:

- good management ability

- good understanding of how the organisation operates and the organisational activities

- good technical expertise in developing and running information systems.

It is easy to see that this range of skills might not always be balanced in an organisation by envisaging where such a person would come from. If the person has a background in management and those skills have been developed, then the first area may be covered. People who make good managers unfortunately do not always have the technical wizardry to have an IT vision for the future, as well as an understanding of the day-to-day computing problems that can crop up. Whilst it may be possible to find a manager with technical ability, it would seem much more difficult to find one that also knew how the organisation operates and all of the activities.

The role of the information director is likely to include the following:

1   Developing the information systems strategy to tie in with the overall organisational strategy. This aspect of the role covers the purchase and use of the technology to fit with the organisation's goals and objectives.

2   Ensuring that there is interaction with the environment. This aspect covers:

- information systems flexibility and connections between other organisations, e.g. electronic data interchange (EDI), shared databases and communications links with customers and suppliers. It also entails looking constantly at the trends in new technology and the new systems enhancements that are being marketed

- the legal environment of IS, which involves the data protection legislation, trans-border flows of information and systems security matters covered in the Computer Misuse Act 1990

- the public relations required to convince suppliers, customers and employees of the benefits of the IS.

3   Responsibility for the information infrastructure, which incorporates the technical and software standards, the establishment of databases and the provision of a systems service function.

4   Setting up and servicing links between the IS staff and the rest of the organisation. This part of the role involves the provision of technical assistance, informal discussion with users about their needs, discussion with finance and management accounting about the payoff of IS investments.

5   Participating in a steering committee to oversee the general direction of IS policy and taking decisions on individual IT projects.

1.2   The role of the steering committee

Because of the size of the investment involved and the importance of key systems to the organisation, many firms are establishing committees to help manage information processing activities.

A steering committee is a collection of members from the various departments within the organisation and is not, therefore, biased toward one particular functional area of the business. The purpose of a steering committee is to decide how to allocate scarce IT resources and to plan for future system developments. Other activities of the steering committee include:

- ensuring that all the IT activities are in line with the strategic plans of the organisation as a whole

- providing leadership at senior level for the exploitation and management of IT

- ensuring that resource allocation decisions are effective

- co-ordinating requirements in any organisational restructuring

- creating the terms of reference for the project teams

- monitoring the progress of the various projects.

Some firms establish a corporate level steering committee for information processing, whose objective is to review plans and determine the size of the firm's investment in information processing. The corporate committee reviews division plans, organises and approves education about systems, and seeks areas for the development of common systems serving two or more sub-organisations, such as two different companies with common information processing requirements. The purpose of a common system is to avoid the cost of developing a tailored application at each site.

Each division has a local steering committee that is charged with the responsibility of developing and approving long-range plans for information in that sub-organisation. The local committee also reviews and approves short-term plans and the annual budget for information processing activities in the division. This committee serves to review proposals for new systems and to assign priorities to them. Finally, the local committee reviews and approves staffing requirements for information services.

The problems that arise with steering committees are

- the experience and skills of the members does not match the purpose of the committee

- having the wrong balance of people on the committee, for example, having those that feel they should be represented rather than those with the actual knowledge required

- a failure in the communication process from the committee to the rest of the organisation

- meetings may be too infrequent and this leads to a concentration on tactical matters and a possible loss of commitment from some of the members.

1.3   Administration

Administration includes the secretarial, accounting and library services associated with the systems department. Department staff will still need secretarial support, for example, to communicate information about changes in information systems to other user departments and to provide standard secretarial functions to managers. The Human Resources department may handle other functions, such as staff recruitment and similar personnel issues, if the organisation is large enough to have one.

Similarly, monitoring actual expenditure compared to budget may be performed by the accounts department, with regular expenditure summarises being provided to the IS department.

Maintaining a library of programmes being used, information about hardware and software issued to staff etc. will be the responsibility of the IS department. It is essential to maintain a record of software issued to ensure that licence agreements are adhered to while basic security of computer equipment means that a database of users and computers issued will have to maintained and updated as each change occurs.

1.4   Database administrator

One very important administrator is the person in-charge of the databases within the organisation; this is the database administrator (or DBA).

The DBA's work can be split into strategic and organisational activities.

Strategic tasks
- working with strategic management to help define the organisation's present and future needs
- choosing suitable file structures for data storage
- analysing the data required for each application
- preparation of a data model
- preparation and maintenance of a data dictionary
- assignment and recording of the ownership of each set of data
- defining hardware needs and planning any changes required
- reconciliation of conflicting information needs.

Organisational tasks
- ensuring data integrity by implementing and controlling database procedures
- production of operating manuals
- provision of training for users and applications programmers on a regular basis
- assessing the ongoing performance of the database.

In some organisations the data administrator's job is split into two parts of a data administrator and a database administrator.

Data administrator

A data administrator will be in charge of coordinating, analysing and recording all data items. The tasks will include:
- analysing the data required by each application
- the preparation of a data model
- the preparation and maintenance of the data dictionary and instructions to users for its use
- the recording of the ownership of all the data.

Database administrator

A database administrator will be concerned with the upkeep and maintenance of the actual database itself. The DBA would be responsible for the following:
- database design and structure, including the planning of any changes required
- the planning of any hardware changes needed
- evaluating proposals to update or upgrade the database

- ensuring data integrity by implementing and controlling database procedures

- the production of operating manuals

- the provision of training for users on a regular basis

- assessing the on-going performance of the database.

1.5 Strategic control and planning

Part of the control function of the IS department involves ensuring adherence to organisational guidelines on purchase of hardware and software as well as the actual use of that hardware and software. For example, staff may not be allowed to play games on computers, so the IT department may regularly audit software on computers for evidence of mis-use.

The main element of control is planning for future use of computers within the organisation. Planning will involve short-term objectives such as developing and setting procedures and standards for use and operation of computer equipment as well as longer term planning. Longer term planning involves developing the IT function to ensure that the overall IT objectives for the organisation are met. For example, proposals for systems changes will be investigated and discussed at the IT steering committee prior to being presented to the Board of the organisation. Similarly, planning will also involve producing a staff plan to take account of changes to the IT systems, and then agreeing an overall budget for changes to those systems, including changes to the number of staff in the department.

1.6 User support

The IS department will provide user support, normally in the form of an information centre or similar system. An information centre would be expected to provide aid and support to people who use computers and to help users develop their own software. It responds to the organisation's need to control technology by:

- establishing hardware standards

- approving a range of suppliers of hardware

- establishing software, testing and documentation standards

- becoming a central point for the release of updated software

- ensuring data integrity in the databases

- enforcing security procedures e.g., backup and virus checking

- other services offered by information centres include

- training in the use of languages and software development tools

- help when searching for reference publications on software, hardware, development methods etc

- specific help with identifying the location of data in the corporate database and ensuring that end-users are not using data that is out of date

- technical assistance in dealing with particular problems when writing applications in programming languages

- guidance when purchasing hardware, software, application packages or external support services to maintain compatibility.

Information centre personnel usually act as consultants and trainers to computing users in departments. They will need a wide range of skills as the end users may be varied in the extent of their computer knowledge. The information centre may provide guidance to a manager purchasing personal computers to be used for word processing *and* give specific technical assistance to a programmer working in an end user department.

User support will also be supplemented with a help desk, to provide assistance on day-to-day problems with computers such as logging on to the network or amending passwords. The help desk tends to focus on small, easy-to-solve issues, whereas the Information Centre will be involved with more long-term projects.

User support staff may also include **data analysts** who are responsible for analysing data within the organisation's databases and presenting this information to the users in accordance with their specific requirements.

1.7 Operations control

It is essential that the computer systems within an organisation continue to function as required throughout the working day, and in many cases 24 hours a day as flexible working means staff need access to computer resources at any time. The main task of operations control is simply to keep the IT systems available and working, and then to troubleshoot any problems that occur.

Particular tasks that operations control will perform include:

- monitoring of network usage including allocation of additional resources to try and alleviate problems such as servers receiving too many user requests or disk space becoming low

- advising users of network problems such as server downtimes

- maintaining the it infrastructure including upgrading it equipment such as telecommunication links where necessary

- fixing faults in the it infrastructure as they arise

- updating anti-virus software and debugging infected machines

Many operations may appear to overlap with the information centre or help desk; clear lines of responsibility will be required to ensure that each department is aware of its activities.

1.8 System development staff

The IS department will maintain a number of programmers and analysts to design and development new in-house software, or amend off-the-shelve software for specific use within the organisation. In fact, the full range of systems analysis and design may be accommodated within the department including:

- systems analysis – carrying out a study of existing systems to ensure they are meeting their objectives

- systems design – designing new systems or amending existing systems to ensure that the system objectives are met

- systems specification – designing a new system in detail including producing the full systems specification document

- systems testing – checking a system works correctly and then implementing that system

- systems review – continually reviewing systems to ensure objectives continue to be met.

1.9   Operational personnel

With the rise of end-user computing, the responsibility of the IS department for basic processing of data has fallen. Most departments tend to input and process their own data rather than batch input documents and send these to the DP department for input.

One major exception to this rule remains with organisations that collect a significant number of payments in the form of cash or cheques (for example electricity or gas supply organisations or banks in the processing of those cheques). These organisations will still require an extensive data entry department to be able to process the large volume of transactions.

1.10 New systems and legacy systems

Many organisations introduce new computer systems for various applications, but continue to use old systems as well. These old systems might be large transaction processing systems, written in an 'old fashioned' programming language such as COBOL. They continue to do their task and have not been replaced with new systems using more 'up-to-date' technology and software. Old 'back office' systems that need relatively little updating and maintenance are often called **legacy systems**.

A point to remember that within the IT department of an organisation, some staff will be employed on the development of new systems. Others will be employed on maintaining and updating existing systems, including legacy systems. If errors are found in a programme, these will have to be corrected, and a new version of the software produced. Programmes might have to be updated from time-to-time, for example for the introduction of new tax rates or tax rules.

Systems analysts and programmers are therefore not entirely involved in new developments.

ACTIVITY 1

Research what skills are required by a Systems Analyst.

Feedback to this activity is at the end of the chapter.

2   Centralisation or decentralisation? The relative merits

The IS department can be maintained in one central location within an organisation, or alternatively, spread out within the organisation. As you would expect, the decision to centralise or decentralise has various advantages and disadvantages, which the individual organisation will have to evaluate before making a decision on the structure of the department.

2.1   Reasons for decentralising

KEY POINT

The main reason for decentralising at least part of the IS department, is to provide a more local service.

The main reason for decentralising at least part of the IS department, is to provide a more local service. However, care must be taken in deciding which sections of the department to decentralise as this may otherwise result in un-necessary duplication of work.

Some of the reasons for decentralising the IS function are discussed below.

Size

The process of decentralisation breaks an IS department up into more manageable units. This enables decision-making to proceed quickly and effectively and, in theory, a closer control to be maintained on the day to day running of each section of department's activities.

FOULKS LYNCH
PUBLICATIONS

One important factor to take into account when deciding whether to decentralise is the size of the firm, and size of the departments: a large company with departments of more than about 15 strong would benefit more from decentralisation than a small firm.

Need for specialists

As a business grows, the nature of its activities often becomes more complex so that each department has to rely on experts to provide appropriate support for that particular segment of the business. For example, a department providing services to customers may require a higher level of (and be prepared to pay for) a higher level of IT support than an internal service department.

Motivation

If managers are made to feel responsible for a particular part of a department then it is generally found that their efforts within that part of the business are improved and, therefore the business prospers.

Uncertainty and better 'local knowledge'

With ever-changing market conditions, decisions cannot be pre-planned or centrally planned. It is important to have local managers who are closer in touch with each particular part of the business environment to be in a position to respond quickly as problems arise. Decentralising the IS department means that changes can be made more quickly to respond to the individual needs of each user department. A centralised solution might not suit every part of the organisation.

Geographical

Decentralisation often refers to the delegation of responsibilities at a single location, an office or a factory; however, it is important for an IS department to get close to different departments in those far-flung locations. On-site support can be a lot more effective than trying to mend a computer by telephone, for example.

Fiscal

Providing a decentralised structure enables user departments to be able to decide on the level of expenditure that they are prepared to make for the service being provided. Placing money into a central resource may not appear to provide any additional tangible benefit, whereas hiring additional staff to work only in one department has an immediate and obvious benefit of more IS staff available within the department.

Training

Training can be focused onto the requirements of the individual department, rather than generic training courses being produced for the whole organisation.

Software availability

For many applications, relatively cheap and well-tried software packages are available. It is therefore easier for local departments or centres in an organisation to select ready-to-install software, without the need for centralised support or systems development work.

 FOULKS LYNCH
PUBLICATIONS

2.2   Centralisation

Some of the reasons for retaining a central IS department are:

Economies of scale

It may be advantageous to acquire one large computer, with greater processing capabilities, rather than several small computers. Centralisation of personnel may also remove unnecessary duplication of activity and allow for regulation and control of analysis and programming functions. It is necessary, however, to balance the cost element against the benefits derived by users (the latter may be greater with decentralisation).

Staff shortages/turnover

Centralisation mitigates the effect of both, so that individuals are less indispensable; they can also be provided with greater scope in their working experience. Fewer employees may be needed so higher quality staff and specialists may be affordable.

Ease of control

Senior management is better placed to control operating functions, particularly when a standard reporting system is being utilised. When IS strategy is an important element in an organisation's overall strategic plan, head office management will want to be able to influence the implementation of strategy, and so are likely to need some degree of centralised control.

To prevent poor 'local' buying decisions

There is a possibility that if IT buying decisions are left to local management, poor-quality decisions are more likely. There might be inadequate control over additional spending, and systems might be purchased or developed that are incompatible with systems used in other parts of the organisation.

3   Outsourcing

Outsourcing refers to organisations hiring/contracting – in services and expertise rather than employing their own staff to perform the functions.

In the context of information technology, computer bureaux were the earliest types of outsourcing. Here a company owning a powerful computer would run clients' programs and carry out their processing. Bureaux are less common now, but **facilities management** has become more common.

3.1   Facilities management

Rather than maintain a computing department of its own, an organisation can choose to contract out its computer operations to a private company, which will be paid a fee for its service. A computer bureau is an external service, whereas facilities management companies operate within the organisation.

Facilities management is defined as the management and operation of part or all of an organisation's IT services by an external source, at an agreed service level, to an agreed cost formula and over an agreed time period. The facilities management contract may further include IT consultancy, the management of IT services, the provision of new services and ownership of hardware and software.

Facilities management companies are contracted to take over part or all of an organisation's computing facilities including:

- project management assistance

- complete control of systems development
- running an entire computing function.

Possible reasons for using facilities management (FM) include:

- the organisation may not have the staff, management time or expertise to organise their substantial data processing requirements
- controlling costs where the contact for services specifies the costs in advance and extra costs will have to be borne by the FM company
- economies of scale may exist where two organisations employ the same FM company, any research carried out by the FM company can be shared between them
- the FM company may employ staff with specific expertise, which can be shared between several customers.

KEY POINT

Some reasons for using facilities management:

- organisation does not have the staff
- cost control
- economies of scale
- FM company has staff with specific expertise.

Advantages

The advantages of outsourcing / facilities management are:

- small organisations might not have the staff, time or expertise to run their own high quality systems
- cost control. the facilities management company will be asked to work to a precise budget, providing the outsourcing company with good control of costs
- economies of scale – for example, for example the client organisation can exploit the contractor's purchasing power on items such as maintenance contracts and purchase of consumables
- specialist staff can be shared over several clients, so that the client company receives the benefit of services from specialist staff it would not otherwise been able to employ.

Disadvantages

Potential disadvantages and problems include:

- the provision of information is an inherent part of management and may be too important to contract out
- technologies that might play a strategic role in an organisation's success should be kept in-house
- work, which has been sub-contracted, can be difficult to switch to a different supplier without jeopardising the smooth running of the organisation. this can give the facilities management company great bargaining power
- the organisation and the facilities management company have different objectives. the organisation will be anxious to improve the information systems and to find new ways of using it to enhance performance and success. the sub-contracting company, however, will be anxious to contain costs and is unlikely to suggest changes
- sub-contracting might be used simply as a way to off-load the problems rather than as the result of an objective assessment of costs and benefits
- once a company has handed over its computing to another company, it is locked into the arrangement, the decision being difficult to reverse. Should the fm company's service be unsatisfactory, then the effort and expense of rebuilding its own computing facility would be enormous.

3.2   Examples of IT outsourcing

You might be aware of some examples of outsourcing of IT work from your own experience. Certainly, you might be asked to comment on the usefulness of outsourcing in particular circumstances, as part of an examination question. Some examples of outsourcing are:

- Payroll. Some companies, particularly small and medium-sized companies, outsource the processing of the monthly payroll to an outside specialist agency.

- Outsourcing the running of an entire computer system. In the UK, there are examples of large government computer systems, such as systems for processing social benefits claims and systems for storing and using criminal intelligence records, that have been 'privatised' and outsourced to private sector companies.

- Software maintenance. Organisations that cannot (or do not want to) afford their own full-time IT staff for maintenance support will use the services of an outside firm. If any problem arises with the organisation's systems, such as a malfunction of the organisation's web site or its system for processing payments for internet sales, the matter is referred to the outside software support firm.

Conclusion

In this chapter you have read about the structures that can be used within an information systems department including the advantages and disadvantages of centralising or decentralising that department. The alternative method of providing information system services by outsourcing the IS department to a third party was also discussed.

SELF-TEST QUESTIONS

Information systems department

1   What activities does the role of the Information Director include? (1.1)

2   What is the purpose of a steering committee? (1.2)

Centralisation or decentralisation? The relative merits

3   Give five reasons for decentralising the IS department. (2.1)

Outsourcing

4   What services does a facilities management company provide? (3.1)

5   Outline the advantages and disadvantages of outsourcing the IS department. (3.1)

EXAM-TYPE QUESTION

Centralising IT

Mugen Industrial plc is an industrial company serving international markets from factories in France, Germany, Portugal and Spain, North America and the UK. The company is a recognised leader in the manufacture of equipment for the automobile and aircraft industries. It also makes a wide range of engine mountings, hoses, plastic mouldings and rubber components. Turnover shown in the last published accounts was £450 million, of which £150 million was contributed by the UK companies.

All the overseas subsidiaries are wholly owned and operate principally in their own country. There is little transfer of goods across national boundaries. The group is managed from a small London headquarters and a great deal of autonomy has been given to the operating units. As a result each subsidiary has evolved its own information systems strategy.

FOULKS LYNCH PUBLICATIONS

In recent months the London headquarters has begun to press for a more centralised management structure. They argue it will enable more efficient use of resources and so cut costs. The Finance Director has asked you to investigate the options and report to him.

Required:

Prepare your report, including the references to key literature you feel appropriate, for the Finance Director setting out:

- the advantages of centralising the IT structure
- the disadvantages of centralising the IT structure
- any non-IT factors that might affect your final recommendation.

(15 marks)

FEEDBACK TO
ACTIVITY 1

A systems analyst must be able to speak with business users and capture their requirements, and then, having analysed the requirements, present them in a format that the developers can understand and work with. Therefore, the skills needed include; business understanding, technical knowledge, systems skills in modelling, and strong interpersonal skills. Each of these areas can be broken down into sub skills, such as awareness of business processes, business objectives, business needs; awareness of databases, programming requirements, technical requirements; data modelling, process modelling, event modelling; written communication skills, interviewing skills, workshop facilitation skills, presentation skills, analytical skills, and so on.

Chapter 3
DELIVERING INFORMATION SYSTEMS: 2

This is a relatively lengthy section covering aspects of charging for computer systems and then providing a summary of the background knowledge required regarding computer hardware and software. You may find that some of this material is familiar to you – in which case concentrate on the areas where you need to increase your knowledge. A complete list of hardware and software and related issues is provided for reference purposes.

Objectives

By the time you have finished this chapter you should be able to:

- briefly describe the types of cost incurred in delivering Information Systems
- describe how the costs of the Information Systems function may be distributed between customer departments
- explain the principles, benefits and drawbacks of cross-charging costs
- discuss the issues raised by establishing the Information Systems function as a cost or profit centre
- describe the advantages and disadvantages of establishing the Information Systems function as a separate company
- explain the problems of accounting for shared infrastructure costs
- describe the typical hardware, software, data and communications infrastructures found within Information Systems functions
- discuss the meaning and need for a disaster recovery plan
- discuss the meaning and need for a risk management process
- describe the meaning and implications of legacy systems
- discuss the relationship of Information Systems with end-users and the implications of the expectations and skills of end-users.

1 Accounting for IS costs

1.1 Costs incurred in delivering an Information Systems

An organisation can incur many different costs in delivering information to its directors, employees, customers and suppliers. These costs can be summarised as follows:

One-off capital costs
These will include:

- hardware and software purchase
- specialist accommodation for computers
- wiring for networks
- installation costs such as new desks for employees.
- new rooms/premises

One-off revenue costs

These will include:

- system development costs including programmers' salaries, system analyst fees, costs of testing the system, cost of converting files etc.
- redundancy payments (if any)
- hiring of new specialist staff
- staff training

Ongoing costs

These will include:

- IS system staff wages
- help desk and information centre salaries
- subscriptions to external information providers such as news services
- data transmission costs (telephone line rental, internet access fees etc.)
- consumable materials such as floppy disks, CDs, paper etc.
- power for computers, VDUs etc.
- any rental costs for hardware not initially purchased
- hardware maintenance and support contracts
- software maintenance and support contracts
- standby and backup arrangements
- regular staff training.

All of these costs will have to be accounted for in some way within the organisation.

KEY POINT

Objectives for an IS charging system:

- improved financial control for the IS and other user departments
- encourage the correct use of IT
- improve morale and motivation of staff.

There are other reasons for re-charging costs of the IS department, apart from re-charging the tangible costs (that is the costs that result in direct expenditure compared to intangible costs such as low staff morale) incurred by that department. The charging system must also accommodate the following objectives:

1 **Improved financial control for the IS and other user departments**. Charging for the service provides an emphasis for the IS department to give good customer service. Similarly, the fact that the user department is paying for the service will mean that the user department will be looking for value for money in the service being provided.

2 **Encourage the correct use of IT**. Providing a charge enables the user department to decide whether or not to actually use specific services being provided by the IS department. If there were no charge for any service, then the use of the service, and the importance of that service to the department would not be regulated. Providing a charge limits the use of any particular service to the parts actually required.

3 **Improve morale and motivation of staff**. Placing a charge on a service helps staff to appreciate the cost of either providing or obtaining that service. User departments will appreciate the cost implications of their IS choices, and hopefully recognise that unlimited service cannot be provided at effectively zero charge. Also, the staff in the IS department will be motivated because they will be earning revenue from providing the services and so provide a better service because a charge is being made.

Given that some costs, like the tangible costs, are essentially fixed, and costs for project work such as providing services for bespoke application development, are essentially variable to the user departments, a two-tier costing structure may arise. Fixed costs are charged separately or not at all and the variable costs charged as incurred. However, before making that decision, we need to investigate the charging methods available.

During the development and operation of Information Systems, there are many costs incurred. List the intangible costs that might result.

There is no feedback to this activity.

1.2   Accounting for costs of an Information System

Having determined what the costs of providing an Information System can be, the next sections investigate the different ways in which those costs are accounted for.

The costs of an information system can be accounted for in three main ways:

- IS is a non-recharged cost centre
- IS is recharged at cost
- IS is recharged above cost, to make a profit.

The advantages and disadvantages of these methods are discussed below.

1.3   Non-recharged cost centre

The costs of the IT department and information systems are charged to an IS cost centre, and treated as a period cost overhead. The costs are then written off to the profit and loss account, without charging them or apportioning them to other cost centres or profit centres that use the IS services.

Advantages
- Simple and cheap. No apportionment of IT costs is needed.
- Might encourage customer-driven demand for innovation. Users might demand better systems knowing that these will have no cost effects on their departments.
- Users can concentrate on the main activities of their departments, as they do not have to worry about IT costs.

Disadvantages
- If a service is free to users, they may demand more and more even when it is not economically justifiable for the organisation to supply more.
- If not recharged fewer people are likely to complain if the service is inefficient and too expensive. The IT department will have little incentive to control costs.
- If not recharged, users can find it difficult to request changes in the service level. They fear the response 'You are getting this for free, be glad with what you get'. Ultimately user departments know what level of service they need and the IT department should be responsive to their needs.
- Performance measurement of departments is distorted if all costs involved in the operation of the department are not accounted for.

1.4 Recharged at cost

The costs of IT and information systems are charged to an IS cost centre. Users of IS services are then charged for the use of those services. The costs might be re-charged to users by apportioning them on a 'fair basis'. Alternatively, the IS cost centre might charge for its services, for example a rate per hour, but the rate charged will not include any element for profit. It will simply be set at a level that allows the IS cost centre to recover its costs.

Advantages

- Simple, as no profit mark-up needs to be agreed

- Depending on how the charge-out is made, users bear the costs of their demand on and use of IT, and so are made aware of the costs they are incurring for the organisation

- Users will complain if the IT charges seem too high, and this could act as a useful control over efficiency and cost-effectiveness in the IS cost centre.

Disadvantages

- If the IT department can charge out all costs, there is no incentive for it to be efficient. A better arrangement would be for it to charge out budgeted costs or standard costs only. That way, any cost overruns in the IT department would stay there and the IT department would have to explain them.

- If recharging is not related to IT usage, users will feel aggrieved. They will feel that a central cost is being arbitrarily passed on to them from a monopoly supplier.

- Even when attempts are made to charge out costs according to usage, it can be very difficult to decide on a fair basis. Some costs will be relatively easy to charge out. For example, analyst's time would be the basis for charging for development work. However, many of the costs will relate to the fixed costs of the IT department and some type of rate per hour of processing may have to be assessed.

1.5 Recharged at a mark-up

Under this basis, the aim would be to charge users for internally-provided IT services with an amount approximating to market rates. In such an arrangement the costs and profitability of the IS profit centre are in the hands of the IS manager and staff. The manager has the power to reduce costs (for example, moving to cheaper accommodation) and increase income by looking for other business opportunities outside the company by offering IS solutions and support to other businesses. Due to increased control over income and expenditure of the company this should allow the manager to offer more attractive and flexible salaries, providing staff with better rewards within an expanding company where there are more opportunities for developing skills and careers.

Advantages

- The IT department should be able to make a profit. This should be motivating for IT managers.

- Making a profit depends on being efficient with costs and offering services that users want to buy and which are competitively priced. The IT department should therefore develop a more commercial outlook.

- Users can compare the in-house cost to costs of hiring outside suppliers. This will help to keep the IT department efficient - provided users have the freedom to contract outside if that is cheaper.

- Users can buy more services if they want to. The IT department therefore becomes the mere supplier of services; the users determine what services they want. The IT department should therefore be more responsive to users' needs.

- Performance measurement of user departments should be fairer if they have to bear the full commercial costs of services.

Disadvantages

- If there is no suitable outside supplier, it can be difficult to decide on the charge-out rates that should be used. Users can be particularly aggrieved if they feel that the IT department is charging out at excessive, monopolistic profit margins.

- Buying from outside can be disadvantageous to the organisation as a whole: the IT department's fixed costs still have to be covered.

- Although a true market may exist for some services (such as specific consultancy projects), it may be impracticable for one department to subcontract to a third party if other departments do not. Most applications are integrated nowadays and it is important to be able to retrieve and use data from many departments.

1.6   Cross-charging of costs including shared infrastructure costs

The charging systems can become more complicated where parts of the IT systems are shared between departments, as it is difficult to determine individual usage of those shared resources. To provide some estimation of usage prior to charging, some or all of the following activities can take place:

- review of network traffic to establish either the number of messages or amount of data being transferred over the shared resource by each department

- checking the number of users of each shared resource and allocating charges based on number of users

- checking the amount of disk space used on network servers and then allocating charges based on this measure

- logging the number of telephone calls made to the help desk and using these as a rough guide to use of resources

Whatever method of charging is chosen, it must be seen to be fair, and incorporate an element of actual usage rather than appear to be an arbitrary amount.

1.7   Establishing Information Systems function as a separate entity

Another alternative to providing IS support within an organisation is to establish the Information Systems function as a separate entity. This is taking the idea of making the IS department a separate profit centre one stage further. As well as being able to make a profit on the services being re-charged, the IS department would effectively be a separate legal entity and so would be run as a separate business. The IS support services would effectively be purchased by the main company as a separate service, in the same way that other goods and services would be purchased.

There is very little difference in this charging system compared to outsourcing the whole Information System support. In such an arrangement the costs of supporting the technology and paying, developing and motivating the IS personnel are transferred to a separate company. The company is essentially outsourcing the supply of systems and services to an external organisation, but in this case an external company which they know has experience in the type of systems and applications they are likely to need. The benefits to the user department include:

- only paying for IS resources and staff when they need them, rather than supporting them internally as a fixed overhead

- increased management time. Senior management's time (and cost) does not have to be spent on organising, motivating and training employees who are not delivering the core business activities of the company.

KEY POINT

Estimation usage prior to charging:

- review network traffic

- checking number of users of each shared resource

- checking the amount of disk space used

- log calls to the help desk.

KEY POINT

An alternative to providing IS support within an organisation is to establish the information systems function as a separate entity.

- access to a larger pool of experienced and motivated staff. The company no longer has to develop, maintain and support such a pool.

- having an agreed contract with specific pre-set service standards

- agreeing a fixed price for the contract

- prices can be easily compared to other IS providers.

The problems for the IS department include:

- how to estimate an appropriate price for all services in advance of provision

- the possibility of paying damages for breach of contract if the service is not provided, or delayed.

Before establishing the IS function as a separate entity, the organisation must ensure that the function is of a sufficient size and maturity to be able to provide this service. The company's systems will also, normally, be established, so provision of IS support is seen more as a service than a necessity. Following the initial set-up of a system, IS support may be expected as a right, not as an additional service that needs to be paid for.

Whatever decision is taken, care is needed to ensure that the basis of making that decision is clearly stated, and that user departments are re-assured that they will be able to obtain the IS services that they require.

2   Computer hardware

All information systems require computer hardware and software to make them operate effectively. This section introduces (or revises, if you are already familiar with this detail) the common hardware and software that are found in most information systems.

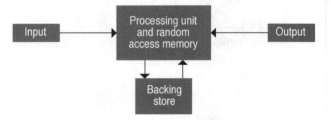

The diagram shown above can represent all computers. Data is entered through input devices, data may be used from the backing store, and output is produced. Records on the backing store may also be updated.

Of course, the sizes of computer can differ greatly from supercomputers down to laptops, and there will be choices as to the types of input, output and backing store devices used.

2.1   Servers

The term 'server' is now used for any shared IT processing or storage device. Although servers vary widely in their technical design, the most important issue for a user such as a management accountant is to recognise the need for a server and specify its performance features. The technical specification of hardware and software is an issue for IT specialists – members of the organisation's IT department or supplier organisations.

The following sections look briefly at the different types of storage and processing hardware available to organisations. Later, we will look at the different ways in which servers can be used in IT architecture.

2.2   Mainframe computers

Much of the computer processing in large and medium sized organisations is carried out on large mainframe computers. This type of computer is well suited to basic operational systems – payroll, stock control, invoicing, etc. – that are crucial to an organisation. Mainframe servers tend to be run by specialist staff, usually employed within the IT department, and tend to run only specially written or bespoke application software. Data may be input by operators within the IT department, or it may be input through VDUs operated by staff within user departments.

2.3   Minicomputers

The minicomputer came to be recognised as such when only mainframe computers existed. Now less powerful mainframe computers equate with the upper end of the minicomputer range and microcomputers cover the bottom end of the range. The term minicomputer is still used for marketing purposes and can be equated with machines such as the larger DEC computers.

Minicomputers may act as the main computing resource in small or medium sized organisations, or may be used as departmental servers within large organisations. Off the shelf software packages are available for minicomputers.

2.4   Personal computers

In recent years personal computers (PCs) have become the most widespread and commonly used computer resource. Their versatility and cheapness, combined with the wide variety of software that is available, allow their use in almost every business.

PCs may be used on a stand-alone basis, or they may be linked together via a local area network (LAN), or they may be linked with minicomputers or mainframes via a wide area network (WAN).

There are four or five common designs of computer chips that have been built into many hundreds of differently labelled PCs. Those chips have made possible the vast expansion of computer production in recent years.

The PC is cheap enough for an individual to have one all to himself or herself either in business or at home. Typically, they cost between £300 and £2,000. Brand names and specifications will be reflected in the price.

Adding extra memory, additional processing power or more peripheral devices can enhance the PC's performance.

2.5   Portable or laptop PCs

In recent years computers have been developed that are truly portable. Many of them use screens that are less power hungry than those on standard PCs, which enables them to be powered by rechargeable batteries. These batteries give several hours of continuous operation before needing to be recharged. This enables portable PCs to be used by business people while travelling.

Portable PCs are compatible with desktop PCs, which enable work carried out on the portable PC to be downloaded on to office computers (either via diskette or via a communications link). Many laptops have a **docking station** into which they can be placed to link them into a local area network.

Portable PCs may also be used for specialist applications such as carrying out market research surveys.

2.6   Peripherals

These are hardware devices other than processors or networks. The term peripherals commonly refers to input, output and communication hardware. Some of these devices are covered below.

2.7   Data storage

Internal storage

Data and programs can be stored in the internal RAM of the computer, or in a hard disk.

RAM (Random access memory) is volatile memory (the contents are lost when the computer is turned off) but it is accessible directly by the computer.

Hard disks provide the permanent storage in a computer. The contents of memory remain intact without the need for power supply, but there is a small time delay involved in accessing data and files stored on the disks. CD can also provide disk storage, although CD / RW drives are needed to read and write to this storage medium.

External storage

The function of external storage is to maintain files of data and programs in a form intelligible to the computer. The principal requirements of external storage are:

- that sufficient storage capacity exists for the system to function adequately
- that the stored data can be quickly input to the computer when required
- that the stored data can be quickly and accurately amended when necessary and the updated files are easily created.

2.8   Computer files

A computer user has to maintain **data files** and **program files**.

There are three types of data file:

Master files	Master files have a permanent existence, and are kept up to date by adding new records, deleting expired records and making changes to records in file
Transaction files (change files)	Transaction files have only a temporary life. They are created by validating input and then writing it to backing storage from where it is used to update the master file. After this they have no further use.
Temporary files	Temporary files are used by a computer program to store data when insufficient memory is available. Although disk space for temporary files must be available to the computer program, they require no human intervention, being automatically created and deleted. A common type of application using temporary files is the sorting of large quantities of data.

The following are examples of master files, with their corresponding transaction files:

Master file	Transaction file (examples only)
Customer (The sales ledger)	Order, payments, Dr/Cr adjustments, new accounts, cancelled accounts.
Supplier (The purchase ledger)	Invoices, credit notes, new suppliers.
Stock	Receipts, issues, returns, new stock items, deleted stock items.

2.9   Computer storage

Magnetic tape

Magnetic tape is still occasionally used as a back-up storage device, where its low cost is a significant advantage, or where it is maintained because other, more recent, systems have not been implemented. Tape can be used to take a fast back up of the contents of the hard disk on a microcomputer. The device used to do this is a tape streamer. It would be normal to keep several editions or 'generations' of backups.

Magnetic discs

Magnetic discs are currently the most important type of external or backing store although CD R/W and DVD are also being used more. The main types of discs are:

Floppy discs

These are about 3'' across and are held in a rigid plastic case, which has a sliding cover to allow access to the disc. They hold about 1.4MB each. Floppy discs can easily be inserted and removed from the computer's disc drive. They are used for taking copies of files and are often used for the supply of new software. They are slow to read and write, and are not normally used as main backing store.

Internal hard discs

These stay permanently in PCs and typically hold up to 80 gigabytes (GB). They are fast and reliable and are used to hold both data and programs.

Disc packs

These are found in larger machines such as mainframe computers. They are typically about 15'' across and can hold very large amounts of data.

Note that when information on a disc is updated, the new information overwrites the old. If a mistake is made, the old data will be irrecoverable. Therefore proper security and backup procedures are needed.

Compact discs

These discs look like ordinary audio CDs and are similarly robust. They can hold about 650MB of data, which makes them ideal for multimedia applications where video and audio data is very space consuming. Re-writeable CD storage (CD-RW) is also available.

Digital Versatile Disks (DVD)

Finally, digital versatile disks are starting to be used as storage devices on some computers. These offer enhanced capacity (from 3.5 gigabytes up to 18 gigabytes of data).

3   Architectures

3.1   Centralised and distributed systems

Over the last few years, there has been a trend towards the fragmentation of large organisations into devolved business units. This autonomy has resulted in an increase in the decentralisation of information technology operations.

 FOULKS LYNCH
PUBLICATIONS

The justification for a decision to **centralise** information technology is similar to the decision to centralise the IS function.

1   **Only one set of files is needed**. Everyone in the organisation uses the same data, which is readily accessible in a standard format.

2   **Economies of scale**. It may be advantageous to acquire one large computer, with greater processing capabilities, rather than several small computers. Centralisation of personnel may also remove unnecessary duplication of activity and allow for regulation and control of analysis and programming functions. It is necessary, however, to balance the cost element against the benefits derived by users (the latter may be greater with decentralisation).

3   **Staff shortages/turnover**. Centralisation mitigates the effect of both, so that individuals are less indispensable, and they can be provided with greater scope in their working experience. Fewer employees may be needed so higher quality staff and specialists may be affordable.

4   **Ease of control**. Senior management is better placed to control operating functions, particularly when a standard reporting system is being utilised.

The arguments in favour of decentralised or distributed systems are as follows:

1   **Local knowledge**. Computer personnel are advantageously positioned when they are close to the problem. They are more likely to arrive at an appropriate solution than if they were remotely located. They will also focus on the business problem rather than technical computer considerations.

2   **Speed of response**. Operational decisions can be made more quickly. Line managers can respond more rapidly to change, as they are better placed to appreciate the local conditions and to be aware of other relevant factors.

3   **Greater appreciation of financial targets**. Costs may be decentralised together with decentralisation of equipment and staff. Senior managers and users will be more attentive to the costs associated with computing activities as this will have a direct effect on the budgets and profitability of their department.

4   **Greater ownership of the information** and hence greater pride in getting it right.

5   **Flexibility**. While centralisation promotes increased efficiency and control, decentralisation permits greater flexibility. Inherently, attempting to attain these two objectives creates a conflict. In practice, new and improved technologies have diluted the merits of either structure; it may be most effective to have some aspects of the information system centralised, and others decentralised.

Some information technology activities can be more satisfactorily accomplished centrally. These include:

- devising an IT strategy for the group

- initiating IT standards

- procuring hardware and software

- monitoring standards

- supply of communication needs

- human resource management

- technical support

- support for computer auditing.

FOULKS LYNCH
PUBLICATIONS

The conflict between centralised and distributed systems caused problems for organisations for many years. In many organisations, parallel systems developed with both centralised mainframe or minicomputer services existing alongside PCs and LANs. It is common to find this type of situation in examination questions, where the theme of the question is 'Can we do better?'

3.2 Client-server architecture

The term **architecture** is used in IT, as in its normal usage, to describe the physical appearance of the system and the way in which its component parts relate to one another. The choice over which architecture to adopt is a difficult one, but recent developments in operating software have simplified this task.

Until about 1990, it was impossible to fully interconnect PC hardware with mainframe or minicomputer processors. This was due to incompatibilities between the operating systems used, as most mainframes and minicomputers had their own operating systems that were specific to each manufacturer, and often to each model of equipment!

In 1990, the first operating systems capable of working on different types of hardware were developed. These **multi-platform operating systems** allowed full interconnection of PCs and centralised hardware, so the users could instruct processing to be carried out on their own workstation, or on any of the shared hardware devices.

This allows users to choose the most appropriate tool to perform the various applications, depending on the organisation's needs and the hardware available.

There are different hardware elements in a client-server system:

Client workstations	These are normally PCs used by individual users.
Local or departmental servers	These are shared by a few users with the same computing needs
A central or corporate server	This is shared by all users throughout the organisation.

These are illustrated in the following figure:

The applications carried out by the organisation's users are split between the available hardware, according to how many users need access to them and how much processing power is required.

Client applications

Client applications are software tools that are used for processing on client hardware. Although a number of client applications have many users (e.g., spreadsheet, word processing), they work as individuals rather than together. Some client applications (e.g., decision support systems) may be unique to one user. Sometimes these tools are called personal applications.

Local applications

Local applications are software tools that are used for processing on a local or departmental server. Local applications are common to users within a section or department and the application is shared by a number of users (e.g., computer aided design (CAD) within an engineering department).

Corporate applications

The processing using **corporate applications** takes place on the corporate server. Such applications are shared by users from many departments (e.g., the organisation's MIS). This allows the use of the very high processing power of the corporate server to be used to its best effect.

4   Computer software

Computer software is the term used to describe collections of instructions to the computer hardware. It is written by computer programmers who are highly skilled and experienced. It is not necessary for you to be able to program a computer, nor are you required to understand the process of computer programming. You do, however, need to be aware of the different types of computer software available.

4.1   Types of software

There are five different types of software available for computers.

- operating systems
- bespoke applications
- off-the-shelf applications
- utilities
- programming tools.

Utilities packages

Utilities packages are software tools designed to improve the way in which the operating system works. These might automate routine operations such as file management or backup (as with 'Norton Utilities'), or might make the whole operating system easier to use (as with 'Windows' when used with a conventional operating system such as DOS).

Programming tools

Programming tools include the programming language itself, the tools to allow programs to be written (such as compilers or assemblers) or more advanced tools such as computer-aided software engineering (CASE) packages.

4.2   Operating systems software

The operating system is the most important piece of software in any computer system, as without it the system will not work at all. It consists of a number of tools to allow the following functions:

- communication between the operator and the computer

- control of the processor and storage hardware

- the management of files

- the use of peripherals such as printers and modems

There are two different types of operating systems in common use in business:

- command-driven operating systems such as DOS, which are sometimes used with a graphical user interface (GUI) utility

- WIMP (Windows, icons, mouse and pointer) operating systems such as Windows 95, which have their own GUI.

The GUI allows a reduction in the amount of training required to use the system, and prevents the selection of invalid or unreasonable options or instructions.

4.3   Bespoke applications

Bespoke, (tailor-made or purpose-written) applications have been constructed to meet the specific needs of the particular organisation in which they are found. The process of programming these is extremely time-consuming and expensive, but is often the only alternative if the application is very specialised.

Advantages of bespoke systems include the following:

- they precisely fit the organisation's information needs

- the organisation has complete discretion over data structures

- the system can be integrated with other applications within the organisation

- the system can be modified to fit changing needs.

If the programs are of interest to other organisations, they can be sold (or licensed). The information services group can thus become a profit centre.

Disadvantages of bespoke systems include:

- development takes a long time, which delays the implementation of the system

- bespoke systems are costly to develop and test

- there is a greater probability of bugs in a bespoke system – most of the errors in packages will have been found by other users. This is normal, and they can be debugged later on.

- support of a bespoke system will be expensive. One now has to bear all the cost..

4.4   Off-the-shelf applications

These are pieces of software, often called application packages, which have been created by a software manufacturer, tested and documented, then copied many times. They are sold in a form that is ready to install and use straight away.

KEY POINT

Examples of off-the-shelf
packages:

- spreadsheets

- word processing

- databases

- accounting

- communications.

Examples of off-the-shelf applications include the following.

- spreadsheets

- word processing

- databases

- accounting

- communications.

These applications tend to be generalist in nature, that is, used by many different organisations for basic word processing and spreadsheet work. Specialist packages are also available for specific areas such as production scheduling, order processing or maintenance of employee details. These packages tend to be more expensive, but again they can be used in many different types of organisation.

Some advantages of off-the-shelf packages

- they are generally cheaper to buy than bespoke packages are to develop

- they are likely to be available almost immediately

- good packages are likely to come with good training programmes and documentation

- new updated versions of the software are likely to be available on a regular basis

- the experience of a great number of users with similar needs to those in the organisation has been incorporated into the design of the package.

Some disadvantages of off-the-shelf packages

- they do not fit precisely the needs of the organisation – the users may need to compromise what they want with what is available

- the organisation is dependent upon an outside supplier for the maintenance of the software; many software suppliers are larger than most of their customers, and are therefore difficult to influence

- different packages used by the organisation may have incompatible data structures.

5   Computer communications

Where an organisation has several locations, it may be more effective to process data locally rather than at one central installation. By doing this individual managers will be able to schedule their own processing and will have more control over the contents of their database systems. Any system that requires computers to communicate with each other will need specialised hardware and software such as:

- modems

- communication programs

- network circuits and software.

KEY POINT

Examples of computer
communications systems:

- modems

- communication programs

- network circuits and
  software.

5.1   Modems

The modem (MOdulator/DEModulator) is the interface between the electronic pulses used to transfer data within the computer system and the signals needed for transmission through the telephone system. It is controlled by communications software running on the computer and provides an input and output link with the telephone system. With appropriate software, intelligent modems (those with built-in control circuitry) can handle communications with minimum manual intervention, allowing redialling of engaged numbers and call answering to be performed automatically. Many models are also capable of adjusting their information reception rate to match the transmission rate of the calling modem.

Modem transmission speeds are quoted in baud rates, which correspond to bits per second.

5.2   Communications software

Despite the sophistication achieved by modems, special software is still needed to handle the communications process itself, and the software used by the transmitter and the receiver must be compatible. To achieve this, certain standard protocols (that is, an agreed format for the communication being used between the different communication devices) have been developed so that systems can signal to each other the start and finish of transmission and reception and any problems experienced with data, and so priorities of use of the communication channel can be properly maintained. It is important in choosing software to ensure that it can cope with all the tasks for which it is likely to be used.

The current trend towards integrated business software for small businesses has led to the incorporation of simple communications software alongside the standard components of such a package – word processor, database, spreadsheet and graphics. In many cases the software will be adequate for an organisation's needs, but it is important to ensure that all potential communications needs will be catered for.

5.3   Local area networks (LANs)

Communication through a modem uses the public telecommunications system. This may be unnecessarily elaborate for an organisation that simply needs its own computers to be able to communicate with each other or to share a piece of expensive hardware. In these circumstances, a local area network (or LAN) may be more suitable. This consists of a circuit, which connects the computers to each other and contains the hardware needed for efficient communication (often in the form of expansion cards which plug directly into the computers' circuitry), and software to run the network. The software provides for appropriate priority control over data transmission and reception and allows the system to cope with multiple users having access to the same files. This involves extra protocols to cover simultaneous access by different users, security over data and so on.

LANs can be made up of several identical computers, often to allow shared access to an expensive piece of equipment, such as a laser printer, to maximise its cost-effectiveness. In some cases several microcomputers provide input to one or more servers, so that they can be used independently within their own locations and as intelligent terminals to the shared machine(s).

Advantages of local area networks
- data can be shared amongst all users
- the network can be gradually extended as the organisation grows. each new machine brings with it additional processing power

- users can share expensive resources such as high quality printers

- if one machine breaks down, the others can continue working – provided the file server has not stopped

- cost effective for large numbers of users

- members of the network can send electronic mail to one another thus reducing the amount of paperwork.

The distance over which a LAN can be set up is limited by the efficiency of the cables connecting the machines, and they are typically used within relatively small areas because of the expense of long distance connections. Within these limits they provide an efficient and secure means of communication and can significantly extend the computing power of an organisation at low cost. It is also possible to set up connections between networks over longer distances using modems and specialised software, so that the range of options available for computer communications within an organisation and between organisations is potentially limitless. An extended network of this sort is often referred to as the wide area network or WAN.

5.4 Wide area networks (WANs)

Wide area networks permit multiple users to have access to a remote computer via the telecommunications network. Network users are required to 'log-on' to the system. A network user would also have a personal password to reduce the risk of unauthorised access.

A modem is often used to gain access to a WAN, though some other devices may be used if the WAN is permanently available. Any device that gives access to a WAN is known as a **gateway**. Although accessing remote computers the response time over a WAN may be only a fraction of a second.

Response time is defined as the interval between data entry by the terminal user and receipt of the result of any processing activity that has taken place.

6   Disaster recovery strategies (contingency controls)

The response to a potential disaster, such as the loss of part of the computer system, should be managed. The best way of doing this is by means of a **contingency plan**.

As the importance of computing within an organisation continues to grow, so the effects of a breakdown of the computer system are potentially even more damaging. In addition, the computer system is increasingly exposed to the potential threat of hackers and the introduction of computer viruses.

For the duration of the downtime, losses can be expected to escalate. It is, therefore, essential that the time when the computer system is unavailable be kept to a minimum.

Contingency planning is the process by which managers prepare to deal with an unplanned and disastrous event. In IT terms this usually means the loss or unavailability of some of the computer systems.

Why is it necessary?

IT systems are usually reliable, but like everything else they are subject to unpredictable events. When these occur, users are faced with a situation where what they believe to be trustworthy has become unusable. The users must be able to continue the business during the period of unavailability, which may be for several months.

Events that cause the unavailability of IT systems may be rare but, when they do occur, they can be disastrous if precautions have not been taken in advance. The reliance on IT is ever increasing. In a modern business there are few areas that are unaffected by IT and consequently there will be few areas that will not suffer if its performance is impaired. In addition the risks are increasing and becoming more varied; for example, IT users now have to contend with the risks of hacking, virus infection and industrial action aimed at the computer staff.

There are four basic steps in drawing up any contingency plan. These are:-

- management commitment

- selection of the option on which the plan is based

- selection of the planning team

- the detailed plan preparation.

Management commitment is necessary due to the considerable costs involved. Before the plan is worked out a stand-by option has to be selected. The planning team should be large enough to provide the expertise needed but small enough to be spared from their everyday duties and responsibilities. Once the details of the plan have been agreed it must be tested. If disaster strikes, the team will be the first point of contact as they have knowledge of the working plan and can put it into immediate operation.

A number of standby plans merit consideration and are discussed below. The final selection would be dependent upon the estimated time that the concern would function adequately without computing facilities.

1   Creation of multiple data processing facilities on separate sites, with the smallest site being capable of supporting the crucial work of at least one other site during the calculated recovery time. This strategy requires hardware and software compatibility and spare capacity. It is calculated that approximately only 20 per cent of computer usage is critical, so the volume selected for temporary transfer can be kept to a minimum.

2   Reciprocal agreement with another company. Although a popular option, few companies can guarantee free capacity, or continuing capability, which attaches a high risk to this option.

3   A more expensive, but lower risk, version of the above is the commercial computer bureaux. This solution entails entering into a formal agreement that entitles the customer to a selection of services.

4   Empty rooms or equipped rooms. The former allows the organisation access to install a back-up system, which increases the recovery time but reduces the cost. The latter can be costly, so sharing this facility is a consideration.

5   Re-locatable computer centres. This solution involves a delay while the facility is erected and assembled and larger computers cannot usually be accommodated.

The effectiveness of the contingency plan is dependent on comprehensive back-up procedures for both data and software. The contingency plan must identify initial responses and clearly delineate responsibility at each stage of the exercise – from damage limitation through to full recovery.

The greater the effort invested in the preparation of a contingency plan, the more effectively the organisation will be able to mitigate the effects of a disaster.

KEY POINT

Examples of contingency plans:

- facilities on separate sites

- reciprocal agreement with another company

- computer bureaux

- equipped rooms

- re-locatable computer centres.

FOULKS LYNCH
PUBLICATIONS

6.1   The need for file security

Vital records are stored on magnetic media and loss of, or damage to, a file may leave an organisation in a serious position. All magnetic storage media are highly vulnerable to a number of dangers – far more so than manual records.

Some of the main hazards that affect the computer installation, in addition to those mentioned above are:

- operator mishandling

- machine malfunction, e.g., disc head crash

- incorrect environmental conditions, e.g., dust, temperature, humidity.

Consequently, safeguards have to be established to prevent loss of files, e.g.:

- procedure standards for operators and librarians

- standby facilities to use another computer in the event of a breakdown

- air conditioning, temperature and humidity controls.

6.2   Back-up procedures

In spite of the safeguards described above, the worst may happen and a file may be destroyed.

The standard way of coping with this potential problem is to maintain proper back-up procedures, whereby copies of files are kept in a 'security store', together with necessary update transactions, so that recreation of copies can be facilitated.

The methods of creating security back-up files and programs include:

- dump the file contents on magnetic disk or other storage medium such as a Jazz drive or exchangeable disk storage (a lot of hard disks in one pack) after each complete update (known as full-copy)

- accumulate update inputs on disk as they are processed and if recreation is necessary reload the previous period's full-copy file and re-process the inputs.

6.3   Meaning and need for a risk management process

All projects have elements of risk. The risk management process is a method of identifying risks in advance and establishing methods of avoiding those risks and/or reducing the impact of those risks should they occur.

The risk management process usually contains the following steps:

- Identifying the potential risks in the project. These are factors that may cause difficulties in the project, or indeed may make the project fail. For example, a risk in a particular project may be 'reliance on too many contract staff'.

- Defining the risk in detail so that it is clear what each risk is actually about. A precise description of the risk will allow a better analysis of its impact and the identification of measures that might be used to counter it. For example, 'inexperienced project managers find contract staff difficult to manage'.

- An assessment of the impact and likelihood of each risk. This allows managers to concentrate on risks that have the greatest chance of happening or those risks that, if they do occur, will have the greatest impact on the project.

- A definition of the actions that should be taken to counter each risk. There are two types of action. Avoidance actions that can try to prevent the risk from taking place in the first place. For example, 'only employ full-time staff on the project'. In contrast, mitigation actions attempt to reduce the impact on the project if the risk occurs; for example, 'send inexperienced project managers on a project management course'.

During the project the risks have to be kept under review and the risk management process must ensure that, if they occur, they are addressed. This will include identifying and dealing with new unanticipated risks that arise during the conduct of the project.

7   Meaning and implication of legacy systems

7.1   Explanation of legacy systems

DEFINITION

A legacy system is an old system, which may no longer meet the organisation's requirements.

A typical business information system at the present time consists of systems that were written many years ago in a conventional programming language such as COBOL or FORTRAN and still use old methods and technologies. They often only support one business unit. These systems are generally called legacy systems.

These systems usually support well-established business processes (such as inventory control) that undergo very little change and whose users are generally satisfied with the information and support the system provides.

Typically, legacy systems were designed to provide information on specific areas, with little or no integration to other applications. However, other newer systems will have been built around the legacy system, meaning that it is now out-of-date. Furthermore, the data contained within the system may not be accessible to the newer systems, which limits information provision within the organisation.

7.2   Replacing legacy systems

As the cost of maintaining two systems (architectures and skill sets of users) is likely to be excessive, one solution to the problem of keeping a legacy system is to replace it with a new system. The data from many legacy systems can be incorporated into one central database or data warehouse, making that data available again to other users and applications in the organisation.

Replacing the legacy system may be easier said than done. Some of the problems that will need to be resolved include:

- determining the file formats (especially where systems information has been lost)
- accessing the data
- reading the data and then transferring it to a new database
- establishing key fields in that data to make the data accessible by other programs.

In all situations, a business case for the transfer of data will need to be made. In other words, there must be some value in making the old data available to the existing business applications.

8   End user issues

End users are the people that are required, or decide, to use directly the information systems in order to complete the tasks they have as part of their work or leisure activities. Users of information systems vary considerably in level of skill from the novice (unskilled) to the expert (skilled), and in the tasks they perform. For example, end users in a business environment may be clerks, accountants, programmers, secretaries, warehouse personnel, engineers, sales representatives, managers and so on.

They can be classified according to the following:

- skill – novice and expert

- function - end users, managers, customers and system users

- nature of use – direct or indirect

- discretion – do users have a choice to use a system or not

- development role – users in the systems development life cycle.

The end user is a very important element in the successful acceptance of information systems. They are more likely to accept the system if they are involved extensively in the specification, development and use of the system and its applications. With the more traditional approach, the final users of the system are likely to be involved in only two stages of development. Firstly, they may be required at the early stage when information is gathered about the present system to establish the nature and activities to be computerised. This may be in the form of interviews. Secondly, they are likely to be involved when the system is tested.

Conclusion

This chapter has introduced some important issues such as risk management and how to charge for Information System services, as well as a long list of information about computer hardware and software. Remember in an examination question you will need to apply this background knowledge to the specific circumstances of the question, so please ensure that you understand all the terms mentioned in the chapter.

SELF-TEST QUESTIONS

Accounting for IS costs

1   List the main ways of re-charging the costs of the IS department. (1.2)

2   What are the benefits to the user department of establishing the IS function as a separate entity? (1.7)

Architectures

3   What are the arguments for decentralised systems? (3.1)

Computer software

4   What are the main types of computer software? (4.1)

Computer communications

5   List the advantages of using LANs within an organisation. (5.3)

Disaster recovery strategies

6   What is a contingency plan? (6)

Legacy systems

7   Define a legacy system. (7.1)

EXAM-TYPE QUESTION

National Counties Hotel plc

National Counties Hotels plc ('National') runs a chain of 40 major hotels. Most of the hotels are in major cities, but some are located in areas of natural beauty and away from towns. Each hotel has a general manager and separate managers for its restaurant, conferences and group bookings. The housekeeper, chef, and senior barman also have some management responsibility.

The company's head office is in London. Each week head office receives a report from every hotel in the chain; this is used for planning and evaluation purposes. Head office also has a reservations section that can take bookings for all the hotels; alternatively, guests can ring up specific hotels. Guests who are touring will often ask the receptionist to make a booking for them at another of the group's hotels in an area they hope to travel to next.

FOULKS LYNCH
PUBLICATIONS

The company is reviewing its information systems, as there have been some problems of late in several of the company's hotels or at head office. These have included:

- Arrangements made by a group bookings manager had not been properly recorded and individual bookings were subsequently accepted when no rooms were available.

- The kitchens did not pick up conference booking information and lunches that had been arranged could not be provided.

- A general manager wanted to review room occupancy by week and profitability. The analysis had to be performed by hand.

- At year-end, head office prepared accounts and it was discovered that an advert that had been placed in a travel magazine had been inadvertently allowed to appear every month. Invoices had been received and paid each month and the cost overrun was in the order of £9,000.

- There has been some revenue lost because room numbers have not been correctly recorded when services to guests have been provided. For example, in the restaurant or bar, guests can charge purchases to their rooms. So far guests have merely had to quote their room numbers without having to show any proof of identity.

You have been asked to advise the company on certain matters and have had a preliminary meeting with a head office official. In response to these problems, the official has said, "What the company needs is a proper operating system. If we had that we would be assured that we would be supplied with the proper information that would allow the company to operate more efficiently".

Required:

Produce a memorandum to the Head Office official that covers the following:

(a) Describe the major components of National in terms of their activities and explain the linkages that may exist between these various activities.   **(10 marks)**

(b) Suggest a data capture method that would improve the accuracy of charging for services. Justify your choice in terms of fulfilling the requirements of National and in terms of guest convenience.   **(5 marks)**

(Total: 15 marks)

Chapter 4
FEASIBILITY STUDIES

The development of a new information system begins with a feasibility study, to establish what sort of system might be required, and whether it would be worth developing or not. This chapter looks at feasibility studies. These should be completed before projects are commissioned and they assess the technical, commercial, social and operational feasibility of proposed new systems and system amendments. The chapters that follow describe the subsequent stages in new system development.

Objectives

By the time you have finished this chapter you should be able to:

- explain the purpose and objectives of a feasibility study

- evaluate the technical, operational, social and economic feasibility of the proposed project

- describe and categorise the benefits and costs of the proposed project

- apply appropriate investment appraisal techniques to determine the economic feasibility of a project

- define the typical content and structure of a feasibility study report.

1   The feasibility study

The development of a new computer system is a major undertaking. It is likely to be costly in both resources and money, and will often cause disruption during development and implementation. It is also likely to have a major effect on the way the organisation operates.

For these reasons, it is vital that the organisation makes sure that the following questions are answered for every computer system that is developed:

- What is required of the system?

- How can the requirements be satisfied?

- Is it technically feasible?

- Is it worth doing?

- Will the organisation have to change its way of doing business?

The feasibility study is carried out to help provide the answers to these questions.

The purpose of a feasibility study is not to carry out an in-depth study into the requirements for a new system. Its purpose should be to gather and present just enough information to enable management to reach a well-informed judgement as to whether to proceed with developing a new system or not.

An in-depth investigation should only be carried out after a decision to proceed has been taken.

1.1 Terms of reference for a feasibility study

Before carrying out a feasibility study the person or team responsible must know what is expected of them. This is set out in a formal document called the terms of reference (ToR). What is contained in the terms of reference will depend on the system being investigated.

The ToR should cover the following:

- **Statement of the purpose of the system.** Why is the system being developed?

- **Scope statement**. This establishes the **boundaries** of the new system and what it should seek to achieve. It specifies the major activities that the system will support. The scope statement is important, because it should prevent 'scope creep' during the project development, whereby additional requirements are added and the system is designed to do extra things. Scope creep delays the completion of a project and adds to its costs. When the scope of the project is clearly stated, any proposal to add to the system requirements can be assessed in terms of additional costs and additional benefits, and a formal decision can then taken about whether to add the requirement.

- **Cost and time estimates.** Although it might be difficult to specify costs and completion times accurately, it is important to set targets. These can then be kept under review as the project development work progresses.

- **Constraints**. If there are any constraints on the project development, these should be stated. In particular, there might be a requirement to develop a new system by a specified target date, or that the system should be developed within a limited budget.

- **Stakeholders**. The ToR should also specify the groups that will have an interest in the system development work and the developed system, and the nature of their interest.

- **Objectives**. There should be a clear statement of the milestones for the project development and the critical success factors. For a project to develop a new information system, these might be stated as follows:

'A System Analysis and Design Model of the current system at stage 1, a Business System Options plan at stage 2, a System Analysis and Design Model of the chosen Business System Option at stage 3, a prototype of the new system at stage 4.

The project will be conducted using Structured Systems Analysis and Design Method (SSADM). The prototype will be developed either using SQL*FORMS accessing an Oracle Database or using an alternative language and platform in keeping with the suggested solution if applicable.'

Timescales for each of these four deliverables should also be stated.

The terms of reference will be agreed between the sponsor of the project (normally the Board or similar decision-making group in an organisation), and the project manager and other people involved in actually running the project. The terms of reference will also be used during the project as a control; that is they can be referred to as the project progresses to ensure that the project is meeting the correct objectives. Finally, at the end of the project, a report will be produced showing that the terms of reference have been met (or occasionally explaining why they have not been met).

1.2   Controlling the project

To control the project, there are likely to be two groups of people, each with their own responsibilities.

The steering committee

The steering committee has the responsibility to oversee and control the development of a system. Sometimes the steering committee will oversee all major projects; other times it will be set up to control a specific project. In either case, it must have the power to ensure that any recommendations are actioned. To provide this power, the people on the committee will usually be senior and will include a senior IS and DP manager, senior representative of different groups of users and financial management.

In addition to their role in overseeing specific projects, the steering committee has a strategic role, being responsible for recommending an overall IS strategy for the organisation and ensuring that systems being developed are consistent with long term strategies and objectives.

The committee will also assign priorities to different projects, and agree (or recommend agreement to the board of directors) specific projects.

Study group

The steering committee will meet infrequently. Another team of people is responsible for carrying out the feasibility study and reporting to the steering committee. This group needs to represent the different interests affected by the system being developed. It is likely to comprise people from the user groups concerned, members of the information systems/data processing department, and possibly an accountant. The systems analyst responsible for the project will usually head it up.

The level of people in the study group is mainly tactical management, but with key operational managers included when appropriate.

1.3   The stages of the feasibility study

The feasibility study can be split into the following stages:

Formation of the steering committee

If an organisational steering committee does not exist then a specific steering committee will be set up.

Setting of the terms of reference

As described earlier, the steering committee is responsible for defining what is required of the system.

Formation of the study group

The steering committee may appoint a systems analyst – or hire one from an outside consultancy – who will then approach people who possess the requisite abilities and experience.

Planning the study

The project team will now draw up a programme of work, with clearly defined timescales and lines of responsibility. An inbuilt level of flexibility should be built in to allow for the fact that feasibility studies often need to cover a wider range of activities that is at first planned.

Problem definition and information gathering

The next stage will produce a formal list of the system requirements and any constraints and problems. This will require the gathering of a great deal of information. In many organisations, the requirements of the system and the way that data flows through the organisation will be recorded using specific diagrammatic models. These tools are discussed in a later chapter.

The list of problems and requirements is likely to cover the following areas:

- the data input to the system
- the outputs (contents, level of detail, timing, etc) from the system
- the predicted future volumes of transactions and data to be processed
- technical feasibility
- the organisational structure of the user departments and their support staff
- the operational costs of the current system
- the current hardware and software available, together with a list of the current applications using the hardware and software.

At the end of this stage a set of documents should have been produced, defining the problems/requirements of the system.

Project identification

This stage will enable the feasibility study group to suggest various options for the project, eliminate unsuitable options and evaluate the others.

When deciding how to develop the system, firstly select a number of criteria that the system must satisfy, e.g.:

- the speed and volume of processing
- compatibility with other systems
- the need for security and the creation of an audit trail.

A number of alternative ways of building the required system can then be evaluated against the criteria defined. Each option that is not rejected at this stage will be evaluated in detail.

Cost-benefit analysis

In order for a project to be carried out, the investment criteria set by the organisation must be satisfied (e.g. 'each project must have an internal rate of return of more than 15%'). Each of the project proposals still under consideration will be the subject of an analysis comparing the costs of developing the system with its likely benefits. In practice, the evaluation of both costs and benefits can be difficult. The different elements of cost may be hard to define and the benefits speculative and hard to quantify.

For example, a new sales system might improve debtors' collection periods, but by how much? Similarly, a new stock system should reduce the frequencies of stock outs and obsolete stock, but it will be difficult to quantify the savings or the improved reputation that the company should enjoy.

Producing a feasibility study report

A report is produced and presented to the steering committee.

The report will include the following aspects:

- The original ToR for the report

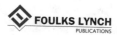

- Description of the business area, department, process under investigation
- The objectives to be satisfied by the new system
- Description of the present system and the problem areas (current physical)
- The requirements for the new system (proposed logical)
- Description(s) of proposed solution(s)

For each estimates of:

- Costs of development and running new system
- Timescales to implement new system
- Resources to develop and run new system
- Impact on staff and the organisation
- Benefits: tangible and intangible

2   The main features to be examined in assessing project feasibility

To be feasible, a project should be justified on the following grounds:

- economic (costs and benefits)
- technical
- operational
- social.

2.1   Economic feasibility

A study into the economic feasibility of a new system is concerned with the costs and expected benefits with each of the alternatives under consideration. Although non-financial benefits will be considered, the economic feasibility should assess the costs and benefits in financial terms.

Costs

Costs can be broken down into three basic categories – one-off costs, on going costs and intangible costs. Sometimes costs can be converted from one category to another, e.g. hardware could be leased (on going) or purchased (one-off).

One-off costs

These can be broken down into capital costs and one-off revenue costs. Capital costs include:

- hardware purchase – computers, peripherals, etc
- software purchase – bespoke software, packages
- communications equipment – cabling, multipliers, etc
- accommodation purchase – to house computers and equipment
- ancillary equipment – desks, security systems, etc
- initial stock of consumables – paper, discs, etc.

One-off revenue costs include:

- consultancy fees
- system development and testing
- file conversion
- use of temporary staff during development and implementation

- printing of documentation, special stationery, manuals, etc
- staff recruitment fees
- redundancy payments
- staff training.

On going running costs

These would include:

- operating staff salaries and overheads
- on going training and recruitment costs
- stationery and other consumable items
- lease of equipment and depreciation of purchased capital items
- maintenance of hardware, software and other equipment
- cost of security and back-up arrangements
- financing costs, e.g. the interest paid on the capital employed.

The running costs of a system will often be around 70% of the total cost.

Intangible costs

The costs listed above are relatively easy to quantify and can be directly attributed to the development of the system. There are other costs that are harder to quantify:

- Staff dissatisfaction and dysfunctional behaviour may well occur when any new system is developed.
- The learning curve. The staff responsible for running the system need to become familiar with the way that the system operates. During the learning curve staff are likely to be slower and to make a greater than usual number of mistakes.
- Opportunity costs. Whenever money is invested in one area of the company, the opportunity to invest in another area is automatically foregone. the benefits of the other investments are automatically lost.
- Lock-in costs. If the organisation strategically chooses to concentrate on a specific supplier or technology, the benefits and cost saving accruing from shopping around are automatically lost.
- Incompatibility between other systems operating within the organisation and the new system will cost money. The old system may need to be replaced or a special data file conversion facility built in.

Benefits

Benefits also range from the easily quantified to those that are more ephemeral and difficult to quantify. In the early days of computing in industry, the majority of projects focused on the mechanisation of manual tasks, and the resulting benefits were cost savings that were easily quantified. This in turn led to the large-scale resentment of computers, which were seen as 'soul-less creators of redundancy and unemployment'. In more recent times the other benefits of better information and competitive advantage have improved the image of the computer in the workplace.

KEY POINT

Benefit types:

- direct benefits/cost savings
- indirect (intangible) benefits.

It is impossible to give a complete catalogue of the possible benefits to be derived from a computer system. Each system is unique in the benefits it offers. Benefits can however be put into two categories - direct benefits/cost savings, and indirect (intangible) benefits. A selection of the benefits in each category is given below:

Direct benefits

- the savings resulting from the old system no longer operating. this includes savings in staff salaries, consumables, etc.

- increased capacity. the new system may be able to deal with a greater volume of transactions, giving savings in overtime as well as increased turnover

- better management of capital by reducing stock levels, and collection of debts.

Indirect benefits

- better and more informed decision-making

- improved customer service, resulting in an increase in customer satisfaction

- freedom from routine decisions and activities, probably resulting in more time being available for long-term strategic planning and innovation

- safeguarding the customers. building direct computer links with customers will often provide them with significant advantages and make it more difficult to find an alternative supplier

- gaining competitive advantage. a fully integrated ordering and delivery system, for example, will give the customers an advantage and make them more likely to buy your products or services.

Partial checklists are often used to help enumerate costs and benefits and these can help to reduce the workload of the feasibility study team.

A specimen summary of costs

	Year					
	1	2	3	4	5	etc
Costs						
Changeover						
Hardware:						
Purchase						
Installation						
Software:						
Purchase						
Development						
Implementation						
Staff[1]						
Operation[2]						
Other						
Information[3]						
Yearly totals						

Notes

1   Including redundancy, recruitment and training costs.

2   The net difference in operating costs between the existing and the proposed system.

3   A quantification of changes in quality and timeliness of existing information and the value of new information provided by the proposed system.

Case study example

MG Hotels presently have two project proposals, but due to cost constraints must decide which project to support.

Project A is a new Accounts Package. This will cost £10,000 to buy and install.

Project B is a new Stock Control Package. This will cost £6,000 to buy and install.

Both projects only incur costs when they are bought and installed.

Project A gives annual savings of £2,500 on fees to our Accountant.

Project B gives a saving of £2,000 per annum on stocks for the first three years, £1,000 for the next two years, £750 for the two years after and then £500 per annum after that.

Both projects we estimate will last 8 years.

Calculate the payback period for both projects.

Calculate the return on investment for both projects.

Answers

Payback A = 4 years

B = 3 years

ROI

Project A

$$APR = \frac{(\text{total savings} - \text{investment}) \times 100}{\text{Investment} \times \text{years}}$$

$$= \frac{[(2,500 \times 8) - 10,000]}{(10,000 \times 8)} \times 100\%$$

$$= 12.5\%$$

Project B

$$\text{Total savings} = (2,000 \times 3) + (1,000 \times 2) + (950 \times 2) + 500 = 10,000$$

$$ROI = \frac{10000 - 6,000}{(6,000 \times 8)} \times 100\%$$

$$= 8.3\%$$

Project A gives a 12.5% APR over 8 years

Project B gives a 8.3% APR over 8 years

2.2 Technical feasibility

The organisation must have the technological ability to cope with the requirements of the system within the allocated budget. The hardware and software must be capable of dealing with the volume of transactions and required response time without significant degradation in the existing systems. Alternatively, there must be enough money available to upgrade the current facilities and to acquire the necessary hardware and software.

A technical feasibility study is therefore concerned mainly with specifying the performance requirements of the system, and then assessing whether a proposed new system will be able to meet those performance specifications. For example:

- There might be a requirement for the system to respond to inquiries input by the user within a maximum time limit, say 10 seconds. A technical feasibility study would assess whether the hardware, files, software and communication links in the proposed system would be sufficient for this performance requirement to be met.

- Similarly there might be a requirement to process certain volumes of input transactions and for an ability to store certain quantities of data in a particular

form (e.g. visual records). A check should be made to ensure that any proposed system is capable of handling the planned volumes in the manner required.

- There might be a requirement for access to central data files by all the employees in the user organisation, from a number of countries across the world. If this is a system requirement, the proposed system must be technically capable of delivering it.

2.3   Operational feasibility

The system must fit in with the way that the organisation runs its business and plans to run its business in the future. It must be capable of providing each user with the required information in a timely manner.

There are two key issues in an operational feasibility assessment.

- Can the proposed system be used in the way intended? Will it work properly? For example, a system might require new data to be input by certain staff in the user organisation before the end of the day on Monday of each week. In practice, however, these staff might not get the data for input until Wednesday each week, and so cannot put it into the system before then. If this is the case, the operational specifications would not be feasible.

- User attitudes to the new system. Will users respond to the new system in a positive way, or will there be strong resistance to using it? Or will the system be used in unintended and unwelcome ways?

2.4   Social feasibility

The system must be compatible with the social organisation of the company, and the company must be sufficiently sophisticated to be able to deal with the complexity of the system being suggested.

This can be split into three basic areas:

- The suggested system should not threaten industrial and personnel relations and motivations.

- The system must not conflict with the corporate ethos and way of doing business.

- The skills and experience within the organisation must be at a high enough level to be able to cope with the complexities of the system.

3   Cost-benefit analysis

There are a number of different techniques used to evaluate projects. After estimating the costs and benefits of a project over a period, each technique results in the calculation of a measure. These measures can be used to compare different investments with one another, or they can be compared with a target value to see if the investment meets the organisational requirements.

The major difficulty in carrying out a cost-benefit analysis lies in the calculation of future cash flows. Since this often has to be done over a period of several years, there is high level of potential inaccuracy, and hence the investments may have a high level of uncertainty and risk. In addition, many of the benefits of information systems projects are difficult or impossible to quantify.

3.1   Payback period

Payback period calculates the length of time that an investment takes to pay for itself. It is easy to calculate and favours low risk investments, but it ignores cash flows after the investment has paid for itself.

Although it is a crude measure of investment, it is extensively used. More sophisticated organisation will generally only use it in combination with some other measure.

Example

		Project 1	Project 2
Cost		(£100,000)	(£150,000)
Net savings			
Year	1	£50,000	£20,000
	2	£50,000	£70,000
	3	£50,000	£70,000
	4	£50,000	£70,000
	5	£0	£70,000

Project 1 has paid back at the end of the second year, whereas Project 2 does not recover its investment until near the end of the third year. By this criterion, Project 1 is the better investment, whereas the total profit from Project 2 is greater.

3.2   Return on Investment (ROI)

Many techniques calculate the profits on a project as a percentage of the money invested in it. The most common measure in this category is the return on investment (ROI).

Example

Two projects have the following cash flows:

Initial investment	£180,000	£220,000
Value after 5 years	£20,000	£30,000

	Net profits	
	Project 1	Project 2
Year 1	£5,000	£0
Year 2	£20,000	£40,000
Year 3	£25,000	£40,000
Year 4	£25,000	£40,000
Year 5	£25,000	£40,000
Total	£100,000	£160,000

To calculate the ROI we use the following formula:

$$ROI = \frac{\text{Average profit p.a.}}{\text{Average investment}} \times 100$$

We first need to calculate the average profits. To calculate this we find the total profits and divide by the number of years.

For Project 1, $\text{Profit} = \dfrac{£100,000}{5} = £20,000$ p.a.

For Project 2, $\text{Profit} = \dfrac{£160,000}{5} = £32,000$ p.a.

We next need to calculate the average investment. Assuming a straight-line depreciation, this is just the average of the initial investment and the final value.

$$\text{For Project 1, Average investment} = \frac{£180,000 + £20,000}{2} = £100,000$$

$$\text{For Project 2, Average investment} = \frac{£220,000 + £30,000}{2} = £125,000$$

We can then calculate the ROI:

$$\text{For Project 1, ROI} = \frac{£20,000}{£100,000} \times 100 = 20\%$$

$$\text{For Project 2, ROI} = \frac{£32,000}{£125,000} \times 100 = 25.6\%$$

On this basis Project 2 is a better investment. ROI is easy to calculate but ignores the timescale in which the money is earned. Early income is less risky and can be reinvested, whereas later income is devalued by the rate of inflation.

3.3   Discounted cash flow methods

Discounted cash flow (DCF) methods take into consideration the time value of money. We will consider the two principal DCF methods of project appraisal: net present value (NPV) and internal rate of return (IRR).

Net present value

This method takes the discounted present value of the future cash flows generated by the project, less the initial outlay. If the NPV is equal to, or greater than, zero the project should be considered as it will at least attain the required rate of return. When the NPV is greater than zero, it will enhance the value of the firm. When using this method to compare projects, the one with the largest NPV should be selected.

Internal rate of return

This method identifies the rate of return that produces an NPV of zero for the project. If the IRR of the project is greater than the firm's required rate of return (usually the cost of capital), it should proceed with the project.

3.4   The feasibility study report

The outcome from a feasibility study will be a feasibility report. This is presented to the manager or management team that has to make the decision about whether or not to proceed with the proposed new system development. A feasibility report typically contains the following sections:

- Introduction
- Terms of reference. This is a statement of what areas the feasibility working party looked at, when and at whose request.
- **Description of the existing system**. The existing system should be described.
- **System requirements**. The existing system will be inadequate for meeting user requirements. The feasibility report should therefore state what the requirements of the new system are. It might also explain how the existing system fails to meet them.
- **Outline of the proposed system**. This should state how the system will operate so as to meet the system requirements. It will specify the inputs to the system and the

outputs and files. It will also specify the hardware, software and staff requirements for operating the proposed system.

- **Development plan**. A description of how the new system will be implemented.
- The likely benefits from the new system.
- The expected costs of developing, implementing and operating the system.
- A **cost-benefit analysis** of the proposed system.
- Suggested software, hardware and suppliers.
- Staff training requirements.
- Suggested implementation timetable.
- Information about other organisations who might be using the proposed system.
- **Alternative systems considered**, and the reasons for rejecting them.
- **Conclusions and recommendations**.

Conclusion

This chapter has looked at the purpose and contents of feasibility studies. It has also looked at methods of assessing costs and benefits likely to arise from new systems.

It finished by looking at the contents of a typical feasibility study report.

SELF-TEST QUESTIONS

The feasibility study

1   What role does the steering IT committee play? (1.2)

The main features to be examined in assessing project feasibility

2   List the four areas of feasibility that a project must satisfy to be acceptable. (2)

3   In a feasibility study what items may be investigated under the three aspects of Technical, Operational and Economic Feasibility? (2.1, 2.2, 2.3)

4   As part of the Economic Feasibility identify some of the costs and benefits which might be incurred in both the development and running of the new system and categorise them into:-

   –   Costs: Capital, one-off and recurring Revenue (2)

   –   Benefits: Tangible, Intangible. (2)

Cost-benefit analysis

5   Name two measures of investment that can be used together, and explain in what circumstances they are both needed. (3)

6   What are the contents of a typical feasibility study report? (3.4)

EXAM-TYPE QUESTION 1

Cost-benefit analysis

A project feasibility study presented to senior management must always contain a detailed cost justification for any proposed computer system.

Categorise and give examples of the costs and benefits that would appear in such a report, including those that might indicate why a project showing a high net present value is not necessarily of greatest benefit to the company.   **(20 marks)**

**EXAM-TYPE
QUESTION 2**

Feasibility report

(a) Outline the main sections of a feasibility report and briefly explain the purpose of the typical contents of each section.

An important part of any feasibility report is a section giving a financial justification for the proposed system.

(b) Describe in detail the costs dealt with in this section.   **(20 marks)**

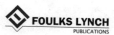

Chapter 5
PROJECT INITIATION, PLANNING AND CONTROL

This chapter deals with the setting up of a systems project. The chapter focuses on the issues of providing control for the project as it starts, and explains the roles of the different members of a project team.

The need for an appropriate management structure is also discussed showing why this structure is appropriate to project management.

Objectives

By the time you have finished this chapter you should be able to:

- define the contents and structure of Terms of Reference
- describe the typical contents of a Project Quality Plan and explain the need for such a plan
- identify the roles and responsibilities of staff that will manage and participate in the project
- define in detail the role and responsibilities of the project manager
- explain the concept of a flat management structure and its application to project-based systems development.

1 Project initiation and Terms of Reference (ToR)

1.1 Project initiation

When a decision is taken to go ahead with developing a new system, the project is initiated (started). The first step is for all the parties who will be involved in the new system and its development (the 'system stakeholders') to agree what the system should be required to do and when the development work should be completed. The outcome of these discussions might be a **project initiation document (PID)**, which is then developed into a more formal statement of the terms of reference for the project.

1.2 Terms of Reference

The Terms of Reference, also called a 'statement of work' and a 'project charter', is a formal document setting out the framework for the new project – its goals and its scope. This document must always be agreed before work on the project begins. The Terms of Reference are usually set by one of the following:

- The Managing Director
- A Systems Steering Committee
- The Systems Analyst's Manager
- The project sponsor

If these are not provided then you should draft them out and seek approval for your own protection. Very often it is not clear what the task of the analyst is, and this is also true of the steering committee. A verbal indication is not satisfactory. A written statement is required outlining the scope and objectives of the project. The document acts as a starting point from which the analyst can investigate the problem area and eventually produce a feasibility report. The content on the Terms of Reference are set out in Chapter 4.

2   Project management

A successful project will require that an effective solution be delivered to the standards required and within the established time and cost constraints. Organisations frequently succeed in achieving only a proportion of these objectives satisfactorily; the result may be that the required standards are met, but costs exceed those budgeted and delivery is much later than planned.

Whether all these objectives are met can be influenced greatly by the management of the project.

2.1   Definition of a project

A project is a collection of linked activities with a clearly defined start and finish point, carried out in an organised manner, to achieve some specific result.

In this examination you may come across any of a range of projects. An individual examination paper may focus on a project for the development or redevelopment of an Information System.

In some examination questions, you may be put in the role of project manager, project finance manager, project team member, project sponsor or external advisor. Whatever context is given to you in the examination, you will need to demonstrate understanding of the project management process, and so this textbook will assume that you are going to be a project manager.

2.2   Sources of projects

Although some projects may be initiated on an ad-hoc basis, it is more common for them to be an implementation tool for the strategic plan of the organisation, as shown in the diagram below.

You will recognise the need to link activities within an organisation to its mission and objectives from chapter one of this manual.

Clearly, some projects are more important than others but, as a project manager, it is important that you recognise the relationship between your project and the strategy of the organisation. It is also quite possible that your project is closely related to others, so you must also recognise any interrelationships with other projects and bear them in mind when managing your project.

2.3   Characteristics of a project

The following are the characteristics of a project according to Trevor Young in his book *The Handbook of Project Management*.

A project:

- has a **specific purpose** which can be readily defined

- is **unique**, because it is most unlikely to be repeated in exactly the same way by the same group of people to give the same results

- is **focused on the customer** and customer expectations

- is **not usually routine** work but may contain some routine-type tasks

- is made up of a **series of activities** that are linked together, all contributing to the desired result

- has clearly defined **time constraints** – a date when the results are required

- is frequently **complex** because the work may involve people in different departments, and even on different sites

- has **cost constraints** which must be clearly defined and understood to ensure the project remains viable.

Whereas in a real business situation it may sometimes be difficult to determine whether a job is a project or not, in the examination the examiner will tell you what the project is. You may, however, find that some of the above characteristics lead you towards a solution to one or more of the problems identified in the question.

3   Phases of a project

Any project, whether it is for the construction of a building or the design of an accounting system, can be viewed as having a life cycle – a series of stages from its beginning to end. Carrying out most of these stages, in roughly the right order, should lead to a more successful solution.

3.1   Project life cycle

The life cycle of a typical project will consist broadly of the stages and tasks shown in the diagram below.

Although a relatively small project may appear to miss out stages completely, this is probably due to the fact that stages are often combined to speed up the project. For example, in a simple project to develop a spreadsheet, a task such as feasibility study may consist simply of a few moments thinking 'is it worth doing?'

Similarly, in some projects you will find that some of the stages simply do not apply. Taking our example of the development of a spreadsheet, there may well be no need for 'options generation' as there are no options! Obviously this would also make the 'options evaluation' stage redundant.

Each stage in the life cycle is discussed in more detail in the following sections of this chapter. The various project management tools associated with each stage are covered in Chapter 6.

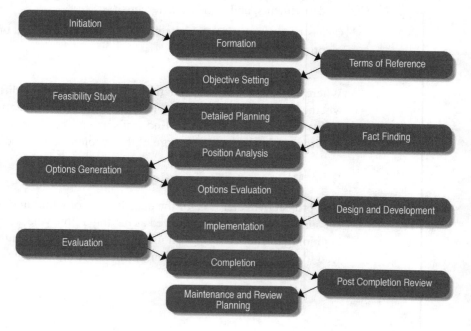

3.2   PRINCE

Some of the stages covered in this chapter include sections relating to the PRINCE (PRojects IN Controlled Environments) methodology. PRINCE is a methodology for project management developed for, and championed by, the UK government. It is used here as an example of the features and benefits of a formal project management methodology. If you are familiar with an alternative, please feel free to use it. The examiner will not require specific knowledge of any single project management methodology; PRINCE may be used as an example although the Examiner will not refer to this methodology in examination questions.

4 Project planning issues

Project managers should be concerned with the following issues, and should consider these when developing a **Project Plan**.

4.1 Outline planning and objective setting

This phase commences when the system proposal is initially generated. It involves:

- establishing objectives and targets for the system
- setting timescale targets for the completion of particular phases
- estimating development expenditures and formulating budgets
- dividing the project into identifiable activities and using this as a basis to prepare an outline plan of the major development stages, identifying the resources required by each and estimating the time required.

The product of this stage will almost certainly be modified several times as a result of discussions having taken place at various levels. After amendments have been made to reflect the additional input, agreement will usually be reached and approval to progress to the next phase will be granted.

4.2 Detailed planning

During this phase, the initial outline plan is developed into a feasible action plan and is undertaken primarily by the project manager and members of the project team. The main activities included in this phase are:

- preparing a detailed schedule of activities to be undertaken; identifying the logical sequence in which these should be performed, as well as the individual tasks within activities; and identifying those activities or a sequence of activities which may be critical. Network analysis techniques may be used at this stage (these are described in detail in Chapter 6)
- assessing the resources available and allocating particular resources to activities identified in the schedule; identifying staffing requirements in terms of recruitment and any training necessary to undertake the project
- preparing a schedule detailing purchases of equipment, software and services required for the system
- preparing detailed budgets for both internal and external expenditure
- developing a system for monitoring and controlling the progress of the activities associated with the system development in respect of time, resource utilisation, costs and standards of quality.

The system will develop to incorporate an information system reporting on progress and offering guidelines for processes to be used in monitoring, reviewing and controlling performance. The latter may include the establishment of steering groups or user groups, the decision to have weekly meetings of the project team and the formulation of terms of reference, membership, occurrence of meetings and the identification of the administrative structure to support them.

At this stage information may be lacking to complete every detail as described above; the significance of this phase is to ensure that all the issues as described have been addressed. The detailed plans are then submitted to management and to the steering committee – if one has been formed. The plans will need to be considered, modified and authorised before proceeding to the next phase.

4.3   Implementation

The implementation of the information system refers to the operational activities necessary to produce the system. Project management is concerned with measuring both the effectiveness and the efficiency of these activities.

4.4   Progress monitoring and review

The process of monitoring and reviewing takes place at varying time intervals and at different stages of the project. The common factor is that the process will measure actual performance against planned performance, with particular consideration to time, resources, costs and quality. Each of these aspects is considered in more detail below.

Monitoring time performance

The primary means of testing this element of performance is by comparing actual completion dates against the planned ones. Management should be supplied with progress reports to enable them to determine whether or not each activity is on or behind schedule.

Monitoring resource performance

In this context the term 'resources' includes human resources working on the project and computer resources, accommodation and other support services. The element attracting the closest attention will, however, be the human resources as this is the element most likely to err.

The aspects of performance to be measured would most commonly be:

- to what extent have resources been made available to the project?

- the degree to which those resources have been utilised to promote the plan

- the degree to which those resources are being utilised efficiently and effectively.

Monitoring cost performance

The monitoring and review process will again involve comparing actual expenditure against planned expenditure. The degree of detail available will be largely dependent on the costing and budgetary control system of the organisation, and will be facilitated by the project being designated its own cost centre; thus, costs which can be identified as attributable to the project can be collected and, where necessary, indirect and direct overheads can be apportioned to the project.

Monitoring quality performances

The measurement of the quality of a service provided is inherently more difficult than, for example, a manufacturing operation where units can be inspected to ascertain whether they reach satisfactory standards. The measurement of a service is more subjective. Performance measurements need to relate to all stages, not just the result – the final information system – which cannot be measured until the project has finished. Therefore the standards of quality actually achieved during the intermediate stages need to be compared against the standards of quality initially agreed.

Despite the possibility of subjectivity, measurement of quality should not be ignored, and could include collecting the users' opinion of the quality of training courses, the extent to which documentation corresponds to the standards initially agreed, etc.

4.5   Evaluation

This phase involves:

- measuring progress in meeting targets of time, cost, resources and quality both during the current reporting period and the cumulative progress date

- assessing the implications of carrying forward work scheduled for the current period to the following period, due to lack of progress

- devising a range of remedial actions to be taken to resolve current or potential future problems, or delays

- analysis of the likely effects of the above alternatives with regard to the four elements – time, costs, resources and quality – when applied to the various different scenarios.

4.6   Control activities

As with the monitoring and review phase, this process takes place continuously throughout the system development and implementation phases. The activities performed during this process should be designed to:

- prevent deviations from the planned activities, unless changes are required.

- correct any deviations from the plan in the previous reporting periods

- prevent any future deviations by revising plans, targets, performance standards and monitoring systems

- implement any other conclusions resulting from the processes of monitoring, review or evaluation.

These control activities will normally require an element of discussion and agreement. The project manager and members of the project team would ordinarily be involved with control activities relating to current operations; however, more senior management would become involved if alterations to future detailed plans, or the project's objectives, targets or budgets were proposed.

4.7   Audit and post-audit review

When the processes of development and implementation have been concluded, the final phase – an audit of the entire development process – is conducted.

Assessment of the following should take place:

- the extent to which the required quality has been achieved

- the efficiency of the system during operation compared with the agreed performance standards

- the cost of the development compared with the budgeted expenditure and the reasons for over- or under-expenditure identified

- the time taken to develop the system compared with the targeted date for completion, and reasons for a variance identified

- the effectiveness of the management process and structures in managing the project

- the significance of any problems encountered, and the effectiveness of the solutions generated to deal with them.

The primary benefit derived from the post-audit analysis is to augment the organisation's experience and knowledge.

Two other areas of activity should be operating throughout all of the above phases: communication and coordination.

Communication – the project manager must ensure that his/her superiors are kept informed and that team members are adequately briefed.

Coordination – at all stages the activities of the project team and the users and other involved parties must be well coordinated.

5   Project Quality Plan

Maintaining the quality of work throughout a project is essential. Not only will the project sponsor expect that the project will progress under appropriate quality guidelines, but the project manager and the project team will also want to deliver a high quality product. Ensuring that the project meets quality control objectives is therefore essential.

A Project Quality Plan should be prepared alongside the Project Plan. The purpose of a Project Quality Plan is to specify all the relevant organisational procedures and standards for making sure that the project is completed to the required level of quality.

The Project Quality Plan covers a wide range of issues, but it is not necessarily a long document. This is because it refers to other document where the relevant organisational standards are set out, and it only describes quality issues in detail when there are no such documents to cross-reference to. This means that a Project Quality Plan is essentially an 'exception document', setting out only exceptions or additions to established organisational procedures and standards.

5.1   Contents of a Project Quality Plan

A Project Quality Plan might contain the following items.

Content item	Comments
Introduction	This should explain how the Plan applies to the project for the system development. Where the need for the Plan has been specified by the system user, as a contractual requirement, this should be stated.
Project overview	This provides a broad description of the project, including its objectives, its main deliverables and the identity of the client/customer. This overview can be extracted from the Project Initiation Document.
Glossary of terms	To avoid confusion and misunderstanding about the use of terms, a glossary of definitions for key terms should be provided.
Product requirement	This section of the Plan provides a description of the work to be carried out in the project development, the project milestones and what has to be delivered to reach each successive milestone. Timescales for achievement of each milestone and to complete the development work in total should be specified. References should be made to the relevant formal project specifications. This section might also specify security requirements, performance criteria, legal requirements and client standards. There should be extensive cross-referencing to the Requirements Specifications for the project.
Project organisation	This should set out the organisation and management specifications for the project development. Each management role should be specified, and the individual filling each role

	should be named. Where management roles are standard, this might be presented simply as a list of roles and associated managers' names.
Monitoring and reporting procedures	This section specifies the procedures for planning, monitoring and controlling the project. For example, how should progress be monitored (perhaps with a critical path chart)? If computer software such as Microsoft Project is to be used for planning, estimating, monitoring and reporting project progress, this should be stated.
Development life cycle	This section specifies the main phases in the 'life cycle' of the system development. For example, these might be systems analysis, systems design, programming, program testing, system testing, user testing an implementation. The phases will normally conform to the organisation's standard project development phases. For each phase, the Project Quality Plan should specify: • start criteria for the phase • methods and procedures to be used in the phase and standards to be applied • procedures for testing and review • phase completion criteria
Quality Assurance	Quality Assurance (QA) is about reviewing the project work *as it progresses*. The aim is to identify errors as early as possible, and put them right. QA checks can be carried out in a variety of ways, and the methods applicable to the project should be stated in the Quality Plan. QA checking methods are: • self-checking • peer review (i.e. checking by colleagues) • formal review by an internal review team formal external review
Testing	This section of the Project Quality Plan should specify the different testing phases that should be undergone (program testing or unit testing, system testing, user testing and so on).
Quality documentation	The results of quality assurance and testing should be documented to verify that the checks and tests have been done, and what the outcomes were. This section of the Project Quality Plan should state how the QA checks and tests should be documented. The organisation might use a standard form, with each check or test documented on a separate form.
Procurement	When there is a requirement to purchase hardware or software items externally for the project, there should be established procurement procedures and standards. The Plan will probably provide a cross-reference to the organisation's established procurement procedures.

Sub-contractors	When the project development work will involve sub-contracting some of the work, the Project Quality plan should specify which work will be put out to a sub-contractor, and what the procedures should be for evaluating and selecting a suitable sub-contractor in each case. There should also be procedures for monitoring the work of the sub-contractor as it progresses, and for acceptance procedures for checking the work when it has been completed.
Changes to the scope of the project	If the scope of the project is changed during the project development, there should be procedures for authorising and documenting the changes. This section of the Plan should specify what those procedures should be.
System version/configuration management	During the development of a new system, it is very common for different versions of the system or different versions of modules within the system, to exist at the same time. To avoid confusion, it is important to know which version is being worked on and which version might need amending. This section of the Project Quality Plan should set out the procedures for controlling the use of system versions. It might call for the use of 'configuration management' software to assist with this work.
Risk management	Risk management involves identifying potential problems and taking measures to eliminate or reduce the risks to an acceptable level. Risk assessment should begin from the start of the project and continue all the way through the project development. Each significant risk should be identified, and a decision taken about how it should be eliminated or reduced (or whether the risk is in fact tolerable).
	For example, a perceived risk might be that using inexperienced staff for systems analysis might result in a poorly-designed system. A measure to eliminate the risk would be to ensure that only experienced systems analysts are used. A measure to reduce the risk might be for senior systems analysts to monitor the work of their juniors very closely.
	Risk management procedures (and documentation requirements) should be set out in the Project Quality Plan.
Delivery	This section of the Plan should set out the arrangements for installing and delivering the completed system to the user.

6   Costing and resource allocation

As mentioned previously, there are four main elements affecting a project:

1   Time – in terms of time taken to complete the project and regarding the opportunity cost of the time invested in the current project that could have been spent on another.

2   Costs – as established in the budget for the project.

3   Resources – including human resources, machinery, space.

4   Quality– in terms of the initially agreed standards of quality.

Let us consider why it is important to allocate resources accurately.

Take the example of human resources in the first instance. Human resources are usually limited. The number of individuals available to do a job at a specific time with a particular skill mix will be predetermined in many cases (offices, factories, etc). In most projects it is necessary to avoid sharp fluctuations in staffing levels. This is partly based on economic reasons – it is expensive to recruit and train staff – but also for social reasons – it is not desirable to hire personnel, lay them off, hire them again, etc. An efficient use of manpower is to aim for a smooth build-up followed by a tapering off – this can often be achieved by rescheduling.

The same principle can be applied to other resources too.

There is typically a relationship between the four elements identified above (time, costs, resources and quality) so that, should one be varied, it will feasibly affect at least one of the other elements: the skill of the project manager is to find the correct balance.

It may be important that the project is completed on time; however, to achieve this there may be a financial penalty in terms of overtime to be paid, or it may become necessary to recruit extra staff. If these financial implications are not an option, then perhaps a compromise on the standards of quality may need to be considered.

7   Role of the project manager

Every textbook on project management contains a similar list of the skills required to be an effective project manager. The core of each list is based on a set of 'leadership qualities' such as that put forward by John Adair. According to Adair, any leader must be able to satisfy three overlapping sets of needs, as shown in the following diagram and described below.

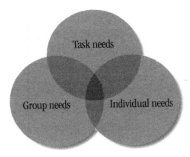

The tasks that a leader carries out to meet **team needs** are as follows:

- building the team and maintaining team spirit
- developing work methods so the team functions cohesively
- setting standards and maintaining discipline
- setting up systems for communication within the team
- training the team

- appointing subordinate leaders.

The tasks that a leader carries out to meet **task needs** are as follows:

- achieving team objectives
- defining tasks
- planning work
- allocating resources
- assigning responsibilities
- monitoring progress and checking performance
- controlling quality.

The tasks that a leader carries out to meet **individual needs** are as follows:

- developing the individual
- balancing group needs and individual needs
- rewarding good performance
- helping with personal problems.

Being able to perform all of these tasks would be a good starting point for any project manager!

7.1 Core skills

KEY POINT

Project manager skills:

- leadership
- technological understanding
- evaluation and decision-making
- people management
- systems design and maintenance
- planning and control
- financial awareness
- procurement
- communication
- negotiation
- contractual skills
- legal awareness.

According to Yeates and Cadle, a project manager requires the following core skills in order to be effective.

- **Leadership.** Project managers should be able to stimulate action, progress and change.

- **Technological understanding.** Project managers need to have an accurate perception of the technical requirements of the project so that business needs are addressed and satisfied.

- **Evaluation and decision-making.** Project managers should have the ability to evaluate alternatives and to make informed decisions.

- **People management.** Project managers should be able to motivate and enthuse their teams and have a constant personal drive towards achieving the project's goals.

- **Systems design and maintenance.** Project managers should be able to demonstrate their individual competence and have a complete working knowledge of the internal administration of their project.

- **Planning and control.** Project managers should be constantly monitoring progress against the plan and taking any necessary corrective action using modern planning and monitoring methods.

- **Financial awareness.** Project managers should be proficient in risk management and have a broad financial knowledge.

- **Procurement.** Project managers should understand the basics of procurement and be able to develop the procurement strategy for their project.

- **Communication.** Project managers should be able to express themselves clearly and unambiguously in speaking and writing and be able to do this in a wide range of situations and with a wide range of people.

- **Negotiation.** Project managers should be skilful in managing their clients and should be able to plan and carry out a negotiation strategy.

- **Contractual skills.** Project managers should be able to understand the contract that defines their project and should be able to manage subcontractors to ensure that the contractual terms are met.

- **Legal awareness.** Project managers should have an awareness of any legal issues that could affect their project.

7.2   Project management training

Many independent training organisations run courses in the basics and advanced tools of project management. Attendance on a course is a good way to develop the skills required, though some of the leadership traits of the successful project manager are difficult to learn as they are related to the personality of the individual.

7.3   Project management qualifications

The Project Management Institute (PMI) is the world's largest project management professional body. It has a certification examination leading to (with appropriate experience) the Project Management Professional (PMP) qualification. The Institute has examination centres throughout the World. The Institute can be contacted via its website at http://www.pmi.org.

8   Project team selection

As a project manager, one of the most important steps is the selection and recruitment of a project team.

In some projects managers may have a team 'forced' on them, or may inherit a team from a previous project manager. If this is the case, little can be done to change the team membership. However, if a project manager is able to select a team, this can be a major determinant of the success of a project.

8.1   Selection

Simply accepting a team member because of their functional specialism and availability is not sufficient. Team members should see that being part of a project team is a privilege, and a formal set of recruitment interviews will help to reinforce this view.

At the recruitment stage, the project manager should consider asking candidates the following:

- What is your relevant technical experience?
- Have you any specialised knowledge relevant to the project?
- Have you worked in project teams before?
- Have you other departmental or project commitments?
- When do these commitments end?
- Can you commit to the project full-time?
- Do you get on well with others?
- Do you like working alone?
- What do you seek to gain from the project?
- Is your line manager in agreement with you joining the team?

On the basis of these questions, and others relevant to the specific project, it should be possible for the project manager to select the right team.

8.2   Induction

Once the team is selected, the project manager might decide to run an induction
program for the group. This will be similar to an induction session for a new recruit to
an organisation, and will be an opportunity to discuss the objectives of the project, the
organisation structure, and other key issues. Induction will also be an opportunity for
team members to identify their role in the team.

8.3   Managing the project team

Once the project is under way, it is one of the project manager's major responsibilities
to develop and manage the work of the project team. In large projects it is the team
who do the work and the manager, although responsible for the quality of the work,
does little of it and concentrates on managing others.

8.4   Communication

One of the keys to success in project management is creating and maintaining a
communication structure within the project team. There are a number of
communication tools that the project manager can use:

Job/task descriptions

Giving each team member a clear written statement of their responsibilities, goals and
performance measures will improve their motivation level and provide a framework for
performance review.

Checkpoint meetings and reports

The PRINCE methodology recommends a regular, often weekly, meeting between the
project team members and the project manager. At this meeting, any issues can be
raised and dealt with in a fairly relaxed environment. The proceedings are often
minuted and reported to the steering committee or project sponsor.

Notice boards

If the project team have an office, a notice board can be used for team-related
correspondence. If the organisation has an intranet, an electronic bulletin board can be
established.

Appraisals

If the project extends over months or even years, the team can have regular appraisals
by the project manager. For details of performance appraisal, see *Organisational
Management*.

Newsletters

The project team can publish and distribute a weekly or monthly newsletter, either in
hard copy form or by e-mail.

8.5   Co-ordination

The project manager must also ensure that the project team becomes a team, rather
than remaining a group of individuals. Regular teambuilding events, such as training
courses and social events, will make the team members feel part of the team and create
a project culture.

Successful co-ordination will create an environment where team members work
together to solve problems.

8.6   Motivation

The project manager is responsible for ensuring that each team member performs at the optimal level. This requires knowledge of motivation theory, and the project manager must take the time to get to know each of the team member's needs.

9   Structures for project teams

The project will progress more successfully when various structures are in place. They are identified below, and the role and responsibilities of each element is described.

9.1   Project team

The project team consists of individuals brought together purely for undertaking a specific project. The size of the team and the period of their existence will be determined by the nature of the project.

The skills and experience required will be dependent on the nature of the system being developed, but typically a project team may consist of individuals selected from the following groups:

- specialist IT staff (systems analysts; programmers, etc)

- specialist functional staff (contributing technical expertise in the relevant area)

- user representatives (who may be inputting or processing data, or using the system output)

- human resource development and training specialists

- external specialists or consultants.

9.2   Team leaders

It is not uncommon, in the case of large development projects, for there to be several leaders.

The team leader will typically be responsible for:

- planning and organising the work of the team members on a regular basis (daily/weekly)

- constantly supervising the activities of each individual team member

- providing advice or taking appropriate decisions in the case of technical difficulties

- coordinating and overseeing intercommunication between user departments and other project teams

- reporting to the project manager and/or user group and, where problems have been encountered, providing advice on feasible solutions

- reporting back to the team members any modifications to the project resulting from decisions made at a more senior level

- supervising the implementation of any changes to the planned activities or schedules resulting from control activities.

9.3   The user group

The user group should, ideally, consist of at least one user from each of the departments affected by the proposals as well as the project manager and team leader/s. This group is an ideal forum for users to express their concerns; to highlight problems affecting users as the system develops; for solutions to be explored; for obtaining user feedback. Although its role is advisory, management generally accept the merits of responding to the issues raised.

FOULKS LYNCH
PUBLICATIONS

9.4 The project steering committee

This committee would typically consist of representatives from the user departments who are members of the user group; the project team leader/s; the project manager and members of senior management who are responsible for either the development staff or the functional areas affected by the developments. The role of the steering committee has been covered in Chapter 4.

9.5 The management sponsor

The management sponsor is responsible for the development of the information system within the organisation, and provides a channel of communication between the project manager and senior management or between the users and senior management in order to report on progress and future developments.

Often the development of information systems involves change – a state that invariably meets with resistance; it is for this reason that the support of senior management is required.

9.6 The project manager

The project manager may be expected to communicate effectively at all three levels (strategic, tactical and operational). Primarily the project manager's responsibility is to ensure that effectiveness and efficiency are achieved across the entire project.

10 Effect of different organisational structures

Different organisational structures need different information systems, and it is essential to thoroughly understand the structure before an information system is designed. The type of organisation and its environment go a long way towards determining how it will be structured, but equally important are the personalities involved and the situation that existed when the organisation was formed. Key factors influencing the organisational structure are: organisational history; internal politics; management style; size of organisation; the nature of the products or services; the type of markets served; how diverse the organisation is; geographical spread.

10.1 The development of structure

Even the smallest business has an organisation structure, though it may be unaware of this. As soon as one person is employed, a structure is established.

If it becomes necessary to appoint an additional member of staff the structure is changed. The duties of the original employee may be reduced, to the extent that some duties are taken over by the new member; or the duties may be shared; or the new member may assume new responsibilities. In any event, the structure will change. At some stage it may be necessary to formalise these relationships.

This simple illustration of sole trader employing another person demonstrates that structures do not remain static. As organisations grow larger, then automatically the structure changes. Strategic management should discuss the type of structure that they want for their particular organisation.

The type of structure will influence the type of information system needed by the organisation. It is necessary to establish such things as the flow of information up, down and laterally across the organisation. It is also necessary to establish who will require the information. Is there an information manager? Do the strategic level of management require on-line real-time information? Is the organisation looking to information technology to remove some of its more mundane processing or is it looking to information technology to provide it with a competitive advantage? These are some of the questions that have to be addressed very early on in any analysis of

information requirements; but before that can be done it is necessary to know how the particular organisation in question is structured and whether it is intending to alter its structure.

The vertical structure of an organisation can be either tall or flat, as in the figure below.

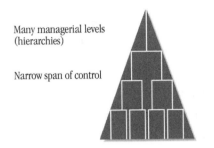

Many managerial levels (hierarchies)

Narrow span of control

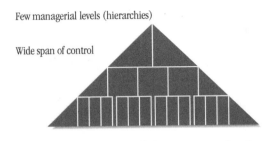

Few managerial levels (hierarchies)

Wide span of control

In order to meet the information needs of the various managers, it is necessary for the analyst to assess the span of control of each manager.

Generally a wide span of control will mean that the manager will be looking after a more diverse group of people and will need a greater variety of information. In addition, flat hierarchies mean that each person is given more responsibility, as there are fewer middle managers. Therefore a flexible information system is needed to allow many people in the organisation to access the information they need.

How wide the span of control is within an organisation will depend on various factors. In general terms, a wider span of control, and therefore a flat management structure, will be more likely where:

- Team members have appropriate project management experience and so they can work will less supervision.

- Tasks being allocated to the team members are less complex, or require only a limited amount of decision making on the part of the team member.

- The ability of the project manager in controlling large teams.

- The project is taking place in one location. A project running in a number of different locations will normally require a manager at each location, placing another layer of management into the control hierarchy.

10.2 Authority and responsibility

There are said to be three different ways in which authority and responsibility can be organised within a structure, but in practice most structures include an element of all three.

Line relationship

This is the form when the lines of authority and responsibility are direct and vertical. There is a rigid relationship between superior and subordinate throughout the organisation.

Advantages

- simple and understood by all employees

- managerial responsibility direct and inescapable

- prompt decisions are promoted

- subordinates get orders from one source only.

Disadvantages

- overall planning and coordination may be inadequate.

FOULKS LYNCH
PUBLICATIONS

Line and staff relationship

In this case line managers retain their executive authority, but functional specialists advise on the standards, methods, procedures etc to be followed.

Advantages

- benefits of specialisation are secured
- planning and coordination are improved
- responsibility can still be fixed and discipline maintained.

Disadvantages

- more complex structure
- decisions may require the collaboration of more people
- possible friction among managers and confusion among workers.

Functional organisations

This form takes account of the relationship between functions, i.e. between different specialist areas. A specialist may be responsible for activities throughout the business that come within his speciality. A functional relationship exists when a specialist, such as the DP manager, contributes a service to line managers. Line managers should follow what the functional manager suggests when acting within his speciality.

10.3 Structural forms

There are different basic forms that an organisation can take:

Product organisation

In the product organisation there are different sections for different products. This is appropriate where the product range varies as to form, process or market when it has the following advantages:

- better coordination – common goals, less conflict
- speedier decisions – communications improved
- flexibility – varying approaches can be undertaken.

It is more likely to be **ends-orientated.**

Separate divisions

Separate divisions are appropriate where the organisation is very large and has many different business products. For example, Tarmac plc has many different divisions each of which is run as a separate business.

Divisionalisation, with centralised specialist divisions, occurs within many different companies and can take various forms

Effectively, each division is a separate business and has an allocation of capital and is entirely responsible for all stages within its scope of activities. Centralisation would remain to the extent that the activities and scope of the divisions would be subject to the overall strategy and policy of the company. Such a process is sometimes known as **federal decentralisation**.

Matrix

The grid/matrix approach came into being because the US Government decided it did not wish to deal with a number of specialised executives when negotiating defence contracts and insisted contractors appointed project managers.

The concept has now been extended to whole organisations, (Lockheed Aircraft, British Aircraft Corporation) as well as to major divisions, as in ICI and in schools, polytechnics/universities, etc.

Marston University Business School

Course → Responsibility (product)	BA Business Studies	BA European Business Admin	MBA	etc
Subject responsibility (function)	D Denny	H Harman	N Neil	
Accounts A Adams	E Edwards	I Ionides	O Olapide	
QM B Brent	F Flack	J Jalal	P Patel	
IT C Charles	G Groves	M Moto	Q Quee	

In this approach the course leaders can be seen as project/product coordinators. They are responsible for course management and share their authority with the subject leaders (functional heads), who are responsible for academic development and research. A staff member, such as E Edwards, is responsible to two people: to D Denny for the BA Business Studies course and to A Adams for academic matters.

Advantages

- retains functional economies and product coordination
- is organic with open communications and flexible goals
- improved motivation through:
  - people working participatively in teams
  - specialists broadening their outlook
  - encouraging competition within the organisation.

Disadvantages

- higher administrative costs
- conflict between functional and product managers leading to individual stress arising from:
  - threat to occupational identity
  - reporting to more than one boss
  - less clear expectations.

10.4 The effect of the organisational structure on Information Systems

In order to properly service an organisation, the information systems must exhibit certain characteristics. They must be:

- sufficiently flexible to deal with the specific needs of each part of the organisation individually
- able to link together in an integrated manner to satisfy corporate information needs
- able to adapt to the evolutionary changes in the organisation caused by growth or by changes in technology or the environment

KEY POINT

Information systems must be:

- flexible
- integrated
- evolutionary
- adaptable
- objective and independent.

- flexible enough to be able to adapt to the specific needs and skills of the individuals – particularly senior management – within the organisation

- objective and independent. The possession of information within an organisation is often the key to power, and some individuals may seek to abuse that power to their own advantage but to the detriment of the rest of the organisation.

11 Human resource management issues

The introduction of a new system inevitably brings with it change. A natural reaction is to resist change; thus, the new system must be introduced with careful and sensitive management. The management of change is a subject that has attracted considerable attention in recent years as its importance has been recognised.

For the system being introduced to be a success, the support of the staff must be gained at an early stage. The changes may involve significant disturbances to their working environment: the recruitment of new staff, redundancies, or the requirement for new skills to be learnt.

The resistance to such measures can be mitigated by means of the project team involving staff in the development of the new system at the earliest stages. It is necessary for staff to be made aware of any changes in the nature of their jobs; details of necessary training; and any anticipated redundancies at an early stage.

The role of the project team in this process is to:

- organise presentations to staff to inform them about the new system and the effects it will have on their work. Fears regarding their own employment should be alleviated by adopting a positive approach, and by encouraging questions

- encourage staff to apply for any newly created jobs in preference to pressuring them into retraining

- ensure counselling services are made available to afford the opportunity for individuals to discuss their concerns

- prepare and circulate a training schedule

- ensure that retraining is undertaken without loss of pay or increase in pressure of work

- encourage senior members of staff to adopt and promote a positive attitude towards the introduction of the new system.

Education and training are the key elements in inspiring confidence in, and commitment to, the new system.

Conclusion

This chapter has dealt with the management of a computer project. This involves being aware of costs, deadlines, quality and resources. Risks assessment and management are also important. By identifying areas of high risk in advance, managers should be able to monitor these closely and have contingency plans for reducing the effects of problems that could arise.

EXAM-TYPE QUESTION 1

Squiggy

The Board of the Squiggy organisation are about to authorise their first systems project to upgrade an old and failing computer system. Unfortunately, no member of the Board has any recent project management experience. The Board has recognised this as being an issue and asked the Finance Director to produce a list of requirements for the project. These requirements will be given to a systems analyst in preparation for a full feasibility study later in the year. The report from the Finance Director includes the following comments. The project will update the current systems of the company.

'The focus of the project is to provide the Board with the necessary information to run the organisation.

We expect the project to take about 12 weeks. During this changeover phase, we will use manual accounting to continue order processing and maintain the customer ledgers.

As we are a small company, the project is unlikely to be complex; so one systems analyst will carry out the work.

An initial budget of £24,000 has been set aside for the project.

As discussed, I will be in charge of the day-to-day running of the project.'

Required:

Evaluate the comments made the FD, showing any weaknesses in those comments.

(18 marks)

EXAM-TYPE QUESTION 2

Skills of a project manager

Yeates and Cadle, identify various cores skills that a project manager requires in order to be effective.

Identify those skills and briefly explain how they apply to a project manager.

(15 marks)

FOULKS LYNCH
PUBLICATIONS

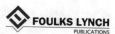

The main steps in planning a project are:

- identify purpose of project

- set objectives – define deliverables

- gather information on resources, timescales

- construct a plan – list tasks, timescales and dependencies, allocate tasks

- decide on the tools to be used and identify control systems

Control systems must be capable of measuring progress, reporting deviations and taking corrective action. The criteria for a good control system includes the following:

- The plan and its control should be viable

- good control relies on good monitoring – keep it simple

- control depends on having measurable objectives and milestones.

In conclusion, three things occur in the planning and control process:

- **A plan is prepared** specifying the project requirements, work tasks, responsibilities, schedules and budgets.

- **The plan is compared** to actual project performance, time and cost.

- **Corrective action taken** if there are any discrepancies and the requirements, schedules and budgets are updated.

Planning and control is very important as it enables people to understand what is needed to meet the goals and reduces uncertainty of outcomes.

1.1 Types of project management tools

A project manager has a range of project management tools available to assist with the planning and control of individual systems projects. These tools have been refined and developed over the years, but they are all designed to improve the effectiveness of the project management process.

The project management tools available include:

- Work breakdown structure
- critical path analysis
- Gantt chart
- resource histogram
- budget.

2 Work allocation

2.1 Work Breakdown Structure

One of the main methods of breaking down work into manageable units, and then allocating those units to members of the project team, is to use a work breakdown structure (WBS).

The basic idea of creating a (WBS) is to take the work involved in the project and break it down into smaller and smaller parts, until the project consists of a series of **work packages**. These can then be put into the project plan as activities.

A hierarchical approach is often taken to WBS production, as shown below.

Top-level WBS

This breaks the project down into stages, often using the project life cycle stages as major sub-divisions of the project.

Second level WBS

This breaks each stage down into groups of tasks. The first group of tasks requires further analysis in this case.

Third level WBS

This breaks the groups of tasks into individual work packages, as shown above. In a complex project it may be necessary to go down to more levels in order to produce a sufficiently detailed WBS. When the individual tasks are identified, then work can be allocated to members of the project team in accordance with their skill and ability.

2.2　PRINCE – Product Breakdown Structure

The PRINCE methodology uses a different approach to analysing the work to be done. The assumption made with PRINCE is that it is easier to see, in a complex project, what is to be produced than it is to know how that will happen. PRINCE therefore uses a system of product breakdown structures (PBS) to analyse the project.

PRINCE always uses the same top-level PBS, as shown below:

Management products are those products associated with the planning and control of the project. They include, for example, the project initiation document (PID), the project plan, etc.

Technical products are those things the project has been set up to create.

Quality products are things associated with the definition and control of quality.

This top level view would then be broken down into a series of more detailed PBS diagrams such as the one shown here for technical products.

PBS for technical products

The next levels would further sub-analyse each type of product, as shown for the hardware products.

PBS for hardware products

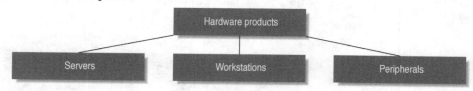

2.3 Planning tools

Having completed the work breakdown structure, it will be possible to construct a project network.

Critical path analysis (CPA) or network analysis

This is a diagram showing the various activities in a project. The aim of the CPA is to identify how those activities link together and to show the **critical path** or the sequence of activities where a delay will result in the overall project being delayed.

Gantt chart

A Gantt chart, named after its inventor, shows the activities of a project, the same as CPA. However, these activities are presented as a bar chart with the start and finishing times clearly identified.

Resource histogram

This is a stacked bar chart showing the number and mix of staff required over the duration of a project.

Budget

The project budget shows for each month of the project, the proposed expenditure. This will be updated as the project progresses with the actual expenditure and the reason for any variances.

Almost all of these tools can be in some form of computer software, For example, a budget or Gantt chart can be presented on a spreadsheet. However, there is also specialist project management software available to produce critical path analysis and Gantt charts directly from the data entered into the software.

The information analysis syllabus requires detailed knowledge of the project networks (network analysis) and Gantt charts. These tools are explained in the remainder of this chapter.

2.4 Project management tools

The development of a computer system must be planned, managed and controlled. The techniques used in managing a computer project are the same as those used in carrying out any other sort of project.

2.5   Network analysis (Critical Path Analysis)

The most commonly used technique for managing projects is called network analysis. There are a number of variants of network analysis. The best known are critical path analysis (CPA), sometimes known as the critical path method (CPM).

With CPA, a project is broken down into component activities that have to be carried out. Some activities can be carried out at the same time, in parallel with each other. Other activities cannot begin until an earlier activity has been finished. For example, you can't test a program until you have written it. For each activity, the activity or activities that must precede it (if any) are identified.

A network is then drawn, showing all the activities to be carried out, and the logical sequence in which they must occur, from the start of the project to its completion.

In addition, the expected time needed to complete activity is estimated and written in the network diagram. Using these estimates, it is then possible to calculate:

- the earliest time at which each individual activity could start

- the earliest time at which the project as a whole can be completed

- the latest possible time at which an activity can finish, without affecting the earliest completion time for the project as a whole.

Some activities will have to be started at the earliest possible time, and completed on time, for the project as a whole to be completed in the minimum time. This sequence of time-critical activities is known as the **critical path**.

Network analysis involves the breaking down of a project into its constituent activities, and the presentation of these activities in diagrammatic form. Please refer back to Section 7 of Chapter 5 for an example of **work breakdown structure** to remind you of how a project can be broken down into its individual activities.

The steps or drawing a CPA chart can therefore be summarised as follows.

Analyse the project

The project is broken down into its constituent tasks or activities. Once this has been done, the way that these activities relate together is examined. This enables the planner to ascertain which parts of the project need to be completed before others can begin.

Draw the network

The sequence of these activities is shown in diagrammatic form called the network diagram.

Estimate the time and cost

The amount of time that each activity will take is estimated. Where appropriate the cost is also estimated. Estimating the time needed to write a new program can be difficult. Experienced analysts will know how long similar projects have taken and can then estimate the time for the current project by adjusting historical times for increases or decreases in complexity.

Locate the critical path

The sequence of activities that has zero float time. If any of the activities should slip behind its schedule, the whole project will be delayed.

Schedule the project

The analysis is used to develop the most efficient and cost effective schedule, if necessary with any alternative way of completing the project being analysed.

Monitor and control the progress of the project

Use the schedule and any progress charts that have been drawn up to monitor progress of the plan.

Revise the plan

The plan is modified to take account of eventualities and problems that occur during the progress of the job.

2.6 Drawing the network diagram

Drawing a logic diagram is a skill requiring practice and ingenuity, and for major projects may require two or three attempts before a satisfactory network or diagram is completed correctly. Computer packages are often used to carry out this process, cutting drastically the time taken.

A network is drawn as a collection of circles (or boxes) and arrowed lines, representing activities and 'events'. An 'event' is when an activity ends or begins. Each activity is likely to be given a number or letter for identification.

There are two types of network chart, an **activity on arrow** diagram and an **activity on node** diagram. In an activity-on-arrow diagram, each activity is shown as an arrowed line, and events are shown as circles. In an activity-on-node diagram, activities are shown as boxes.

In this section you will be shown activity-on-arrow diagrams. If you are required to draw a network in your examination, you may use whichever approach you are most familiar with.

The following diagram represents the sequence of activities involved in *turning on the television and selecting a channel to watch*; larger diagrams can be used to represent situations that are more complicated.

This diagram is called a **network** and represents the whole project.

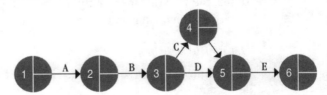

Each of the straight lines connecting the circles represents a task that takes time or resources; these lines are called **activities**. The arrowheads show the direction of the activity.

The circles are called **events**, and represent a point in time. Each event represents the beginning of an activity, and/or the completion of an event. Event 3 represents the point in time when activity B has been completed, and activities D and C begin.

The dotted line connecting events 4 and 5 is called a **dummy activity**. Dummy activities do not take any time or resources, are drawn in to make the diagram clearer, and they ensure that none of the rules or conventions for drawing diagrams is breached.

The activities represented in the diagram are shown in the table below. The network contains the assumption that you will use both the TV guide and review television programs on the TV at the same time, while trying to find a program to watch.

Choosing a TV program

Activity	Description	Immediate preceding activities
A	Find TV guide	-
B	Turn on television	A
C	Review channels on television	B
D	Review programs in TV Guide	B
E	Select program to watch	C, D

The network was drawn using the following rules and conventions:

2.7   Rules for drawing a network

1   A complete network should have only one point of entry – the start event, and one point of exit – the finish event.

2   Every activity must have one preceding event – the **tail**, and one following event – the **head**.

3   Several activities may use the same tail event, and several the same head event, but no two activities may share the same head and tail events. Thus the following diagram would not be allowed as part of a network:

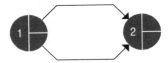

Instead, a dummy activity is used, shown by a dotted arrow, so the correct version of the above would be either of the following two diagrams:

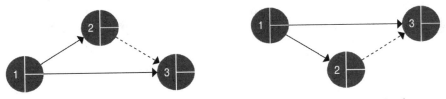

4   An event does not happen until all activities into it are complete. In the network for selecting a TV program for example, event 5 is not complete until both of the activities C and D are complete. You cannot choose the TV program you want to watch until you have reviewed the alternatives in the TV guide and on the television.

5   **Loops** are not allowed. You cannot have a series of activities leading from an event that lead back to the same event. The essence of drawing a network is that it represents a series of activities moving on in time. **Neither of the two following diagrams is allowed**:

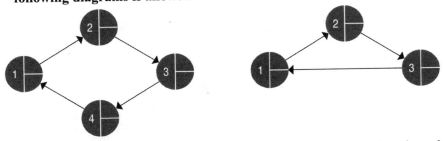

6   **Danglers** (events that do not represent the completion of the project, but which have no activity coming out of them) are not allowed. All activities must contribute to the progression of the network or be discarded as irrelevant.

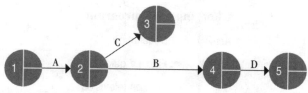

The dangling activity should only be included if it contributes to the progress of the project, in which case it should link to the end event as in the following diagram:

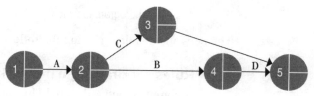

2.8   Conventions for drawing networks

In addition to the rules described above, certain conventions are followed for the sake of clarity and conformity.

• networks proceed from left to right – the start event is at the left hand side of the diagram, and the end event at the right hand side

• networks are not drawn to scale

• arrows representing activities should have their head to the right of their tail unless it is impossible to draw the network in that way

• events or nodes should be numbered so that an activity always moves from a lower numbered event to a higher one. This convention is relatively easy to accomplish in a simple network but in a complex network it may be necessary to number in tens to allow for extra activities to be added without the need for a complete renumbering of the whole diagram

• lines that cross should be avoided if possible

• the start event may be represented as a line instead of a circle, particularly when several activities may begin at the start point.

2.9   Finding the critical path

The **critical path** through a network is the chain of activities whose times determine the overall duration of the project. Activities on the critical path are known as **critical activities**, and any increase in the duration of a critical activity will result in an increase in the project duration.

Finding the critical path is a routing task to identify the longest path in a network. In the network diagram below, there are two possible paths from the start event to the end event: namely ABE and CDE. The time taken for each of these paths is 26 days for ABE and 18 days for CDE. Because path ABE takes the longest time, it is called the Critical Path.

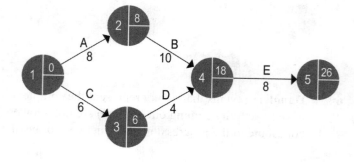

The basic technique of finding the critical path is as follows, taking each node in turn:

Event 1 is the starting event, reached after time 0. Event 2 is reached after activity A, and therefore the earliest it can be reached is after 8 days. Event 3 can be reached after 6 days. Event 4 can be reached either through activity D from event 3, or via activity B from event 1. The earliest it could have been reached is via the longer of these two paths, i.e. 10 days from event 2. Activity E cannot begin until event 4 is reached i.e. after activity 4 is completed. Even though activity D has been completed 8 days before B, E must wait.

Information concerning the time for each of the activities in the network is recorded in the events at the end of each activity. The top right of each event records the earliest finish time for each activity that is the working from left to right, the quickest time that an event can be reached. . For example, activity A takes 8 time units, so the top left of event 1 shows a 0, the start of the network, and event 2 shows 8. Similarly, activity B takes 10 time units to go from event 2 to 4, making the earliest finish time at event 4 of 18. The earliest finish times for other events can be calculated in the same way.

Event 4 has an earliest finishing time of 18, not 10 (activity C plus D) because both activities B and D must be complete by this event. The activities with the later finish time is always included, otherwise this activity would still be running when the event occurred.

The next process is the **backward pass.** The bottom right of the event records the latest finish time. This is the latest time an event can finish in order to reach the end of the network when the last activity finishes.

The latest finish time for 5 is the same as the earliest time – 26 secs. This is always the start point for calculating the backward pass: the final event has the same earliest and latest times.

The latest finish time (LFT) for each of the previous events is obtained by subtracting the activity durations from the preceding events along the backward route, taking the minimum value where there is more than one route back into an event.

The LFT for event 4 = 26 – 8 = 18 secs

The LFT for event 3 = 18 – 4 = 14 secs

The LFT for event 2 = 18 – 10 = 8 secs

The LFT for event 1 = the minimum of 8 – 8 = 0 secs (from 2), and 14 – 6 = 8 secs (from 3).

Event 3 has a latest finish time 8 greater than the earliest start time. A delay of up to 8 secs would not affect the total project duration. The other events have earliest times equal to the latest times, and so any delay in reaching them would increase the project duration. These events are on the critical path. The critical path therefore follows activities A, B and E.

The critical path is found by calculating earliest times first by means of the forward pass, and then the latest times by means of the backward pass. Events whose earliest time equals their latest time are by definition on the critical path. The critical path should be traceable from the start event through to the end event. It is possible for a project to have more than one critical path.

2.10 Calculating the float

Some activities in a project, like C above, have spare time, so that when delays occur on those activities, the overall project duration may not be affected. This spare time is called the **float**. In a typical project, only about 20% of operations are critical, so the other 80% have a float time. All activities on the critical path have, by definition zero float time; delaying those activities will have the effect of increasing the overall time for the project.

Calculation of the float can be illustrated using the same network:

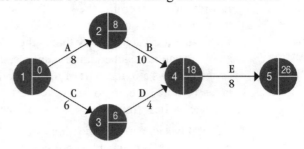

The critical path goes through events 1, 2, 4, 5 – or activities A, B, E. There is no float time on those activities. You know there is no float because the start and finish times at each event are the same.

The float time on activities can be obtained from the formula:

Total float = Latest finish time – Earliest start time – Activity duration

Float for C = 14 – 0 – 6 days = 8 days

Float for D = 18 – 6 – 4 days = 8 days

The Float for C is therefore the latest finish time of 14 (from event 3) less the earliest finish time of 0 (from event 1) less the duration of the activity of 6. This gives a float of 8. In other words, as long as activity C reaches event 3 by time day 14, the network can still be completed. Activity D will take 4 and activity E 8 time days to reach the last event of 5 by time day 26.

Similarly, D has a float of 8, (event 4 latest finish time of 18 less event 3 earliest start time of 6 less activity duration of 4). As long as activity D reaches event 4 by time unit 18, again the network can be finished.

The float is used to identify whether any delay in starting or carrying out an activity will cause a delay in the project completion time.

A delay in either activity C *or* D of up to 8 days will not cause an increase in the project time, but if there is a delay in activity C, the earliest start time for D will be delayed, reducing its float. The two floats are not independent of each other; when calculating a float a check must be made to identify progress from previous activities, as late running activities will limit the floats of subsequent activities.

The example above has been made very simple, to demonstrate the principles. A real development project is likely to have far more activities, with more complicated dependencies between them. However large the project, and however many parallel activities there may be, the principles of calculating forward and backward passes is exactly the same, and so are the principle for deriving the critical path, and amount of float on all non-critical activities.

2.11 Gantt charts

The ideal project reporting system is a mixture of graphics and tables. One form of graphical presentation that is commonly used as a part of network analysis is the Gantt chart.

A Gantt chart is a kind of horizontal bar chart where the length of the bar represents the duration of the activity as in the figure below. When a Gantt chart is used to help in the control of a project, two bars are used to represent each activity – one the planned duration and the other the actual duration.

Activity

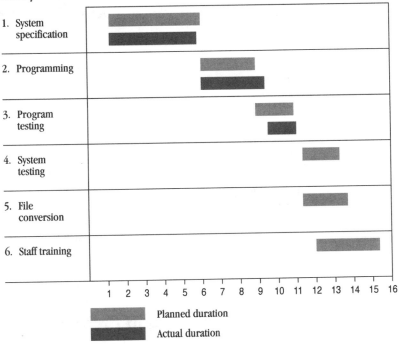

Example: The use of project management

The following network could be monitored using the chart and table beneath it.

Activity B was delayed by late delivery, but weekend working, and the transfer of resources from activity G to activity E enabled activity E to be completed on schedule and the project to be put back on course.

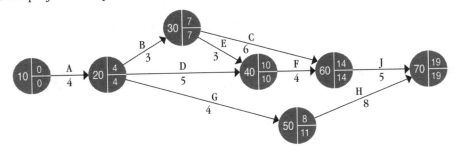

Activities

Activities

Scheduled activity	Actual event	Descr.	Float	Start	End	Start	End	Comments
A	10-20	-----	0	04/07	28/07	04/07	26/07	------------
B	20-30	-----	0	01/08	19/08	27/07	26/08	------------
C	30-60	-----	1	22/08	06/10	29/08	07/10	------------
D	20-40	-----	1	01/08	02/09	01/08	04/09	------------
E	30-40	-----	0	22/08	09/09	27/08	09/09	------------
F	40-60	-----	0	12/09	07/10	12/09	07/10	------------
G	20-50	-----	3	01/08	19/08	27/07	26/08	------------
H	50-70	-----	3	22/08	14/10	29/08	16/10	------------
J	50-70	-----	0	20/10	11/11	20/10	11/11	------------

3 Problem areas and project slippage

All projects include some risk: cost overrun, missed deadlines, poor outcome, disappointed customers, and business disruption. Identification and management of risks is therefore important as they will cause project deadlines to be missed resulting in overage slippage of the project timetable.

3.1 Risk management

Risk management consists of the following steps:

1   Identification of the risks.

2   Estimate of their downside effects i.e., the implications of what could go wrong.

3   Estimation of the probabilities of the events occurring. It will be difficult to establish precise probabilities, but it will be necessary to establish some type of prioritisation: some risks will be much more likely than others. Attention must first be paid to the more important threats.

4   Decide how the risks will be handled.

Risks can be handled as follows:

*   do nothing. This is appropriate where the effect is small or the chance of occurrence very remote

*   insure against the risk

*   off-load the risk, for example by arranging for third parties to complete part of the project

KEY POINT

Risk steps:

*   identify risks
*   estimate downside effects
*   estimate the probabilities of the events
*   decide how the risks will be handled.

- investigate the risk further and try to protect against it. For example arrange to have additional staff available in case of project overrun.

4   Threat identification and slippage reduction

4.1   Possible threats

The following can threaten the success of a project. Suggestions are included as to how to minimise the slippage involved with those threats.

Poor management

Many project leaders will be from technical backgrounds and they may not have the proper management skills for controlling large projects.

Project leaders should be properly trained so that they have managerial skills as well as technical skills. They should not be given large critically important projects until they have proved themselves on smaller exercises.

Poor planning

Managers have not made use of the various planning methods available: network analysis, Gantt charts. They have not broken the project down into its various activities and estimated a time and cost for each.

Lack of control mechanisms

It is essential to be able to monitor the progress of projects otherwise it is impossible to decide whether they will meet cost and time budgets.

Reporting mechanisms and review dates should be set out in advance.

Unrealistic deadlines

There is often pressure from users for projects to be completed quickly. Project teams, particularly if they have had to win the job competitively, may have suggested times that are unrealistic.

Project managers must look critically at the deadlines. They should identify the critical activities of the project and ensure that these do not slip.

Insufficient budget

Too few people are employed on the project, inadequate hardware is bought, the cheapest (not the best) solutions are always sought.

Of course, organisations cannot ignore costs and should try to get good value for money. However, it is important to be objective about what a given cost budget can produce by way of project outcomes. If money is tight, it might be better to do a smaller project thoroughly than a larger one poorly.

Moving targets

The project specification keeps changing as the project progresses. This will certainly add costs and delay to the project.

Users requirements should be thoroughly examined and the analyst should check understanding before the project is started. Techniques such as structured walkthroughs and prototyping will help here.

Additional information on risk management can be found in chapter 14, section 7, where the production of a risk management plan is explained in more detail.

4.2   Project change procedure

One of the most effective methods of dealing with the need to amend projects is to have a project change procedure. Although this procedure will not remove some of the risks discussed above, it will enable some changes to be made to the project with minimal disruption and slippage occurring.

The main issue to be aware of in changing a project is that the later into a project that a change is made, then the more difficult it will be to accommodate that change and the greater will be the expense of that change.

A change management procedure for a project will normally involve the following activities:

Identifying the need for change

This may arise from many sources including user input, technical difficulties with implementing part of the project, time or cost efficiencies identified by the project team etc. Any change will be discussed with the Project Manager initially.

Change recommendation

A more formal explanation of the change is produced, stating clearly the need for the change, what the change will be and the costs and benefits associated with the change

Feasibility of change

The project manager and senior members of the project team will check that the change is actually possible in terms of technical and social feasibility

Steering committee approval

When the case for a change has been checked, the change document will be placed before the Steering committee for discussion, and approval if the change is accepted

Project sponsor approval

Major changes will also require the authorisation of the project sponsor and possibly the Board or similar decision-making body of the organisation

Amending project plan

The project plan will be amended to take account of the change. Deadlines and costs will be revised.

Make change

The change is actually carried out and, where necessary, tested to ensure that there are no conflicts with other sections of the project.

4.3   Advantages of project management tools

The following are the main advantages afforded by using critical path methods:

1   **Easier visualisation of relationships**. The network diagram that is produced shows how the different tasks and activities relate together, making it easier to understand a project intuitively, improving planning and making it easier to communicate details of the project plan to interested parties.

2   **More effective planning**. CPM forces management to think a project through thoroughly. It requires careful and detailed planning, and the discipline imposed often justifies its use even without the other benefits.

3   **Better focusing on problem areas**. The technique enables the manager to pinpoint likely bottlenecks and problem areas before they occur

4   **Improved resource allocation**. Manpower and other resources can be directed to those parts of the project where they will have the most effect in reducing cost and speeding up the completion of the project. Overtime can be eliminated, or confined to those jobs where it will do the most good.

5   **Studying alternative options**. Management can simulate the effect of alternative courses of action. They can also gauge the effect of problems in carrying out particular tasks and can, therefore, make contingency plans.

6   **Management by exception**. CPM identifies those actions whose timely completion is critical to the overall timetable, and enables the leeway on other actions to be calculated. This makes it possible for management to focus their attention on the important areas of the project.

7   **Improved project monitoring**. By comparing the actual performance of each task with the schedule, a manager can immediately recognise when problems are occurring, can identify when those problems are important and can take the appropriate action in time to rescue the project.

One of the most significant benefits of network analysis is that it enhances management's ability to monitor the project as it is being carried out. After the project has been analysed a series of charts, diagrams, graphs, narratives and tables are drawn up. These can be used as a reporting system that will identify immediately a critical activity that is out of control, or a non-critical activity that has used up its float.

Once problems have been identified, extra resources can be brought in or transferred between activities. Managers are thus in a better position to correct the situation before the problems become insoluble.

5   Project management software

There are many project management software tools available. We will look at a sample of products that are available. These product descriptions are intended as a basic introduction. Due to the ever changing software products, it might be useful to visit the Web sites of the individual software manufacturers to get up-to-date product information. Many sites provide downloads and free trial usage of their products.

5.1   Microsoft

Microsoft Project (MS Project) dominates project management software systems. It must be installed on every user's computer and is compatible with Microsoft Office. This allows team members to save to the database documents created in any Office application. Users become familiarised more quickly due to the same tool bars being used in MS Office. There are no limits as to the number of tasks it can handle.

One very good feature of MS Project is that it allows multiple projects to share a common resource pool; use existing e-mail infrastructure to communicate with other team members; "flag" certain tasks as reminders; split tasks; analyse project using "worst" and "most-likely" cases and many more.

5.2   Project Scheduler

This is compatible with MS Office and with an SQL database. It enables multiple projects to be merged to see the total resources used within the company.

5.3   Trakker

This offers a variety of products including, tools for risk management, activity-based costing, earned value management, as well as the usual planning, budgeting, and tracking tools.

5.4   Features of project management software

A project planning package will usually require five items of information to be input.

- the start date of each activity
- the duration of each activity
- the dependencies between activities
- the resources available
- at what stage resources will become available.

The first step in using project management (PM) software would normally be to define general management information, which would include the project name, name of project, with the start and end-dates of the project. Each activity, as it is entered, will be allocated a unique ID, and the dependencies between it and other activities.

The input screen is often similar to a spreadsheet, in that the user is presented with a grid of cells in which to enter the data to be converted into a schedule. The software will convert the input data into a Gantt chart, or a network diagram as requested. Another screen may ask for resources that are to be allocated to each of the activities, and produce a resource scheduling diagram or table for the manager.

As with CASE tools, (described in more detail, in Chapter 12) the software is considerably more than a drawing tool, incorporating a repository of rules and data on both the rules for the management techniques, and the individual project.

The pictures below come from the scheduling input for the package *Project Manager*, from Softkey Multimedia Inc. The first view is the blank input screen, and the second shows a Gantt chart derived from the input data, (as the years on each screen show, they are from different projects!)

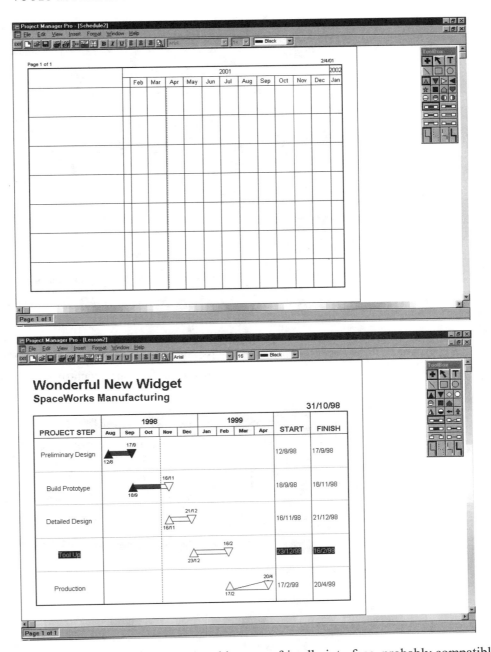

The software will also be presented in a user-friendly interface, probably compatible with Windows®. Microsoft Project® is one of the more commonly used project management software tools.

Most project management software packages will generate Critical Path networks, Gantt Charts, Resource histograms, billing information, cost estimates, actual times and costs incurred, reports for project managers and the Steering Committee. As with most packages, it achieves what traditional, human, project management has always achieved, but with greater efficiency and speed, and with the ability to handle much greater complexity.

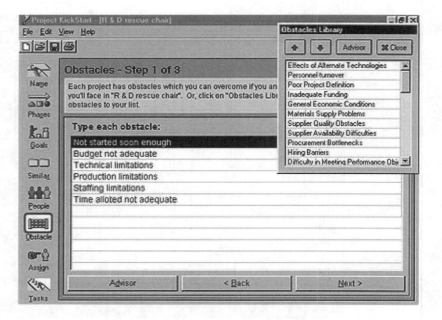

The screen above, from a package called Kickstart, helps the project manager to identify and cater for risks or obstacles to successful completion of the project.

The following picture, also from Kickstart, identifies the human resources available for then project.

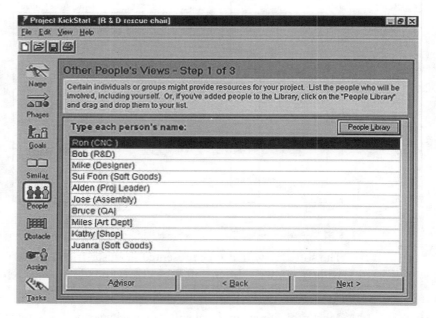

5.5   Advantages of using project management software

- the use of project management software allows the manager to achieve the more tedious, clerical tasks quickly and efficiently. The challenge for the project manager is not to draw the diagrams, but to identify dependencies, and manage the resources available

- the software is able to perform the calculations for deriving critical paths and floats available much faster than humans can

- the software can help to track resources used across multiple projects

- having the plans available on software makes maintenance and adjustments easier

- billing complications, arising from cross-project allocation, can be handled more simply by the software

- project management software should also handle the configuration management (version control) of all project documentation

- document management: all documents produced for the project can be stored, and their quality criteria set and checked, using the software.

- The software is able to generate reports on the progress of the project, and automatically flag any delays to the critical path, with recommended action.

Conclusion

This chapter has introduced you to the range of project management software tools available to the project manager, and provided guidance on the production of networks and Gantt charts.

SELF-TEST QUESTIONS

Project planning and control

1   Identify the most commonly used project management tools. (1.1)

Work allocation

2   What is the critical path in a network? (2.3)

3   Explain purpose and structure of a GANTT chart. (2.11)

Threat identification and slippage reduction

4   What factors may cause project deadlines to slip? (4.1)

5   What are the advantages of using project management tools? (4.3)

EXAM-TYPE QUESTION 1

Drawing networks

(a)   Identify the errors of logic and the departures from convention in the following diagram:

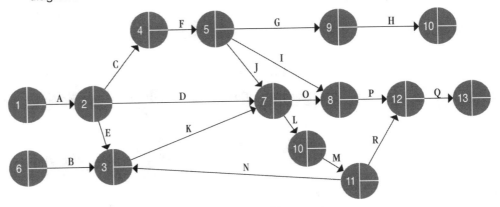

(b)   Draw a network diagram from the following information

Activity	Immediately preceding activity
A	-
B	-
C	A
D	A, B
E	C, D
F	D
G	E, F

(15 marks)

Finding the critical path

Draw networks and find the critical paths for the following projects:

(a)

Activity	Preceding activity	Duration
A	-	5 days
B	A	5 days
C	B, D	5 days
D	-	15 days
E	B, D	10 days
F	E	5 days

(b)

Activity	Preceding activity	Duration
A	-	4 days
B	A	2 days
C	B	10 days
D	A	2 days
E	D	5 days
F	A	2 days
G	F	4 days
H	G	3 days
J	C	6 days
K	C, E	6 days
L	H	3 days

(15 marks)

Calculating the float

Activity	Duration	Cost	Preceding Activities
A	5	£1000	-
B	2	£200	A
C	2	£400	B
D	4	£1500	C
E	3	£6000	D
F	5	£2000	E
G	5	£1600	E
H	4	£6000	F, G
J	3	£250	A
K	4	£1550	J
L	12	£600	K, M
M	10	£100	A
N	11	£2000	M

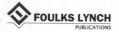

Activity	Duration	Cost	Preceding Activities
A	5	£1000	-
B	2	£200	A
C	2	£400	B
D	4	£1500	C
E	3	£6000	D
F	5	£2000	E
G	5	£1600	E
H	4	£6000	F, G
J	3	£250	A
K	4	£1550	J
L	12	£600	K, M
M	10	£100	A
N	11	£2000	M

In addition to the costs above, extra costs are incurred at £1000 per day.

Draw the network, find the critical path, and estimate the total cost of the project.

Activity N can be reduced by 1 day for an extra £200. Is it worth doing? One person can be diverted from activity D to activity L, increasing D by 2 days, but decreasing L by 1 day. Is this worth doing?

(15 marks)

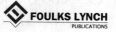

Chapter 7
DEVELOPING AN INFORMATION SYSTEM

This section charts some of the history of how information system projects have been controlled, as well as investigating some of the more commonly used methodologies for developing those information systems. The chapter commences with an introduction to the Systems Development Life Cycle, which can be used as a framework for system development projects. Variations such as the waterfall, spiral are described, and two current standard methodologies, SSADM and RAD, discussed in the context of the SDLC.

Objectives

By the time you have finished this chapter you should be able to:

- define the participants in the systems development process – managers, analysts, designers, programmers and testers

- describe the waterfall approach to system development and identify its application in a representative systems development methodology

- describe the spiral approach to systems development and identify its application in a representative systems development methodology

- discuss the relative merits of the waterfall and spiral approaches, including an understanding of hybrid methodologies that include elements of both.

1   Participants in the system development process

The Project Manager is responsible for the planning, developing and delivery of the products produced in the project. The Project Manager manages the team that has been brought together to undertake the project; allocating work, monitoring and reporting the progress of that work as well as motivating the members of the team. It is the project manager who usually develops and maintains the project plan and who identifies slippage against that plan and takes the appropriate action to correct this.

It is common for a project to be initiated because someone has identified a problem with the existing system. Alternatively, an opportunity is perceived that will lead to an improvement in the present system. In both cases the **Users** of the existing system will play an important role. The users can provide information on the current system. They will also be able to specify, in their own terms, the requirements of the new system. They will also be involved towards the end of the project when they will be able to give feedback on the suitability of the working system.

Understanding and documenting the current system and defining the requirements of their successors is the task of the **Systems Analyst**. The analyst usually carries out a series of interviews with the users to determine how they currently work and how they wish to work in the future. Other fact finding methods they use may include observation, questionnaires, document analysis and so on. From such fact finding, the analyst formalises these requirements in a document called a Requirements Specification where the required processes and performance of the proposed system are described in both graphical models (for example, Data Flow Diagrams, Entity Relationship Models) and textual models. The analyst is usually responsible for all the stages of the system cycle except the program development. Final testing and implementation is usually the analyst's responsibility.

The Requirements Specification produced by the system analyst is further refined into a design specification which shows how the organisational requirements specified by the user will be delivered by a computer-based solution. Part of this design will be the detailed specification of processes. This detailed specification is passed to the **Programmer** who has responsibility for writing the code to implement the processes. The program is written in an agreed programming language. This code has to be functionally correct (that is, it must meet the business requirements) as well as agreed standards of program design and syntax. The program is usually subjected to a formal structured walkthrough where the program is checked for correctness and adherence to organisational standards. It is the responsibility of the programmer to perform a series of unit tests before releasing the program into the wider system. To summarise, programmers write, test and document computer programs from the system specification provided by the analyst.

Another important part of the design is the data specification usually consisting of a graphical entity relationship model supported by tables describing the content of each entity. **Data Analysts** often perform the production of this data specification and indeed they may be involved in earlier specification work, providing assistance to the systems analyst. The data analysts report to the database administrator. They are also involved in detailed design of files and databases, producing robust and efficient database design to support the business processes specified in the requirements.

2 The evolution of the systems development life cycle

In the very early days of computing, the use of computers was mainly limited to scientific applications. When they started to be in widespread use in the business world – in the late 1950s and early 1960s – the high capital costs had to be quickly justified. The early applications to be mechanised were those that gave a quick payback. These applications were ones involving the automation of existing procedures.

Systems development was largely haphazard and little strategic thought went into how IT would be exploited. The programs that were developed often left much to be desired. User input was limited, testing and documentation were poor, and there were many bugs.

In the 1960s, the National Computer Centre (NCC) developed a more structured approach – the Systems Development Life Cycle (SDLC). Although their approach had some weaknesses, it was a great advance on what had gone before.

2.1 The systems development life cycle

The systems development life cycle is a term used to describe the five stages of systems development. These five stages are known as the:

- planning stage
- analysis stage
- design stage
- development stage
- implementation stage.

The initial letters of these stages spell PADDI, which can help in remembering the phases. We will use a slightly modified description of the phases, as shown below.

Each stage consists of a number of smaller steps.

2.2   PADDI

There are three key words to each stage of PADDI and students who can remember the key words will be able to discuss each stage with reference to any scenario given to them. The words are as follows:

Planning

Recognise	It has first to be recognised that some type of problem exists. The question asked at this stage therefore is: In what way does the problem manifest itself? Investigations would be carried out to ascertain the answer.
Diagnose	It may not necessarily be the case that the way in which the problem manifests itself is the problem itself. So, with the facts gathered at the 'recognise' stage, the analyst must then diagnose the problem.
Define	Once diagnosed a definition of the problem can then be reached.

Analysis

Review	A review of the existing system needs to be undertaken
Gather	Information relating to the existing system should be gathered
Measure	The performance achieved by the existing system should be measured for effectiveness. This provides a benchmark for the new system.

Design

Consider	Alternatives to the existing system need to be considered. There may be a variety of alternatives but obviously the most effective and economical for the actual company concerned is required.
Select	Once the alternatives have been considered then a selection must be made.
Design	Once the selection is made then the design of the new system can begin.

Development

Develop	The new system must be developed either in house or externally dependent upon the system chosen.
Purchase	The requirements (both hardware and software) must be written or purchased and tested.
Test	The system should be tested to ensure that it works and that it meets the needs of the users

Implementation

Document	User and technical documentation must be produced
Changeover	The new system must be brought into operation
Review	The system and project must be reviewed, so we can solve any problems and learn from our mistakes

3   The phases of the systems development life cycle

3.1   A model of the life cycle

The life cycle can be represented by the model in the following figure:

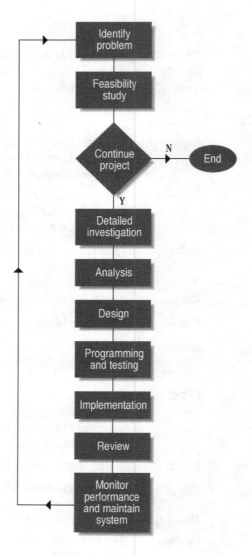

3.2   Identify problem

The need for a new or replacement system is identified by the users, or as a result of the strategic analysis of requirements.

3.3   Feasibility study

A study is carried out to reveal possible solutions to the problem that has been identified, and to see if the cost of developing a new system is justified. A more detailed description of how a feasibility study is carried out was given in Chapter 4. Some of the work completed during the feasibility study may be used at the investigation, analysis and design stages.

During the feasibility study a steering committee may be set up to oversee the project, and a development team be appointed to carry out the systems analysis work. Again, substantial analysis work may be conducted during the feasibility study.

3.4   Giving the go-ahead to the project

The steering committee may give the go-ahead to the project (or recommend its acceptance to the board) if it is justified. As well as the recommendation of the feasibility study report, the steering committee will also consider the project's priority amongst other projects under consideration, and its technological, economic, operational and social feasibility.

3.5   Detailed investigation

The systems analyst of project team will proceed with a detailed and thorough fact-finding exercise using a number of methods to investigate current system requirements and problems (for example, interviews, questionnaires, observation, document analysis). It is a detailed study of the existing system. This may be conducted, substantially, during the feasibility study.

3.6   Analysis

The information that has been collected must be summarised, sorted and critically judged. This will help to identify any problems, inefficiencies and bottlenecks in the current system. The information will be recorded in a series of dataflow diagrams (DFDs) and entity-relationship diagrams so that the system can be designed. These methods are covered in more detail in the following chapter. Detailed analysis work might be conducted during the feasibility study.

3.7   Critical evaluation

All the facts recorded have to be established in a format that allows critical evaluation. The format would normally include:

- **narrative**: costs, equipment, main difficulties, coding, forms/documents
- **dataflow diagrams and organisational charts**: communication lines, departments, outputs, main areas causing bottlenecks, etc
- **tables**: volumes of data processed, frequencies
- **documentation files**: containing samples of documents, forms occurring in each system.

The present system can now be reviewed critically in order to assess the actual need for the data and the level of effectiveness. This also applies to the processing procedures and the costs.

3.8   Systems design

The analyst will specify details of the system being developed. The design is broadly based on that suggested during the feasibility study, but will go into considerable detail:

- data inputs, processes and outputs
- file structures
- program specifications for each program in the system
- a test schedule for each program
- a test schedule for the overall system
- the method of implementation
- a detailed time schedule for hardware/software acquisition or creation
- operating instructions
- training schedule for users
- system performance measurement.

At this stage a systems specification will be produced, specifying what the chosen option of new system will look like.

3.9   Programming and testing

Each program is produced and tested according to the specifications developed above.

3.10 Implementation

Data files will be converted to the new format and the company will change over to the new system.

3.11 Review

This process will immediately follow implementation. The system's performance will be compared with earlier targets. Modifications will be required if the system does not meet user requirements.

3.12 Monitoring and maintenance

This is required to keep the system going and up-to-date. The system will be continually monitored to identify when problems occur. It may require maintenance to adapt it to changes in user requirements, to bugs in the system and to shortfalls in performance.

4   The importance of the NCC life cycle

4.1   The impact of the life cycle

The NCC approach to the systems development life cycle has a very positive effect on the standard of computer systems. The systematic approach led to a substantial improvement in the quality and efficiency of systems development.

Within the SDLC, individual models such as the waterfall and spiral models can be used to apply the overall methodology into different situations and projects. The SDLC provides the general framework for the model, while the specific model shows the exact activities to be carried out and specifies the inputs and outputs in each phase of that model.

Within the SDLC, the feasibility study should have established that the new system could be justified. Proper analysis and design increase the chances that the new system will meet users' requirements. The cycle also recognises that systems will have to be continually monitored and updated as necessary. Systems that do not keep up with the information needs of the organisation are next to useless.

4.2   Structured methodologies

Some limitations to the waterfall approach were soon apparent:

- Most applications were straightforward automation of transaction processing systems. The way that the system was mechanised did not exploit the opportunities offered by IT, and largely followed the existing system.

- Users were relegated to a passive role in the development of systems. The definition of their requirements was technical and relied very heavily on the abilities of the systems analysts. This often resulted in the information needs of managers being ignored, poorly defined user requirements and a lack of involvement of users in the development process.

- there was no major rethink of the way things were done, and that systems were developed independently of one another.

These shortcomings prompted other approaches, still based on the waterfall. The most important approach that evolved through the 1970's and 80's was the Structured Approach to analysis and design, based largely on the work of Ed Yourdon and Tom De Marco.

The growth of other ways of developing systems such as Structured Systems Analysis and Design Method (SSADM), helped to reduce the effect of many of the drawbacks of the systems development life cycle. These methods helped in the following ways. They:

1   **Involve users more closely** in the development process. Users are involved with reviewing products throughout the design process and in formally accepting or rejecting those products at specific stages during the design.

2   **Separate logical and physical designs**. There is a separation between *what* is to be achieved and *how* this is to be implemented. The benefit of this approach is that the focus of the project can be on business benefits rather than issues arising from implementing the actual system into an organisation. It also helps to avoid the danger of a business being tied to a single supplier.

3   **Emphasise data**. The models tend to focus on the data within the system rather than the processing to be carried out within the system because data tends to be more stable and less likely to change over time.

4   **Produce easily understood documentation**. The documentation tends to be diagrammatic rather than text based to avoid the problems of not reading or checking large text documents in sufficient detail.

5   **Integrate the development process** with the disciplines of project management. The models have an overall structure associated with them allowing for a more consistent and complete approach to the work. Progress through the project can be easily determined and there are no sudden or unexpected jumps with the structure of the project.

In the next sections, the waterfall and spiral approaches to system development are explained, and then these processes are applied to a generic systems development system, and the more specific SSADM.

5   The waterfall model

The waterfall model of systems development was originally published in 1970 by W Royce. The aim of the model was to introduce some formality into the system design process. Prior to this time, there had been a number of significant failures of systems projects. The main reason for those failures appeared to be a lack of formality in the design and control of those projects.

In the waterfall model, systems design is broken down into a number of sequential stages, with each stage being shown as a separate box in the model. The development process was not allowed to move onto the next stage until work on the previous stage had been completed. The outputs from each stage formed the inputs to the next stage; hence each stage had to be completed in turn to maintain the links between the inputs and outputs.

 FOULKS LYNCH
PUBLICATIONS

5.1   Detail of the waterfall model

The waterfall model can be represented by the following figure:

The waterfall model of the system development life cycle

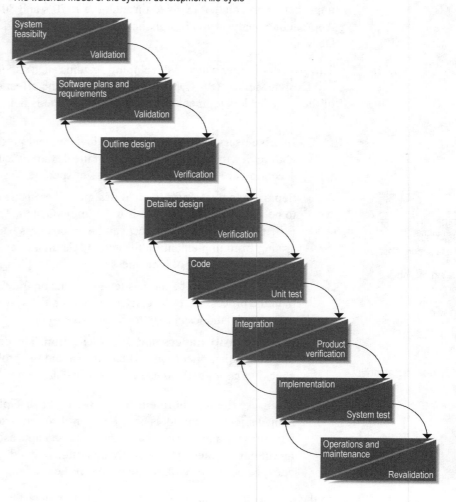

The model itself has eight different stages. Each stage is divided into two parts: the first part covers the work to be carried out in that stage and the second part is the validation or verification procedures on that specific work. Within this model the terms verification and validation have specific meanings:

Verification means checking the link between a product and the specification for that product. In other words, this is a check that the product is being built in the correct way.

Validation means checking whether the product is fit for is operational mission, that is, checking whether the correct product is being built.

The process of building a product moves from stage to stage, with very little interaction between the different stages apart from the transfer of outputs and inputs between each stage. At the extreme, this means that amendments to products take place within the waterfall stage that particular product is at. For example, a change at the code stage does not mean re-visiting the previous four stages. Any amendments are made within the coding and any subsequent stages. However, rework may also be necessary on some products that have already been delivered.

KEY POINT

Verification means checking the link between a product and the specification for that product.

Validation means checking whether the product is fit for is operational mission.

FOULKS LYNCH
PUBLICATIONS

Within more recent systems design projects, the waterfall model is taken to mean any sequential model that is divided into consecutive stages and which follows the general structure of the original model. The naming of the stages is not important, and appropriate names can be used for the particular project being undertaken.

Each step in the system development life cycle is seen as part of an irreversible sequence of events. One step cannot begin until the previous step has been finished. Once a step has been started, there is no going back to an earlier step.

The image is therefore of water flowing down steps in a waterfall, one step at a time, towards the bottom.

In the example show here, detailed system design cannot start until outline system design has been finished, and program coding cannot begin until detailed system design has been completed.

5.2   Advantages and disadvantages of the waterfall model

The advantages of the waterfall model can be summarised as follows:

- It provides a clear and easy to follow sequence of activities.

- Issues of quality management are addressed through the verification and validation sections in each stage of the model.

- Project management and control is facilitated by the need to complete each stage before moving on the next.

The disadvantages of the waterfall model include:

- There is no formal means of exercising management control over a project, and planning control and risk management are not covered within the model itself.

- Estimating times and costs is difficult for each stage.

- Users may not see the progress of work between requirements, in stage 2, and implementation, in stage 7.

- The life cycle can take so long that the original requirements may no longer be valid by the time the system is implemented.

- There is little scope for prototyping in the waterfall lifecycle

The model works best when any reworking of products is kept to a minimum and the products remain unchanged. If the systems are likely to undergo significant change, then a different approach from the waterfall model is recommended.

The waterfall model is now used as the basis of structured methodologies such as SSADM. This methodology is explained in more detail in section 7 of this chapter.

6   The spiral model

The spiral model is another approach to systems development, first devised in the 1980s. It differs from the waterfall model mainly in that it includes an iterative/repetitive approach to systems development. The spiral model is represented in the figure on the next page.

Like the waterfall model, the spiral model has a sequential sequence of stages, with each stage having to be completed before moving on to the next. The main difference with the spiral model is that although the systems development work moves all the time towards eventual completion, the works goes back several times over to earlier stages and the sequence of stages is gone through over and over again.

However, in practice, user requirements are difficult to determine, and it is difficult to see how the system will perform in practice. The spiral model responds to these problems by providing an iterative approach to development. The same activities may be repeated in order to clarify issues or provide a precise definition of requirements. The systems development life cycle may therefore be repeated a number of times for the same project. At the end of each turn of the spiral, a piece of functionality may be delivered to the users, so that the system evolves during the life cycle development.

The spiral model may therefore be summarised as follows.

- The user's requirements are not fully specified when the system development work begins.

- The project goes through a series of iterative cycles of events or development stages. At each stage of the development, a new **prototype** (working model) of the system is produced.

- A prototype is a working model, which can be put into active use, but it is not the completed system.

- New prototypes are produced, one after the other, each getting closer to the user's final requirements. Eventually, a final system version is produced, and the system development work has reached its end.

The spiral model of the system development

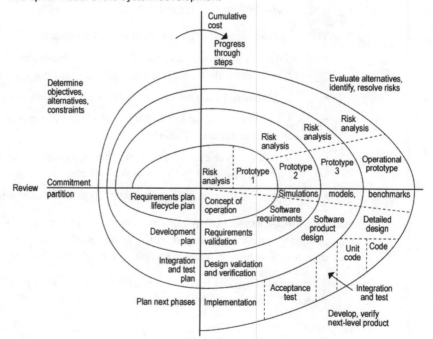

6.1   Development of the spiral model

The spiral model was proposed and developed by Barry Boehm. It is termed the spiral model because the path from start to finish in the model means spiralling out from the start at the centre of the model to the implementation phase at the outside of the model.

The model is divided into four quadrants. The purpose of each quadrant is:

- **top-left** – the objectives of the project are determined and any alternatives and constraints identified

- **top-right** – the different alternatives are evaluated and the risks of each alternative are evaluated and resolved.

- **bottom-right** – the development of the system takes place. this is the quadrant that corresponds to the waterfall model

- **bottom-left** – the next phase or iteration of the model is planned (if necessary).

The main benefit of the spiral model over the waterfall model is the introduction of objective setting, risk management and planning into the overall development cycle. These are essential aspects of system development so the spiral model tends to be preferred over the basic waterfall model. Another significant benefit is that the user can be given some of the working functionality before the entire system is completed. It is an *evolutionary* method of delivering working systems.

7   Structured Systems Analysis and Design (SSADM)

SSADM is a method that was adopted as a standard for all British government projects in 1980. It represents a data oriented approach to systems development and is based on a threefold view of the system:

- **data**, as modelled with entity relationship models

- **function**, as modelled with data flow diagrams

- **events**, as modelled with entity life histories.

These three models are described in more detail in chapter 9.

One reason for making it a standard was that every analyst in the Civil Service working on a project used the same techniques and models, so they could move from project to project, and in some cases to new departments, and could still work effectively in the same way. This was intended to help management control the progress and quality of the systems under development.

SSADM is a highly structured and complex methodology. It divides the development of a system into modules, which are further broken down into stages, then into steps, and finally into tasks. Each task produces a deliverable, so helping the project management monitor both progress and quality.

The ethos of SSADM can be expressed in three statements:

- an accurate understanding of the system being examined can be obtained from looking at it in three ways – the processes, the data and the events

- the logical design of the system is separated from the physical design and implementation. This allows the analyst to break free from the existing way of doing things and to be more innovative

- user involvement and client liaison at significant points in the process, in order to ensure that the development always meets business needs.

7.1   The stages of SSADM

SSADM covers the early parts of the life cycle, from feasibility study through to physical design, and expresses them in five module stages..

Module 1: Feasibility study

This is not mandatory in SSADM but when it is carried out it includes a preliminary investigation into the system being developed and the production of a cost-benefit analysis. The management can assess whether it is worth the expense and time of continuing to the system analysis and design phases of SSADM.

Module 2: Requirements analysis

This phase of work is broken down into two stages – the analysis of the current way of operating with the specification of the requirements. Data flow diagrams and logical data structures are the main techniques used. This is followed by the presentation of business systems options to allow the users to select the way forward.

Module 3: Requirements specification

This module defines the required data model, the required functions and models the event handling behind the functions. Prototyping and user modelling are also carried out. It will specify what the new system will look like on the chosen option. The main document produced here is the System Specification.

Module 4: Logical system specification

A list of technical options is drawn up if new hardware or communications technology is needed. After that, the on-line functions are expanded so that the dialogues can be designed for the user interface. The logical processing for all enquiries and updates are designed.

Module 5: Physical design

In this module the logical data structure is converted to a physical data design, to be mapped on to whatever DBMS has been selected for the system. The functions are mapped on to the physical model, and converted to program specs.

SSADM contains many more models and documentation than this overview suggests, but for the purposes of this syllabus, the description above gives the flavour of the methodology. Another principle behind the later versions of SSADM is that a project manager can customise the method to use whichever set of techniques is most appropriate for the scope of the project.

7.2   Comparison of SSADM to the waterfall and spiral models

SSADM is based on a WATERFALL model as can be seen from the structural nature of the model. Each stage of the SSADM is to be completed prior to the next stage starting. There are specific sign offs to be obtained at the end of each stage of SSDAM, implying this close correlation with the waterfall model. However, SSADM has also been criticised for being too procedural and bureaucratic, while the need to tailor it for individual projects has been noted.

There is some element of iteration within SSADM, which provides some comparison with the spiral approach. Specifically, SSADM provides for the use of prototyping at various stages in the model, implying requirements and specifications may be changed at certain stages of the model.

8   Rapid Application Development

Another approach that is becoming popular is Rapid Application Development (RAD). This is based on an iterative (spiral) life cycle model. Its philosophy is to involve the end-users by means of workshops (to elicit all their requirements promptly) and prototyping (to involve them in the design effort), and to deliver systems that meet the requirements quickly.

RAD is a method of developing information systems that involves: a development team incorporating end-user clients and IS specialists, the use of rapid development software tools, and the staged delivery of a working system by means of iterative prototyping of solutions to business requirements.

8.1   Time boxes

Another feature of RAD is the use of **time boxes**. A time box is a period, say three months, agreed by users and developers. Within that period, a life cycle of analysis, design, build and test will be completed for a piece of functionality. This will be followed by another time box with its own agreed functionality and so on, until the system is complete. The advantage of this approach is that the users are able to utilise important parts of their new system earlier than if they had to wait for the entire waterfall to be completed.

8.2   RAD and the development team

The teams are made up of developers and users. Among the developers is someone known as a SWAT (skilled with advanced tools). The team should not be larger than four or five strong, but all members should be equal, i.e. the users are genuine team members, not 'guests' who are tolerated by the developers. Because of the intense time pressures, the team should be made up of highly motivated people.

8.3   RAD and the spiral model

As mentioned above, RAD fits relatively well into the spiral model of system development. If you refer to the spiral diagram on page 124, then RAD fits in as follows:

Determine objectives, alternatives, and constraints. The objectives for the software will still need to be determined. However, with RAD, the analyst will spend a lot of time with the users of the system to ensure that their requirements are precisely specified and agreed at the beginning of the project. While this is favourable outcome of the RAD process, the main reason for the analyst spending this time now is the extreme difficulty in amending those objectives later in the development process. The objectives need to be clear at the beginning of the development to ensure that changes are not required.

Evaluate alternatives, identify and resolve risks. With RAD, the main alternative is likely to be some form of database system, so the main risk will be ensuring that data can be accessed in the format needed by each user. The risk at this stage is not specifying the appropriate links into the database, so reports that the user requires will not be available.

Develop and verify. The software will be written using 4GL tools, (See Chapter 12) providing user prototypes that can be turned into the final software relatively easily. Again, users need to be fully involved in this process, and review prototypes as they become available. Within the first iteration of the spiral model, amendments to screen design etc will be relatively easy. Although some amendments, such as the positioning of fields can be made on subsequent iterations, other amendments such as including missing fields in the design do become more difficult as the software nears completion.

Plan next phase. Planning the next phase means essentially checking that the prototype meets the user requirements, and then ensuring that any amendments or changes to requirements are included in the next iteration of the spiral.

If all goes to plan, then the final software will be available in a matter of months, rather than a year or so.

8.4   Conditions for RAD

RAD is especially appropriate for particular situations:

- if users are not clear about their requirements, RAD can quickly help clarify them
- if users are reluctant, or unwilling, to sign off a detailed specification, RAD can work from a high level requirements statement and refine the requirements to the correct level with user workshops
- if there is a culture of user involvement in systems development, a RAD team can work productively
- there is a need for faster delivery than conventional development can provide
- the target system is limited in scope
- the target system is not expected to be implemented on a new platform.

8.5   Disadvantages of a RAD approach

- RAD is not to be confused with an approach known as 'Just do it', or JDI. JDI is an undisciplined approach that will generally create far more problems than are solved.
- large and complex IS are probably not suited to RAD
- it is harder to ensure the meeting of targets such as response times and integration using piecemeal development
- there is a danger that users will keep suggesting changes or enhancements that are not realistically achievable, and will not accept being told that they can't have them.

Conclusion

This chapter has introduced some of the systems development models that have been used over the last ten to fifteen years to help control system development projects. It has looked specifically at the waterfall life cycle (exemplified by SSADM) and the spiral life cycle (exemplified by RAD). Remember that the SDLC provides the overall framework for these models; the model then provides the method of applying the life cycle to a specific situation.

SELF-TEST QUESTIONS

The evolution of the systems development life cycle

1   What are the main stages of the SDLC? (2.1)

The waterfall model

2   Explain the waterfall model of systems development. (5)

The spiral model

3   What are the four quadrants of the spiral model? (6.1)

SSADM

4   What are the five modules of SSADM? (7.1)

RAD

5   What is a time box? (8.1)

WRF Inc

WRF Inc trades in a dynamic environment where it is essential that information is presented quickly and clearly to its staff. The information can come from the company's database or from other staff members. Significant processing of the information is also required on each individual's personal computer (PC) before effective decisions can be made.

WRF Inc intends to upgrade its computer system to improve speed and clarity of information. Each member of staff will have a PC linked to a local area network (LAN). Each PC will run Windows 3.1 and a word processor and spreadsheet on its local hard disk. The network will be used for centralised backup, access to a central database, and storage of data files. The LAN will also be used for communication within the office by e-mail.

The systems analyst in charge of the project thinks that users will require a Pentium 4 processor running at 1.5 Gherz with 256 megabytes of RAM. The network will incorporate a central file server and run at a low baud rate. He is pleased that the system will cost only $US 3,000 per user (about £2,000). The systems analyst is on a fixed-term contract that terminates when the system installation is complete.

Users have broadly welcomed the move although they have not been formally told of the systems change. The requisitioning department of WRF Inc has now questioned the order for the computer hardware and software because of lack of authorisation from the Board.

Required:

Write a report to the Board:

(a)   briefly explaining the systems development life cycle (SDLC); and

(b)   explaining why it is preferred to the situation outlined above as a means of providing a systems changeover for WRF Inc.   **(20 marks)**

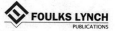

Chapter 8

USER REQUIREMENTS

This chapter investigates the various methods of obtaining information concerning user requirements during the analysis phase of systems development. The issues where users find difficulty in expressing their requirements are also discussed.

Objectives

By the time you have finished this chapter you should be able to:

- define the tasks of planning, undertaking and documenting a user interview
- identify the potential role of background research, questionnaires and special purpose surveys in the definition of requirements
- describe the purpose, conduct and recording of a facilitated user workshop
- explain the potential use of prototyping in requirements definition
- explain how requirements can be collected from current computerised Information Systems
- discuss the problems users have in defining, agreeing and prioritising requirements.

1   Obtaining user requirements

1.1   Gathering requirements from the current system

Defining user requirements demands an understanding of how the system works and looking at what the problems are. There are many ways of obtaining the information required, such as: interviews, questionnaires, special purpose documents (usually for activity sampling), observation (both formal and informal), and analysis of current documents.

There are also many issues to consider in getting a clear picture of a system. One is to look at the current business processes and identify the tasks or particular system functions. These tasks are examined in more detail to identify the users, the users' interaction with the system and each other, and whatever tools they use in the task. It is important not to go into an investigation of a system with preconceived ideas.

There are four main ways of collecting information:

- Asking questions, by e.g. interview, surveys, email questionnaire, a discussion database

- Observational studies, including formal observation of a task, shadowing a user through their working day, ethnographic studies, participating within the user environment

- Prototyping the requirements that have already been identified at a high level, and prototyping the interface for usability requirements

- Formal sessions, including group discussions, focus groups and facilitated workshops

The aim of obtaining user requirements is to produce an accurate requirements specification (RS) for a project. To produce the RS, the analyst will have to will have to obtain information from a range of different users, with the availability of some of those users being very difficult to determine.

Having obtained this information, it is also important to consider the methods used for describing the user requirements. Documenting and modelling user requirements will be covered in Chapter 9.

1.2　Elicitation

Elicitation is concerned with extracting from a group of users a description of the requirements for a system from the users' point of view. Building this picture of requirements has three stages:

Firstly, identification of the information sources that will be used to provide detail about the system, in terms of people and documents. Existing documentation such as organisation charts, and procedure manuals can be used to try and check the completeness of this list of sources.

Secondly, establishing the relationships between the information sources that have been identified. It is important to establish both direct relationships (where information passes from one user to another) and hierarchical relationships (where one user carries out part of the actions of another user). The information flows in particular need to be correctly documented.

Lastly, elicitation can take place by analysing documents and performing user interviews. More detail on interviews is provided below.

After information on requirements has been obtained, this will be verified and validated, as explained later.

1.3　User interviews

The systems analyst or project team will begin the analysis phase with a detailed information gathering or fact-finding exercise, using a number of techniques, such as interviews with users and systems specialists, observation of the system in operation, questionnaires, simulation and document review.

The facts that the analyst seeks revolve around:

- current processes
- data and documents currently used
- problems with the current way of working
- the users' requirements from the new system.

A face-to-face interview is an excellent way to obtain detailed, in depth information. It is one of the major investigative methods and requires good communication skills from the analyst. Interviews should always be planned, even when conducted in an informal manner. Whether to interview formally or informally by conducting a structured or unstructured interview will depend upon the type of person being interviewed and the atmosphere the interviewer wishes to create. This is where communication skills play a major part.

The interviewer needs to plan:

- **whom to interview**: obviously he or she will be unable to interview everyone unless the project scope is very small. Each user will have different information to offer, and different levels of requirements, depending upon their own place in the organisation.

- **when to interview**: there is the need to avoid times which will be particularly disruptive to the day to day business of the company. The interview should begin neither too early nor too late. Timing will depend in part on the number of interviews to be conducted.

- **what to ask**: The questions asked will depend on the requirements of the proposed system, and users' feedback reflecting their own needs and concerns. Background information on the current workings of the system, and any problems arising, is also important.

- **where to interview**: if the interviewee will need to demonstrate his/her tasks or refer to documentation, then the interview is best conducted at the location of the interviewee. This also serves to put the interviewee more at ease, as well as allowing the analyst opportunity to informally observe aspects of the workplace.

- **how to begin** the interview: Will a formal or informal approach be best suited to the interviewee? What is the best way to obtain the interviewee's confidence?

- **how to analyse** the notes, recordings, etc. made during the interview.

When planning the interview, the analyst could do worse than prepare a set of questions based on Rudyard Kipling's 'six honest serving men':

- what
- how
- when
- how
- where
- who.

These enable precise questions, and so precise answers, to be offered. In controlling the interview, the analyst should make use of a judicious mixture of **open** and **closed questions**. An example of an open question is,

'Tell me about your relationship with the Purchasing Department'

while an example of a closed question is,

'Does the manager authorise the purchase before or after you complete this form?'

During the interview, the interviewer will need to make detailed notes of the conversation taking place. Rather than make written notes, the interview can be recorded for later playback and analysis. This is not always a good idea, though; some people feel more inhibited in the presence of a tape recorder, and may be more guarded than is useful.

The analyst should also have a list of pre-prepared questions and some form of reporting template so that answers can be placed in the appropriate section of the form for later analysis and comparison to other responses.

As with any other interview situation, the analyst will need appropriate training in how to conduct an interview. The analyst will need specific skills in asking questions and obtaining responses from interviewees, because the latter may feel threatened by a system project and so not be particularly co-operative.

FOULKS LYNCH
PUBLICATIONS

Interviews may also be used to obtain additional information following a questionnaire. Users' comments concerning the questionnaire can be investigated in more detail and any other concerns from the interviewees discussed in more detail.

1.4   User workshop

Information concerning user requirements can also be obtained in a user workshop. The main purpose of this activity is to discuss with users as a group their requirements for a system. Making the collection of data part of a discussion will help to improve the accuracy of the data collected because the users will start to see how, for example, the outputs from one department of the organisation will start to affect other departments. This form of workshop is known as a Joint Requirements Planning workshop, or JRP.

The workshop will normally be conducted at a pre-arranged time and place, with user representatives from various departments in the organisation. As an alternative, the workshop can be run with representatives from one department, only to provide a brainstorming session for that particular department. The workshop will be conducted by a trained and impartial **facilitator**, whose job is solely to move the workshop towards a consensus by the appointed time. The facilitator should not be one of the actors or stakeholders in the system, lest they be suspected of pushing the workshop towards their own favoured outcome.

The agenda of the meeting is to discuss the information requirements of different user groups, with specific reference to identifying situations where outputs and inputs between different departments are not matched (as noted above) or where outputs are produced which other departments did not know about, but would still find useful. There is the danger that different users or departments have requirements which conflict with each other, or both believe to be a higher priority than anyone else's. In these cases, it is up to the facilitator to help the workshop negotiate an acceptable resolution. To keep the session focused, specific areas of the information will be discussed in turn. It is preferable to have frequent breaks to allow for informal discussion and check work carried out so far to ensure that links between information have not been missed.

The workshop can be recorded in various ways, although popular methods range from flipcharts and post-it notes through to workgroup software. The latter recording method means that all participants have their own PC; these are networked and the output is displayed on a large screen where common documents are being worked on. As participants spot ideas or linkages in the information, the main document can be updated for other participants to see.

At the end of the workshop, detailed minutes will be produced and circulated to all participants to ensure that information concerning the workshop has been recorded correctly. Any amendments can be sent to the workshop administrator. The analyst will use the workshop information to update the systems notes and ensure that logical design of any new system takes into account the information obtained from users.

1.5   Background research

Information about a system will also be available from other sources such as questionnaires and studying documents that are used within a system. Information is sometimes available in the form of written instructions or procedures manuals. The systems analyst should study these to become familiar with the system and avoid asking elementary questions at interviews. Information obtained from such sources should be treated with caution, as it is often out of date or misleading.

If the system under investigation is already computerised then the analyst will also fully investigate all the documentation relating to the analysis, design and development of that system. He or she would peruse the original system specifications and compare the requirements with the original test results.

1.6   Observation

The analyst will watch the current systems in operation. When investigating by means of observation it must be realised that the results will be distorted by the observation activity itself. Human nature dictates that different behaviour will occur when an individual is aware that he is being observed.

Participation in the task in question is sometimes a way of diluting the distortion caused by observation.

Observation provides the analyst with the chance to ask the user how and why they are performing their current task exactly as they are. This can help in capturing requirements which the analyst had missed in his/her questioning at interview, and which the user had not thought to mention.

Workers and trade unions alike tend to become suspicious of direct observation and it is therefore necessary to inform them fully of the reasons for conducting such an observation. The lesson to learn is that it is the *job* that is being observed, not the person performing it.

Informal observation is simply being sure, during an interview or when visiting the site, to notice various aspects of the working environment, such as bottlenecks, tidiness or otherwise, working conditions, sense of business or leisure, amount of interaction between people carrying out tasks etc.

1.7   Questionnaires

Questionnaires can be used to collect large amounts of information from large numbers of people. Questionnaires must be properly designed in order to extract meaningful information. The following factors should be considered:

- the objectives of the questionnaire
- the tone of the questionnaire
- the style of the questionnaire
- Questions must be short and straight to the point
- The ability to statistically analyse the answers
- its length
- whether to pilot it
- how responses will be analysed e.g. use of optical mark reading might be appropriate
- the timescale for return and analysis.

Questionnaires can also be used if the users are scattered over a number of different sites.

It is difficult to get more than basic data from questionnaires, and it is not easy to follow up contradictory or cryptic answers. The data elicited will be more related to levels of satisfaction, usability requirements or frequencies and volumes.

1.8 Prototyping

The operation of a system can sometimes be understood by construction of a small-scale model, with dummy data. It is a useful way to identify interface requirements, and to give users a 'look-feel' appreciation of the system. Frequently, an extra requirement may be found when a user tries to work with a prototype and finds an important function missing from their menu screen. The user needs to be made very aware that this is only a model, without the full data, and that they are not being offered the completed system. This form of prototyping is known as 'throwaway' prototyping, because the mock-up will feed into the design process, without itself being delivered as part of the solution.

1.9 Special purpose surveys

These are designed by the analyst to gain extra data about the current operations of the system; for example, s/he may need to know how long a clerk spends in a day on a particular task. A special purpose survey will ask that clerk to record exactly when the task begins and when it finishes, for a period of a week or fortnight or whatever is suitable. From this, the analyst can identify peaks and troughs in this activity, and measure its impact on the rest of the system. This is useful for calculating how much time can be saved if the task is to be performed by the new computer system. Special purpose surveys are a way of sampling the activities carried out by the users, in order to find out how much time is spent, on average, on each task.

2 Recording information

2.1 Types of documentation

Fact-finding leaves the systems analyst with a large amount of information, often in a disorganised form. The analyst now has to prepare documentation of the existing system. This should include:

- sources of information (people interviewed, documents studied, etc.)
- a narrative description of the system
- comments on the system, with particular attention to any weaknesses, e.g. errors, delays, excessive costs, bottlenecks, etc.
- recommendations for improvements
- flowchart(s) and data flows of the systems processes
- specimen documents, both blank and completed
- organisation charts
- tables giving staff numbers, work volumes, costs, etc.
- graphs, bar charts and diagrams, where appropriate.

This report serves as a record of the existing procedure. It may be checked by a senior systems analyst to ensure that everything has been covered. It is used as the basis of subsequent systems design.

2.2 Evaluating fact-finding techniques

The following table gives the main advantages of the various methods of fact-finding.

Method	Advantages	Disadvantages
Interview	• personal contact • good relationships can be established • follow-up questions can be asked at once • analyst can assess quality of staff and work	• time-consuming • interviewee may be uncooperative • interviewee may ramble or be incoherent • interviewee may describe what he *should* do, not what he *does* do • delay may occur in arranging appointment
Observation	• cross checks information obtained by interview • gives in-depth knowledge of system • reveals quality of work	• time consuming • exceptional items may be missed
Questionnaire	• time-saving • saves cost if information needed from remote points • suitable for small amounts of specific information	• difficult to design • unpopular • may not be returned • not suitable for large amounts of information • non-reactive to unexpected responses
Study of other documents	• saves interview time, etc. • gives useful background information	• may be out of date • may describe what should be done, not what is done
Prototyping	• allows the system to be studied off line • Can prompt the user to identify other requirements • Can allow the user to explain how they wish to perform a task	• expensive to produce • may not be representative

2.3 Verifying and validating requirements.

After information about requirements has been obtained, it must be verified and validated.

Verification attempts to ensure that the information supplied by different users is consistent and complete. Checking consistency can be carried out by comparing the information obtained from different users or documents, and then asking additional questions or undertaking more document analysis to resolve those differences. However, completeness is more difficult to check, because the omission of critical information is more difficult to determine.

The process of validation means to ensure that the requirements specification is a complete and accurate representation of what the users require. Validating the RS had to be carried out by reviewing it, because there is no existing documentation to show what is actually required. If this documentation were available then the RS would not be required!

The RS can be validated in a number of ways including structured walkthroughs and use of prototypes, as well as simply reading the RS itself.

2.4   Use of prototyping

One method of checking the accuracy of the recording of system information and the subsequent production of a requirements definition is to use prototyping. However, the principles of using prototyping for producing some form of working model of a system remain the same.

Prototypes produced at an early stage in the requirements definition are not intended to be an accurate representation of the final specification or screen design of the finished product; their purpose is to confirm with the users that the functional requirements have been understood, and in some cases to capture requirements that had not been identified before. The main point of producing the prototype is to ensure completeness of information provision, rather than the precise layout of that information. The users can check information provision in the prototype, enabling the analyst to clarify or identify requirements that had been ambiguously expressed, or even omitted altogether.

2.5   Problems users have in defining requirements

It is important to provide users with different methods of checking a requirements specification, to try and ensure that all requirements have been identified and included in that specification. Users may not be familiar with providing detailed information on their requirements, either due to inexperience of actually stating those requirements or due to other factors such as lack of understanding of the processes in producing a requirements specification. Some of the common problems facing users in this area are briefly described below.

1   **Users uncertainty of the system boundaries**. Users may not be clear exactly where the system they are using finishes, and the next system starts. For example, simply because the sales system accesses details on finished goods, does not mean that sales staff have responsibility for updating the finished goods stocks. Part of the requirements specification for the sales system may include access to this information, but maintenance of the stock file may still be the responsibility of the production department.

2   **Balance of computer and human processing**. Users may be unclear what balance of **computer** and human processing will best meet the system objectives. Users may specify that certain tasks should be manual, when using a computer system could provide greater accuracy or efficiency in completing that task. For example, product codes can be obtained from manual lists or from the stock master file. If users are not familiar with the computer system, the latter may not be specified although it will be more efficient.

3   **Lack of users' knowledge in the capabilities of hardware and software.** Users may not ask for specific functions to be performed, due to misunderstanding of computer and/or software capabilities. If the user does not understand what the computer can do, then their requests may be inaccurate due to lack of knowledge.

4   **Fundamental differences** may require a lot more work, with a final verdict on whether conflicting requirements can be met coming from the software supplier. Frequently, the project sponsor, on the user side, will resolve such conflicts.

5   **Evolving requirements**. Some requirements will change over time, and users will expect the requirement specification to be updated automatically to take account of those changes. While this may be possible, a clear record of any changes must be maintained

6   **Untestable requirements**. Some user requirements are simply not testable or possible to include within a requirements specification. For example, users may require a system to be robust or user-friendly. While these appear to be good objectives for a system, actually specifying that a system is user-friendly can be quite difficult, mainly because these is no precise definition of this term.

        The normal method of carrying these requirements into the requirements specification is to include features that users would like in that specification. Users can then review prototypes or other initial system builds later to ensure that their requirements have, in fact, been met.

7   **Obvious information**. It is quite normal for users to omit information that is obvious to them, and then be surprised when this information does not appear in the requirements specification. The error made by the users is to assume that the information is obvious to the analyst as well, which it almost certainly won't be.

8   **Not obtaining all the requirements** is one of the fundamental problems of elicitation, as discussed above. Various methods can be used to try and limit the amount of assumed knowledge of requirements, including group discussions, brainstorming and interviewing new members of staff. The latter are more likely to state their requirements in detail because they will have only just started to use the system.

9   **Terminology differences**. Systems analysts, purchasers and suppliers may well use a different terminology that users are not familiar with. This can result in users perceiving that an analyst has understood some requirement, simply because some jargon is used to explain it. However, because the jargon is not understood, then the misunderstanding of the requirement is not identified.

Having some form of glossary of terms used can be helpful to users. However, the best remedy to this error is not to use inappropriate terminology in the first place. If the analyst is to use jargon, it should be the users' jargon for their work.

2.6   Prioritising requirements

In the same way that users may find it difficult to identify all their requirements, they may also find it difficult to actually prioritise their requirements. All information may be seen to be important, and so all information has the same high priority in being received.

The analyst may be able to help users to prioritise requirements by looking at factors such as frequency of use of information or whether information is critical to the specific job being undertaking. Providing some critical success factors for the users may be helpful because information requirements can be mapped against these. Requirements that are important to meet the success factors will then receive a higher priority rating than other requirements.

Although this setting of requirements may appear to be haphazard, it does assist the analyst by giving some idea as to the information that *must* be received now compared to information that is simply *nice to have* within the next few days.

A prioritising measure that is widely used is known as MoSCoW rules. This classifies each requirement as:

Must have

Should have

Could have

or

Won't have this time (but maybe in the next stage)

Conclusion

This chapter has investigated how user requirements are obtained, and looked at the various methods available to the analyst.

Obtaining user requirements

1   What is elicitation? (1.2)

Recording information

2   What are the main advantages of the methods used for fact-finding? (2.2)

Prototyping

3   What are the limitations of prototyping at the requirements specification stage? (2.4)

Analyst

The analyst is responsible for identifying and defining the user requirements and problems within the current system. This is usually carried out as part of the feasibility study and during the detailed investigation stage. During these stages the analyst will use a number of fact-finding techniques to obtain this information, the end product being a Requirements Specification Document.

Required:

Briefly explain the following fact-finding techniques that are available to the analyst in their investigation.

(a)	Interviews	**(4 marks)**
(b)	Observation	**(4 marks)**
(c)	Questionnaires	**(4 marks)**
(d)	Prototypes	**(3 marks)**
		(Total: 15 marks)

Chapter 9

DOCUMENTING AND MODELLING USER REQUIREMENTS

Having obtained the details of the current system, and requirements for the new, the analyst needs some methods of describing user requirements either at the level of individual computer programs, or at the level of the entire business processes.

The process models only give a single view of the subject. It is also important to model the structure of persistent data (a static model), and how the system responds to events, which dictate what **state** the persistent data can be in. These three views combined allow us to understand the requirements of the system as fully as possible.

Note that structured English, decision tables, decision trees and data flow diagrams are all within the syllabus and are covered in this chapter. However, these process models do overlap to some extent, and it is not likely that more than one will be required in the examination at any time.

Objectives

By the time you have finished this chapter you should be able to:

- describe the need for building a business process model of user requirements

- briefly describe different approaches to modeling the business process

- describe in detail the notation of one of these business process models

- construct a business process model of narrative user requirements using this notation

- explain the role of process models in the systems development process

for processes, static structures and events.

Once the investigation is complete, the information needs to be documented and analysed, that is, building a model of the system showing its problems, working methods, bottlenecks, inefficiencies and so forth.

1   Building a business process model of user requirements

Systems design will involve two key stages; namely the production of the requirements definition (that is, specifying what the system is to do) and the actual design itself (deciding how the system is to be constructed to meet the requirement). This section provides additional detail on specifying what the system is to do, rather than the precise specification on how this will be achieved.

KEY POINT

Stages of requirements definition:

- acquisition

- expression of this information in a notation

- analysis of requirements

- specifying each requirement.

The stages of requirements definition are:

- **acquisition**, or capture of information from the user

- **expression** of this information in a notation which explains those requirements and will prompt further questions about the requirements

- **analysis of requirements** to ensure that they are consistent with each other and expressed in a suitable level of detail, and

- **specifying each requirement** in a definitive statement.

The capturing of information from the user has been considered in Chapter 8; the other stages of the requirements definition are explained below.

1.1   Requirements notation

Business processes can be modelled in various ways. Simple flowcharts are one such way in which we can follow business processes, observing time dependencies and sequencing; data flow diagrams shows how data is maintained in a system, and how the system interacts with the outside world, but it does not show time dependencies or sequencing. Detailed algorithms of processing can be modelled using structured English or pseudo code.

KEY POINT

A **requirements notation** is normally some form of diagram or text that provides information on the requirements definition.

A **requirements notation** is normally some form of diagram or text that provides information on the requirements definition. Examples of the notation used include structured English or similar formal notations and decision tables. The amount of formality used varies between the different types of notations; however, the more formal the notation, the greater degree of structure there will be within the model.

In general terms, greater formality results in:

- a more precise specification, with a higher degree of internal consistency and completeness

- the need for more specialist skills in producing the notation. However, more design tools are available to help produce that notation

- a specification that is more difficult for users to understand. Care will therefore be needed in communicating information to the users.

In most situations, a mix of notations will be used to provide an appropriate trade-off between accessibility to users and preciseness of logical design.

This chapter will give extended examples of one or two types of these notations, but these sections are not exclusive. You can use a simple flowchart, or a multi-level data flow diagram; decision tables, structured English, or any notation to model processing that you are comfortable with.

1.2   Types of notation available

The types of notation available relate to the degree of formality of that notation.

Informal approaches

These notations employ no fixed syntax and consist of English statements supported by diagrams, again with no formal structure. There are also no formal means of elicitation, validation or verification.

The main advantages of this approach are that it requires little training and is easy to apply. However, the specifications are usually ambiguous, inconsistent and incomplete, which limits their use for producing accurate and workable systems.

KEY POINT

Types of notation:

- informal

- semi-formal (structured)

- formal methods.

Semi-formal or structured approach

This approach uses diagrams with well-defined syntax and structured English. Examples of the notations used include data flow diagrams, CORE and SADT.

This approach provides a much greater scope for achieving consistency, completeness and clarity in the requirements specification, and can normally be understood by the user and the analyst. The main limitations are the lack of some design tools to fully express system requirements and the need for some basic training to produce and understand the documentation.

Advantages of using a structured design method

- the structured method used will result in some picture of a system being produced. the use of this notation within the overall systems design method does have some distinct advantages

- the design method will decompose the design task into many smaller activities, meaning that process monitoring is more effective and management control for the design project is improved

- standardising the development process and the form of the products enhances communication and maintenance, and assists transferability of staff between projects

- the discipline imposed by the method helps to ensure that important design issues will not be forgotten

- the quality control procedures incorporated into the design will help to ensure that the quality of the final design is satisfactory

- the probability of a successful development is increased because the methods use best practice from a number of different design projects.

2 Business process models

Methods are needed for capturing information about an information system. This next section looks at a method of modelling the business structure at a more strategic or higher level.

One such technique is the use of Data Flow Diagrams (DFD).

For your examination, you should be able to read a DFD and comment on it. You might even be expected to identify errors in it. It is less likely that you will be expected to draw one, from data given to you about a system.

Most computer systems involve the input, processing and output of data. A DFD is a graphical representation of how data is moved through the system. DFDs are split up into a series of levels. The top level gives a general definition of how the data flows, and each further level gives a more and more detailed description of the system. DFDs therefore use a top-down structured approach to understanding system needs.

Dataflow diagrams use fewer symbols than flowcharts although there are a number of different symbol sets in use today. The notation used by structured systems analysis and design (SSADM) is very popular.

Example: Data flow diagrams using SSADM symbols

The set shows 4 constructs:

- *External Entities:* these are any body, person or organisation external to the system, but which interact with it.

- *Data stores:* these are any place that data comes to rest. They may be manual (M), such as filing cabinets, card index files, a diary, a wall chart, a notebook; Data (D) such as an entry in a spreadsheet, or a database; Temporary (T), such as a transaction file, or an in-tray/out-tray.

- *Process:* a process that transforms the data in some way. It may be to perform a calculation, or to file some data, or to answer a query, or to generate a related report or output. The process has an Id, a unique number that has no sequence implication at all, a stripe that indicates the location, i.e. where, or by whom, the process is carried out.

- *Data Flow,* shown as an arrow, which represents where data moves, either as a document, or as an electronic message.

If you are familiar with other notations, be free to use them instead; it is the logic behind a DFD that counts, not the precise shape of a box.

2.1   Symbols used

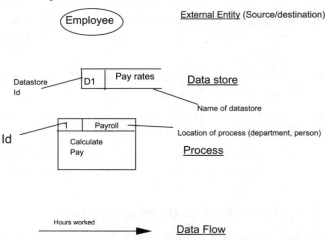

2.2   Level 0 (Context) diagram

The highest level of DFD is a context diagram. A **context diagram** shows *one* process only, the source of the data and its destinations. The example shows the context diagram for an Order Processing System.

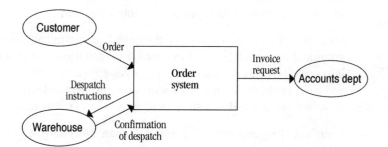

2.3   Level 1

Level 1 of a dataflow diagram explodes (decomposes) the diagram into more detail; it looks at the main processes that take place within an order system.

A level 1 diagram would still show the original external entities as on the next page.

Each of the processes within the level 1 diagram would be exploded separately to show the main processes taking place within that particular process itself. However, for the

sake of our example, we will look at process number 2: *Check order details*. This is exploded in the next figure.

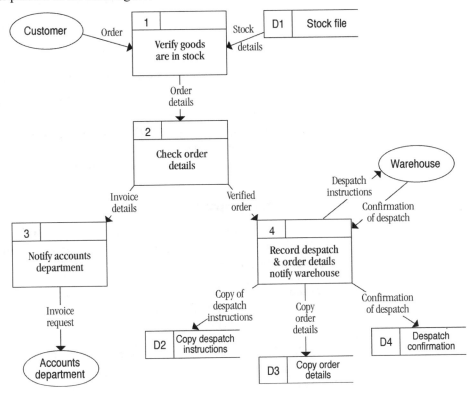

2.4   Level 2

Looking at the level 1 diagram again it can be seen that *Verify goods are in stock* (1) led into Process 2 (*Check order details*), which, in turn, led into the Process 3 (*Notify accounts department*), and Process 4. These must be shown on the level 2 diagram, which in this case expands Process 2 to show in more detail what is happening inside.

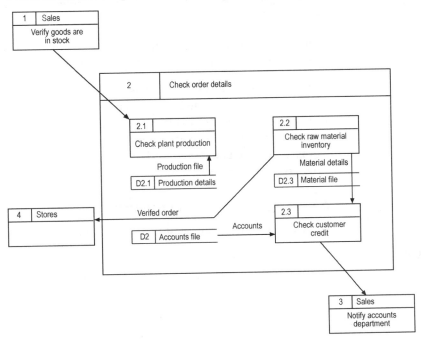

Note that the reference ID of the boxes does **not** imply any sequence or dependency – they are purely reference. At level 1 – and level 2 if appropriate, the box at the top of each process identifies which department, or which user, performs the process.

There are certain rules that the DFD notation must follow:

- no data store can access another data store directly: only a process can pass data from one store to another

- no external entity can access a data store directly, only via a process

- every process must have at least one input flow (its trigger) and one output flow. It can't generate data from nothing, or swallow data

- DFDs, structured English, decision tables and decision trees are all examples of process models. It is not necessary for you to try and learn all of them. In the examination you may well be asked to describe a situation using a process model – which technique or notation you use will be left entirely up to what you personally feel most comfortable with.

3   Structured English

Other methods or techniques are used to describe or specify systems at the lowest level of process detail. These include the informal tools of structured English, decision tables and decision trees.

You don't need to learn structured English, only know what it is and how it might be useful in systems development work. However, you might be required to prepare a decision table in your examination.

English is a rich and fertile language, capable of expressing and conveying both simple and complex ideas. It is understood by a great number of people, including many for whom it is not their native language. Describing the steps in a program in English has a number of advantages, making the program definition readily understood by both programmers and users.

Unfortunately like most living languages, English is capable of ambiguity – if you instruct somebody to 'get the shirt and iron', one person may fetch a shirt and an iron, whereas another will fetch the shirt and start to iron it. This tendency to ambiguity and lack of clarity makes normal English unsuitable as a means of defining what a program should do.

Structured English eliminates this problem of ambiguity while retaining the benefit of using a narrative to describe the stages in a program.

There are several different 'dialects' of structured English, but they all use the same approach – using a limited subset of the main language with the addition of a few extra words (such as ENDIF) to clarify the specification of what the program should do. All unnecessary words (such as pronouns and adjectives) are eliminated, and certain key words are defined unambiguously to denote particular actions. In many versions of structured English, these key words are written in capital letters.

3.1   Logical program structures

There are three basic kinds of logical activity that may form part of a program:

- **sequencing** – where activities follow one after another

- **selection** – where choosing which activity is to be followed is conditional upon a certain logical condition

- **repetition** – where activities take place several times, either while a condition remains true or until a condition becomes true.

3.2   Sequencing

A sequence instruction will be followed once and only once.

Statements to read a record from a customer file and display the results on a VDU
screen might appear as follows:

```
GET customer record from cust-file

DISPLAY customer record ON screen
```

Sequence instructions may incorporate input and output as seen above, but may also
incorporate calculations, as below:

```
SUBTRACT person allowances FROM gross pay to give taxable pay

MULTIPLY taxable pay BY tax rate to give income tax

ADD bar items to client-reference no to give total cost of
stay
```

3.3   Selection (conditional statements)

Some processes are only carried out under certain circumstances. Structured English
uses a number of constructions to show this.

The IF statement is the most basic way to show a choice. This is used in conjunction
with indented text to show which statements are selected. Many versions of structured
English use an END IF keyword to show the end of the scope of the IF statement.

An example of how the IF statement works can be seen below, where the calculation
of national insurance contributions is shown:

```
IF employee not of pensionable age

    THEN calculate NI contribution on salary

ENDIF
```

Another common situation is where one set of actions is carried out if a condition is
true, another set of actions carried out if the condition is false. This situation uses the
IF ... THEN ... ELSE construction.

```
IF actual-arrival-time > expected arrival time

    THEN

        ADD 1 to total no of trains late

        SUBTRACT expected arrival time FROM actual arrival time
        GIVING minutes late

        ADD minutes late to cumulative minutes late

    ELSE

        ADD 1 to total no of trains on time

ENDIF
```

The section of narrative above could be used to help calculate statistics on the
punctuality of trains.

Sometimes the condition used to select which of the statements is carried out is more complex. This can be catered for by using compound conditions – combining choices using AND or OR.

For example, to decide if an employee is past retirement age:

```
IF employee age > 59 AND employee sex is female

    THEN print retirement notice

ENDIF
```

or

```
IF (employee age > 59 AND employee sex is female)OR (employee
age >64 AND employee sex is male)

    THEN print retirement notice

ENDIF
```

In the second case, brackets are put around the two conditions to avoid ambiguity.

IF statements can sometimes be nested – with one condition being completely enclosed within another.

For example, to calculate the grade assigned to a student:

```
IF exam-mark < 50

    THEN DISPLAY student failed message

    ADD 1 to total number of failures

ELSE

    IF exam mark < 75

        THEN DISPLAY student passed message

        ADD 1 to total number of passes

    ELSE

        DISPLAY student distinction message

        ADD 1 to total no of distinctions

    ENDIF

ENDIF
```

The indentations make it clear which ELSE and ENDIF statements apply to each condition.

Narrative using nested IF statements can be quite complex and confusing. The case statement can be used to simplify matters when a number of mutually exclusive conditions are to be evaluated.

The nested IF statements above could be expressed as follows:

```
*EVALUATE exam marks
 DO CASE
```

FOULKS LYNCH
PUBLICATIONS

```
    CASE exam mark less than 50

       DISPLAY student failed message

       ADD 1 to total no of failures

    CASE exam mark between 50 and 74

       DISPLAY student passed message

       ADD 1 to total no of passes

    CASE exam mark between 75 and 100

       DISPLAY student distinction message

       ADD 1 to total no of distinctions

  ENDCASE

* END of EVALUATE section
```

The lines beginning with an asterisk are comments, used to make the narrative easier to read.

3.4   Repetition

KEY POINT

WHILE can be used to repeat statements.

A set of instructions may need to be repeated several times, either while a condition remains true, or until a condition becomes true.

For example, use of WHILE to calculate train punctuality record:

```
*PUNCTUALITY CALCULATIONS

DOWHILE any more trains

   GET train arrival details

   IF actual arrival time > expected arrival time

      THEN

         ADD 1 to total no of trains late

         SUBTRACT expected arrival time FROM actual arrival
         time GIVING minutes late

         ADD minutes late to cumulative minutes late

      ELSE

         ADD 1 to total no of trains on time

      ENDIF

   ENDIF

ENDDO
```

There are code generators that allow the automatic production of programs from pseudo code, or structured English.

4   Decision tables

Decision tables are used as a method of recording in tabular form a decision-making process and the consequent actions. They may be more convenient to draw and use than flowcharts when a large number of logical alternatives and procedures exist.

The decision table has four quadrants together with headings for the title and rule number and takes the following form:

Title	Rule number
Condition stub	Condition entry
Action stub	Action entry

Draw thick or double lines between the four quadrants.

1   The **condition stub** lists all the possible conditions that may exist within the system.

2   The **action stub** is a list of all the actions that may be taken depending upon the circumstances that may exist.

3   The **condition entry** section gives the various combinations of conditions that can exist in the system. Each combination (or rule) is equivalent to a particular route through a program flowchart.

4   The **action entry** indicates what action to take for each particular rule. It indicates what operation symbols appear on a particular route through a program flowchart.

4.1   Types of decision tables

There are three main types of decision tables:

1   **Limited entry** – in which a condition in the condition stub is phrased to provide a yes or no answer. The condition entry section has 'Y' or 'N' to indicate the condition. Only 'X' is entered into the action entry section to indicate the actions required.

2   **Extended entry** – in which various conditions are included in the condition entry section and the description of an action is given in the actions required.

3   **Mixed entry** – is a mixture of (1) and (2).

We will consider the limited entry decision table first and deal with the other types afterwards.

Example: Limited entry decision tables

William is a student studying for an accountancy examination. If it is Saturday he does not study, but goes downtown. On other nights when it is not raining, he goes jogging. On any other night he studies.

Produce a decision table for this situation.

Solution

(a)   The conditions that affect his action are:

         1   is it Saturday?

         2   is it raining?

(b)   These can be entered into the condition stub.

         The actions that he might take are:

         1   go out

         2   go jogging

         3   study for examination.

(c)   Calculate the number of condition combinations. The maximum number is 2^n where n = the number of conditions calculated in (a). Here there will be 4 condition combinations, which is 2 squared. Draw one vertical column for each condition combination in the entry section of the table.

(d)   Complete the condition entry section of the table by using the **halve-rule**. This means that you halve the number of columns in the entry section $(4 \div 2 = 2)$ and write Y twice and N twice in the condition entry. Then halve the number to write alternative Y and N in the condition entry.

(e)   Complete the action entry writing an X if an action is appropriate to the condition combination.

Condition	1	2	3	4
Is it Saturday?	Y	Y	N	N
Is it raining?	Y	N	Y	N
Go out	X	X		
Go jogging				X
Study			X	

(f)   Now remove redundant rules. These are identified by looking for columns where the action entries are the same, and the condition entries differ in one condition only.

         This applies for rules 1 and 2 and the decision table can be reduced to:

Condition	1	2	3
Is it Saturday?	Y	N	N
Is it raining?	-	Y	N
Go out	X		
Go jogging			X
Study		X	

 FOULKS LYNCH PUBLICATIONS

Harry allows his customers a discount of 5% if both:

(a)   the balance on the account is less than £200

(b)   all items outstanding are less than two months old.

If one of these conditions is violated, the discount allowed is 2%. Customers who have been trading for more than three years are allowed an additional 2% provided that neither of the above conditions is violated.

Draw a limited entry decision table.

Feedback to this activity is at the end of the chapter.

Delivery charges are calculated as follows:

(a)   If the value of the order is £100 or more and the distance is less than 50 miles, no charge is made. If the distance is more than 50 miles, the charge is £5.

(b)   If the value is less than £100 and the distance is less than 50 miles, the charge is £5. If the distance is 50 miles or more, the charge is £10.

(c)   If the customer requests urgent delivery, a fixed charge of £20 is made.

Draw a decision table for delivery charges.

Feedback to this activity is at the end of the chapter.

4.2   Extended and mixed entry

It is possible to draw a decision table including other conditions (e.g. age, price, quantity) in the condition entry, and to enter the description of the action in the action entry. The table is then referred to as extended entry.

If both limited and extended entries are used, the table is called mixed entry.

Examples of the types follow:

Example: Extended entry (to show action on overdue accounts)

Discount	A	A	A	B	B	B
Age of debt	1 month	2 months	3 months	1 month	2 months	3 months
Action	Nil	Personal letter	Refer to manager	Stock letter	Warning letter	Final warning

Example: Mixed entry (to determine credit rating)

References	Y	Y	Y	N	N	N
Size of debt	£500	£250	Nil	£500	£250	Nil
Credit rating	A	B	C	B	C	Cash

There are three types of customer, A, B and C as follows:

(a)   Type A receives a 10% discount on all orders, except that for orders above £2,000 in value the discount is 12%.

(b)   Type B receives a 7% discount on all orders except that for orders above £2,000 in value the discount is 8.5%.

(c)   Type C receives a 5% discount on all orders regardless of value.

Using the above date, draw a mixed entry decision table.

Feedback to this activity is at the end of the chapter.

4.3 Advantages and disadvantages of decision tables

Advantages

- **analysis** – the construction of a table is a valuable aid to analysing a decision-making process, to ensuring that all possible conditions have been explored, and unnecessary conditions eliminated

- **communication** – a decision table is a convenient way of explaining a decision-making process to someone else

- **conciseness** – the decision-making process is represented clearly in the minimum of space. it is sometimes easier to see what decision is taken in particular conditions than by tracing the lines of a flowchart

- **convenience** – a decision table is easier to reproduce (e.g. using a spreadsheet) than a flowchart

- **standardisation** – standard forms can be used for the completion of decision tables far more readily than with flowcharts

- **programming** – some high-level languages allow a decision table to be converted into a program. This is possible only with limited entry tables

- **intelligibility** – the layman understands decision tables more easily than program flowcharts.

Disadvantages

- they become cumbersome when the number of conditions and the number of rules is high

- they cannot show an intermediate action in a decision-making process

- they are not always suitable for planning programs. (Generally, program flowcharts are better.)

4.4 Decision trees

A decision tree is an alternative way to present the logic of a decision. It shows the courses of action available together with possible outcomes for each course of action.

To describe the various factors influencing a decision, two symbols are used: a square to denote a decision point, and a circle to denote a chance point. A decision point allows a firm course of action to be chosen. Chance points mean that the outcome is uncertain.

FOULKS LYNCH
PUBLICATIONS

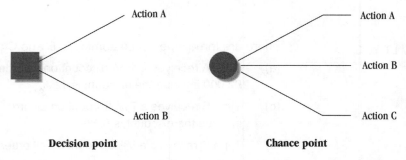

Decision point   **Chance point**

By convention, decision trees are expressed from top to bottom or from left to right.

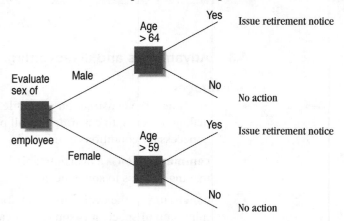

Decision trees are a useful tool for displaying logical choices, but can be a very cumbersome tool when the choices are very complex.

5   Modelling static structures

5.1   The Entity Relationship Model (ERM)

As well as modelling the business processes, we need to identify and model the persistent data held by our system. There are a number of ways this can be done. A common technique over the last twenty years or more is the Entity Relationship Model (ERM).

An **entity** is something of significance to a system about which data must be held. This may be something tangible, such as a product that we sell; it may be more conceptual, such as an account, or it may be something active, such as a delivery.

An **entity relationship model** (sometimes known as a **logical data stru**cture or LDS) reflects a static view of the relationship between different entities. The ERM is an important part of several systems development methodologies.

5.2   Entities, relationship and attributes

The three basic concepts of an ERM are entities, attributes, and relationships. An entity is an individual person or object that is important to an organisation; an attribute is an individual piece of information to help describe that entity; and a relationship is a logical link between two entities.

The attributes of a customer include name, address and telephone number. The relationships between the three entities show that one customer may place several orders, and each order may be for several products.

5.3   The symbols used in an ERM

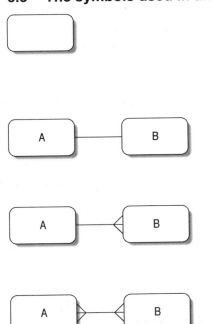

Represents an entity

An entity must be capable of having more than one occurrence (i.e. the environment itself is not an entity – the data subjects it uses are).

Represents a 1-1 relationship

An occurrence of A is related to only one B; an occurrence of B is related to only one A.

Represents a 1-M relationship

An occurrence of A is related to 1 or more occurrences of B; an occurrence of B is related to only one of A.

Represents a M-M relationship

An occurrence of A is related to one or more occurrences of B; an occurrence of B is related to one or more occurrences of A.

The rules of data modelling state that a M:M relationship cannot exist; it usually implies that there is further analysis to be carried out to identify more data in the systems than has yet been discovered. When you find a M:M relationship, the solution is to draw a **link entity** between them, so that the link forms two 1:M relationships instead. That principle is illustrated in the next section.

5.4   Building an entity model

The entities *Department and Employee* will have a relationship. This can be shown as follows:

However, the model being developed needs to show that a department has many employees, but that a specific employee order can belong to only one department:

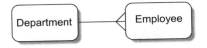

This model can be further extended to show that the employee can possess many skills. Each skill, conversely, can belong to many employees.

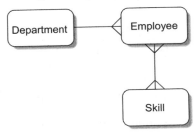

However, we have said above that M:M relationships are not allowed. We put another entity, a link entity, between the two M:M entities. In this case, the link entity would be an *Employee Skill*. So, each Employee can have many Employee Skills, while each

Employee Skill belongs to only one Employee; similarly, each Employee Skill will be for only one Skill, while each Skill will appear on many Employee Skills. This is always the case when using a link to resolve M:M relationships: the **crows' feet** always go at the link end of the relationship lines. This is shown below.

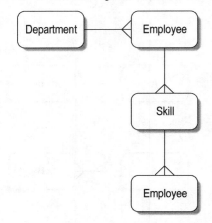

The model now shows that each Employee can have many Employee Skills. Each Employee Skill is for a particular Employee. The entity Skill however, will have many Employee Skills on different Skills:

We can continue building the model, with entities found for Job and Job-Type, and whatever other features the business needs to store about its employees. Employees at MG Hotels are often asked to cover for a member of staff who is away, and therefore it is important to see the skills they have in order to make a good choice.

Each entity will be made up of a number of attributes, i.e. data items that together describe the entity. Thus, *Department* will have as its attributes

Department-ID

Department-Name

Telephone Extension

Head of Department

Office-number

Employee may have the following:

Employee Number

Name

Address

Telephone Number

Date-of-birth

Grade

Department-ID

The most important attribute is the key, a unique identifier that will be used to identify each occurrence of an entity. In the examples above, the key is shown in italics.

Building models of the relationships allows an analyst to develop a logical view of a system. An analyst must primarily identify the entities that exist within the system.

5.5   Showing optional relationships

The diagram developed in the previous section showed no distinction between the types of relationships. Some relationships may be conditional, whereas others are mandatory. These may be differentiated by using broken or partially broken connecting lines to show that a relationship may or may not exist.

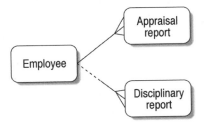

This shows that a fully established employee *must* have one or more appraisal reports, but *may* have one or more disciplinary reports. A disciplinary report *must* have an associated employee.

This optionality is one way of modelling the rules that govern a business. For example, some businesses may create a customer record only when they place the first order; in that case the relationship between customer and order will be solid, a *mandatory* relationship. Another business may create a customer record before the first order is placed, when authorised by the sales director after negotiations. This would be shown as a dotted line, an *optional* relationship.

This simple piece of notation illustrates the different rules under which these businesses handle customer records.

5.6   Validation of ERM

The ERM can be used to help validate the data flow diagram: the data inside the entities must correspond with the data inside the data stores. Each piece of data should have a process at least to create it and one to delete it. There may also be processes to update it.

A more direct way, though, of validating the ERM itself is to test the model against the requirements. One method is to navigate the model with an access map. Here is an access map showing how we can answer an enquiry: 'Identify the different skills of employees in the booking department, along with a date of when the skill was obtained.' To answer that enquiry our model must let us find the particular department, and track all the skills the employees within that department have.

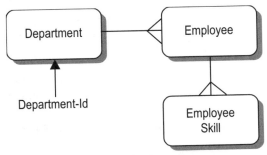

The arrows show how each department has many employees, but we can track each one in turn, and for each employee we can find the employee skills, together with the data the skill was obtained for that employee. This exercise should be carried out for each functional requirement, to be sure that the model can support all the requirements.

5.7   Importance of ERM

The first draft ERM can be drawn as part of the feasibility study. This helps to give a feel for the size and complexity of the area being studied.

A more detailed model will be drawn for the detailed analysis, and that one will be refined and added to for the required system design. The full models should identify all the data and its identifiers, all the logical relationships between them and as many of the business rules that can be supported by the data.

When the required system relationship models have been completed, the physical design of the database files can be undertaken. In the physical design, each entity is likely to become a database table, or record. Each attribute on the model is likely to become a physical data item.

The ERM is just one way of modelling persistent data.

6   Event models

6.1   Modelling user requirements - events

While an entity relationship model reflects a static view of the relationship between different entities, an **event model** or **state model** shows details of the different events that cause an entity to be updated, from its creation right through to its deletion from the system. There are a number of ways that this can be modelled – the two commonest types of model are **Entity Life Histories** and **State Transition Diagrams**. This section will concentrate on entity life histories, but for the purpose of the examination, familiarity with any one technique or method for modelling states of an entity will be sufficient.

An **event** is something which happens in the world that causes us to make a change to the data in our system (our entities).

The three types of event

- **External events**, such as a customer placing an order (this will lead to creation of order and order line records, modification of product record, and possibly creation of customer record).

- **Time-based events** (e.g. at month end, interest will be added to overdrawn credit accounts).

- **Internal events**, such as a management decision to discontinue a product line, which will result in modification, then deletion of the record.

As far as modelling the events goes, you do not need to distinguish one type from another – it's just that knowing the types helps you know where to look to find the events.

If you have drawn a data flow diagram, you will discover the events as flows from an external entity into a process that then updates a data store.

6.2   Entity life history (ELH)

An **entity life history** is a diagrammatic representation of the events that affect an entity, tracking the entity from 'womb' to 'tomb'. As such, it is another tool to help model the business rules. For example, some businesses will not send an invoice until goods are delivered to the customer; another, similar, company may issue an invoice on receipt of the order, or demand payment before the goods are despatched. Whichever sequence is laid down by the company can be reflected in the sequence of events on the ELH.

There are various conventions for recording entity life histories. The following diagram uses the conventions from SSADM and shows a selection of the events that can affect a bank account.

The structure is a **tree structure**, with the root at the top. The root is a single box with the name of the entity.

At the bottom of the tree are the events. Drawing from left to right, we begin with the **birth event**, i.e. what event causes our system to create the record. At the end, (the right) of the diagram is the **death event**, i.e. what causes us to delete the record from our live system. In between are the **mid-life events**, i.e. those that cause us to update the values of attributes during the record's active life.

As many entities can experience a lot of mid-life events, the diagram can grow to a quite complicated level. However, there are only three basic constructs to be aware of in the diagram. The illustration following has examples of each. The explanation is underneath.

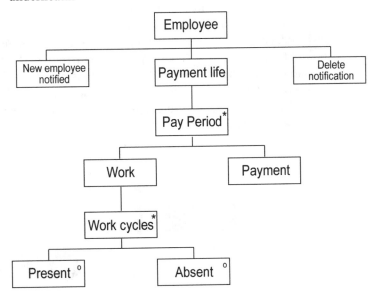

Notation rules

The rules of the notation are:

- the diagram is in the form of a tree, with the entity as the root

- the order of the boxes, from left to right, shows the time sequence (so in this example, the payment cannot be made until the work is carried out.)

- the events are at the bottom of each branch. Boxes in the middle are known as **structure boxes**, and are for navigation from event to event only

- moving from top to bottom in the diagram describes the processes carried out in a greater level of detail

- an asterisk (*) in a box represents an **iteration**, or a repeated process. Everything on the branch below the Iteration can be repeated. An iteration will mean that the event can affect this entity 0, 1 or many times

- a circle (o) in a box shows a **selection**, or a possible choice of events. During the time an employee should be at work, it is possible to be either present or absent, but not both.

Thus, an asterisk in the box labelled 'payment period' shows that there may be many pay periods being monitored, for each of which the employee may be either present, or absent.

6.3   Validation of ELH

The Entity Life History allows a cross reference to both the DFD (or other process model) and the ERM. Each event should be visible on the process model, and it often happens that this technique uncovers events – and hence required processing – that the analyst failed to capture earlier. Similarly, every entity should be modelled, to ensure that there is at least a creation and deletion (birth and death) event for each one. If that is all that happens in an entity's life, it may not be worth drawing them all, but those events should at least be identified.

6.4   The value of an ELH

The ELH diagram provides a pictorial representation of what happens to an entity. This provides a way in which the analyst can understand what is likely to happen, and provide a clear means of communication. The analyst must design methods to permit each event to occur.

Just as important, the analyst must make sure that the events can only take place in the correct sequence for that entity, according to the business rules. When the system is designed, each event will trigger a process to update the record; if the entity is not in the right state – i.e. the event happens at the wrong place in the life history, that transaction must be rejected with an error message. In an ELH for a customer, if the business declares that a customer cannot place an order if no payment for previous orders has been made, that rule must be shown on the diagram, so that the business rules are kept. The extract below shows this. *Either* the debt is still owing, *or* the order is met.

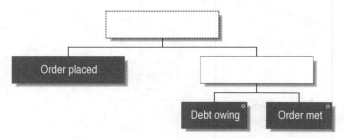

In this way, the ELH (or whatever state model is used) helps to preserve both the business rules and the integrity of the database.

6.5 State transition diagram

A State Transition diagram is an alternative way of modelling the state of an entity or object. The notation is simply a series of boxes, each box showing a state that the object can be in. The links between states is shown as an arrow. Iterations would be shown as an arrow leading from a state back to the state. Each transition represents an event, leading to the change in state. The Employee life history shown above can be represented in terms of a State Transition Diagram as follows:

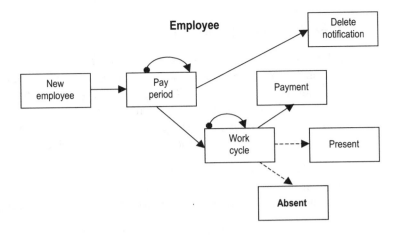

Conclusion

This chapter has looked at how the requirements are included within system documentation such as structured English and data flow diagrams. The former provide the detail of the individual computer programs while the latter focus on the business processes taking place. Two other perspectives to be modelled are the static models and the state models of the system.

Data Flow Diagrams

1   What symbols are normally used to produce data flow diagrams? (2.1)

Structured English

2   What are the benefits of using structured English? (3)

Decision tables

3   What are the four sections of a decision table? (4)

Modelling static structures

4   What do the terms entity, attribute and relationship mean? (5.2)

Event models

5   What are the three constructs used in the ELH diagram? (6)

Process model of a mail order firm

A large mail order firm operates through several thousand local agents, who sell mainly to close friends and relatives. An agent receives a new catalogue every spring, summer, winter and autumn. Friends select goods from the current catalogue and then pay the agent the appropriate amount, receiving in return a receipt detailing goods ordered and moneys paid. The agent adds their order to an order form and pays their money into a separate account used solely for business.

Every Saturday the agent posts the order form (now containing items ordered by a number of people) together with a single cheque drawn on the business account, retaining a copy of the order form, which is kept in a red ring binder.

The company sends items ordered by return of post together with a delivery note. The agent checks the items received against both the delivery note and his/her own copy of the order, using telephone calls to resolve any discrepancies. If all is satisfactory, the agent then throws away the order form but retains the delivery note in a blue ring binder.

At the end of every quarter the agent receives, along with the new season's catalogue, a statement of all items ordered in the quarter, together with a commission cheque for 10% of their total value. After checking the details against the delivery notes in the blue ring binder, the agent pays the commission into his/her own personal bank account.

Required:

(a)   Draw a suitable process model depicting the above procedure.   **(14 marks)**

(b)   Briefly describe two graphic tools in common use in structured systems analysis to amplify the logic of the processes identified in a process model used in part (a).   **(6 marks)**

(Total: 20 marks)

Limited and extended entry decision tables

EC Ltd supplies a range of industrial cleaning materials and gives discounts on orders as follows:

Total order value	Discount
Less than £50	2%
£50 and over	5%

These discounts are only given if the customer's account is less than four weeks in arrears. If the account is more than eight weeks in arrears a pro forma invoice must be sent and settled before despatch.

Required:

(a)   Prepare a limited entry decision table to determine the correct discount for any order.

(b)   Explain the difference between limited entry and extended entry decision tables.

(c)   State and justify three advantage that decision tables are claimed to have in this context.   **(20 marks)**

EXAM-TYPE
QUESTION 3

Dataflow terms

With reference to dataflow diagrams, explain the meaning of the following terms:

(a)	external entity	**(3 marks)**
(b)	context level	**(3 marks)**
(c)	decomposing	**(4 marks)**
(d)	top down approach.	**(4 marks)**

(Total: 14 marks)

FEEDBACK TO
ACTIVITY 1

(a)   Calculation of number of rules

The first step is to count the number of conditions; in this example, three:

1   Balance   £200

2   Items   2 months old

3   Trading   3 years

The number of rules needed can then be calculated by the formula 2 to the power of the number of conditions:

i.e. $2^3 = 8$ rules

(4 conditions would require 16 rules, 5 would require 32 rules and so on). The table can now be drawn with the condition and action stubs completed and entry portions left blank.

(b)   Completion of condition entry by 'halving'

'Halving' completes the condition entry.

- the first half of the first line is filled with Ys and the second half with Ns

- the number of Ys and Ns is halved and they are entered alternatively on the second line

- this halving is continued until on the last line alternate single Ys and Ns are entered.

(c)   Completion of action entry

Next entering Xs against the appropriate actions completes the action entry. This also is illustrated in the following table:

(d)   Full table showing halving

Discount	1	2	3	4	5	6	7	8
Balance ‹ £200	Y	Y	Y	Y	N	N	N	N
Items ‹ 2 months old	Y	Y	N	N	Y	Y	N	N
Trading › 3 years	Y	N	Y	N	Y	N	Y	N
No discount							X	X
2% discount			X	X	X	X		
5% discount		X						
7% discount	X							

(e) Removal of redundant rules

The next step is to remove redundant rules. In this example Rule 4 is redundant, because if either of the first two conditions is violated the customer received no extra discount even if he has been trading for more than three years. Rule 4 can therefore be removed and a '-' entered in Rule 3. The same is true of Rules 5 and 6 and Rules 7 and 8. The simplified table, with the redundant rules removed is shown below.

Remember, rules can be combined together systematically, two columns at a time. Two columns can be combined together if these two conditions apply:

- the actions relating to the two columns are the same

- the conditions on the two columns differ in only one position.

If these conditions apply, the two columns can be written down, as one with a hyphen replacing the entries in the conditions where the difference mentioned above exists.

(f) Table with redundant rules removed

Discount	1	2	3	4	5
Balance £200	Y	Y	Y	N	N
Items 2 months old	Y	Y	N	Y	N
Trading 3 years	Y	N	-	-	-
No discount					X
2% discount			X	X	
5% discount		X			
7% discount	X				

FEEDBACK TO
ACTIVITY 2

Your table should be as follows:

Delivery charges	1	2	3	4	5
Urgent delivery	Y	N	N	N	N
Value $\geq$ £100	-	Y	Y	N	N
Radius $\leq$ 50 miles	-	Y	N	Y	N
£20	X				
£10				X	X
£5			X		
No charge		X			

FEEDBACK TO
ACTIVITY 3

Your table should be as follows:

Type of customer	A	A	B	B	C
Order > £2,000	Y	N	Y	N	-
Discount	12%	10%	8.5%	7%	5%

Chapter 10
EXTERNAL DESIGN

This chapter provides an explanation of the design features for the parts of the computer that you can see – that is the human-computer interface and the different reports that are produced by a computer system. Providing a good clear design is important to help users communicate with the computer system itself, and help them to understand the outputs being received from the computer system.

Objectives

By the time you have finished this chapter you should be able to:

- define the characteristics of a user-friendly system
- describe the task of external design and distinguish it from internal design
- design effective output documents and reports
- select appropriate technology to support the output design
- design effective inputs
- select appropriate technology to support input design
- describe how the user interface may be structured for ease of use
- explain how prototyping may be used in defining an external design.

KEY POINT

External design concerns the interface between users and the system.
Internal design doesn't concern the end user, but is concerned with the technical aspects of the system.

1   External and internal design

External design is concerned with the interface between the users and the system. Many changes have taken place and computation has seen a number of major themes:

- The first is that the user population is growing (for example, the number of users on the internet. In 1980 there were approximately 100 registered sites, and in 1994 the number reached 100,000,000). This means that there is now a huge market for even relatively specialised products.
- The application range is growing. From very specialised devices for calculating navigational aids to general purpose computing devices. These systems are being applied to a vast range of user tasks. The problem at the moment is that we are very poor at matching the systems we build to the user's needs.
- The degree of expertise is growing. Users are more discriminating than they used to be. The introduction of graphical presentation facilities has 'increased the stakes' in user interface design. The impact of multimedia and the games industry has meant that the more 'interactive' systems are more appealing than the original text-based interfaces. It is now less easy to satisfy many user groups.
- If user participation is increased it is likely to produce a more user accepted system.

Internal design doesn't concern the end user. It is concerned with the technical aspects (for example, database and program design).

2   Input devices

For an information system on a computer to be able to run effectively, it must be able to interact with the world around it. It receives data and instructions through its input devices; it sends the results of its processing via output devices; and it stores data and programs for later use on its storage devices. It may also communicate with other computers via communications channels.

Not all devices are solely for either input or output devices; some provide both capabilities. Devices such as touch screen terminals provide the ability to send messages to users and to receive instructions from users.

The outputs of a MIS or DSS might be in the form of a display in answer to an on-line query, or to acknowledge a successful transaction, or it might be in the form of a report aggregating transactions of a particular kind, to provide important control information to management. The result of this might be input to the system from management to correct, say, falling sales, or bad pricing decisions.

2.1   Data collection and input

Before a computer can process data, that data must be input to the computer in a machine-intelligible form. The general term of data collection is used to cover the following activities.

Originating the data

In most cases this will be done through the receipt or creation of a clerical document, although there is a trend towards the elimination of documents. Many systems now enable an order to be taken by telephone and keyed directly into the computer.

Data transmission

This is the transfer of data from its originating location to the server being used for storage or processing. In some cases data transmission may involve telephone links between the computer department and remote locations.

Data preparation

In some cases particularly in large corporate server operations, the data must be prepared before it is input to the computer, e.g. data may be keyed onto tape or disc off-line.

Data input

The data is read by the input device and transferred to the internal storage of the computer where it is processed. A wide variety of methods have been developed to meet differing needs and we will consider many of these methods here.

The collection and input of data presents a major problem to many computer users because:

- if adequate controls are not maintained, there may be errors at the preparation stage, which will lead to incorrect or incomplete information being produced

- it may be a time consuming process to prepare and input the data especially in comparison with the fast processing speeds of the CPU.

The cost of data collection, transmission, preparation and input may be high.

2.2   Choice of data input method

There are various input methods, and selecting the one with the optimum cost, speed and accuracy characteristics is often a critical success factor in systems development. Any errors at the data input stage can have serious consequences for the quality of the information output from the system.

The following sections look at most of the common data input methods available for information systems and the criteria used to select between them.

In selecting the method or methods for data input for a new system, the system designer will consider:

- how to reduce the risk of errors and mistakes in the input

- what type of input method might be appropriate for the requirements of the system.

2.3   Keyboard input (and visual display unit)

An integral part of almost all terminals, work stations and PCs is the keyboard. By hitting one of the keys the user is able to transmit the relevant character code to the computer. Characters are set out on a keyboard in various ways, but most have the letters set out as on a traditional typewriter keyboard. Because of the way that the letters on the top row are arranged, these keyboards are called 'QWERTY' keyboards (AZERTY in France).

There are special function keys that have meanings depending on the sort of software being used. The shift, control and alt keys can be held down at the same time as one of the other keys is depressed to modify the character that is transmitted to the computer.

Keyboards are used with screens (visual display units or VDUs) so that the individual inputting data by keyboard can carry out a visual check on what is being keyed in, and can be directed by the program to enter the data into particular boxes or locations on the screen.

Although keyboard input is now common in computer systems, a major problem can be the level of keying-in errors that occur. Accuracy relies on the keyboard skills of the individuals inputting the data. The greater the volume of data to key in, the greater the number of input errors will be.

Where keyboard input is used, the system designer should therefore try to limit the amount of data that has to be keyed in, or should try to make the task of input easier, through the additional use of a mouse or tracker ball, and WIMP features.

2.4   Default values

Default values are values that are entered automatically by the computer program into given 'fields' of information in a record on the computer screen. They can be used when the value to be entered into a particular box on screen (field of data) can be predicted with a reasonable degree of certainty. For example, there might be a field in a record for Value Added Tax. Since VAT is normally charged at 17.5%, the value 17.5 could be entered as a default value into the VAT data field. If 17.5 is not the value required, it can be altered by clicking on the field with a mouse and entering the correct value by keyboard.

Default values help to reduce the time spent keying in data, because they are entered automatically. They also reduce the risk of input errors due to keying-in mistakes.

2.5   Mouse and tracker ball input

Computer mice and tracker balls are extensively used as input devices on PCs, particularly if graphical user interfaces (GUIs) are used.

A mouse consists of two or three buttons mounted onto a body containing a ball.

As the mouse is moved around on a desktop, the ball-bearing rotates. The rotation is sensed and transmitted to the computer. The movement of a cursor on the screen reflects the movement of the mouse on the desktop. The cursor can be made to point to an option displayed on the screen and a button clicked to select that option.

A tracker (or roller) ball works in a way that is similar to the workings of a mouse, but the ball is rotated by hand. It is often used as an alternative to a mouse on a portable PC.

2.6   Optical mark reading (OMR)

The OMR technique assigns values to marks made on a document according to their position. For example, marking one of the boxes in the diagram below may represent a number between nought and nine:

(The number 7 has been marked as an example.)

A common use is on **meter reading sheets** and on **examination answer sheets** with individual sheets being scanned in a matter of seconds.

The main advantages of mark reading are:

- its simplicity

- cheapness

- the volumes of transactions that can be processed in a short time.

Since a reading device reads the marks on the input document, the probability of input error is less than with keyboard input.

2.7   Optical character recognition (OCR)

The OCR reader can identify specially printed characters or carefully hand-written characters. The reader incorporates a light beam, which follows the outline of the character being read, which it compares with a stored reference of characters. The system can normally read and verify with the operator a page of A4 text in about a minute.

Care must be taken with this input, as there is no verification other than visual scrutiny.

OCR applications include meter reading forms for some **gas and electricity bills** and is also becoming popular in some word processing systems which allow **documents prepared using a normal print or typewriter to be scanned in as input** to the computer.

In recent years, a number of systems have come on to the market, which claim to be capable of **handwriting recognition**. The first of these was the Newton from Apple Computers, which was essentially a small laptop computer with a touch-screen display. The manufacturers claimed that the system could quickly learn to recognise the user's handwriting. Low sales and reliability problems soon forced this machine off the market, but other systems are now available that are said to be more reliable.

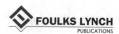

2.8   Magnetic ink character recognition (MICR)

Magnetic ink character recognition uses highly stylised characters are printed onto documents using inks that contain iron oxide. The document is then passed through a magnetic field before being read by special equipment. Input speeds are up to 2,400 documents per minute.

This method is used mainly for **banking applications** and is used on cheques and paying-in slips. The cheques have the account number, branch code and cheque number pre-printed and after use the amount of the cheque is printed using the same font. MICR is generally much more accurate than OCR; however, it does require high quality printing and expensive reading equipment.

2.9   Plastic cards and badges

There is a wide range of applications in which plastic cards can be used as a means of data capture. The card can be used to print the account number in OCR characters on a document for subsequent input to a document reader, e.g. credit card systems such as Barclaycard or Visa.

The card may bear magnetic data which are read when it is inserted into a slot, e.g. cash and credit card systems operated by many banks for electronic funds transfer at the point of sale (EFTPOS).

The card may be used to gain access to secure areas and as a form of unique identification for staff.

2.10 Bar coding

Bar coding uses a pattern of black and white strips representing a code. It is seen widely on retail goods in supermarkets where the coding system is known as the Universal Product Code. The following are typical examples of such markings:

The code is read by a bar code scanner or light pen which converts the bar coding into a magnetic form for input to the computer. It is often used in electronic point of sale (EPOS) systems. These are systems used at cash desks in **shops and supermarkets**. Items to be purchased contain a bar code, which is put under a reading device that recognises the item and its price from the data in the code.

The input method is extremely quick, taking only as long as the 'beep' to confirm that the code has been read and verified against the stock master file. In such systems the code is used to provide continuous stock recording and re-ordering as well as providing the customer with a detailed receipt. Bar coding reduces user input error, and saves time and money.

 FOULKS LYNCH PUBLICATIONS

2.11 Scanners

A scanner uses a beam of light to scan text or an image so that it can be automatically input into the computer. Any image can be scanned by a normal scanner. Coloured images can also be input using special colour scanners. Scanners can be hand-held, flat-bed or overhead. In conjunction with optical character recognition (OCR) scanners can automate the data input of large text documents for further processing.

2.12 Other input devices

There are a number of other input devices that are either experimental or in use in very specialist applications. It is likely that some of these input devices will become much more widely used in the general business community in the near future.

Voice recognition/voice data entry

A microphone is used to input the words spoken by an operator or user. This method of input is in its infancy, with the computer having a limited understanding of certain key words and comments. There is also a problem in recognising different accents and ways of speaking. A frequency analysis of the different tones in a voice can be used to recognise an individual whose voice patterns have been stored in the computer. This can be used as a security device, limiting access to a computer system or secure area.

The software to support speech recognition requires a minimum specification of a Pentium computer with 32 Mb RAM, and over 100MHz processor.

Two examples of speech recognition are: Naturally Speaking, by Dragon Systems, and Via Voice, from IBM.

Touch screen/light pen

If light-sensitive or touch-sensitive devices are connected to a VDU, then the screen can act as an input device. By touching the screen with one's finger or the light pen, the user can select a specific application from a menu displayed on the screen. This form of input is used in ways similar to the use of a mouse.

Stylus

A stylus device is often used to input technical drawings or graphic designs to a computer. The stylus looks like a pen with a small ball bearing in its tip. A graphic artist or technical drawing expert can trace a drawing on a drawing board, with the image thus being reproduced on screen.

Image to text software

An optical scanner (described earlier in this chapter) can be used to transfer images into the computer. These images can either be of graphics or of text. Although textual image can be entered into a computer in this way, it cannot immediately be treated as text by, for example, modification by word processing software. This is because text files are stored in a different way than graphic computer files. Special computer software is needed to modify a graphic file containing text into a computer text file. To date this kind of software has not been 100% successful in converting both typed and hand-written data, although in future it is possible that this will be a major way of entering data from documents.

2.13 Selection of data collection methods

It will be clear that the user has a wide variety of data collection methods from which to choose.

The main considerations in the design of a data preparation system are set out in the table below.

Economy	Costs must be kept to a minimum. The high proportion of total DP costs spent on data capture makes this a crucial area in overall system costs. There is often a conflict between cost and the other considerations described below.
Accuracy	Errors should not be created in the process of data collection. Any errors that do occur should be detected and corrected.
Time	The time spent in collecting data should not be excessive in relation to the needs of the system as a whole.
Reliability	The system should be reasonably free from breakdown.
Flexibility	The system may have to cope with different types of data and with changes in the amount of data.
Volume	The amount of data to be collected has an important effect on the method selected.
Existing equipment	An organisation will use data collection systems it already possesses, unless there are strong reasons for a change.

3   Input data validation

In most systems, the accuracy of data input depends to some extent on the accuracy with which the source data is collected and recorded, or the accuracy of the input. Whenever human intervention occurs, the risk of errors is likely to be high.

One way of identifying errors in data on input is to write data validation checks into the computer program. Input data validation is checking of input data for accuracy by the program. It consists of a number of different checks on data input to the system. Each check normally relates to a particular item or field of data.

A program can identify some input errors where there is a logical error. A check can be written for a particular field of data, and if the input data fails the check, an error report is produced, and the error can be checked and corrected. Input will not be accepted where a data validation check is failed.

Common types of data validation check are as follows.

Format checks

Each data field might have a specified length and format. A format check ensures that data entered into this field conforms to these requirements. For example, a customer's account number might be a code in the format two letters followed by five numbers (AANNNNN). A validation check can make sure that all records entered into the system have a customer code with this format. Codes with a different format, such as A582493, will be rejected with an error report.

Valid value and range checks

Certain fields of data may only have a limited range of valid data values. For example, product codes might all be in the range 1,000 to 4,999. A field to indicate the sex of an individual might have to be the value M or F. A range check can make sure that data is entered with a value in the acceptable range. A valid value check can make sure that the entered data has one of the acceptable values.

Consistency checks

Consistency checks compare the input into one field of data with the input into another field of data, to make sure that the two items of data are consistent with each other. For example, a company might sell a range of products and despatch them from one of four warehouses. It might be that products with a stock code beginning with the number 3 are held only in warehouses B and C. A consistency check could be written into a program to ensure that if a stock code is entered beginning with a 3, the warehouse code entered must be B or C. If it is not, an error report will be produced.

Item counts and totals

Calculated total and item counts are concerned with consistency between values at the time of data entry. For example the marks for each question must (when added together) equal the total mark for the paper and the number of questions answered must tally with the number of marks recorded.

Check digit

Certain fields may have codes to which a check digit can be attached. This digit usually becomes the last character or number of the code. When the code is entered the check digit is recalculated and validated against the one entered by the operator. Check digits are particularly useful in supporting range checks. For example, the entered candidate number may have two digits transposed (71233452 instead of 72133452) and still pass the range check (70000000-79999999). However, if the code had used a check digit system to produce the last character then this transposition would have been picked up.

One check digit system is the modulus 11 system. Suppose there is a basic 4-digit code. Using a check digit, the code will be expended to a 5-digit code by adding a check digit. One 4-digit code might be, say, 2478. The check digit would be derived as follows.

Code digit	Weighting	Weighted total
2	5	10
4	4	16
7	3	21
8	2	16
		63
Check digit	1	3
		66

The check digit is a number that, when added to the weighted total as shown in the total, produces a grand total figure that divides exactly by 11. Here, a check digit of 3 takes the total to 66, which is divisible exactly by 11.

The code is therefore 24783.

If this code is keyed in incorrectly, a check digit check in the program will spot the error. For example, if the code 24783 is entered as 24873, the program would do the following check.

Code digit	Weighting	Weighted total
2	5	10
4	4	16
8	3	24
7	2	14
3	1	3
		67

This does not divide exactly by 11, so the code must be wrong.

Check digit checks are particularly useful for checking the accuracy of key codes, such as customer codes in a sales system.

Data verification

Data verification involves a double entry of data values by different operators. The second time that the data is input, it is checked by program against the data that was input the first time. The data input the second time should be identical to the data input the first time. If it isn't, an error report is produced. The input operator can then check the error, and make sure that the correct data is entered.

4 Output devices

Most computer systems will use a range of output devices to communicate with users.

Output devices work in a number of different ways:

Temporary display

Devices such as Visual Display Units display information on a temporary basis. Usually messages would be displayed until the user acknowledges that they have been read, but sometimes messages will scroll off the screen as more information is displayed. Many VDUs are attached to local printing devices and provide the capability of producing a screen print so that a more permanent copy of the screen output can be displayed.

Printed output

The most common form of output device where a hard copy is required is one of the many kinds of printer.

Process control

When the computer is running a production process, its major outputs will be direct to the equipment that is controlling the process.

4.1   Printers

There is a wide range of equipment available and management needs to make a decision based upon their anticipated requirements. Not surprisingly the faster the speed and the higher the quality then the greater the cost of the equipment. Speeds vary from about two pages per minute for ink-jet printers to about 35 pages per minute for high quality laser printers. In the following sections we deal with the more common types and features of computer printers.

Character printers

So called because they print one character at a time; they are found in most small business systems and there is no requirement for very fast printing speeds. The main type of character printers is:

Ink-jet printers and Desk jet printers

Printing is achieved by guiding a high-speed stream of ink drops onto the paper. They provide faster, quieter and better quality printing than the traditional dot matrix impact printer. Colour ink-jet printers are now common, and many ink-jet printers are portable enough to be used with a laptop PC.

Laser printers

Laser printers print whole pages of text or graphics at once, and use techniques developed for photocopying to achieve high speeds.

4.2 Computer output on microfilm (COM)

With computer output on microfilm, the output is recorded directly onto microfilm. The film bears a miniature image of what appears to be a printed document, although no original in fact exists.

The microfilm can be in the form of a strip or sheet. The microfilm can be made user-intelligible by special enlargers and printers.

The COM method is becoming increasingly popular. Its advantages are:

- stationery costs are reduced: reproductions made from a master microfiche are quite inexpensive
- transport is simple and cheap
- retrieval of information is easier: a reel of film can be coded and an automatic search facility provided in the viewer.

The disadvantages are:

- special equipment is needed to view the film (an enlarged image has to be projected onto a screen) and to provide a full size hard copy if required
- COM equipment is expensive (many organisations use a bureau service instead of buying their own)
- microfilm can only be used internally because of the need to provide viewing machines..

An example of the use of microfilm is in the motor trade: price lists of spare parts are now often supplied to dealers on microfiche, however CD-ROM is rapidly overtaking COM for high volume document storage.

5   Selection of output methods

The selection of output methods depends upon the needs of the user. The sorts of factors to consider are indicated below.

VDU
- Is the display suitable for long periods of continuous use and can the brightness and position of the screen be adjusted?
- How often is the display updated (i.e. refreshed)?
- Does the display flicker minutely, causing strain on the eyes?
- How many lines can be simultaneously displayed?
- How many characters per line can be displayed?

Printer
- What is the printed output to be used for? Is the print of an acceptable quality for (a) (i) internal use and (b) external use?
- Is the printer speed acceptable?
- Is the paper width compatible with the characters displayed on the VDU?
- Are supplies of stationery, ribbons or ink/toner cartridges readily available and reasonably priced?

- How noisy is the printer?
- What maintenance contracts are available?

Inevitably, the better the quality, design and flexibility of the equipment, the more expensive it may be and there is a continuous play-off between costs of those features and the benefits of them.

5.1   What makes a system user friendly?

A system is user friendly if the user is completely satisfied with the interaction they have with it. There are distinctly two types of user: novice and experts, and when designing the user interface it is important that all types of user are taken into consideration.

6   Human-computer interface

The human computer interface is the interface between the software system and the user of that system. The user is not interested in the internal workings of the system. It is about how the information is provided to and captured from the users. It is important to design this with full participation from the users to ensure the users are happy with the end product.

Once you know what the input, output, interface, dialogue and database for the system are, you can design the inside of the system, the part that will make the interface operate, generate output and access and update the database.

Getting the external design correct is vitally important for any computer system, partly because the users must be happy using the system, and partly because there are various legal obligations to adhere to regarding this design.

6.1   Components

A critical element in any system design is the human-computer interface. The components that make up the interface are the terminal and keyboard design, screen layout and appearance and the dialogue between the user and the system.

We shall first look at the characteristics that a well-designed human-computer interface will have. We then look at how different users have differing requirements of the interface. Finally, we look at the main components of the interface in detail.

6.2   Characteristics of a well-designed human-computer interface

The feature that defines a human-computer interface is the dialogue between user and machine.

A **human-computer dialogue** is an exchange of information between a user and the computer system, via an interactive terminal.

The dialogue consists of an exchange whereby, for example, the user will initiate a transaction by selecting a menu option. The system will prompt the user to input details of the transaction, or parameters of an enquiry, and will respond by acknowledging the transaction, or displaying the result of the enquiry. The acceptance of otherwise of a new information system may come to depend entirely on how 'friendly' this dialogue is to the users who have to learn and work with it.

Dialogue requirements

Dialogues should be:

1. **Natural.** The language of the dialogue, and the sequence of tasks, should be compatible with the user's view of the task being performed. Data should be presented in a logical way, and in the order that the user is accustomed to seeing it.

2. **Consistent.** There will normally be a style guide published both for the application system and the company that is installing it. This style guide will define the norms for screen layouts, colours used, date formats etc, so that users who need to access more than one system or dialogue in the system will recognise the layout and conventions and move from one to another without difficulty.

3. **Supportive.** Users should be guided as to how to enter any data, and should they make a mistake. There should be on-line help facilities to help people navigate through a dialogue, and to give context-specific assistance.

4. **Comfortable.** This can mean that the ergonomic design of the work station is comfortable for the users; it can also mean that the response time of the system is comfortable for the users. If it takes 20 seconds to display a response to a query, the users will feel anything but comfortable; they are more likely to feel frustrated or anxious. Conversely, if the system responds within 1/10 of a second, they are likely to feel intimidated by it, and so make more errors. A response time of 1-3 seconds is most comfortable for most users.

5. **Visible.** If a system is going to take many seconds to respond to a user's input, it should not leave an unchanged screen display with no clue for the user to follow; when that happens, the user is more likely to keep repeating the operation, or pressing the enter key, and delaying even more. Instead, there should be a message on screen saying that the transaction is being processed. An alternative would be to show an icon, such as an hourglass, or even a bar filling with a solid colour as the operation is carried out, with a percentage figure showing how much of the job is completed, and how much still to do. Whichever choice is made, the users are clear that their input is still being processed, and that they should wait.

6. **Helpful.** Error messages should be clear and meaningful. 'Capture Error X2259' does not help a user understand what they have done wrong; 'You have typed alphabetic characters into a numeric field' gives them a clearer insight into their mistake. As well as pointing out errors, the dialogue should allow them to correct the mistake, telling them what corrective action to take, rather than have to either carry on or abort the transaction.

7. **Recoverable.** It is very frustrating for users to be most of the way through a long transaction, only to lose everything if the system crashes. There should be the scope for saving work periodically through a data entry task, so that the users can pick up from where they left off when the system is restored

8. **Flexible.** The dialogue may be used by both experienced and naïve users. Naïve users (either brand new or occasional) will be glad for plenty of on-screen help; experienced users would not want the screen cluttered with unnecessary messages and guidance. There should be a way for users to select the interface and help level that suits them, rather than having to adapt their working practices to someone else's design

9. **Navigable**. Users should be able to see what to do at the end of any screen – whether they wish to repeat the action, perform another task, quit the system, or save the work they have completed. There should always be clear instructions for how to proceed.

KEY POINT

Usability describes how a
computer meets the dialogue
requirements.

The term given to the manner in which these criteria are met is **usability**.

Much of the development in personal computer software over the period since about 1987 has focused upon the interface. Certain characteristics may be identified in many modern PC packages that are common to any well-designed human-computer interface. These are that it should be:

- consistent in its appearance and underlying logic

- flexible in the way that the user interacts with the system, catering for users of differing skills levels

- perceived as being under the control of the user in terms of the order and pace of work.

Most of these objectives are met within the modern graphical user interfaces (GUI's) such as Windows®. However, communication between the user and the computer has not always been this easy, as this section will explain.

Much of the communication between the user and the computer takes place with the user facing a VDU screen, issuing commands via a keyboard and/or a mouse. This is the most flexible and interactive way for the system to relate to the user. The user is able to select programs for the computer to run, to enter data, and to control how the program runs. The key to good dialogue is user friendliness, and this is what the analyst must seek, building in suitable help facilities, tolerance for errors and permitting the user to easily correct typing errors.

KEY POINT

Ways to communicate with a
computer:

- answer questions

- select a menu option

- hot buttons

- fill in a form on screen

- use a graphical user
  interface.

There are five common ways for the user to communicate with the computer:

- by asking/answering questions posed by the computer

- by selection of an option from a menu

- by using **hot buttons**

- by filling in a screen based form

- by use of a graphical user interface (GUI).

6.3   Questions

This method of prompting a user response is less popular than it once was because of the possibility of error, but is still found in older systems and where appropriate in newer systems. It is very important to make it plain to the user what is expected of them, and to allow for the likely range of responses.

Thus:

Is this company an existing customer (Y/N)?

prompts the answer, but the program should still allow the user to type in either upper or lower case or to answer in full (yes or no).

Similarly:

Is the employee M (male) or F (female)?

should allow both upper and lower case or for the answers to be in full.

There is still a trap in the way this second question is posed, inviting the answer 'Yes' from a particularly facetious (or dim-witted!) user.

6.4   Menus

When there are a number of mutually exclusive options, a menu is a useful way to prompt input from a user (see figure below). The user may type the number relating to his or her choice, or may alternatively highlight the option required and press the enter key (or click the mouse button).

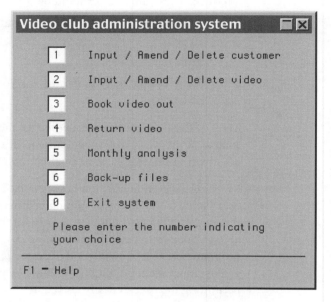

There may well be a series of menus, with one choice bringing a second menu on screen and so on as in the next figure.

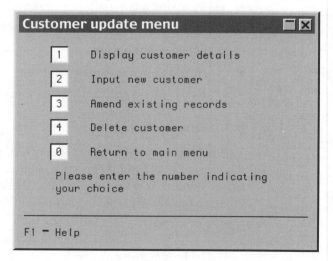

The F1 key is used to provide context sensitive help in the system shown above. Note that option 0 allows the user to go back to the main menu, perhaps to exit the system or to choose different processing options.

Menu systems are still found on many legacy DOS packages (or Windows packages that are based on an original DOS program). The main examples of these types of packages include stock enquiry systems and some sales systems, particularly in DIY and household furniture superstores. The package appears to be Windows-based, but you will notice a list of options on-screen that are the older DOS menu being made available, although the mouse can be used to click on the required menu number or option.

6.5   Hot buttons

When a user becomes very experienced at using a system, the menu can become a very tedious and long-winded process. To shortcut this process, an individual key can be used to enter a specific command. In the example used to illustrate the way that menus work, the user may be able to directly go to the 'input new customer' routing by pressing Control + E, i.e. holding the control key down while pressing E.

Many heavily used packages allow a choice of menu or hot button operation. Word for Windows, for example, allows the user to select operations using menus or using a combination of the control, shift and alt keys and letters on the keyboard (for example Control + S = Save).

6.6   Form filling

In many systems where records containing a number field have to be entered, they will be typed onto a screen-based form as in the figure below. The form will be laid out in attractive and clear format using different colours and boxes drawn on the screen to make it clearer and easier to fill in. Reverse video may be used to make it obvious to the user how wide a field is, and blinking messages and sound used to show when the user has made an error. The user may move from field to field using the tab or cursor movement keys, or may be moved automatically to the next field.

```
┌──────────────────────────────────────────┬───┐
│ Video customer entry screen               │▭ ✕│
├──────────────────────────────────────────┴───┤
│                                               │
│       Account number 9406012                  │
│                                               │
│     Surname      ┌──────────────────────┐     │
│                  └──────────────────────┘     │
│     Forenames    ┌──────────────────────┐     │
│                  └──────────────────────┘     │
│     Style (Mr/Ms/Mrs) ┌─────────────┐         │
│                       └─────────────┘         │
│     Address      ┌──────────────────────┐     │
│                  └──────────────────────┘     │
│                  ┌──────────────────────┐     │
│                  └──────────────────────┘     │
│                  ┌──────────────────────┐     │
│                  └──────────────────────┘     │
│     Post code    ┌─────────────┐              │
│                  └─────────────┘              │
│  ─────────────────────────────────────────   │
│  F1-Help  F2-Store record  F3-Abandon operation │
│              PgDn-Next screen                 │
└───────────────────────────────────────────────┘
```

In this system the account number may be generated automatically, and a second screen used to enter personal details (such as date of birth, telephone number, sex).

Many systems use forms that mimic the hard copy originals. For entry of details from a cheque, for example, an exact duplicate of the cheque is displayed on screen and the user fills-in the relevant fields. This helps make inputting information relatively quick and easy, as the user is already familiar with the style of the form being input.

6.7   Graphical user interface (GUI)

Graphical user interfaces use images as well as words to prompt user choice. They are designed to dispel techno fear and make operation of the computer more intuitive for inexperienced users. Some GUIs are designed to make the screen look like an ordinary desk top, with folders representing applications or documents that the user can open as desired. GUIs are more commonly found on PCs but are also used in conjunction with 4GLs (fourth generation languages).

FOULKS LYNCH
PUBLICATIONS

Examples of GUIs include Windows, LUNIX and the operating systems pioneered by Apple on their Macintosh Computers.

Many PC applications packages use graphical user interfaces, including Excel, Word for Windows, WordPerfect for Windows, etc.

With the development of object orientated programming languages such as Visual Basic and Visual C++ which specialise in graphical applications, bespoke applications programs with GUIs are also becoming more common.

Graphical user interfaces are characterised by the following attributes:

- some form of pointing device, typically a mouse
- the ability to have multiple views of data and applications open simultaneously
- a high degree of command consistency between applications
- applications, data and commands represented on the screen by icons
- access to commands through pull down menus.

In this environment the command language has been replaced by manipulation of objects and icons on the screen. For example, if the user wanted to move a file from one directory to another, he would locate the file by opening the directory (in this environment a directory would be represented by an icon of a folder) in which it was stored, and then use the mouse to drag the file to the new directory (**drag and drop**). In this situation the user would not have to use the keyboard or recall any commands. GUI's can be described as employing WIMP – windows, icons, mouse and pull-down menu.

6.8 WIMP interface

Many graphical user interfaces are designed as WIMP interfaces. WIMP is an acronym, with the letters standing for Windows, Icons, Mouse, Pull-down menus.

(NB: Some authorities decode the acronym as standing for Windows, Icons, Mouse, Pointer).

Windows

A window is a section of the screen that is dedicated to a specific application or document. Windows can be opened or closed; moved around the screen; and changed in size by using a mouse and a pointer. Several applications can be operated at the same time, and the user can switch from one application to another just as could be done on a real desktop.

Icons

Icons are little images or graphical symbols representing objects or applications. The icon may be a proprietary trademark, or may represent an abstract idea graphically. To delete a file, for example, the file may be moved with the mouse until it has covered a 'trash can' icon. A file or disc recovery program might have a red cross as an icon and a help facility might be represented by a question mark.

Some examples of icons are as follows:

Trash can	Disk Doctor	Help	File manger
File deletion icon	Disk recovery routine	Help screens	File utilities

The user will click on an item with a mouse to select an application to run or an operation to carry out.

Mouse

A mouse is a small device consisting of a ball, a sensor to detect how the ball moves, and two or three buttons which can be clicked to initiate actions or held down to continue actions (such as moving a file, or changing the size of a window).

The mouse is moved around the surface of a desk or of a special mouse mat. As the mouse moves, the ball bearing rotates. This rotation is measured by the sensor and the movement of the mouse is reflected by the movement of a **pointer** on the screen.

Pointer

The pointer is an arrow that moves around the screen as the mouse is moved around the table. When the pointer is over the relevant icon, the mouse button is clicked to select the action of object being operated upon.

Pull-down menu (Pop-up menus)

An initial menu bar will be displayed along the top (or down the side) of the screen. One of the options will be selected and clicked upon with the mouse, and a second menu will be displayed.

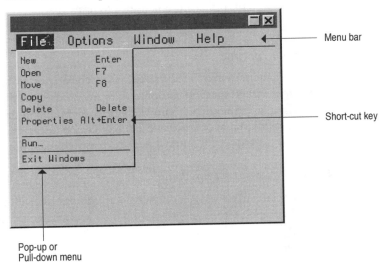

To save time for experienced users, some menu choices may be represented by specific keys or combinations of keys on the keyboard. The user then has two ways of selecting an operation – following the menus or hitting the shortcut keys.

6.9 Consistency

As the cost of hardware and software has fallen in recent years the major cost in systems has become the manpower to operate the system throughout its life. This is one of the factors that have led commercial software developers to focus upon the human-computer interface. In the early 1990s, Apple Computer Inc. publicised the findings of independent research that suggested the cost of operating the Apple Macintosh was significantly lower than with other kinds of personal computer because of its consistent user interface.

Consistency may also apply to the way that two different software packages function. For example the command to save a file may be the same in a word processing package as in a spreadsheet. If there is consistency of this kind the cost of training staff who already have some experience can be reduced. Microsoft products are also able to provide a consistent user interface.

6.10 Flexibility and user control

Another factor driving the improvement in the human-computer interface is the growing understanding among employers of the cost of low staff morale. Many factors affect staff morale, one of which is the degree of control the employee has over the pace and order of the work they are required to carry out. Computer systems that are designed to optimise the use of the hardware will rarely give the user any discretion over how the work is carried out. Employers were prepared to accept poorly designed interfaces when the cost of hardware was significantly higher than it is today. As the cost of high staff turnover and low morale have become widely understood, the economic argument has moved in favour of designing interfaces that do not interfere with the users' discretion over how to carry out their jobs.

6.11 Classification of users

The design of the user interface should take account of the kind of user likely to be using the system. It therefore is useful to draw distinctions amongst users and based upon differing requirements of the user interface.

Computer literacy

Computer literacy may be classified into two categories: general computer literacy and software package specific computer literacy. A user may be an expert in the use of a particular package but lack knowledge of computers in the wider sense, and obviously someone could have extensive knowledge of computers without any knowledge of a particular package. A well-designed system will meet the needs of both kinds of user.

General computer knowledge

Commercial software developers have tried hard to enable users who have good general computer knowledge to apply that knowledge to new systems. The design principle here is consistency. Various means have been used to achieve command consistency between software produced by different firms. In the case of Apple Computer Inc. and Microsoft inc. both have a set of standards which developers of software for the Apple Macintosh and Microsoft Windows are recommended to follow. Other firms have also developed guidelines to aid consistency of software developed internally and, in the case of some larger firms, these standards have been adopted outside the firm. Quasi-autonomous bodies set up to agree standards on many aspects of technology and computing are addressing the question of consistency.

Knowledge of a particular package

Where a user lacks knowledge of both the particular system and general computer knowledge, they should be able to gain assistance, guidance and help from the system itself without outside guidance.

Methods include:

- help screens
- tool tips. Information about the functions of buttons appear on-screen if the mouse pointer lingers over the button
- wizards. The package talks users through a procedure.

The same system should allow the user with good general computer knowledge, but new to the specific package, to make intuitive assumptions about operating the package with a high degree of success. As both types of user become more familiar with the system they should easily be able to memorise the commands and increase their productivity by means of short cuts that by-pass help messages and assistance.

Package developers and users of the package

System developers use software and systems to develop applications for use by end users who will work with the system to input and manipulate data. The difference between these two groups is important when dealing with complicated systems. The developers will need access to the full range of the system and its capabilities – this will impact upon the kind of interface they prefer. The end users of the same system will rarely need access to the full system, and to allow them this could suggest that the system was overly complex for the kind of task they need to carry out. End users normally need a simpler interface that reflects the nature of the tasks they need to do.

Occasional and frequent users

Distinctions may be drawn between the occasional and frequent user in terms of the extent of package specific knowledge each acquire of the system, the use they put the system to, the training they require and their tolerance to a poorly designed interface. Frequent users, typically:

- learn and retain a greater range of specific knowledge
- use the system to execute a fixed range of functions. The occasional user will typically use the system to make varied enquiries.
- require formal training because use of the system is an important aspect of their work
- have no alternative method of carrying out their jobs, so they are more likely to persevere in learning a system that has a poor interface.

6.12 Design elements of the human-computer interface

Work station ergonomics

Work station ergonomics includes all aspects of the terminal and keyboard design as well as the furniture, lighting and general environment. Here we identify just those aspects that relate to the terminal and keyboard design.

Terminal design

The screen should be adjustable in terms of height, angle and distance from the user. This should be independent of the keyboard adjustment described later.

Characters should not flicker or move. The use of certain kinds of fluorescent lighting with some terminals can cause these problems.

The screen should be free from glare and reflections. This should be a design feature of the terminal and not reliant upon adjustments to the ambient lighting.

The user should be able to choose either dark characters on a light background or vice versa. The contrast between the characters and background should be adjustable, as should the brightness.

The resolution of the screen should be capable of displaying sharp character images.

6.13 Keyboard design

Keyboard design is a factor that needs consideration in work station ergonomics. As individual preferences with regard to keyboard design can be quite different, the keyboard design should include adjustment in as many aspects as possible. The following are some of the design features that need consideration:

1   **Key force.** The pressure required is a function of the frequency of use. Frequent users may prefer a light touch, while infrequent and inexperienced users may prefer keyboards that require greater pressure.

2   **Key shape.** The top surface of the key should be concave with a reflection free finish.

3   **Keyboard height.** The height of the keyboard should be adjustable. There should be some device that users can rest their wrists on, and this should also be adjustable.

4   **Keyboard angle**. This should be adjustable and in the range 10 to 15 degrees from horizontal.

6.14 Screen design

Layout of the display

The location of data on the screen can greatly affect the ease with which the user can locate the precise information required, and this affects the stress associated with using the system. The following suggestions are based upon what any user would expect to find on a paper-based form.

- ensure that there is sufficient space between items to ensure that they appear separate and distinct.

- place important and frequently used data on the left side of the screen and arrange in descending order of importance from top to bottom.

- where columns are needed give the eye something to follow when moving from one column to another to avoid accidentally changing rows

- group items together logically, and possibly put boundaries around the groups to indicate the grouping.

What to display

The screen design should always be easy to read, presenting its information in a clear and tidy manner. It should be free from any information not relevant to the task the screen or system is intended to aid. Good design principles are:

- clearly show the users what they are required to do

- display only the information essential to carrying out an action or making a decision

- display all the information needed to execute a task on a single screen. The user should not need to refer to other screens.

Input screens

The layout of input screens should be influenced by the source of the data.

1   **Data from paper forms.** Where the data is to be input from a paper form, then the screen layout should follow the paper form. This approach is recommended because users in these circumstances will typically be high frequency ones, with good package specific knowledge. This means that they will only infrequently look at the input screen whilst entering data, because their attention will be on the paper form. Therefore they can enter the data in each of the boxes on the paper form and press, say, the enter key to confirm the entry of that part of the data and automatically move to the next box which corresponds to the next box on the paper form.

2   **Capturing data at source.** Where data is supplied from other sources the screen itself becomes the form that asks for the information the system needs. Here the screen should be designed using the same principles of paper form design, where the label for each box that needs to be completed clearly indicates the data to be entered into the box.

6.15 Response time

There are two aspects of response time which concern the human-computer interface:

- time between the user giving a command and the command being completed

- time taken to refresh the screen when new characters are entered from the keyboard.

Screen refresh rates are critical for any application where the user will enter large quantities of data. Examples include word processing and database entry. This aspect of response time is largely a function of hardware or communications capacity.

The following guidelines are pertinent to response times applying to commands:

1   **Frequently used commands** should take less than one second.

2   **System response to commands.** When a user has given a command he should be able to see that the system has acted upon it, and then see the result of the command. For example, where the user closes a window on a screen, that window should not instantly disappear; instead, it should either shrink or turn into a shadow and then disappear.

3   **Consistent response.** A consistent response time for a particular command should be sought. This may mean slowing down some variants of the command.

4   **Notice of delayed response.** If the response time will be longer than the user has become accustomed to, the system should either state that the request is being worked upon or state how long the request will take to complete. More sophisticated systems will show the user details of the progress in performing a lengthy command, and also give the user the opportunity to abort the request.

6.16 Error handling

Error handling is an important part of the user interface particularly during the learning stage. Often users are reluctant to start learning the package for fear of making irrecoverable errors.

The system should prevent errors taking place by always showing the user what is required next. The system should cater for the inexperienced user by clearly showing how to get detailed context sensitive help.

Where a user carries out an incorrect action, the system should immediately identify this before any harm is done. The system should then explain to the user why what was done was incorrect. When an error is detected, only that part of the input that is incorrect should need to be re-keyed. Deficiencies in this aspect of the user interface can infuriate users with limited keyboard skills; having to re-key a screen of data because the wrong date format has been used can alienate a new user at a critical phase in their introduction to the system. Correction of the date format is an example of where systems can often correct invalid entries. Where there is a fairly limited range of codes or commands, the system can suggest a correct entry after an invalid one has been detected.

Systems should enable users to reverse commands they have given. Whilst the command may have been a valid one in terms of the system definition, users may change their minds or realise they have made an error. The ability to reverse back through the most recent commands will reduce the stress levels upon new users who are unnecessarily slow in the use of the system whilst they double check all of their entries and command choices. This facility is equally useful to the expert who carries out commands very quickly but is still likely to make mistakes.

6.17 The dialogue between the system and the user

The dialogue between the user and the system can take a number of different forms. Which one is chosen should be contingent upon:

* the kind of users (frequent or infrequent, new or experienced)
* the other dialogues in use in the environment
* the nature of the tasks to be carried out.

The following is a description of the main categories of dialogue between the user and the system.

Menus

Menus are the most popular type of dialogue. The user is presented with a menu of choices and is required to choose one. This is done by highlighting it with the cursor, or by keying the menu item number, or by use of the arrow keys, or by keying in all or part of the menu item name.

Menus are usually assembled into a hierarchy, with main menus leading on to sub-menus and so on. Users with knowledge of the package may navigate around the system, by-passing the menu hierarchy by memorising menu references. Therefore the menu system can satisfy both novice and expert users.

Forms

Forms, as the name suggests, appear like a paper-based form, where the user is required to fill in boxes. This approach is typically used in database applications to enter data and with some applications also to retrieve it. The use of colour to distinguish between labels and data is helpful. Some systems provide additional information on the data to be entered into each box. This additional information appears when the cursor is placed in the box concerned.

Command language

Command languages are becoming a less popular method of user interface, generally being restricted to use by the computer specialist. However nearly all computer systems incorporate an operating system which is operated by a command language, and many users will occasionally use a very restricted range of commands e.g., copying files, making and renaming directories.

Typically, command languages have a strict format for each command, which is then followed by the **arguments**, which specify the details for the command.

7   Input and output design

For a computer system to perform effectively, it must be able to interface effectively with its environment. The most important elements of the environment are people – the people preparing and inputting the data, the people running the system, the people receiving output. It is crucial to ensure that communication between these people and the system is as effective as possible. A great deal of effort must be put in to designing the forms, dialogue and output for the system.

Communication between the system and its users can be put into four categories:

- input design
- document and code design
- dialogue design
- output design.

Input design

Input design must concern itself with a number of factors – with the collection of data itself, with the entry of data into the computer, and with the validation of the data. The systems analyst must be concerned not only with the needs of the system, but also with the capabilities of the people inputting the data.

A number of things should be considered when planning the input for the system:

- What sort of program-run mode is this designed for – will it be run on a batch-processing basis, or will there be an on-line system?
- Is it possible to input data directly by machine? The use of devices such as bar code readers or magnetic ink character readers will streamline data input and reduce the risk of error.
- What is the volume of data input? It is important to consider not only the average volume of input but also its range and seasonality.
- Will data need to be transcribed from its original source before it is input?
- Is some part of the data already entered into the system?
- How should the accuracy of the data be ensured? The analyst should consider not only that data should be entered as accurately as required but also that no data is missed or entered twice. The data control routines will vary according to whether the system is run in batch or on-line mode, and whether data input is mechanised or not.

7.1   Document and code design

Input documents have two roles to play. Data is collected onto them, and they are then used as a base for entry onto a computer. There are a number of techniques available for helping to reconcile these sometimes conflicting requirements, but document design is largely a matter of common sense.

The careful design of documents is an essential ingredient of an effective system. Documents should provide an efficient means of transmitting information. There are many costs associated with the use of documentation and inefficient document design will cause additional costs to the business. Costs associated with document design include:

Cost of printing

As a general rule, standard size documents are preferred (e.g. A4, A5) as they are less expensive than special sizes. Documentation used solely for internal purposes may use lower quality paper and printing than those used for external purposes where the company will wish to use top-quality stationery to impress customers and others. Multi-part stationery is more expensive than single part.

Handling costs

Input forms must be easy to complete and to enter into the computer. If a form is inefficiently designed it may not be used properly. For example a customer sends a cheque for the current month balance only, rather than the total sum due, because a statement does not clearly show the total due. Internal documents may cause delay or additional management time if they do not contain all the information that is needed. A form that is not clearly identified may be mistaken for a different document. Some documents may be handled frequently and so must be capable of standing up to regular use, e.g. audit working papers.

7.2   The document description/document analysis form

When an analyst is recording facts about the existing system he will be interested in the documents that are used in the system. The documents will often help to clarify the existing procedures and controls. In a similar way an auditor may well examine documents within a client's accounting system. The analyst may wish to include in his own files copies of documents used in the system, both blank documents and some with specimen data entered.

The documents themselves cannot give a complete picture and to supplement them the analyst may complete a **document description** form. An example of such a form is given below with a brief explanation of the data to be included in it:

1   **Title** – gives the form title and number with details of any alternative name commonly used for this document in the company.

2   **Purpose** – a brief description of the purpose of the document. This may help to identify unnecessary documents/copies.

3   **Originated by** – gives the place and means of origination and may identify the means of combining existing documents.

4   **Used by** – this should be related to the purpose of the document to ensure that it is only sent to those who need it. It may indicate the suitability of the layout for the user's needs.

5   **Number of copies** – minimum, average, maximum, seasonal fluctuations.

6   **Contents** – it is essential for each data item to be clearly indicated on the document. The size column indicates the maximum number of characters making up that field.

7   **Sequence** – used where the sequence of field names is different from that in the previous section.

8   **Data dictionary reference** – organisations with complex database systems will often have a data dictionary. The document may affect data on the database, and the database dictionary will refer to that document. A unique reference is needed.

Shown below is an example of a document description form.

Title of document				Project Name Date	
Purpose					
Originated by					
Used by					
Number of Copies			Minimum Average Maximum	} Per	
No	Field Name		Size	Comments	
Sequence of data fields					
Remarks					

7.3   Document design hints

The content and design of a document will be governed largely by its purpose and the system of which it forms part.

There follows some general advice on the design of a document for an examination answer.

Determine the purpose of the document

In an exam, read the question carefully and decide what the document is for. You may find that it is created to provide information (e.g. to management). You may conclude that this information (the output) should be contained along the bottom row or along the right hand column of the document.

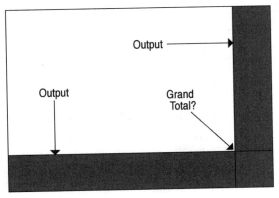

Determine the input data required

Your document will probably have to show the data items that are used to determine the output. For example, to determine the value of an invoice (output) one needs to show what has been sold, the unit price, the price net of VAT, the VAT amount and the gross price (input).

Decide the order in which to record the data

You should work from left to right across your document or work down from top to bottom (i.e. the process is left to right or top to bottom).

Size of the document

It was suggested earlier that documents should be a standard size. The document must be big enough to contain all the data and be easily read but not so big as to be difficult to handle and file. The solution in the examination is normally easy – use one whole sheet of A4 for each document that you have to design. This means that you have a suitably sized document and you do not have to draw the borders.

Title

The title of a form is important. It should be descriptive and preferably short. If the question in the examination gives the form a title, then use that in your answer. Write the title of the form IN BLOCK CAPITALS across the top of your answer.

Reference numbers

These are useful for re-ordering purposes. The document number should be placed in a corner of the document so that it can easily be identified when held in a file.

Headings

It is important that as much data as possible is pre-printed on the document so that only variable data needs to be entered when the document is used. Watch out in particular for the need to include:

- dates, e.g. DD, MM, YY. This is important in multi-national systems, since different countries have different standard ways of displaying dates.
- units, e.g. hours, kilos
- instructions, e.g.   Write your name here. Please return this remittance advice with your cheque.

Multi-part sets of documents

It is often effective to print several copies of a document together on multi-part stationery, usually each copy being a different colour. Remember that it is essential to have the same data at the same position on each copy but that lower copies may have information blanked-out of them. For example the price of goods is shown on the invoice copy but not on the despatch note copy.

Control and authorisation

Many documents will be sequentially pre-numbered and may have space for authorisation, perhaps at various levels. If you think the control and authorisation methods are appropriate include them.

In the examination, it is important above all that your answer *looks like a document* that could conceivably *meet the objective described in the question.* You may find it useful with the examination in mind to study documents which you come across at work. Consider the contents and layout. Why has a particular design been used? Could it be improved in any way? You will find some examples of questions requiring document design in the next section of the manual.

7.4   Output design

Output must be clear, precise and informative. A considerable amount of thought and effort is put into designing the output since, for users, it is the most important part of any system.

The first choice that will have to be made is the output medium. The two most common output media are the VDU, for temporary (or soft) copy, and printers for permanent (or hard) copy. Other output media that are sometimes useful include COM (computer output to microform), graph plotters and 35mm cameras (for directly produced slides).

Output design may also be assisted by the use of prototyping. Particularly in the case of Windows applications, example screens can be produced very quickly using 4GL's and screen designers. These will help the user understand the look and feel of any screen before software is written to produce that design. Many 4GL's will produce code that can be incorporated into the final design software design, saving extensive re-programming work.

7.5   VDU display

The VDU is an excellent medium when decisions must be made immediately, or where the user is working interactively. If a sales order clerk is speaking on the telephone to the customer, the computer will report whether stock levels are high enough to service the order, and the clerk can accept the order.

When designing an output screen the analyst must be sparing with the amounts of information displayed, and ensure that the screen is clear and easy to understand. The screen should identify what is being displayed and screen layouts should be designed to fit a common style – making it easy for the user to know precisely where to look for the information displayed. Usually information will continue to be displayed until the user takes some action – such as pressing the enter key. Many systems allow users the option of producing hard copy of what appears on the screen when required.

Print-out design

After the systems analysis process has identified what output is required, it will need to be designed. Its structure will depend upon the use that will be made of it. There are basically two categories of printed out documents:

- working documents – invoices, purchase orders, statements, etc
- information presentation documents – analysis of sales, reports, etc.

7.6   Working documents

For working documents everything is subordinated to making the document functionally efficient and effective. Many such documents are printed onto multi-part pre-printed stationery. This stationery will be designed to fit the standard house style of the organisation. The information, which varies, is printed on to the stationery at the time of document production.

The information printed at the bottom of the following statement can be read directly using an optical character reader (OCR). This cuts down the amount of clerical work required to input the details of payment received. This sort of document is known as a 'turn around' document.

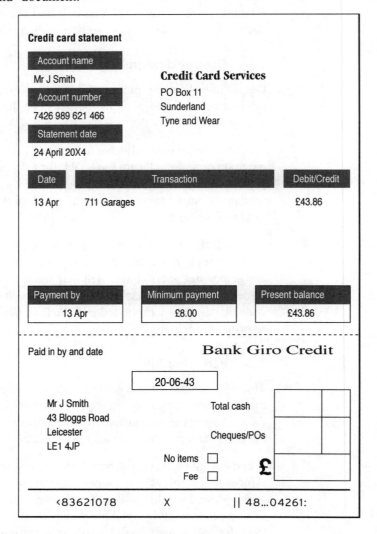

7.7   Information presentation documents

These documents are designed to be clear and understandable. As can be seen in the example below, the report specified when it was produced, what information is being presented, and what time period is covered.

J Bright

Pareto report

List of customers in diminishing size

Produced: 16.4.X4

Period covered: March 20X4

Customer	Total Sales	Cumulative sales	
A Jury plc	£66,486	£66,486	(33%)
B Kenwright	£33,204	£99,690	(50%)
C Lamb & Co	£20,310	£120,000	(60%)

Conclusion

In this chapter, you have learnt about the importance of provide good output design, whether that is the VDU screen or paper print-outs. The issue of how to ensure that the design is acceptable to the users has also been explained.

SELF-TEST
QUESTIONS

Input devices

1   List the main forms of input to a computer system. (2)

Output devices

2   What factors affect your choice of a Visual Display Unit? (4)

Human-computer interface

3   What are the three most important characteristics of a well–designed human computer interface? (6.2)

4   What are the main attributes of a GUI? (6.7)

Input and output design

5   What is the purpose of a document description form? (7.2)

FOULKS LYNCH
PUBLICATIONS

Report layout

The extract below from a report shows information about stock levels.

The report has two main purposes.

- to highlight products that are below their re-order level
- to compare the total 'value at re-order level' with the total 'stock value'. The organisation requires that total 'stock value' should not exceed total 'value at re-order level' by more than 10%.

Required:

(a)   Most organisations have standards for the layout of such reports. For example, the standards may require that each report should have a title (as in stock level report).

List *five* further standard items that might apply to any system generated report. These standards may or may not have been adhered to by the stock level report extract.   **(5 marks)**

(b)   Briefly describe three ways in which the usability of the stock level report might be improved taking into account the main purposes of the report. (Credit will not be given for standards issues already listed in part (a) of this question).

(6 marks)

(c)   The accurate data entry of stock information is essential. In what way can errors be reduced when entering data into the system?   **(4 marks)**

(Total: 15 marks)

Report extract

Stock level report						
Product code	*Cost per unit*	*Units in stock*	*Stock value*	*Re-order level*	*Below re-order level*	*Value at re-order level*
98765	30	20	600	15		450
98766	60	7	420	5		300
98767	59	30	1770	40	********	2360
98768	45	21	945	23	********	1035
98769	23	53	1219	70	********	1610
98770	40	112	4480	110		4400
98771	30	67	2010	50		1500
98772	10	9	90	5		50
98773	40	7	280	5		200
98774	30	23	690	25	********	750
98775	25	45	1125	50	********	2250
98776	45	32	1440	30		1350
98777	12	10	120	10		120
98778	15	15	225	10		150
98779	45	45	2025	50	********	2250
98780	10	30	300	25		250
98781	45	67	3015	50		2250
98782	23	54	1242	50		1150

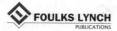

FOULKS LYNCH
PUBLICATIONS

98783	80	20	1600	10		800
98784	12	78	936	15		180
98785	56	58	3248	50		2800
98786	12	12	144	10		120
98787	6	90	540	100	********	600
98788	50	2	100	5	********	250
98789	78	1	78	5	********	390
Total	881	908	28642			27565

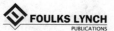

Chapter 11
SOFTWARE DELIVERY

This chapter investigates the different methods of obtaining software for use within an organisation. The approach to selecting software via the invitation to tender is looked at in some detail, along with the various methods of actually writing that software when the successful tenderer has been chosen.

Objectives

By the time you have finished this chapter you should be able to:

- define the bespoke software approach to fulfilling the user's information system requirements

- briefly describe the tasks of design, programming and testing required in developing a bespoke systems solution

- define the application software package approach to fulfilling the user's information system requirements

- briefly describe the tasks of package selection, evaluation and testing required in selecting an appropriate application software package

- describe the relative merits of the bespoke systems development and application software package approaches to fulfilling an information systems requirement

- describe the structure and contents of an Invitation To Tender (ITT)

- describe how to identify software packages and their suppliers that may potentially fulfil the Information Systems requirements

- develop suitable procedures for distributing an ITT and dealing with subsequent enquiries and bids

- describe a process for evaluation the application software package, the supplier of that package and the bid received from the supplier

- describe the risks of the application software package approach to systems development and how these might be reduced or removed.

1　Software solutions

There are various ways to produce a software solution for a systems project.

- purchase a standard software package and use this without any modification

- purchase a standard software package and make suitable amendments to customise this for the organisation's specific requirements

- purchase a standard software package and add company specific modules as necessary

- pay for a bespoke system to be developed using existing hardware.

KEY POINT

Software sources:

- standard package

- customised standard package

- standard package plus additions

- bespoke package.

This chapter investigates the two main forms of purchase, namely the use of an **application package off-the-shelf** and the writing of a **bespoke package** (a purpose-written system). The other purchase options have similar advantages and disadvantages, particularly when compared to the bespoke solution, so they are not mentioned again in detail in this chapter.

FOULKS LYNCH
PUBLICATIONS

2   Bespoke software (purpose-written systems)

Bespoke (i.e. tailor-made or purpose-written) applications are constructed by programmers to meet the specific needs of the particular organisation in which they are found. The process of programming is extremely time-consuming and expensive, but is often the only alternative if the application is very specialised.

2.1   Preparing a bespoke system

Before a bespoke system can be implemented into an organisation, there are various design and build stages that must be completed in order to provide a relevant and robust package for that organisation. Writing bespoke software is similar to producing any other software in that the software development and testing cycle must be followed.

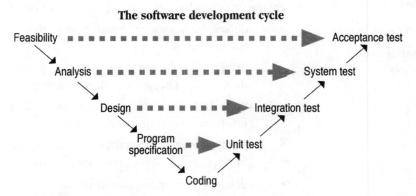

The software development cycle

The feasibility and analysis stages will normally have been covered as part of the standard system development life cycle (chapter 7). This means that the analysis of the requirements of the software will be available.

The design phase will involve producing a systems design specification, probably in the form of a requirements specification that can be distributed to potential writers of the software. This document will form part of the Invitation To Tender (see below) which is sent out to suppliers. Responses to the Invitation To Tender will have to be evaluated and a supplier chosen prior to the detailed program specification being produced.

Alternatively the software can be written in-house using the organisation's own software development team.

Once the builders of the new system have been selected, and the requirements specification for the new system completed, the team will consider the options of writing completely new software programs, or amending existing programs to meet the organisation's requirements. Part of this choice may be within the Invitation To Tender responses, especially where a software house has identified time and cost savings from amending some of the existing software. As usual, users' input will be requested at the design stage to ensure that the final system will meet their requirements in terms of functionality and usability. Prototyping may also be used to assist in trapping user requirements.

Detailed work will also be required to check the structure of existing databases and field design in the existing programmes that the bespoke system will need to communicate with. The bespoke software will need to exchange data with other programs, so it is important that the file organisation written into this system is compatible with existing software in the organisation.

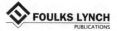

After coding of the software, the three testing stages (unit, system, user) will be undertaken to test the individual unit of the software, then the integration with other modules in that particular program suite, and finally the integration with other software programmes in the organisation. Testing is crucial in the bespoke solution to ensure that proprietary and bespoke programs can 'talk' to each other correctly.

Finally, the users of the software will perform an acceptance test, prior to sign-off of the software and its implementation into the organisation.

2.2   Advantages and disadvantages of bespoke systems

Advantages
- They are written to fit the organisation's information needs precisely.
- The organisation has complete discretion over the design of data structures.
- The system can be integrated with other applications within the organisation.
- The system can be modified to fit changing needs of the user over time.
- Bespoke systems might give a company a competitive advantage in the market place, if they can do more than competitors' computer systems.

If the programs are of interest to other organisations, they can be sold (or licensed). the information services group can thus become a profit centre.

Disadvantages
- System development takes a long time, which delays the implementation of the system.
- Bespoke systems are costly to develop and test.
- There is a greater probability of bugs (software errors) in a bespoke system.
- Support for a bespoke system will be expensive. The organisation has to bear all the cost.

2.3   Risks of bespoke application software development

The risks of using bespoke application software mainly relate to the disadvantages listed above. These risks can be overcome by:

- ensuring that users are involved at all stages in the design of the software. Any amendments to the design must be discussed with the users, and acceptable compromises found

- either, taking the support and maintenance of the software in-house, or continuing the contract with the supplier with an escrow agreement in place. Providing maintenance in-house has the distinct disadvantage that programmers may not be fully aware of how the software was written. Trying to provide support will therefore be time consuming and potentially very costly if the software is amended incorrectly

- the data structures for the other software programs to be accessed must be stated clearly within the invitation to tender or subsequent software analysis documentation. While this may not overcome all errors in design, placing the data structures in a formal document will ensure that the supplier has notice of them, and must legally attempt to adhere to that specification.

FOULKS LYNCH
PUBLICATIONS

3   Invitations To Tender

An Invitation To Tender (ITT) is a document inviting suppliers to make a bid for the supply of some specific software (or hardware) to the purchasing company. The invitation may be sent out to specific suppliers, or made as a general invitation to any supplier, perhaps via an advert in a trade journal.

The invitation to tender is likely to be for hardware, a substantial application package or for the development of a bespoke system by an outside contractor.

The ITT will define what needs to be done to achieve the system objectives and act as a basis for suppliers to put together and present their proposals.

3.1   Contents of an ITT

The invitation to tender will normally contain the following sections:

- letter of invitation
- instructions to tenderers
- conditions of contract
- form of letter and schedules
- requirements specification
- software engineering requirements.

The same format can be used for purchasing bespoke solutions or off-the-shelf packages, although in the latter case, details of software engineering may be very limited as the package is likely to require only minimal amendments.

Letter of invitation

This is the formal invitation to tender. It will specify:

- the date for submission of tenders
- contact names for technical queries
- contact names for contractual queries
- a warning that tenders received after the due date may not be considered.

Instructions to tenderers

These instructions advise the tenderer what to do and how to tender for the contract. Many of the points may seem obvious, but they have to be stated to avoid any mis-understanding. The instructions will include:

- alternatives and options where the tendered may suggest different methods of achieving a requirement in the requirements specification, but with improved efficiency or reduced cost.
- additional information that may be available from the supplier
- period of validity of the ITT
- a statement indicating whether or not prices can be varied for changes in labour rates or materials costs
- statement on the basis for prices
- statement on compliance – that is areas of the tender that the tenderer cannot comply to, with reasons for this non-compliance.

Conditions of the contract

The conditions of the contract apply to the terms of the supply of the software itself. The important areas to be included in this contract will include:

The conditions of the contract apply to the terms of the supply of the software itself. The important areas to be included in this contract will include:

Visibility of the supplier's activities during development	The purchaser needs to be able to contact the supplier as the contract progresses to ensure that the software being designed actually meets the requirements specification and that the contract is running to schedule. As some of the work may be undertaken away from the supplier's premises, then providing appropriate contact arrangements is important.
Purchaser response to queries	The contract will specify timescales for the purchase to respond to queries raised by the supplier. The aim is to ensure that work is not unduly delayed by slow response times.
Ownership rights in software	The actual ownership of software is not always clear. The contract needs to state that ownership passes to the purchaser, normally after the supplier has been paid, to avoid subsequent dispute in this area.
Patents, design rights and copyright	The main issue here is intellectual property rights, and whether the software written infringes on copyright of any existing software. The supplier will normally indemnify the purchaser against any breach of copyright; in effect, the supplier is confirming that the software is original work and does not infringe any other copyrights.
Indemnity and insurance	The supplier will need to arrange for appropriate insurance covering areas such as professional indemnity, product liability and legal expenses. Third party consequential damages may also be considered, although consequential loss may also be excluded by the contract.
Acceptance	How the supplier will know whether or not the purchaser has accepted the software. Some formal sign-off agreement will be stated with an acceptance certificate being produced as evidence of this.
Warranty period	This is the amount of time during which the supplier will amend the software for errors found in it. The warranty will include any errors noted in the acceptance certificate, but will exclude defects caused by the purchaser amending the software.
Maintenance and enhancement	The purchaser may ask the supplier to continue to support the software by providing ongoing maintenance and upgrades to the software. Alternatively, responsibility for these can be taken in-house.
Insolvency or bankruptcy	In case of insolvency or bankruptcy of the supplier, the purchaser will normally need access to the source code of the software so that it can be amended and upgraded in the future. One method of achieving this aim is to place the source code with a third party, to be released only if the supplier is insolvent or bankrupt. This arrangement is commonly called an 'escrow' agreement.
Performance and completion time	The contract will provide a timetable showing important milestones and estimated completion time for the software.
Confidentiality	Both the supplier and the purchaser will agree to keep confidential information that is not in the public domain. Confidentiality constraints apply to any sub-contractors as well as the main contractor.
Insurance copies	An explanation of whether additional copies of the software are available in case of loss or damage at the purchaser.

Form of letter and schedules

The tenderer will need to commit, in relatively high-level terms, to some additional information regarding the supply of the software and subsequent support after successful installation.

Price and timescales for completion of the work and also for amendments and maintenance in the future.

The tenderer will be required to state whether they comply with the requirements in the ITT. If compliance to specific sections cannot be given then these will be stated within the response to the ITT.

The tenderer will also have to supply some basic technical and project information concerning the software to be written and the method of writing the software. This information may be supplied in a form which the supplier produces

The requirements specification

The ITT will also include the detailed requirements specification. Details of a requirements specification are covered in chapters 7, 8 and 9.

Software engineering requirements

This section asks the tenderer to provide an overview of the life-cycle method that will be used to produce the software. It provides the supplier with confidence that recognised design principles will be used to write the software.

3.2   Identifying suitable suppliers

Identifying potential suppliers of software can be difficult. Although there is no absolute rule for identifying all possible suppliers of software on the market, there are a number of avenues that can be explored:

1   **Suppliers to other organisations**. An examination of the hardware or software used by comparable organisations can reveal the existence of suitable products, and how popular they are with their current users.

2   **Trade magazines**. A trawl of trade magazines will find appropriate advertisements and trade reviews and articles. Each of these must be examined critically – it should not be assumed that the articles and reviews are necessarily independent or unbiased.

3   **Consult an expert.** The company may consult with an expert. This expert may be a computer consultant with experience in the application being computerised, or may be employed by a dealer or retail establishment. It is important to consider the independence and motivation of the advice given – a dealer, for example, may receive a higher profit margin on one product than another.

When a list of suppliers has been drawn up, then the ITT can be sent and responses to this awaited!

4   Evaluating supplier proposals

Once the proposals have been received from potential suppliers, they must be compared with what was requested in the tender document, and the best one selected. The criteria used to judge the proposals can be put into three categories:

Technical performance

How closely do the suppliers' proposals tally with the hardware and software requirements specified in The Invitation To Tender Document?

Cost

What is the overall cost of the package offered by each supplier?

Customer support

How good is the after-sales service and warranty offered by the supplier?

Attempt to obtain the hardware and software from the same source and with a guarantee that they will be compatible. If bought from different sources and the system does not work, one supplier can blame the other's product.

4.1   Evaluating software proposals

There are many points to consider when evaluating possible purchases of application software (off-the-shelf packages). It is often useful to make out a checklist of the points that are most salient to the user. Some of the points that may be included on the checklist are:

How well the software fits the needs of the organisation.	This does not necessarily imply that every single requirement is satisfied – the users may be able to compromise, or to satisfy their information needs in some other way.
Can the software be tailored to fit the organisation's needs?	Sometimes packages can be modified by the supplier (at a cost) and, on other occasions, a package may have sufficient flexibility to allow the users to adapt it as required.
Other facilities.	Has the software any extra facilities that can be exploited by the organisation?
How well does the organisational structure fit in with the demands placed on it by the software?	The users should only acquire the software if no changes in structure are needed, or if any such changes will increase efficiency. A centralised system to help the sales force plan its calls efficiently would not be suitable where the sales people do not regularly visit the head office.
Will existing hardware need to be upgraded or replaced?	Many modern PC applications are very hungry for internal memory or hard disk space, and may not be capable of running on older machinery.
Is the software compatible with existing software and file structures?	A change to a new word processing package, for example, may require all existing documents to be converted to the new format. A supplier that is eager for business may well agree to carry out the conversion process.
Is the software compatible with the organisation's future requirements?	The users may be planning to migrate to a new operating system, which would make it necessary to acquire software compatible with the new operating environment.
Under what conditions is the software being supplied?	Extra payments may be payable each year; use of the software may be restricted to single machines; a site licence may be needed for use on more than one machine; use may be restricted to machines at a single location.

What protective measures has the supplier taken against unauthorised duplication?	Although suppliers are justified in protecting their software, the measures they take can sometimes cause operational problems. The user may be unable to take a back-up copy of the original disk that the software was supplied on. If the system becomes corrupted the user may have to obtain a replacement from the supplier. There may be a delay of several days before the system can be used again.
How fast does the system run?	The user will need to be assured that the system can cope with the volumes of data that will need to be processed and stored – some software that can look satisfactory when demonstrated by a salesperson can be unusable when asked to deal with volumes of data that are greater than it was designed for.
Can the software be adequately demonstrated?	The supplier is often able to show a special demonstration version of the software running. Sometimes a restricted version (or even a full version) of the software can be lent to the user for a period of time. Many suppliers make lists of existing customers. These can be visited to see the system running in a real situation. Seeing software running can give the user a 'feel' for how it works and can provide reassurance as to its suitability.
How user friendly is the software?	It must be both easy to use and tolerant to user error. Menus, graphical interfaces and clear prompts make the software easier to use, and attractive and uncluttered screen designs make the system enjoyable to use. One strategy used by software designers to make their products user-friendly is to mimic the look and feel of more familiar software. Lotus 1-2-3, for example, is often used as a pattern for other software – both spreadsheets and other types of software.
Documentation must be both comprehensive and comprehensible.	Documentation can be at several levels, ranging from brief reference cards, through easily understood user guides to system manuals that can act as a technical reference to specialist and experienced users.
How will the user acquire the expertise to run the system?	Most suppliers offer training, and both internal and external courses may be appropriate ways for users to learn how to operate the system. Well-known packages often have many experienced users who may already be employed or who can be hired in. On-screen and written tutorials allow users to learn at their own speed.
How wide is the customer base of the software?	The existence of a large number of customers provides several benefits. Most of the bugs in the software will have been identified and corrected. There is likely to be a reservoir of expertise that can be exploited by the user, and books may have been written and training courses developed. The user can be assured that they will get what they expect from the software.
Does the software have any security features?	User numbers, passwords and encryption are useful for protecting confidential data on all types of software, and are absolutely vital in multi-user and networked systems.
What sort of maintenance and after-sales service is offered?	Maintenance and after sales service is just as important for software as it is for hardware. A maintenance fee will usually be payable for bespoke software just as it is for hardware. The availability of a help desk is very helpful to an organisation. Many suppliers charge a subscription for access to a help desk, and some suppliers charge for each call asking for advice. The existence of this kind of charge should be a disincentive towards buying a particular software package.

Are future versions of the software likely to become available?

Many software suppliers allow users to obtain updated versions of packages at advantageous rates. If an updated version is *not* bought, the users must assure themselves that the supplier will continue to support the older versions. The user can suffer disastrous problems if support is not kept up. An example of what can happen is as follows:

A small business acquired one of the biggest selling PC accounts packages. The version of the software that they bought was one for a different type of microcomputer. This particular version of the package did not allow for a non-integer percentage Value Added Tax. By the time the software house had found someone capable of updating the package, the small business had been forced to go back to a manual invoicing system.

What is the cost of the software?

All aspects of cost must be included in the user's calculations – purchase price, site licenses, maintenance, the cost of access to help, training costs, etc.

4.2   Selecting an application package

Organisations have a great deal in common with one another – the core information processing activities are likely to be very similar from one company to the next. The basic accounting functions, for example, apply to a large majority of businesses. Many applications are served by packages that can be obtained off-the-shelf, although care must be taken in choosing the appropriate package for the specific organisation.

The selection of application package will depend on a variety of factors including those summarised in the table below:

User requirements	The package will be reviewed to check that it meets the functional requirements of users in terms of volume of data to be input and processed, format of output, number of users etc.
Cost	Although the organisation needs primarily to purchase a package that will meet the user requirements, cost will still be important. Where there is a trade-off between these items, care must be taken to ensure that user requirements are not unduly compromised.
Interface design	The package should be easy to use and follow conventional interface design (such as Windows) to allow for ease of use and training.
Controls	The package must include appropriate controls to confirm the completeness and accuracy of processing of all data input. Access and security controls will also be required.
Updates	Appropriate and timely updates must be available. Updates are particularly relevant for software that changes frequently due to legislation or similar changes (e.g. wages software).
User manuals	Full documentation will be required in the form of detailed reference guides and probably some quick reference or similar brief guide.
Compatibility with existing hardware and software	The package must run on the organisation's existing computer systems. Software compatibility will be particularly important where data needs to be exchanged between different packages.
Support and maintenance	Support contracts to provide automatic upgrade of the software will normally be available, as will telephone support lines to help users resolve queries arising from using the software.

Information will also be required on the supplier of the package regarding areas such as:

1   **Length of time in business.** This provides an indication of the financial stability of the supplier and is indicative that the company has a good chance of remaining in business to support the software in the future.

2   **References from other users.** These reference sites can be used to test the appropriateness of the software for the situation in the purchasing organisation, and also to check on the reliability of the supplier in providing support for the software.

3   **Availability of demonstration copies of the software.** Running the software on the organisation's own computer systems will provide one of the best methods of evaluating that software.

The normal tasks involved in choosing the application package are:

- produce a requirements listing and send this with an invitation to tender to a number of suppliers

- review the tender documents and make an initial selection of, say, three software packages

- obtain copies of those packages and test on the organisation's own computer system. alternatively, the supplier may be asked to make a presentation to show why the purchasing company should use their particular package

- obtain user input and evaluation of each package

- obtain technical input and evaluation of each package to ensure it is compatible with existing hardware and software and provides the necessary processing capability

- test the package with test data from the organisation, paying particular reference to unusual items

- provide a final purchase recommendation, taking into account other factors such as after sales service – see below.

4.3   Advantages and disadvantages of off-the-shelf packages

Advantages

- They are generally cheaper to buy than bespoke packages are to develop.

- They are likely to be available almost immediately.

- Any system bugs should have been discovered by the vendors before sale.

- Good packages are likely to come with good training programs and excellent documentation and on-screen help facilities.

- New updated versions of the software are likely to be available on a regular basis.

- The experience of a great number of users with similar needs to those in the organisation has been incorporated into the design of the package.

- Different packages will be available for different operating systems or data structures

Disadvantages

- They do not fit precisely the needs of the organisation – the users may need to compromise what they want with what is available

- The organisation is dependent upon an outside supplier for the maintenance of the software; many software suppliers are larger than most of their customers, and are therefore difficult to influence

- Different packages used by the organisation may have incompatible data structures.

- Using the same packages as rival organisations removes the opportunity of using IS for competitive advantage.

Application packages can be altered and tailored to a buyer's requirements, but amendments to an existing package have to be paid for, and so add to the purchase cost of the software.

4.4   Comparing supplier proposals

Often, an organisation will need to weigh up a series of competitive tenders and choose the best. The tenders that they are comparing may well have different strengths and weaknesses, with no one offer providing the perfect solution. They may be tested using benchmark and simulation programs, or they may be compared using a formal procedure called weighted ranking.

4.5   Weighted ranking

A number of factors that are important to the system under consideration are listed. Each factor is given a numerical weight to indicate their relative importance to the users. Both the factors and the weighting they are given will vary according to the system being evaluated.

Example: Weighted ranking

Factor	Weighting
User friendliness	10
Cost	7
Quality of output	8
Speed of processing	4
After sales service	5
Security features	8

Each supplier is then ranked against each factor, thus:

		Rankings		
Factor	Weighting	Supplier A	Supplier B	Supplier C
User friendliness	10	1	2	3
Cost	7	2	3	1
Quality of output	8	3	1	2
Speed of processing	4	3	1	2
After sales service	5	1	2	3
Security features	8	1	2	3

FOULKS LYNCH
PUBLICATIONS

Suppliers are then given a score that matches their ranking. In the example above, since there are three suppliers, a ranking of 1 is given a score of 3, a ranking of 2 is given a score of 2 and a ranking of 3 received a score of 1.

| | | Score | | |
Factor	Weighting	Supplier A	Supplier B	Supplier C
User friendliness	10	3	2	1
Cost	7	2	1	3
Quality of output	8	1	3	2
Speed of processing	4	1	3	2
After sales service	5	3	2	1
Security features	8	3	2	1

Each score is multiplied by the appropriate weighting, and the total calculated for each supplier.

Thus the total scores are:

Supplier A $= (10 \times 3) + (7 \times 2) + (8 \times 1) + (4 \times 1) + (5 \times 3) + (8 \times 3)$

$= 30 + 14 + 8 + 4 + 15 + 24$

$= 95$

Supplier B $= (10 \times 2) + (7 \times 1) + (8 \times 3) + (4 \times 3) + (5 \times 2) + (8 \times 2)$

$= 20 + 7 + 24 + 12 + 10 + 6$

$= 89$

Supplier C $= (10 \times 1) + (7 \times 3) + (8 \times 2) + (4 \times 2) + (5 \times 1) + (8 \times 1)$

$= 10 + 21 + 16 + 8 + 5 + 8$

$= 68$

The highest score is achieved by supplier A, whose proposal would be the one chosen.

This procedure may distort the result, since a slight preference for one supplier over another has the same effect as a significant preference. This problem can be overcome by allocating each supplier a score for each factor instead of a ranking. This amended procedure is more complex to carry out but is likely to lead to a more accurate result. The maximum score for each factor is given as a value of 10.

Thus the previous example might yield the following table:

| | | Score | | |
Factor	Weighting	Supplier A	Supplier B	Supplier C
User friendliness	10	10	9	5
Cost	7	7	6	10
Quality of output	8	5	10	9
Speed or processing	4	8	10	9
After sales service	5	10	9	5
Security features	8	10	9	8

The total score is calculated in a similar way:

Supplier A $= (10 \times 10) + (7 \times 7) + (8 \times 5) + (4 \times 8) + (5 \times 10) + (8 \times 10)$

$= 100 + 49 + 40 + 32 + 50 + 80$

$= 351$

Supplier B $= (10 \times 9) + (7 \times 6) + (8 \times 10) + (4 \times 10) + (5 \times 9) + (8 \times 9)$

$= 90 + 42 + 80 + 40 + 45 + 72$

$= 371$

Supplier C $= (10 \times 5) + (7 \times 10) + (8 \times 9) + (4 \times 9) + (5 \times 5) + (8 \times 8)$

$= 50 + 70 + 72 + 32 + 25 + 64$

$= 313$

Using the amended weighting, it can now be seen that Supplier B is offering the best package.

Example: Use of weighted ranking

A small organisation wishes to computerise the production of their accounts. They run two separate companies, each with their own accounts staff but under the control of the group financial manager. They do not wish to change the way that they operate, so they need a system that can be networked over three computers, one for each company and a third for the group financial manager.

Each company's accounts staff are responsible for the day-to-day running of their business, while the group financial manager is responsible for producing consolidated accounts for the two businesses and for the management accounting function. The accounts for each of the two companies must be kept confidential.

The organisation makes out a list of factors that are important to them, allocating appropriate weights.

Factor	Weight
Ability to provide all basic accounting functions required	Essential
Networking capability	Essential
User friendliness	8
Cost	10
Management accounts capability	6
Hot line support	2
Security features	8
After sales service	4

A short-list of four accounts packages is drawn up. The packages are called Alphabet Accounts, Flying Horse, Heaven Sent and Wise. Each of these is scored against the factors described above.

Factor	Supplier Scores			
	A	F	H	W
1 All basic functions supplied	✓	✓	✓	✓
2 Networking capability	x	✓	✓	✓
3 User friendliness	7	9	10	8
4 Cost	10	2	2	4
5 Management accounts capability	3	10	8	6
6 Hot line support/training	0	5	6	10
7 Security features	6	10	7	8
8 After sales service	0	6	8	10

Solution

The first thing to note is that Alphabet Accounts does not satisfy the essential requirement of being able to be networked. Although it is by far the cheapest package, it is not a satisfactory solution to the organisation's needs, and is not considered further.

The scores for cost are corrected to 5 (Flying Horse), 5 (Heaven Sent) and 10 (Wise). Factors 1 and 2 are satisfied by all three packages and do not need to be considered further. The amended table is reproduced below.

Factor	Weight	Supplier Score		
		F	H	W
3	8	9	10	8
4	10	5	5	10
5	6	10	8	6
6	2	5	6	10
7	8	10	7	8
8	4	6	8	10

The total scores for each supplier are calculated by cross-multiplying the factor weights by the appropriate scores.

Flying Horse

Total score $= (8 \times 9) + (10 \times 5) + (6 \times 10) + (2 \times 5) + (8 \times 10) + (4 \times 6)$

$= 72 + 50 + 60 + 10 + 80 + 24 = 296$

Heaven Sent

Total score $= (8 \times 10) + (10 \times 5) + (6 \times 8) + (2 \times 6) + (8 \times 10) + (8 \times 7)$

$= 80 + 50 + 48 + 12 + 80 + 56 = 326$

Wise

Total score $= (8 \times 8) + (10 \times 10) + (6 \times 6) + (2 \times 10) + (8 \times 8) + (4 \times 10)$

$= 64 + 100 + 36 + 20 + 64 + 40 = 324$

It can be seen that Heaven Sent is marginally ahead of Wise, and is the package selected. It should also be noted that the difference between Heaven Sent and Wise is very small, and further factors may be taken into account to further compare these two packages. Additional price discounts may also be available by negotiating with these two suppliers.

Conclusion

This chapter has explained the different methods of purchasing and tailoring software for specific use within an organisation.

SELF-TEST QUESTIONS

Bespoke software

1   What is a bespoke software application? (2)

Invitation to tender

2   List the main contents of an invitation to tender. (3.1)

Evaluating supplier proposals

3   What are the three main categories under which supplier proposals are evaluated? (4)

EXAM-TYPE QUESTION

Software packages

Scenario

ZYNC Plc is a large manufacturing company. It has traditionally developed many of its information systems in-house and the data processing (DP) department currently employs about 120 staff.

The following main applications are currently supported.

Application	Package / Bespoke	Year implemented	Development language
Process control	Bespoke	1989	FORTRAN
Integrated accounts	Package	1995	
Payroll	Package	1996	
Order processing	Bespoke	1991	COBOL
Quality control	Bespoke	1993	COBOL
Marketing information	Bespoke	1996	4GL

There are approximately 25 smaller applications developed in-house to respond to the needs of individual departments. However, the DP department does not have a good reputation. User departments frequently complain about missed deadlines, poor quality software and lack of functionality.

A new IT director has recently been appointed. He believes that most of the problems have been caused by the organisation's emphasis on building bespoke solutions.

His view is that 'Packages are the way forward. We can no longer afford the luxury of building our own systems.'

He is also critical of the systems development life cycle in place at ZYNC.

He claims that 'We have made the mistake of forcing all our system developments – whether they are bespoke systems, application packages or small one-off systems through a standard systems development life cycle (SDLC). This SDLC (listed below) has led to unnecessarily long elapsed times on projects.'

Stage 1	Feasibility study
Stage 2	Systems specification
Stage 3	Programming and unit testing
Stage 4	Systems testing
Stage 5	User-acceptance testing
Stage 6	Implementation

The new IT director proposes that all future systems will be implemented using standard application software packages. He claims that;

'*Standard packages offer cost and time savings as well as guaranteed quality.* We will be looking for packages that fit 80% or more of our business requirements. We will not be commissioning any changes to the functionality of the package. If the package does not exactly fit the business then the business must change to fit the package. We have already successfully implemented packages for accounts and payroll. We must now repeat that success in other areas of the business.'

The IT director has agreed that staffing will be kept at the current level for the foreseeable future. He states that: 'We obviously need staff to implement our package policy, although I will be looking for a significant contribution from the user areas.

Required:

(a)   Briefly explain what is meant by a:

– software package   **(3 marks)**

– bespoke solution.   **(3 marks)**

(b)   The IT director identifies three benefits of adopting the application software package approach.

'Standard packages offer cost and time savings as well as guaranteed quality.'

Briefly explain how the software package approach can offer each of these three benefits to ZYNC Plc.

– cost savings   **(3 marks)**

– time savings   **(3 marks)**

– guaranteed quality   **(3 marks)**

(Total: 15 marks)

Chapter 12
COMPUTER AIDED SOFTWARE ENGINEERING

This chapter looks at two methods of producing software with the aid of productivity tools. The first approach is that of Computer Aided Software Engineering (CASE) tools. These are automated software tools used by systems analysts and designers to develop models and data for information systems specification.

The second approach uses Fourth Generation Languages and prototyping in the design of software, along with some of the advantages of using these methods.

Objectives

By the time you have finished this chapter you should be able to:

- define a Computer Aided Software Engineering (CASE) tool and give a brief list of representative products

- describe a range of features and functions that a CASE tool may provide

- explain the advantages of using a CASE tool in the system development process

- define a Fourth Generation Language and give a brief list of representative products

- describe a range of features and functions that a 4GL may provide

- explain how a 4GL contributes to the prototyping process.

1   CASE tools

Computer Aided Software Engineering (CASE) is one of the ways the analyst and designer can speed up the development of new systems, while improving the quality of control over the work that they do.

CASE tools mechanise some of the more routine and tedious tasks in systems and program development. They are used to speed up and make more consistent the systems development process.

There are a number of tools in existence, some of which cover the analysis phase of the Lifecycle, some the design, some the build, and some the project management and control aspects. There are also some integrated CASE tools (ICASE) that cover the whole lifecycle.

DEFINITION

CASE tools are automated software tools used by systems analysts and designers to develop information systems.

INFORMATION SYSTEMS

The diagram below shows the facilities offered by CASE.

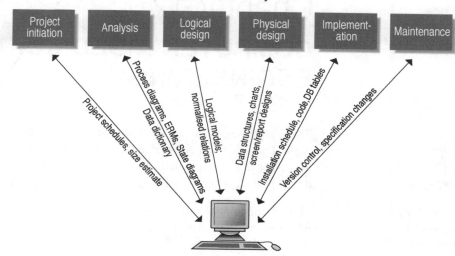

(Source: Hoffer, George and Valacich 1996 Modern Systems Analysis and Design. Benjamin Cummings.)

1.1 Objectives of CASE

Organisations may choose to use CASE in systems development in order to:

- speed up the development process
- standardise the development process
- ensure the quality of development models
- improve the quality of the systems
- improve and standardise the documentation produced during the development
- simplify maintenance
- improve the management of the project.

1.2 Levels of CASE

CASE tools can be categorised according to what part of the lifecycle they cover.

Upper CASE tools

Upper CASE covers tools used in the analysis phase. They include:

- **diagramming tools**, to draw process models, data models and state models according to the rules of those specific notations and methodologies
- **analysis tools** that check for completeness and consistency in diagrams, forms and reports
- **a repository** to enable integration of specification, diagrams, reports and project management information

Lower CASE tools

These include:

- **document generators**, to help produce technical and user documentation in standard formats
- **display and report generators**, to enable prototypes of the interface to be made

- **code generators** to enable automatic generation of program and database definition code directly from the design documents.

1.3   Components of CASE

Repository

The repository is at the heart of CASE tools, especially integrated-CASE. It is a centralised database that holds all the information needed to create and maintain a software systems project, right the way from initiation through to code generation and even maintenance.

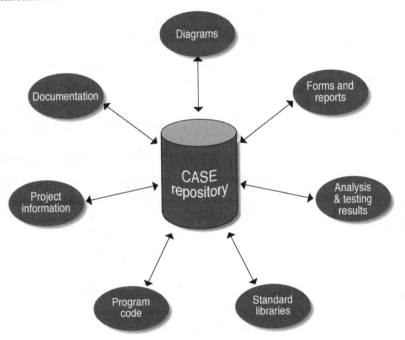

(Source: Hoffer, George and Valacich 1996 Modern Systems Analysis and Design. Benjamin Cummings.)

Data dictionary

This is a tool that is used to manage and control access to the repository. It will keep a record about all the data items in the system. Descriptions that the dictionary will hold might include: item name, textual description, synonyms, type and format, range of acceptable values, programs, inputs, outputs etc that use that item.

Diagramming tools

The CASE tool is built to draw specific types of diagram, to specific notations. Thus a CASE tool might be built to support all SSADM diagrams, such as SELECT. Another might be built to support the UML notation, such as the RATIONAL suite. As well as being able to draw the shapes for that method, the tools also has the rules that support the method built into it. Thus, a diagramming tool for SSADM would not allow a diagram that showed a data store interacting with another data store. Similarly, when a level 1 diagram is to be decomposed to level 2 the CASE tool would ensure that all the flows in and out of the level 2 boundary mapped on to the level 1 process.

Documentation generator tools

Each stage of the SDLC is responsible for further system documentation. The documents may be diagrams or reports, or data specifications. CASE will have appropriate templates, and the information from each phase is fed into the repository, so that the documents can be generated and maintained automatically.

1.4 Traditional systems development versus CASE-based development

The following table compares the main differences between traditional systems development and CASE-based development:

Traditional systems development	CASE-based systems development
Emphasis on coding and testing	Emphasis on analysis and design
Paper-based specification	Rapid interactive prototyping
Manual coding of programs	Automated code generation
Intensive software testing	Automated design checking
Maintain code and documentation	Maintain design specification

(Source: Hoffer, George and Valacich 1996 Modern Systems Analysis and Design. Benjamin Cummings.)

2 Fourth Generation Languages and prototyping

2.1 Generations of computer languages

Computer languages have passed through four different generations:

First generation

This was machine code with programs being written in binary code only. The programs were very complex to write and extremely difficult to read and debug. Maintenance was equally difficult. The programs were written for a particular machine, and could not be installed on another machine afterwards.

Second generation

Assembler languages. These used symbolic code to provide instructions to the computer. While they were slightly easier to understand, they were still very similar to machine code, which limited their usability. These too were written for just one machine, and were not portable.

Third generation

High-level languages such as FORTRAN, COBOL, PL/1 and BASIC. The languages were much easier to use as many of the commands were close to English. Portability between different operating environments tended to be limited as the program was written for one type of computer, but use of a piece of software called a **compiler** made portability much more feasible than it had been for 1st and 2nd generations.

Fourth generation

There is no precise definition of a fourth generation language, although the main points are given below.

2.2 Fourth Generation Language

While there is no precise definition of the language, Martin (1982) provides a list of the desirable features of this type of language. The main points from this list are:

- centred on a relational database
- links to other propriety databases to assist overall system development
- integrated and active data dictionary

- simply query language to allow programmers and users to access the data

- integrated screen design tool, or screen-painter

- a dialogue design tool to facilitate production of dialogue boxes including the use of graphics

- a report generator

- procedural coding facility to document procedures in written or software terms.

One of the main aims of the fourth generation language (4GL) is to provide a development facility for the programmer, analyst and end-user. The 4GL must therefore contain all the tools required not only to write a program, but also to enable users to test that program prior to final coding. Most 4GLs will be written to fit in with existing software, otherwise substantial re-coding will be required to transfer the 4GL code into a full working version of the software. The screen painter and dialogue design tool will build the interface for the user, while one of the other main purposes of 4GL is to develop a prototype, as described in the following sections.

4GLs are also used to access databases using English-style commands such as FIND ALL RECORDS WHERE NAME IS 'SMITH'. The languages are therefore quite user-friendly allowing users with little or no programming experience to use them.

2.3   Example of user-based 4GL

Many 4GL's, at least in application development, tend to be used by programmers and are rarely seen outside of this environment. However, there are some programmes written for users which provide a similar look and feel to a full 4GL programme development tool. An example of one of these programmes is shown below.

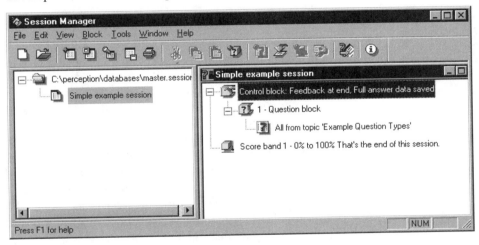

© QuestionMark Computing Ltd 2001

This screenshot shows part of a application designed to produce Computer Based Training and question/evaluation packages. Like many Windows® packages, it has a Graphical User Interface and toolbar showing commonly used tools. However, the main work area has a variety of different icons and text. Some of the important features of this package are listed below.

- Icons representing some quite detailed programming instructions to the user, however, the user does not have to worry about writing those instructions out, simply placing the icon on the screen means that the software will perform those instructions.

- Icons can be moved around the screen by drag and drop (or cut and paste) making re-arranging the order of activities easy.

- Additional steps can added to the CBT by selecting the appropriate icon from the toolbar.

- Many icons can be 'opened', and specific programming instructions provided. For example, the large red question mark icon is currently displaying one particular question set, this can be amended to display other question sets simply by double clicking on the icon and choosing a new set. The 4GL package itself then finds those questions, not the user.

Using the 4GL not only saves the user time, it also means that the detailed programming language does not have to be learnt. As long as the user understands what the different icons can do, and how to place these onto the screen, then quite detailed, in this case, CBT packages can be built.

3 Prototyping

Prototyping is the production of a working model of a system. Working models are used in many areas of business, from the production of new cars to the training of pilots to fly new aeroplanes. The use of prototypes minimises the risk that the item being designed will not fit the needs of the organisation and allows experimentation without the high cost of failure.

Under the traditional methods of system development, users specified their requirements to the analyst and project team, who then developed the system based on those requirements with little or no further user involvement. Prototyping lets the user view the system during development and to make amendments or corrections as required.

3.1 Throwaway and working prototypes

The throwaway model acts as a communications device between user and developer and aids in the learning process. The user is better able to explain his requirements from the model developed by the prototyper and the prototyper is better able to demonstrate how the proposed systems is intended to operate. This kind of prototype is usually built very quickly and would not include aspects of the system such as security, performance, error handling procedures, etc.

An example of a throwaway prototype is one developed for screen-based dialogues. There would not be any underlying database, nor would there be facilities and codes for storage or data manipulation. Screen-based dialogue simulation enables the analyst to lead the user through a series of screens and explain how each screen is used. The user is able to relate to the system and is in a better position to say whether the system meets his requirements and expectations. This kind of system may be a simple shell and contain no working capacity.

The working prototype is an extension of the throwaway model and will incorporate and implement some of the system's important features.

The prototype will be constructed using similar tools to those used in the construction of an actual system. The user interface style will be similar to that of the final implementation, thus enabling better evaluation of the system. As the data dictionary screen and data definitions will have been preserved, these can be used for the final construction. A sub-system is taken and developed into a working prototype, which is in turn used to form the basis of the new system.

3.2   Working prototypes

Working prototyping (or evolutionary prototyping) is an alternative approach to developing systems, akin to RAD (Chapter 7). The developer constructs a prototype of part of the functionality of the new system. S/he tests and refines it with the user until it reaches the desired quality. At that point, it is actually handed over to the user as a working system, with all of the data converted and the non-functional requirements implemented. Another set of required functions are then developed in the same way, and that prototype added to the original handover. In this way, the system is developed with the users' help in a piecemeal fashion, but in a way that means they can use the most urgent parts of it sooner.

3.3   Advantages of prototyping

The final design is highly likely to fit user needs

It is often difficult for inexperienced users to visualise what the computer can do for them and to define what they need. By having concrete examples it is easier to visualise what the computer can do for them and to define their needs fully and precisely.

Employees are involved in the systems development process

Because of the dynamic way that prototyping develops systems, employees working in the user department are fully involved in the development process. They are more likely to identify the system as being *their* system. This will help to ensure that the system is properly defined, and will reduce the likelihood of dysfunctional behaviour.

Identification of problems

Once a full system has been developed, it is very expensive to eradicate any bugs in the programs or difficulties in the way the users relate to the system. With prototyping, the systems analyst or users can identify any problems or omissions and eliminate them. The user-friendliness of the system can be guaranteed.

Code generation

Many 4GLs are capable of automatically producing a series of programs written in a third generation language. This makes prototyping a very cost effective way of developing systems.

3.4   Disadvantages of prototyping

There are some disadvantages with prototyping:

- many 4GLs and other prototyping tools are hungry for computer processing resources and expensive to buy

- the development process may become sloppy and unstructured, wasting money and resources and making planning difficult. The greatest danger here is 'requirements shift' whereby users, seeing how much the computer can do, think of more and more extra requirements to add on to the specification. With suitable controls, this disadvantage can be overcome

- prototyping tools often require data to be in a specific format. Existing data files may require conversion before they can be input into the prototype

- some prototyping tools are restrictive in the way that systems can be developed, and may not allow hand written codes to be linked in

- code produced by code generators may well be less efficient than that produced by an experienced programmer

- error recovery routines
- the ability to work in direct mode, or to create 3GL code.

Conclusion

This chapter has explained the importance of testing and checking software to ensure it is as error free as possible, and outlined some of the main techniques that are used to carry out that testing. It is unlikely that you will have practical experience of testing, so ensure that you understand the principles of testing, and can spot weaknesses in any testing system you may find in an examination question.

SELF-TEST
QUESTIONS

CASE tools

1   What is a CASE tool? (1)

2   Explain the advantages of CASE tools in system development. (1.4)

4GL and prototyping

3   Describe the main features of a Fourth Generation Language. (2.2)

Prototyping

4   What are the advantages of prototyping? (3.3)

EXAM-TYPE
QUESTION

Prototyping

In the context of systems development:

(a)   Explain what is meant by a prototype.   **(3 marks)**

(b)   Describe two advantages and two disadvantages of using a prototyping approach to systems development.   **(8 marks)**

(c)   Select two facilities usually found in a fourth generation language (4GL) and explain their application in developing a prototype system.   **(4 marks)**

(Total: 15 marks)

Chapter 13
TECHNICAL INFORMATION SYSTEMS REQUIREMENTS

KEY POINTS

Performance of a system
covers:

* Response and turnaround
  times
* Ability to deal with volumes
  of transactions
* Availability of system
* Accuracy of results

These are known as non-
functional requirements.

DEFINITION

Response time is the interval
between data entry by the terminal
user and receipt of the result of
any processing activity that has
taken place.

This section of the manual discusses some of the technical requirements of a system, such as performance and volume requirements, various 'housekeeping' activities and the purpose of an audit trail. Many systems need to interface with other working systems in the organisation and, in some circumstances, outside the organisation, too.

Objectives

By the time you have finished this chapter you should be able to:

* define and record performance and volume requirements of information systems

* discuss the need for archiving, backup and restore, and other 'housekeeping' functions

* explain the need for a software audit trail and define the content of such a trail

* examine the need to provide interfaces with other systems, and discuss the implications of developing these interfaces

* Understand requirements for data conversion and data creation.

1   Performance and volume requirements

When the requirements document is completed, there will be entries for what is known as **non-functional** requirements. Non-functional requirements are descriptions of the expected performance of the system. They will typically refer to issues such as response and turnaround times, availability, usability, security and privacy. Usability requirements were described in Chapter 10; security and privacy requirements will be covered in Chapter 14. The requirements document and the functional specification will also state expectations and requirements relating to volumes of both data and transactions.

1.1   Performance

Turnaround and response times

A justification for many systems is that they will turn transactions round faster than the system being replaced, so saving time and cutting costs. The analyst may have discovered, for example, that to respond to a customer order by taking the order, despatching the goods and sending the invoice currently takes 1 hour of effort, and 8 elapsed hours. The integrated ordering-stock management and invoicing system built to replace this was justified by the calculation that the computer time is reduced to half a minute and the elapsed time reduced to 2 hours, most of which is the manual work in the warehouse and despatch bay. A further justification was that this increase in turnaround time means that the system can cope with a massive increase in throughput, resulting in greater profits for the company.

Testing may have shown, on a small test database and a single terminal, that this target performance was met comfortably. On implementation, however, the performance may significantly degrade because in fact there are a hundred sales staff accessing the system simultaneously, reading and updating a database several hundred times larger than the test one, and so the whole cycle is slowed significantly. We would hope that it is still faster than the current system, but the expected turnover of the business will be lower than predicted.

There have been cases where the turnaround times have been disastrously slow. In the 1980s, the UK Passport Office, for example, installed a new system that took two months to turn passport applications around, as opposed to the fifteen days that the old system took.

A manager may have requested the facility to make enquiries on stock levels, or customer details, or on line sales summaries, and expect to be able to call them up on screen within 3 seconds. If, because of weight of traffic and quantity of data, the system cannot give him/her the information for 10 seconds, they will be disillusioned and sceptical about the system. The requirements document must capture the expected response time, and the system designed to ensure that it is met. This may be captured as a part of each individual requirement, or it may be specified as a 'global' non-functional requirement, meant to apply to every enquiry in the system.

Volumes of transactions

In October 1989, the Brussels Stock Exchange was out of action for two days after the computer systems crashed, unable to handle the unexpectedly high volumes of transactions. An air cargo system was unable to deal with the volume of transactions passing through it, and the ensuing backlog caused the company's warehouse to overflow. After two weeks, the whole system was shut down. Sadly, there are many other horror stories of systems that failed to deliver what they promised, and led instead to very costly embarrassment and, in some cases, business failure. As with the two cases cited here, it was not *what* the systems was specified and programmed to do that led to failure, but *how* it achieved it, i.e. the non-functional, performance measures.

When collecting and specifying requirements for the new system, the analyst must identify what the volumes of traffic are expected to be:

- how many users will use that function
- what will be the minimum number of transactions per day, or hour
- what is the expected maximum number of transactions per day, or hour
- what growth is expected in the number of transactions over the next 6 or 12 months. Without a clear picture of these figures, the designer cannot build an optimum system.

Availability

Another important non-functional requirement is the availability of the system. Some systems, especially those supporting e-commerce, and safety critical systems, need to be available for 24 hours a day, 7 days a week; others only need to be working for standard office hours.

Whichever, the desired availability of a system, and of the functions within the system, must be specified in the requirements document, and will be part of the assessment of its performance. There should be a realistic expectation: to say that a system must be fully available 100% of the time does not allow opportunity to take back-ups and perform other necessary housekeeping. To say that it must be available 99.99% suggests that it can be down by no more than 1 hour in a year. This is not a realistic expectation, and should be challenged. More likely is that part of the system can be taken down, and the rest of the system work on a degraded performance for an agreed period. For example, if a system is built to capture orders, validate them, allocate stock, prepare despatch notes and invoices, while generating purchase notices where necessary, it may be allowable for most of the system to go off-line, as long as orders can be captured, to be processed later when that part of the system comes back on line.

MG Hotels have stipulated that they require their booking systems to be available from 6. Am until midnight for seven days a week. They have found that these hours allow prospective visitors from most of the time zones to call to make reservations. However, should the central database crash during those hours, they will accept a level of service that will let them take the visitor's details, and details of their requirements, so that as soon as the system is restored they can make the reservation and call them back with either confirmation, or alternative provision.

They originally wanted the system to be available for 24 hours a day, 365 days a year, but the designers pointed out that while this could be achieved, it could only be done at a greater cost than MG thought worth paying. This level of service could have been achieved by running a duplex system, i.e. two precise copies of the system running simultaneously for the whole time, so that if one system failed, the other could cut in at once and preserve the service. This is acceptable in a safety-critical system, such as air traffic control, or nuclear power station control, but not for a system such as MG wish.

The lesson from this is that any level of availability is obtainable, but the more rigorous the requirement, the greater the cost to achieve it. The users, designer and project manager must address the results of losing service for a certain period, and its cost to the operations; if it results in substantial loss of business the company may decide that it is preferable to pay a great deal extra for the service; if it might result in loss of life, there is no question, but the company must pay what is needed to ensure continuous availability.

Accuracy

Another test of a system's performance will be accuracy of its output. This is a feature that will be checked during each phase of testing. Accuracy covers both the stored data and the output. Thus, the invoice produced by the system must tally with the value of the goods despatched, which in turn must tally with the original customer order. In the process, the quantity of stock held must be decreased by the appropriate figure once it has been allocated to the order. A combination of initial testing, and continuing audit, should ensure that this aspect of performance is satisfactory.

Level of accuracy is significant in management reporting. A list of orders taken and their value must be accurate to the exact penny, so that it can be reconciled with the monies received and due. However, a senior manager who is looking at summary information regarding sales figures for such and such a region for the last six months will only expect the figures to be accurate to, say, the nearest 100,000. Any finer level of accuracy than that will become meaningless. Each level, therefore, of a reporting system or MIS has its own requirements for levels of accuracy. These too will be identified and recorded in the requirements document.

The Directors of MG Hotels will be concerned to see how many bookings take place across the whole chain over a year, to the nearest 100,000. Directors of a particular country's division will be concerned to see how many bookings there were over the year to the nearest 1,000, and a regional manager within the country will look to the nearest 500. Managers and supervisors in each individual hotel need to know the precise number of guests due to arrive day by day, and the precise number who have stayed and paid.

FOULKS LYNCH
PUBLICATIONS

2　Housekeeping requirements

2.1　Archiving and back-up

Archiving

KEY POINT

Data files need to be archived periodically, so that they are available for enquiry purposes, but do not take up undue storage space on the main operational database.

When data pertaining to a transaction is completed, it can be either deleted from the system completely, or put into storage elsewhere, perhaps for later reference. For some form of transactions, there are legal requirements (see below), while for others, such as personnel systems that store details of employees, there may be a need to keep details of ex employees for the purpose, say, of providing references for future employers. This storing of old data is called *Archiving*. Archiving will be on either magnetic media such as tapes or disk packs, or on optical media such as CD Rom. If the company is only seeking to save space (see below), it may hold the archive in a human readable form such as microfilm or microfiche. The operational system will never be able to access such data again, but human eyes can find and refer to it if desired.

There are two reasons for archiving old data.

1　To save space on the operational system

2　To have old data available to answer enquiries, and to be able to conduct trend and pattern analyses on them.

Saving space

The longer the system is in operation, the larger the database grows. An order processing system will, by definition, add new orders and new customers every day of its operation. There will come a time when, if old data is not purged, there will not be space to add new records. Before that time, allocated file space will become so clogged with new data that the speed of processing degrades to an unacceptable level as the programs try to work through two or three levels of overflow in order to find the required data for the transaction. After a certain time following a transaction, it is unlikely that the record will be needed for further action, so it should be removed from the operational database. For legislative reasons, financial data should be kept for seven years following the transaction; this does not mean that it should be kept with 'live' data for the full seven years. More probable is that perhaps a year after the transaction is completed, it will be archived on secure storage elsewhere. Optical disks are frequently used for archive purposes. The archived data can be retrieved and read, but will not be updated.

Available for enquiries

KEY POINT

Back-up copies of data, programs and transactions enable the organisation to recover from disasters.

After data is archived, the organisation may still want to interrogate it using various techniques to try and identify trends in customers' buying patterns, or to determine a product's long-term viability. If the data was completely deleted when the transaction time was completed, the company could not make use of it for these purposes. This would severely handicap its operations and decision-making ability in a competitive environment; keeping the information available in an archive allows it to be interrogated, while not interfering with the performance of the live system.

MG Hotels could use the reservation information gathered over the last five years to assess not just simple trends such as which times of year are most popular for bookings, but could identify demographic trends, such as demand for single rooms among certain age groups, or reasons for group bookings over a particular period, in order to target their advertising campaigns, and perhaps to put together packages that will appeal to identified sectors of the market.

2.2   Back-up and restore procedures

KEY POINT

Back-up systems:

- magnetic disk

- accumulate update inputs on disk

- tape streamer.

Every system should be prepared for accidents, disasters and failure. The simplest way to prepare for these is to take regular backups of all data, transaction and program files. This involves copying all files on the database, particularly the most volatile and commonly accessed file, onto a safe medium away from the live system. The principle is the same for a stand-alone PC or for a mainframe system. Typical backup media would be CD ROM, or a Tape Streamer. These allow large volumes to be saved at high speed.

For the duration of the downtime, losses can be expected to escalate. It is, therefore, essential that the time when the computer system is unavailable be kept to a minimum.

Requirements for backup

Strategies for recovery can be based on a number of strategies; whichever strategy is employed will affect how the technical requirements are specified. Three common strategies are:

KEY POINT

Technical requirements to cater for back up procedures will include stipulations for:

- File generations

- Checkpoints

- Logs

- File generations

- Checkpointing

- Logs/journals

These are described below:

1   File generation

These refer to master files on the database. In M.G. Hotels case these would include Guest files, Reservations files, Bills files, Corporate files.

Each of these files is backed up on to a storage medium at the end of a business cycle (perhaps a day); the transactions that updated them during that period are also backed up. The backups are usually kept for two periods, so that three versions are kept in total: the current one and the two previous ones. These are known as Grandfather – father - son generation. This allows re-constitution from two earlier versions of the files, if there should have been a major disaster. Usually, re-constitution is normally required from the Father generation only. Is form of backup – restore is commonest on mainframe applications. Technical requirements would include the filespace needed to store the generations, and time needed to take the backups.

2   Checkpoints

A checkpoint is a mechanism used on large batch applications, not on on-line applications. A checkpoint is a point in time during the run when the progress and status of the work is recorded. Should there be a crash subsequently, the run can be restarted from the checkpoint rather than going back to the beginning of the run.

A requirement would be to stipulate which transaction runs are to be checkpointed, and at what frequency.

3   Logs/journals

The journal (or log) electronically records the processing history of the whole system. It records the transactions, updates, errors, faults. As part of its function, it will record the state of the data record before it is updated, and after (Before-image and After-image). This allows an audit trail (see below) for the system, as well as an immediate diagnostic source in case of trouble or suspected corruption.

Requirements would be to stipulate the details recorded in the log, and how it is to be reported.

The purpose of the housekeeping functions is to ensure both accuracy and performance, congruent with the users' stipulation. This entails recognising that mishaps and breakdowns do occur, for many reasons, and the system must be able to recover from them.

System recovery

The response to a potential disaster, such as the loss of all or part of the computer system, should be managed. The best way of doing this is by means of a **contingency plan**. The plan itself will be specified as a response to the technical requirements.

As the importance of computing within an organisation continues to grow, so the effects of a breakdown of the computer system are potentially even more damaging. In addition, the computer system is increasingly exposed to the potential threat of hackers and the introduction of computer viruses.

For the duration of the downtime, losses can be expected to escalate. It is, therefore, essential that the time when the computer system is unavailable be kept to a minimum.

A number of common standby plans are discussed below. The final selection would be dependent upon the estimated time that the concern would function adequately without computing facilities.

1   Creation of multiple data processing facilities on separate sites, with the smallest site being capable of supporting the crucial work of at least one other site during the calculated recovery time. This strategy requires hardware and software compatibility and spare capacity. It is calculated that approximately only 20 per cent of computer usage is critical, so the volume selected for temporary transfer can be kept to a minimum.

2   Reciprocal agreement with another company. Although a popular option, few companies can guarantee free capacity, or continuing capability, which attaches a high risk to this option.

3   A more expensive, but lower risk, version of the above is the commercial computer bureaux. This solution entails entering into a formal agreement that entitles the customer to a selection of services.

4   Empty rooms or equipped rooms. The former allows the organisation access to install a back-up system, which increases the recovery time but reduces the cost. The latter can be costly, so sharing this facility is a consideration.

5   Re-locatable computer centres. This solution involves a delay while the facility is erected and assembled and larger computers cannot usually be accommodated.

The effectiveness of the contingency plan is dependent on comprehensive back-up procedures for both data and software. The contingency plan must identify initial responses and clearly delineate responsibility at each stage of the exercise – from damage limitation through to full recovery.

The greater the effort invested in the preparation of a contingency plan, the more effectively the organisation will be able to mitigate the effects of a disaster.

3   Audit trails

It is often useful to be able to trace the path of transactions through a computer system. Part of the value of this kind of audit trail is to enable the system to be thoroughly tested during project development, but it also allows management to investigate any cases of fraud, or false transactions.

An audit trail for a computerised accounting system can be defined as 'a register of the details for all accounting transactions' (Sage plc).

The specific trail for a system will be designed with the aid of the Internal Auditor. The trail must give certain information about each transaction: who made the transaction, at which terminal; on what date and at what time the transaction was carried out, and which files/records were accessed.

Some operating systems have logging/journal facilities as an integral part of them. Essentially, however, an audit trail is a list of transactions entered into a system and of transaction activities. It can be printed out in detail or in summary form, when required. External auditors often ask for a printout of the audit trail when they carry out their audit work.

Sensitive data, e.g. payee codes, should be subject to a separate audit report showing when the data was read, written to or updated. It should show also the before and after state and the data causing the change.

As well as it being a convenient tool to monitor the progress of a system, it is a legal requirement in many countries, including UK, to provide *audit trails* of all financial transactions in public and other companies.

AUDIT is an inspection, verification and, in some cases, correction of business accounts. The auditor must be an independent person, with no vested interest in what is being inspected. External auditors are appointed to look after the interests of shareholders or owners; internal auditors ensure corporate management that resources are being used wisely and well, and that its assets are safe.

Auditors may sample outputs rather than inspect every single transaction. They will also ensure that controls and procedures are faithfully observed.

3.1   Work of the internal auditor

The work of the internal auditor regarding information systems management will include the following:

- Liasing with the project team and providing recommendations on the controls that can be implemented in systems. These controls are likely to focus on establishing an audit trail within the information system so that transactions can be followed through the system.

- Reviewing controls within existing systems and recommending improvements to those controls.

- Reviewing the work of the project team; specifically ensuring that the project quality plan is being followed and that documentation being produced meets the quality standards.

- Monitoring any systems change and reviewing the completeness and accurate of data being transferred from one system to another.

- Liaising with the external auditor to provide information on the controls within information systems, and where necessary performing tests of those controls for the external auditor.

The important distinction in all of this work is that the Internal auditor is reviewing and checking systems and the work of the project team; production of original documentation is normally avoided. If the Internal auditor produced documentation, then an independent check on the accuracy of that work could not be carried out.

An accountant will also be involved more in the budgeting, monitoring and reporting on the financial aspects of a project. The extent of involvement will normally depend on the size of the project, and then need to specialist assistance in determining the financial success of a project.

4   Interfaces with other systems

Very few computer systems work in isolation; they will almost certainly have some links to other systems whether this is via the Internet or to other network servers. As computer systems are developed, or as they are used over time within an organisation, there will be a need to ensure that appropriate links between computers are established and maintained.

In the case of a new system, part of the analysis and design phases of the SDLC will be to review what links are actually required for the new system, and then plan to provide those links. For example, if a user requires up-to-date information from a specific source, then links to that source will be included within the system.

Needs for links to other systems may also develop over time as users' jobs change or new systems and sources of information become available. Upgrading an existing to provide the required links may be difficult, especially where the existing system was implemented without any thought to the future requirements of users. Specific problems that may be faced include:

- lack of appropriate cabling for network or other access

- lack of hardware capabilities, for example to fix additional network cards into the computer

- insufficient memory to run upgraded software

- incompatible software

- lack of it staff to check and test any changes.

The analyst will need to test any amendments to the system carefully to ensure that there are no clashes with existing software and to check that existing systems do work correctly following any amendment. In many cases, minor amendments will simply not be made; instead, many minor amendments will be grouped together and one 'major' change will take place.

Links to other computer systems may be required for various reasons including:

- access to third party information (including Internet access)

- provision of services to third parties (such as Extranets)

- communication between departments in an organisation, where each department maintains its own servers

- access to value added networks and electronic data interchange services

- sharing of information worldwide within an organisation (using Lotus Notes or similar system)

- communication via e-mail.

5   Data conversion and data creation

Data conversion means the transfer of data from one system onto another system, which normally involves some reorganisation of the data itself, such as creating new fields. Data creation involves setting up or creating new data from scratch. Data creation is likely to be needed in most data conversion situations, especially where new master files or databases are to be established.

Data conversion will be required in situations such as:

- a new software system is introduced which is not immediately compatible with any existing systems.

- two information systems, which provide similar data are amalgamated into one system

- two organisations, with different information systems, merge and one common information system is required

- details of how to approach the data conversion process is to be found in chapter 16 of this text.

During the analysis and design phases, the format of all data fields will have been specified; if the system is being mapped onto an existing computerised system, there may be a mismatch between the data fields across the two systems. In this case the specification must stipulate how the mapping is to be achieved.

Another problem that can occur during the conversion relates to the volatility of the data, i.e. how rapidly and how much of it changes. All standing reference data can be transferred early in the process; when the new system is to go live, all the data must be accurate and up to date. This means that the changeable data can only be converted at the last minute; as an alternative, all the most recent transactions can be saved, to be run against the data just prior to implementation. The technical requirements for conversion must identify the changeable data, and what strategy is to be used to ensure accurate and timely conversion.

Conclusion

This chapter has described the technical requirements for a new system and the importance of specifying these in tandem with the functional requirements and technical design of a system.

Performance and volume requirements

1   Why is performance information on computer systems recorded? (1.1)

Housekeeping requirements

2   What is the difference between archiving data files and backing up data files? (2.1)

Audit trails

3   How can the internal auditor assist in the systems development process? (3.1)

Interfaces with other systems

4   What are the implications of a system having to interact with other computer systems? (4)

Data conversion and data creation

5   Explain the problems involved in converting data before implementation. (5)

Disaster Recovery

'Disaster Recovery' is a charity that flies aid to the sites of natural disasters such as floods, earthquakes, volcanic destruction etc. It keeps stockpiles of provisions such as blankets, tents, water purification units and tablets, preserved foods and some clothing. When there is news of a disaster, the provisions are loaded onto trucks and landrovers, and flown to the site as soon as possible. It raises money by public donation, fundraising campaigns and a large network of retail outlets in UK towns.

Disaster Recovery has commissioned a new integrated information system to manage the stock levels, and also to track the whereabouts of volunteer drivers, trucks and aid that is in transit.

Because most of its money is earmarked for disaster relief, the Directors have stipulated a low budget to cover basic functionality, not wanting to divert too much money from the core activity.

You are a consultant working on the specification. Write a report for the Directors explaining the technical requirements that the system may need to meet, and explaining why this may demand a higher investment than they wish to make.

(15 marks)

Chapter 14

SECURITY AND LEGAL REQUIREMENTS

Information systems have to be monitored to ensure that they continue to work efficiently, to ensure that they comply with relevant legislation and to check that they are safeguarded from threats such as viruses and hackers. All of these issues are discussed in this chapter with specific reference being made to UK legislation.

Objectives

By the time you have finished this chapter you should be able to:

- describe the principles, terms and coverage typified by the UK *Data Protection Act*

- describe the principles, terms and coverage typified by the UK *Computer Misuse Act*

- discuss how the requirements of the UK data protection and UK computer misuse legislation may be implemented

- explain the implications of software licences and copyright law in computer systems development

- discuss the legal implications of software supply with particular reference to ownership, liability and damages

- describe methods to ensure the physical security of IT systems

- discuss the role, implementation and maintenance of a password system

- explain representative clerical and software controls that should assist in maintaining the integrity of a system

- describe the principles and application of encryption techniques

- discuss the implications of software viruses and malpractice.

1   The Data Protection Act 1998

The Data Protection Act was initially introduced into UK law in 1984 for two major reasons.

- To counteract the threat to privacy caused by the increased ability of computers to hold, transfer and process personal data. Personal data is information about an individual.

- To enable the UK to meet its obligations to ratify the Council of Europe Data Protection Convention. When fully operational, this convention will enable the countries that have signed it to refuse to allow data to be transferred to other countries that do not have equivalent data protection laws.

The Act was amended in 1998, the new Act becoming law on March 1st 2000. This was required to comply with the EU's *Data Protection Directive*, which extended the scope of the legislation from just computer records of personal data to manual records as well.

KEY POINT

The transfer of personal data
outside the EU is restricted.

One feature of the Act is that the transfer of personal data outside the European Economic Area (basically the EU) is restricted. Personal data may only be transferred outside the EU if the other country has a similar level of data protection law.

Another feature of the 1998 Act is that it gives more powers to individuals whose details are being held; for example, the individual's explicit consent is required when processing sensitive data such as racial origin, criminal convictions or political opinions.

1.1   The scope of the Act

KEY POINT

The Act applies to personal data
of data subjects that is processed
by, or on behalf of, data users.

The Act applies to **personal data** of data subjects that is processed by, or on behalf of, data controllers.

The Act gives rights to individuals:

- to access personal data held about them by a data controller

- to seek compensation for any loss or damage suffered from the misuse of such personal data.

For the purposes of the Act, data is information recorded in any form. This can include data processed by equipment operating automatically, or data kept in manual records. There are various exclusions from the need to notify under the Act, including data held for standard business purposes. Note that manual records that have some logical filing system (structured data in terms of the Act) are included under the Data Protection legislation. However, if those records are simply used to maintain an organisation's accounting records, then there is normally no need to notify (that is register under the Data Protection Act).

KEY POINT

Personal data is data relating to a
living person who can be identified
from the data itself.

Personal data is data relating to a living person who can be identified from the data itself, and which is in the possession (or likely to come into the possession) of a data controller. However, data concerning deceased persons or companies is not within the scope of the Act. A person who is the subject of personal data held by a data controller is known as a **data subject**.

KEY POINT

Data is held when all of the
following apply:

- it forms part of the data
  processed or intended to be
  processed by, or on behalf
  of, that person

- the person controls the
  contents and use of the
  data

- the data is in the form in
  which it has been, or is
  intended to be, processed.

A data controller is a person who determines the purpose for which, and the manner in which, personal data will be processed and used. The 1998 Act refers to 'data controllers' whereas the 1984 referred to 'data users' in this context. Data is held or controlled when all the following conditions apply:

- the data forms part of the data processed or intended to be processed by, or on behalf of, that person

- the person controls the contents and use of the data

- the data is in the form in which it has been, or is intended to be, processed.

The implication is that a data controller does not have to own the computer on which personal data is held. For example, a computer bureau could process the data on behalf of the data controller, but it is the data controller who decides how the data should be processed. On the other hand, physical custody of a floppy disk containing personal data does not make that person a controller if he has not, and does not intend to, process it.

1.2   The Data Protection Register

This is a register of data users and bureaux compiled by the Data Protection Commissioner.

The register lists names and addresses of all users and bureaux together with general details of the nature of the personal data held and the purposes for which it is held. One or more addresses will be provided to which data subjects may write to request access to the data that relates to them.

1.3   Provisions of the Act

The 1998 Act gives a data subject, with some exceptions, the right to examine the personal data that a data controller is holding about him or her. Individuals may write to a data controller to ask whether they are the subject of personal data, and they are entitled to a reply.

The data controller may charge a nominal fee for providing the information, but is required to reply within a certain time.

Where personal data is being held, the data subject has the right to receive details of:

- the personal data that is being held

- the purposes for which the information is being processed

- the recipients to whom the information might be disclosed.

The data subject is also entitled to receive this information in a form that can be understood. In practice, this usually means providing the data subject with a printout of the data, and an explanation of any items of data (such as codes) whose meaning is not clear.

Any individual who suffers damage as a result of improper use of the data by the data controller is entitled to compensation for any loss suffered.

1.4   The Data Protection principles

The Data Protection Act establishes eight general principles or standards to be observed by data users and bureaux. Failure to comply with these principles can result in seizure of data and unlimited fines. The Secretary of State has the power to amend the principles. The principles are as follows:

Personal data held by users

1   The information in personal data should be obtained and processed fairly and lawfully.

(Obtaining the data fairly means that it should be collected from the data subject, and the data subject should know why it is being collected. Personal data must not be collected by deception or coercion.

Processing the data fairly means that the data subject should have given his or her consent, or that the processing is necessary to perform a contract to which the data subject is a party, or that the processing is necessary to comply with a legal requirement, and so on.)

2   Personal data held shall be held only for one or more specified and lawful purposes, and shall not be further processed in any manner incompatible with that purpose or those purposes.

(This means, for example, that a data controller cannot collect personal data for one purpose, such as to provide an internet service to a private customer, and then use the data for another purpose, such as marketing other services – unless the data controller has specified those purposes.)

3   Personal data shall be adequate, relevant and not excessive in relation to that purpose or purposes for which they are processed.

(A data controller should not collect more personal data than is actually needed. In this respect, a **data dictionary** can play a useful role in system development. A data dictionary sets out the role and purpose of every item of data held in a system, so that all the personal data held on the system can be justified.)

4   Personal data shall be accurate and, where necessary, kept up to date.

(The data controller should take reasonable steps to make sure that the data is accurate and up-to-date. One way of doing this is to write to data subjects periodically, and ask them to verify their personal data, or to notify the data controller if any details should be changed.)

5   Personal data held for any purpose or purposes shall not be kept for longer than is necessary for that purpose or those purposes.

(When the original purpose for collecting and holding the personal data no longer exists, the data should be destroyed. For example, when an employee leaves an organisation, the organisation should destroy all records relating to past appraisals of the employee.)

6   Personal data shall be processed in accordance with the rights of data subjects under this Act.

7   Appropriate technical and organisational measures shall be taken against unauthorised or unlawful processing of personal data and against accidental loss or destruction of or damage to, personal data.

8   Personal data shall not be transferred to a country or territory outside the European Economic Area unless that country or territory ensures an adequate level of protection for the rights and freedoms of data subjects in relation to the processing of personal data.

One of the main duties of the Commissioner is to encourage data controllers to comply with these principles. The registrar will investigate complaints that these principles have been contravened and may issue the following:

•   an enforcement notice requiring the recipient to comply with the principles within a set time

•   a deregistration notice threatening to remove the recipient from the register

•   a transfer prohibition notice forbidding the transfer of specified data out of the EEA.

If a data controller is deregistered and may no longer process personal data, that could effectively put them out of business. The controller may appeal to a Data Protection Tribunal against these notices.

Reasons for processing

Personal data cannot be processed unless one of the following exclusions for processing is met:

•   The data subject consents to the processing. Consent must be explicitly obtained; it cannot be implied. In other words the data controller must ask the data subject whether personal data can be processed prior to that processing taking place.

•   Processing is the result of a contractual agreement, perhaps by providing a report to a client.

•   Processing is a legal obligation.

•   To protect the vital interests of the data subject.

•   Processing is in the public interest.

•   Processing is required to exercise official authority.

There are exemptions to the legislation. These might be exemptions from the Act altogether or from certain parts of the Act. Typical exemptions relate to information held for national security purposes, information about crime, information about taxation, data held for health, education and social work, payroll and accounting applications, the domestic use of computers and personal data held by unincorporated clubs and societies.

KEY POINT

Processing of personal data is forbidden except in specific circumstances.

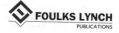

Sensitive data

Also, data which is deemed to be sensitive cannot be processed without the express consent of the data subject. Sensitive data is data relating to racial origin, political opinions, religious beliefs, physical or mental health, sexual preferences or trade union membership.

2   The Computer Misuse Act 1990

Until the introduction of the *Computer Misuse Act* in 1990, two highly damaging activities were not against the law. These were hacking into computers, and the deliberate infection of computer systems with viruses. Although an offended organisation could use the civil courts to seek damages for losses suffered, there was no effective legal protection against these two misdemeanours.

2.1   Hacking

Hacking is the gaining of unauthorised access to a computer system, and perhaps altering its contents. Hacking might be done in pursuit of a criminal activity or it may be a hobby, with hackers acting alone or passing information to one another. Hacking is often a harmless activity, with participants enjoying the challenge of breaking part of a system's defences, but severe damage can be caused to the computer system owner.

Although computer hacking is commonly associated with outsiders breaking into a computer system, the law also applies to unauthorised access to an organisation's computer systems by its own employees.

2.2   Viruses

A virus is a piece of software that seeks to infest a computer system, hiding and automatically spreading to other systems if given the opportunity. Most computer viruses have three functions – avoiding detection, reproducing themselves and causing damage. The damage caused may be relatively harmless and amusing ('Cascade' causes letters to 'fall' off a screen), but are more often severely damaging. In recent years two viruses in particular ('Melissa' and 'I Love You') were spread by email address books around the world within a very short time, and inflicted considerable damage to systems, and the businesses that depended on them.

Hackers and viruses are examined in greater depth later in this chapter.

2.3   The criminal offences created by the Act

This act was designed to outlaw hacking, the introduction of viruses and the unauthorised copying of data. Three new offences were created by the Act:

Unauthorised access to a computer (hacking)

It has become illegal to gain access or to attempt to gain access to a computer system without authorisation. It is not necessary to succeed in gaining access to be guilty of this crime.

The maximum penalty is up to six months in prison and/or a fine.

For example, an employee of a company might gain unauthorised access to the payroll records, perhaps by using the password of an authorised user, and look at the salaries paid to the company directors.

KEY POINT

Offences created by the Act:

- unauthorised access (hacking)

- unauthorised access with intent to commit another offence

- unauthorised modification of data or programs.

Unauthorised access with intent to commit another offence

The maximum penalties for this crime are significantly greater than for unauthorised access alone:

- On summary conviction an offender is liable for up to six months in prison and/or an equivalent fine.

- On conviction or indictment an offender may be imprisoned for up to five years and/or an unlimited fine.

For example, an employee of a company might gain unauthorised access to the employee records, and find information about an employee that he or she can then use for blackmail.

Unauthorised modification of data or programs (introduction of viruses and computer sabotage)

A person is guilty under this offence if the intention is to prevent or hinder access to any program or data or to compromise the reliability of data or programs.

The penalties for this crime are the same as for the crime of unauthorised access with intent to commit another offence.

2.4   What you need to know about data legislation

You need to be aware of the scope and terms of the Data Protection Act and the Computer Misuse Act, and the data protection principles.

You should also give some thought to how the requirements of the Act can be enforced. For example:

- How can an organisation enforce the requirement of the data protection principle 5 that personal data should not be held for longer than its purpose? A comment has already been made about the possible use of a data dictionary in this context.

- How can offences under the Computer Misuse Act be prevented or detected if they occur? Control over access to computers (both physical access and access through passwords and user names) and the use of firewalls and anti-virus software are all possibilities.

3   Copyright law and software contracts

Copyright in general terms is the right to publish, reproduce and sell the matter and form of a literary, musical, dramatic or artistic work. The owner of the copyright can therefore sell the item that the copyright relates to, and can stop other people from selling the same work because they are breaching the copyright obtained by the original author.

KEY POINT

The Copyright, Designs and Patents Act of 1988 provides the same protection to the authors of computer software as it does to literary, dramatic and musical works.

Within the UK, the *Copyright, Designs and Patents Act* of 1988 provides the same protection to the authors of computer software as it does to literary, dramatic and musical works. However, selling software is slightly different to selling a book or painting, for example. When computer software is sold, it is not sold outright to the purchaser. Instead, the purchaser is granted a right to use that software as explained in the user licence. This normally means that only one person at a time can use the software, and that making of copies of the software is limited to back up purposes only. The purchaser cannot therefore simply copy the software onto another CD or floppy disk, as this would breach the copyright.

Most software suppliers allow more than one person to use one copy of the software, where, for example, the software is loaded onto a network server, and a licence to use multiple copies of the software has been purchased.

Some software can be copied legally; this is **shareware**. The software can be loaded onto a computer and tested; however, if the user decides to keep the software, then a royalty payment is due to the author. **Freeware** is software that can be copied and used without charge, although the software author retains the copyright to that software. Finally, **public domain software** is freely available and sharable software that is not copyrighted.

Anyone convicted of an offence under this Act can expect a fine of unlimited amount plus a prison sentence of up to two years.

3.1   Software contracts – off-the-shelf software

Software contracts can be in respect of either packages or bespoke software. The contracts governing most packages are standard. As explained above, users are normally licensed to use a copy or copies of the software; they do not own the software as such and the licence can be withdrawn if the contract is breached.

The important terms found in package software contracts govern the user's rights of use and limit the software vendor's liability.

A typical licence agreement is reproduced below:

Software Licence Agreement

1   **WHAT THIS IS.** This sheet contains the Software Agreement (the 'Agreement'), which will govern your use of the ABC Company software package 'XXXXX'.

   YOU AGREE TO THE TERMS OF THIS AGREEMENT BY THE ACT OF ORDERING OR RUNNING OR INSTALLING THE SOFTWARE.

2   **GRANT OF LICENCE.** On acceptance of your order, ABC Company will grant you, and you will accept, a limited licence to use the ordered software, user instructions, and any related materials (collectively called the 'Software' in this Agreement). You may use one copy of the software. If installed on a network, only one user may use the software at any time.

   You may not transfer or sublicense, either temporarily or permanently, your rights to use the Software under this Agreement without the prior written consent of ABC Company.

3   **TERM.** This Agreement is effective from the day you receive the Software and continues until you return the original magnetic media to ABC Company. You must also certify in writing that you have destroyed any copies you may have recorded on any memory system or magnetic medium.

4   **ABC COMPANY'S RIGHTS.** You acknowledge that the Software is the sole and exclusive property of ABC Company. By accepting this Agreement, you do not become the owner of the Software, but you do have the right to use the Software in accordance with this Agreement. You agree to use your best efforts and all reasonable steps to protect the Software from unauthorised use, illegal reproduction, or illicit distribution.

5   **YOUR ORIGINAL DISKETTE/HARD DISK COPY.** You may use the original diskette to make a hard disk copy for the purpose of running the Software program. You should not use the original diskettes when running the Software program. After making a hard disk copy place the original diskette in a safe place. Other than the authorised hard disk copy, you agree that no other copies of the Software will be made.

6   **LIMITED WARRANTY.** ABC Company warrants for a period of ninety (90) days from the effective date of this Agreement that, under normal use, and in accordance

---

with the installation instructions, the magnetic diskette will not prove defective, that the program is properly recorded on the diskette and that the accompanying instructions are substantially complete and contain all the information which ABC Company deems necessary for the use of the program. If, during the ninety day period, a defect in the Software should appear, you may return the software to ABC Company for replacement without charge. Your sole right with respect to a defect in the Software is replacement of the Software.

EXCEPT FOR THE LIMITED WARRANTY DESCRIBED IN THIS PARAGRAPH, THERE ARE NO WARRANTIES, EITHER EXPRESSED OR IMPLIED, BY THIS AGREEMENT. THESE INCLUDE, BUT ARE NOT LIMITED TO, IMPLIED WARRANTIES OF MERCHANTABILITY OR FITNESS FOR A PARTICULAR PURPOSE, AND ALL SUCH WARRANTIES ARE EXPRESSLY DISCLAIMED.

7   **LIABILITY.** You agree that regardless of the form of any claim you may have, ABC Company's liability for any damages to you or to any other party shall not exceed the license fee paid for the Software.

ABC COMPANY WILL NOT BE RESPONSIBLE FOR ANY DIRECT, INCIDENTAL, OR CONSEQUENTIAL DAMAGES, SUCH AS, BUT NOT LIMITED TO, LOSS OF PROFITS RESULTING FROM THE USE OF THE SOFTWARE OR ARISING OUT OF ANY BREACH OF THE WARRANTY, EVEN IF ABC COMPANY HAS BEEN ADVISED OF THE POSSIBILITY OF SUCH DAMAGE.

8   **TERMINATION OF AGREEMENT.** If any of the terms and conditions of this Agreement are broken ABC Company has the right to terminate the Agreement and demand that you return the Software to ABC Company. At that time you must also certify in writing that you have not retained any copies of the Software.

9   **GOVERNING LAW.** This Agreement is to be governed by, and interpreted in accordance with the law of England.

3.2   Software contracts – bespoke software

The user should have more say when negotiating for bespoke programs to be written. Of particular importance will be who owns the copyright to the program and the source code. Unless otherwise stated, the law will assume that the software writer will own these. The full list of matters that should be addressed is as follows:

- precise description and specification of the software
- performance warranties (that it will operate with certain response times)
- price
- terms of payment
- dates for completion
- acceptance tests and period for acceptance
- penalties for late delivery and poor performance
- conditions of use
- ownership of copyright
- ownership of source code
- documentation
- training
- warranties
- after-sales service and levels of support

- protection against copyright infringement
- confidentiality (client's business matters).

All these items will be included in an agreement to write the software, prior to that writing being commenced.

4   Security, privacy and threats to the organisation

Security and privacy are both important considerations in the design and operation of information systems in an organisation. Their importance is evidenced by the fact that both have been the subjects of legislation within the last few years. The protection of the organisation's security and the individual's privacy must be key aspects of the organisation's information technology strategy.

4.1   Security

Security can be defined as:

- the protection of data from unauthorised access, change or modification
- the protection of programs from unauthorised change or modification
- the assurance that systems operate as designed, and that users continue to receive the services that they need
- the protection of hardware against damage
- the protection of humans against injury and harm.

The damage to data, software and hardware can be caused deliberately or accidentally, and may be caused by 'act of God' or by human malice or error. The assurance that systems operate as defined implies that system faults are also within the broad definition of security problems.

Security, therefore, is a wide and important part of the management of IT, and must be taken very seriously. A security policy should consider the avoidance or minimisation of threats, the prediction and detection of problems and the recovery from problems.

4.2   Privacy

Privacy is the right of an individual to control the dissemination or use of data that relates to him or herself.

The volume of data that can be held on a computer, the speed with which it can be transmitted, and the ability of the computer to link several sets of data pose especial problems. Personal information can be misused much more effectively on computer than with manual systems. The dangers of this misuse led to the *Data Protection Act* (above).

4.3   Threats

There are always threats to an organisation during the operation of any system, whether the system is manual or computer-based. Computer systems are much more vulnerable to risk because of the power and speed of the computer, and because problems are more difficult to identify.

The extra problems of computer systems are:

- Data stored on magnetic media is much more liable to undetected corruption or loss.
- The computer can be accessed remotely via the public communications network – unauthorised people can access and change data.

- No automatic trace of computer transactions is created. If a problem occurs, it may be impossible to correct or even detect inaccuracies in the data.

- The computer can carry out processes so fast that a great deal of damage can be done by the time that an error has been detected.

- The computer does not have an automatic 'feel' for what is reasonable.

Types of threat

Five basic types of threat to an organisation relate to information technology.

DEFINITION

Five basic threats:

- physical damage to hardware or computer media

- damage to data

- damage to humans

- operational problems

- industrial espionage/fraud.

Physical damage to hardware or computer media

Malicious damage, poor operating conditions, natural disasters and simple wear and tear can physically damage machinery and storage media such as disks, tapes and diskettes. These carry a triple threat – the cost of repair or replacement of hardware; the danger of damaged data or program files; and the cost of computer down time. This is discussed in greater detail below.

Damage to data

Hackers, viruses, program bugs, hardware and media faults can all damage data files. The havoc caused by damaged data is made worse if it is not detected and rectified quickly.

Damage to humans

Computers and peripherals can cause hazardous conditions for operators and users, who can receive electric shocks, trip over wires, gash themselves on sharp corners, or be injured in fires. Sometimes physical precautions against computer damage can themselves create danger. Some units, for example, are protected against fire by being flooded by CO_2 gas. If someone were trapped when this happens, serious injury or death may result.

RSI – repetitive strain injury is an injury caused by constant repetition of specific activities such as the use of keyboards. It can cause long-term problems and has forced many individuals into premature retirement and their employers have had to pay large damages claims.

To avoid physical trauma to users of computer equipment, attention should be paid to their needs when designing workstations and setting up the computer installations. Measures that can be taken to protect staff include:

Good ergonomic design

Workstations should be designed for comfortable use by the people who are going to use them. The lighting must be such that there is no glare or reflection from screens. The screens themselves should be designed to reduce the amount of flicker, which is extremely tiring to the eyes. Furniture must be of a comfortable height for the average user, and should be adjustable to fit the needs of the non-average user. The designers of workstations should also avoid sharp corners and projections that users could accidentally hurt themselves on. Wires should not be in a position where people can trip over them.

Ducting and false floors

To avoid the damage to both users and equipment that can be caused by tripping over cables, these should be fed through ducting or passed through false floors and false ceilings.

Safety awareness and training

Most accidents are caused by human error, so it is important to stress awareness of safety in the workplace. A high priority must be placed on the well-being of staff, which will cut down on absenteeism and sickness, reduce costs and increase the effectiveness of staff.

Operational problems

Program bugs and operational mistakes can cause significant problems, ranging from the need to resuscitate files and repeat computer runs, to the possibility of losing customers.

Industrial espionage/fraud

Industrial espionage and sabotage can yield significant advantages to competitors, and fraud and blackmail is a significant threat.

4.4   The underlying causes of problems

The basic causes of problems are:

1   **Human error.** The most prolific cause of problems is human error.

2   **Technical error.** Hardware or software malfunction is another significant risk, with communications equipment giving especial problems.

3   **Natural disasters.** Natural disasters (bad weather, earthquakes, fire, flood, etc.) cannot be avoided completely, but their possibility must be catered for.

4   **Fraud, espionage, sabotage.** The deliberate actions of individuals can result in significant loss, whether these actions are for personal gain, for competitive advantage or for revenge or malice.

5   **Poor personnel relations.**

5   General protective measures

Although many of the measures discussed below will be described in more detail later on, it is relevant at this point to list a number of measures that organisations should take to protect themselves whenever they build information systems.

1   **Physical security.** Access to hardware should be controlled and restricted to authorised personnel. This will reduce the chances of physical sabotage, accidental damage and hacking.

2   **Protection against remote access.** Passwords and user numbers can be used to limit the chances of unauthorised people accessing the system via the public communications network.

3   **Back-up procedures.** Data should be backed up on a regular and systematic basis. This will enable problems to be recovered with the minimum of trouble.

4   **Strict operating procedures.** Imposing strict operating procedures and controls reduces the chances of human error.

5   **Attention to health and safety.** All dangers should be eliminated from the working environment by passing cables through ducts and being alert to safety hazards. The danger of RSI and eyestrain will be reduced by the careful ergonomic design of workstations and the use of flicker-free visual display units.

6   **Encryption of data.** If data is encrypted, the only people who can read the data are those who have the key to the encryption technique. This means that even if an industrial spy were to gain access to a computer system or intercept a communications link, the damage they could do would be limited.

7   **Vigilance.** The most dangerous situation is where people become overconfident and blasé. All people in the organisation should be alert to danger at all times.

6   Physical threats to computer installations

Poor security may result in physical damage to a computer installation – either accidental or deliberate. It may also allow unauthorised access by ill-intentioned or ham-fisted people. In either case, protective measures must be taken.

For an organisation to plan its defence against any kind of threat, it must make a catalogue of the dangers that it faces before counter-measures can be developed.

6.1   Physical threats

Physical threats can result in many kinds of damage to an installation. All parts of the system are vulnerable, including the machinery, the environment, computer media, software and the people using the system. The resulting damage can be so crucial that companies can be completely bankrupted by physical disasters that they have not properly protected themselves against. Physical threats include:

Fire

Fire is a very serious hazard to a computer system. It can damage or destroy every part of a computer installation – hardware, software, data files and the original transaction documents. Even the people involved and the fabric of the computer installation are at risk from fire.

It is not just the flames that cause the damage; heat, smoke, dust and the substances used to fight the fire are all very destructive.

Flood

Water can be extremely damaging to any kind of electrical equipment. Rivers and seas overflowing may cause flooding, or it may be caused by the results of fighting fires within the building. Computers sited in the basement or ground floor of buildings are more susceptible to flooding than those sited on upper floors, although the floor immediately underneath a water tank may also be at risk.

Weather

Bad weather can harm an installation by physically damaging the fabric of the building, by damaging hardware or computer media, or by interrupting the power supply. The worst damage is caused by extreme weather such as high winds, torrential rain or thunderstorms, but long term erosion of weathering can also degrade the fabric of the building and harm the computer installation.

Although the threats posed by wind, rain and extreme temperatures are significant, the most common weather-based threat is lightning. This can act in a number of ways:

- A lightning strike on a building may damage its fabric or burn out electrical cabling and other equipment.

- The cabling connecting different machines in a network may be struck. This can damage several machines at the same time, and disable the network.

- Overhead pylons carrying high voltages are very commonly struck by lightning. This can cause power surges and spikes in the electricity supply to the computer installation and damage equipment several miles from the lightning strike. Data files corrupted by this occurrence must be reconstructed and can cause a great deal of down time in an unprotected organisation.

Natural disasters and terrorist attack

Earthquakes and explosions are potentially disastrous to people, machinery and buildings. They are also likely to disrupt communication lines. Damage caused by terrorists may be an accidental side-effect of an attack on another target, or it may be specifically aimed at a commercial or military organisation.

Uncontrolled physical environment

A great deal of equipment and computer media needs to be operated in a controlled physical environment. Although it is less important for PCs, they are still susceptible to many hazards. Dangers include:

- dust
- heat
- cold
- humidity
- spillages (e.g. coffee, tea, soft drinks and food)
- static electricity
- magnetic fields
- power failure, irregular current, surges and spikes.

Deliberate physical attack and fraud

In addition to the sort of terrorist attack described above, computers are also liable to attack from disgruntled employees, ill-disposed members of the public, thieves, industrial spies, blackmailers and extortionists, and other criminals. There are a number of such hazards that installations need protecting against:

- hardware sabotage
- hardware theft
- software piracy
- blackmail and extortion
- copied or stolen data
- unauthorised alteration of programs
- false transactions being applied to data files
- loss of confidentiality
- physical interception of data communication
- the use of detection equipment to show what is being displayed on computer monitors. Equipment similar to television detector vans can intercept the radiation from a monitor and display a facsimile of what is displayed on the screen. This equipment can operate over a distance of many yards.

7   Countering physical threats

Once the physical threats to an installation have been catalogued, measures can be developed to counter them. Many of these measures will cost money, but others may just entail the introduction of good working practices.

Those counter-measures that do cost money need to be cost-justified. The cost-justification will not always be formally carried out, but management will need to know how much their counter-measures are costing.

The actions that can be taken to protect against physical threats can be categorised as follows:

1 **Preventative measures.** All possible measures must be taken to stop problems from occurring.

2 **Detective measures.** If a problem has occurred, the organisation must find out what has happened so that the effects are minimised.

3 **Corrective measures.** After a problem has been discovered, its effects must be minimised and the organisation must take action to return the situation to normality.

The problems that do escape the net of the preventative measures adopted by the organisation may reveal weaknesses that need to be countered in the future. Planning against threats must be regarded as an ongoing process.

7.1   Protection against fire

There is a range of measures that can be adopted to protect against the risk of fire or alleviate its consequences:

• training of staff to be alert against fire

• control of combustible materials

• regular fire drills

• smoke and heat detectors

• fire alarms

• fire doors and automatically closing doors

• automatic extinguishers: carbon dioxide and water sprinklers (where appropriate)

• manual foam-based extinguishers

• regular backing up of files and transaction data

• fire-proof, water-proof safe for back-up media

• holding back-up materials off-site

• regular servicing of machinery and maintenance of electrical equipment

• the use of computer bureaux if machinery is damaged

• planned redundancy – the availability of more than one machine, so that work can be transferred onto another machine if one is affected

• insurance cover.

Not all of the above measures are adopted in every organisation – some measures are alternatives to others – but there is often a synergy between some of the above measures, with several measures being more effective if they are used in combination. Insurance premiums are likely to be reduced if insurance companies are satisfied with the other measures adopted. Regular backing up of data is of little use unless the back ups are stored in a fireproof safe or at another location.

7.2   Protection against floods and the weather

Several of the measures to protect against fire have a more general value. The regular taking and safe storage of back ups, the use of external bureaux or planned redundancy, and the use of insurance policies to mitigate the results of disasters are examples of general-purpose protective measures.

Some of the more specific measures are:

Careful siting of hardware

Computer machinery should be installed away from dangers. Organisations will usually avoid the basement and other areas that are vulnerable to flooding. Most computers of any kind, including PCs, micro computers, will not be put into temporary office buildings unless operational reasons dictate that they should be.

Regular building maintenance

If the building is well maintained, there is less chance that leaks will cause major problems.

Shielded cabling

Cables and wires are vulnerable to water as well as to lightning strike. If there is a weakness in the cable, electricity will track across a damp surface causing further degrading.

7.3   Power failure

Back-up generators

In the event of a power failure, a back-up generator can be switched on to enable processing to continue. These generators may be tripped automatically to minimise disruption.

Current isolators

Specialised equipment can be connected to the power supply to flatten out spikes and other uneven patterns in the amount of electricity coming through. Spikes can cause computers to make errors and damage disk contents.

Current isolators minimise the danger of damage to computer media or hardware.

7.4   Physical attack

Shatter-proof glass

Shatter-proof glass will minimise the problems caused by explosions and similar terrorist activities.

7.5   Environmental control

One of the most powerful protections against physical threats is to isolate the computer installation as far as possible from the rest of the world. The degree to which this can be done will depend upon the size and value of the computers and the importance of the systems that run upon them. Mainframe computers are likely to be enveloped in a protective cocoon, whereas personal computers have fewer external protections and must be more inherently robust – more tolerant to imperfections in their environment. Some machines are built to withstand extreme conditions, especially those that are designed to be used outside.

More generally, however, business computers have protective measures built into their environment. These measures include:

Separate area

A separate or segregated area will enable the section of a building containing the computer facilities to be totally controlled. Air conditioning and dust controls will ensure that the computer equipment operates under optimum conditions.

Static control mats

Static control mats dissipate static electricity before it can build up into a damaging charge.

Separate electrical supply

Spikes, surges and dips in the electricity supply are not only caused by problems in the public network. There may also be problems caused locally within the building itself. A particular danger is when more than one piece of electrical equipment shares the same circuit. Switching on a power-hungry piece of equipment is likely to cause a significant dip in the power available to machines that are already switched on. Even machinery such as electric kettles and vacuum cleaners can cause problems to computers. It is unwise, therefore, to connect sensitive equipment such as computers to circuits shared by other machinery.

Restricted access

Many of the physical threats to a computer installation that we have discussed earlier are caused by unauthorised individuals gaining access to the computers. Restricting access to the computers by the installation of security mechanisms will minimise these risks. A discussion of some of these security measures can be found later in this chapter.

7.6   Protection against fraud and data theft

Once people have gained access to computer facilities, they may try to enter false transactions or to copy data. There are a number of measures that can be taken to detect when this is happening and to avoid likely problems. The measures that can be taken include the use of physical devices, operational procedures and security software.

The sort of security procedures that may be adopted include:

Strict controls over input/processing/programs and division of duties

There should be no confusion over which person should be doing each job. In this way, the chance of problems occurring is very much reduced; if problems do occur then it is much easier to establish what has happened and to rectify the situation.

Internal audit review systems

It should be possible to trace back all the events that affect data files. An audit trail will enable management to identify when any problems have occurred and find out what the causes of those problems were.

Encryption of data

Data may be coded so that it is not understandable to any casual observer who does not have access to suitable decryption software. Encryption provides a double benefit. It protects against people managing to gain access to the system, and it protects against the tapping of data whilst being transmitted from one machine to another.

Shielding of VDUs

To protect against people with detection equipment being able to view remotely what is being displayed on VDUs, the units may be shielded to prevent the transmission of radiation that can be detected. Computers containing sensitive material can also be sited so that they are out of the range over which detector vans can operate. Some defence establishments have been known to install PCs accessing sensitive information in metal-lined rooms with no outside windows, to eliminate the chance of unauthorised individuals viewing what is being shown on the screen.

8   Physical access control

Reducing access to sensitive areas can cut down considerably on the risks posed by intruders. It will minimise the probability of hardware theft, espionage, sabotage and all other kinds of computer crime. It also reduces the chance of non-criminals causing inadvertent damage.

There are various basic categories of controlling access to sensitive areas. These include:

- security guards
- physically lockable working areas
- safes and lockable cabinets.

An organisation may have a mixture of different devices to restrict access.

There is likely to be a security guard controlling access to the whole building. Especially sensitive areas are likely to be very tightly controlled – this would include the main computer facilities. Security in other parts of the building is likely to be much lighter, sometimes depending on the operating procedures of an individual department.

Physical security within the computer department

Security in the computer department itself is likely to be very tightly controlled. Some of the controls that may be operated are:

- the computer department being sited in a secure part of the building, often on an upper floor
- access past a separate reception or security desk
- access being via locked doors which may be opened in a number of different ways:
    - typing in a personal identification number (PIN)
    - an electronic key card
    - conventional keys may be issued to authorised personnel
    - combination locks requiring a person to type in a set sequence of digits, which can be periodically changed
- closed circuit TV used to monitor what is happening in a particular part of a building – this may be backed up by security video cameras.
- doors automatically locked in the event of a security alarm
- computer equipment electronically or physically tagged to activate an alarm if an attempt is made to carry it out of the building or computer area.

Other devices, such as machines which can identify fingerprints or scan the pattern of a retina, are often seen in TV programs, but are not in general use, either for technological reasons or because they are too expensive.

8.1   Data security

The first line of defence against interlopers is to control physically who is allowed near to the computer. The second line of defence is to reduce the damage that can be caused when the first line of defence is breached.

This can happen when an interloper succeeds in getting past the security measures or when a hacker manages to access the computer remotely.

In either case, it is vital to prevent unauthorised users from changing or viewing data, and to limit the damage that they can do. There are a number of points to consider:

Theft of disks

Diskettes and CDs (both referred to hereafter as disks) are vulnerable to theft and to damage. Although the disks themselves are not valuable, the data they hold can be. They can be easily smuggled out of a building in a briefcase or a pocket, and disk security is often a weak link in an organisation.

Disks should not be left lying around on desks and working surfaces. They may be lost, stolen, inadvertently reused or damaged by spillages of hot drinks. Disks should be locked away when not being used, and should be filed for easy reference. All disks containing important information must be backed up on a regular basis.

Theft of printout

Computer printout may well contain confidential data. Many industrial spies make a habit of investigating the rubbish for useful titbits of information. Disks are also sometimes discarded and, even if files have been deleted, the data on them can be recovered. Both printout and disks should be shredded or otherwise destroyed before being thrown away.

Unauthorised access

Passwords and user numbers are used as a way of identifying who is authorised to access the system. There may be several levels of password, with particularly sensitive applications protected by multiple passwords. There may also be a system of electronic handshakes; these enable the computer to recognise which terminal is accessing it. This allows some applications to be restricted only to certain terminals. These protections can also be used to help track down the culprits when a security breach has occurred.

It is important to maintain strict security over the passwords used. Unauthorised users may discover passwords in several ways. For example, a written reference to the password may be secreted somewhere near the computer (often taped to the underside of a desk drawer). The hacker may be able to guess the password from knowledge of the private life of an authorised user; the password or user number might be worked out through trial and error (sometimes carried out systematically by a computer program); the password may have been 'lent' or otherwise discovered because of carelessness.

PIN numbers are used in certain circumstances. These personal identification numbers can be used in combination with magnetic strip cards to reinforce security. Cash dispensers are a typical example of this kind of protective measure.

FOULKS LYNCH
PUBLICATIONS

9   Passwords

The British Computer Society's definition of a password is: 'a sequence of characters that must be presented to a computer system before it will allow access to the system or parts of that system.'

The sequence of characters referred to above can be any combination of letters, numbers or symbols. The system in use will determine such factors as the maximum/minimum length of password permitted; characters which may not be allowed (*, ?, -, for example), whether the password is case-sensitive, etc. The administrators of the system can usually set the properties of the individual's account: when/if the password expires (obviously the security of the system is improved if a user has to change the password regularly); if the user is able to change their own password, etc.

When a password is entered, the characters entered should not appear on the screen (but may appear as, for example, asterisks; this confirms to the user the number of characters entered). This will prevent disclosure of the password to any onlooker.

The use of passwords is to increase data security and restrict access. These objectives, however, need to be balanced against the resultant inconvenience and, if taken to extremes, a reduction in value of the system to users.

A password may be required at boot-up, i.e. when the machine is first switched on. If this level of security is used, care must be taken to ensure that this password is not forgotten; great inconvenience ensues if no one can easily gain access to the machine at this level!

In the case of a LAN, a password will usually be entered in conjunction with the user identity. The user identity will be displayed as it is typed in – or the user ID of the last person to log on may even appear by default – whereas the password should not appear as it is typed.

It is possible to set a screen saver to require a password to re-enter the system. This actually provides nothing more than a deterrent, as rebooting the machine will circumvent this restriction to access and, indeed, it is possible to identify the password which has been used by looking at the appropriate system file.

9.1   Problems with passwords

Password systems can only be effective if users use them conscientiously. There are several inherent problems with such a system:

- Authorised users may divulge their password to a colleague: this may arise because allowing temporary access in this way may be perceived as being more convenient than going through the process of setting up the colleague with their accounts.

- Many passwords may have associations with the user (e.g. son's name and age: brian14; house name and number: 19bellfield); these can be discovered by experimentation.

- Passwords are often written down close to the computer (e.g. pinned to the notice board inside the office), left on a yellow 'post-it' in a desk drawer or even attached to the terminal!

To protect passwords and user numbers against discovery, a number of precautions should be adopted:

- Users should be required to change their passwords regularly.

- Passwords should be memorable but not obviously related to a user's private life (common password choices such as children's or pets' names or birthdays).

- Users should be encouraged never to write down their passwords. Mnemonic methods should be suggested as an *aide-mémoire* (e.g. making up a phrase or nonsense sentence using the numbers and initial letters).

- Passwords should be case-sensitive and passwords should be a combination of numbers as well as letters.

- There should be strict controls over passwords – they should never be 'lent' or written down where they can be easily seen.

- There should be automatic sentinel or watchdog programs to identify when a password has been keyed incorrectly.

An alternative to passwords is for the user to have a card or badge; this can be used to establish the identity of the user, but passwords may then be required in conjunction with the use of the card.

10   A logical access system

10.1 The role of a logical access system

Physical access involves restricting unauthorised access to the hardware of a system. In comparison, logical access controls the access of those who do have access to a computer or terminal; this may take the form of restricting access to specific data application software.

A **logical access system** involves a system of facilities developed and maintained to protect data or software from the potential dangers of unauthorised access.

The potential dangers to data that may exist resulting from unauthorised access are as follows:

- It may be **inaccurate**. This situation may be difficult to detect as the system itself will ostensibly be functioning normally, but will in fact be producing inaccurate figures. The danger here is that management decisions may be reached using fallacious information.

- It may be **falsified**. This may be done to gain some advantage, to the detriment of the organisation.

- It may be **disclosed**. Information may be made available to individuals who have not been granted access to it, or to the public in general.

- It may be **lost**. This may occur at any stage (i.e. before, during or after processing).

10.2 The operation of a logical access system

Initially, the security risks with regard to computer-based should be assessed considering the potentialities identified above.

The next stage entails classification of data in terms of sensitivity. Suggested classifications may be:

- **public data**: giving wide access to read/copy

- **limited access data**: specific users in personnel or finance

- **private data**: access to identified individuals only.

A logical access system should, therefore, be capable of the following:

KEY POINT

A logical system should:

- establish user's identity

- verify user

- confirm that user has authorised access to requested data.

- establishing the user's identity by means of an ID code

- verifying the user, usually by means of a password

- confirming that the user has authorised access to the requested data.

To accomplish this the system should be capable of:

- identifying each user by means of a logical identifier

- matching the identifier with the terminal being used, to ascertain that access is from an authorised location

- controlling access to specified data and resources by users, terminals/computers

- logging accesses and usage of resources to facilitate auditing.

11   Hacking

Hacking is the deliberate accessing of on-line systems by unauthorised persons.

DEFINITION

Hacking is the deliberate accessing of on-line systems by unauthorised persons.

Management often requires that the contents of certain files (e.g. payroll) remain confidential and are only available to authorised staff. This may be achieved by keeping tapes or removable disks containing the files in a locked cabinet and issuing them only for authorised use.

The introduction and growth in the use of on-line systems has meant that alternative precautions need to be taken. Security at the terminal should be adequate; the terminal can be locked and/or kept in a locked room. Access and use should be properly recorded and controlled.

As organisations have grown to depend more and more on systems and the data stored on them, individuals and other organisations have become increasingly interested in gaining access to those systems and the data.

Since the 1980s, a class of highly intelligent individuals has emerged. These people use their knowledge of systems to gain unauthorised access to systems for their own purposes. The perpetrators, hackers, often consider hacking to be fun, and it is not necessarily done with malicious intent.

As modems and micros have become more widespread, the threat of hacking has increased. Due to changing working practices, many systems now have dial-up facilities; this facilitates entry into the system by the hacker after the telephone number has been obtained or by means of an auto dialler. To exacerbate the situation, hackers, having obtained numbers, make these available over the Internet.

11.1 The dangers stemming from hackers

A knowledgeable hacker can conceal any evidence of their deeds by disabling the journal or console logs of the main CPU.

Once hackers have gained access to the system, there are several damaging options available to them. For example, they may:

- gain access to the file that holds all the ID codes, passwords and authorisations

- discover the method used for generating/authorising passwords

- develop a program to appropriate users IDs/passwords

- discover maintenance codes, which would render the system easily accessible

- interfere with the access control system, to provide the hacker with open access to the system

- generate information which is of potential use to a competitor organisation
- provide the basis for fraudulent activity
- cause data corruption by the introduction of unauthorised computer programs and processing onto the system (computer viruses)
- alter or delete files.

11.2 Controls to help prevent hacking

By specifically identifying the risks that the hacker represents, controls can be designed to help prevent such activity occurring. Examples include:

Physical security

Check that terminals and PCs are kept under lock and key, and ensure that, where dial-in communication links are in place, that a call-back facility is used. (In call-back, the person dialling in must request that the system calls them back to make the connection. The system will only make a call to a pre-defined telephone number that is assigned to that specific user. This stops unauthorised users using a modem attached to the system to log in from an unidentified location.)

User authentication systems

There should be software controls over access. User authentication systems have two elements: user names and passwords.

User names

Each employee with authority to access some of the computer system files and programs is given a user name. Typically, each computer terminal will display the username of a particular individual, although this can be altered by keying in a different name. An individual user might be allowed access to some parts of the computer system but not others.

Passwords

In addition to user names, access is also protected by passwords. Each user of the system has an individual password, and has to key in the password correctly in order to gain access. To prevent an unauthorised person from 'stealing a password' by looking over the shoulder of an authorised person as he or she keys in a password, the screen displays asterisks as the password is keyed in, rather than the actual letters and numbers of the password.

The controls over passwords must be stringently enforced and password misuse should represent a serious disciplinary offence within an organisation. Associated with the password is a list of files, and data within files, which the user is allowed to inspect. Attempts to access unauthorised files or data will be prohibited by the operating system and reported at the central computer. For example, an order clerk using a VDU would be allowed access to the stock file, but not to the employee file. Similarly, the clerk would be allowed access to the customer file for purposes of recording an order, but would not be able to inspect details of the account.

Data encryption

Files can be scrambled to render them unintelligible unless a decoding password is supplied. Encryption can also be applied to data before transmission, so that it is unintelligible to eavesdroppers. (See below for more on Encryption.)

System logs

Every activity on a system should be logged and be subject to some form of exception reporting, e.g. unusual times of access could be reported.

Audit trails

Sensitive data, e.g. payee codes, should be subject to a separate audit report showing when the data was read, written to or updated. It should show also the before and after state and the data causing the change.

Sensitive users

Every facility must be accessible by at least one person. This should not mean that the same person has access to every facility. The system should allow a different user to be assigned to specific facilities as a form of segregation of duties, so that at least some form of collusion would be required, e.g. to generate an automatic payment on a non-existent supplier account.

Random checks

The 'constable on the beat' approach checks who is doing what at random intervals on the system, and ensures that they are authorised for those activities.

12   Encryption

Encryption provides a defence to enhance physical security measures.

Encryption is the technique of disguising information to preserve its confidentiality; this should occur during transmission and when stored. Encryption derives enciphered text from plain text, thus transforming the latter into an unintelligible form; in simpler terms, it is a method of scrambling the data in a message or file so that it is unintelligible unless it is unscrambled (or **decrypted**).

The process of encryption and decryption comprises an algorithm and a key; the algorithm is the operation itself, which transforms the data into cipher, and the key controls the algorithm; changing the value of the key can alter the effect of the algorithm so that the conversion for each key value is completely different.

Computers, because of their computational power, facilitate sophisticated encryption techniques that would otherwise be unrealistic. The cryptanalyst must devise a system with a cost of decoding which is sufficiently high to deter a potential unauthorised decoder but which has, at the same time, a level of sophistication no higher than necessary, as this slows down the processing time – which costs money.

Cipher keys may be different for each file or message, but they will usually be applied to groups. Often the same key is used for encryption and decryption, so both the sender and the receiver must know it, which increases the possibility of it becoming known to an unauthorised user.

If the encryption and decryption keys are different, they can be constructed so that a potential eavesdropper may gain complete knowledge of the encryption process and key and yet still be unable to unscramble the data, even with the aid of sophisticated computer equipment. The encryption key may be made generally available, and then it is know as a **public key.** The person receiving messages encoded with the public key retains a different (**private key**) that is needed to decrypt the message. Because the private key is kept secret, the person sending a message with the public key will know that only the intended recipient of the message can decrypt and read it.

KEY POINT

Encryption is the technique of disguising information to preserve its confidentiality.

KEY POINT

Encryption uses a **public key** that may be made generally available, plus a **private key** known only to the recipient. Without the private key, no one can decrypt the message.

So, if you make a purchase on the Internet, almost all vendors will confirm that you are on a secure link so your credit card details are safe. All this means is that your credit card details are encrypted using the vendor's public key; only the vendor has access to its own private key, making the transfer of data very secure.

Of course, you may argue that computers are so fast they can break encryption systems quickly. However, as noted above, the power of computers to search for decryption keys has lead in recent years to producing keys that would take a significant amount of computer time to break. Two encryption systems, PGP (Pretty Good Privacy) and RSA (named after the inventors Rivest, Shamir and Adleman and marketed by RSA Data Security Inc.) are examples of this type of encryption system. It has been estimated that with today's computing power, a message encrypted with RSA could not be broken before the universe ends!

13   Computer viruses

13.1 Types of computer viruses

A further security and control issue, which has been highlighted in recent years, is the growth of computer viruses. A **computer virus** is a small program that, having been introduced into the system, proliferates; its purpose is to spread extensively, impairing both data and software. As the name suggests, they have the ability to infect a whole computer system. The infected programs may then act as carriers for the computer virus, with the end result that the infection process can have a spiralling effect. The potential for the damage a virus can cause is restricted only by the creativity of the originator. Given the mobility between computerised systems and the sharing of resources and data, the threat posed by a viral attack is considerable.

Viruses can be categorised as:

- **trojans** – whilst carrying on one program, secretly carry on another
- **worms** – these replicate themselves within the systems
- **trap doors** – undocumented entry points to systems allowing normal controls to be bypassed
- **logic bombs** – triggered on the occurrence of a certain event
- **time bombs** – which are triggered on a certain date.

Once a virus has been introduced into the system, the only course of action may be to regenerate it from back up. However, some viruses are written so that they lie dormant for a period, which means that the back ups become infected before the existence of the virus has been detected; in these instances restoration of the system becomes impossible.

13.2 Preventative steps against computer viruses

It is extremely difficult to guard against the introduction of computer viruses. Steps may be taken to control the introduction and spread of viruses, but these will usually only be effective in controlling the spread of viruses by well-meaning individuals. The actions of hackers or malicious employees are less easy to control. Preventative steps may include:

- control on the use of external software (e.g. checked for viruses before use)
- use of only tested, marked disks within the organisation
- restricted access to floppy disks and CDs on all PCs/workstations.

Anti-virus software is available to protect against viruses, although the focus of these programs is to detect and cure known viruses; they will not always restore data or software that has been corrupted by the virus. As new viruses are being detected almost daily, it is virtually impossible for the virus detection software to be effective against all known viruses. More recent anti-virus software includes algorithms, which look for particular signatures or patterns of computer code, which imply a virus may be present. These programs have decreased the success of virus attacks, although one of the effects of these types of programs is to provide a new challenge for authors of computer viruses.

It is now usual for users connected to the internet to receive regular updates of their anti-virus software by downloading a new version of the software from the software supplier's web site, in response to an on-screen prompt.

14   Disaster recovery plans

An unexpected disaster can put an entire computer system out of action. For large organisations, a disaster might involve damage from a terrorist attack. There could also be threats from fire and flood damage. A disaster might simply be a software or hardware breakdown within a system.

Disaster recovery planning involves assessing what disasters might occur that would pose a serious threat to the organisation, and trying to ensure that alternative arrangements are available in the event that a disaster occurs.

In the case of a computer system for a clearing bank, this would mean having an entire back-up computer system in place that could be brought into operation if a disaster puts the main system out of action.

Not all organisations have extensive disaster recovery plans. Certainly, however, back-up copies of major data files should be kept, so that in the event that the main files are destroyed, the data can be re-created with the back-up files.

Conclusion

This relatively lengthy chapter has provided the background to maintaining the security and integrity of computer systems. The need to comply with legislation and implement appropriate controls to guard against specific risks facing an organisation's computer systems has also been discussed.

The following table might provide a useful summary of measures for dealing with risks to systems.

Potential threat	*Counter measure*
Physical damage, due to fire or flooding. Also damage caused by physical conditions such as dust, heat, cold, humidity, power failures, magnetic fields	Make sure that the procedures in event of a fire are well documented and that staff are trained in what to do. Provide fire extinguishers and smoke/heat detectors, fire-doors. Obtain insurance cover. Computer equipment might be located in a segregated area in which air conditioning and dust controls operate effectively. Static control mats and uninterrupted power supplies can be used.

 FOULKS LYNCH
PUBLICATIONS

	Off-site facilities can be pre-arranged to cater for the possibility of total destruction of the in-house computer equipment.
	Off-site back-up copies of data files should be maintained.
Damage caused by human interference, such as unauthorised access resulting in theft, piracy, vandalism	Access to the computer room should be restricted to authorised personnel only. Doors to the secure area should be locked and require either PIN code, conventional key, combination locks, or electronic keys to open them.
	Closed circuit TV and security guards are also possible solutions.
	The hardware itself can be physically or electronically tagged to sound an alarm if it is removed from the building. Where possible hardware can be locked down, or locked in cabinets.
Operational problems, such as program bugs and user operational errors	Thorough testing of new programs should help to minimise the risk of software errors (bugs) although it is unlikely that testing will eliminate the risk of software errors entirely. The procedure to follow in the event of finding a bug should be clearly documented and made known to all the staff.
	Strict operating procedures should be followed to control and reduce the number of user errors. Adequate training of all staff members will help.
Data corruption, e.g. viruses, hackers	Sentinel software, such as virus checkers should be run and updated regularly to prevent corruption of the system by viruses. Firewall software should provide protection against unauthorised access to a system from the internet.
	Passwords and user numbers can be used to limit the chances of unauthorised people accessing the system via the public communications network.
Data theft, e.g. fraud, industrial espionage, loss of confidentiality	Data encryption techniques prevent all but those individuals with the encryption key to view the data in an understandable form.
	Passwords and user numbers can be used to limit the chances of unauthorised people accessing the system via the public communications network.

	Physical access controls should also apply here.
Human resource risks, e.g. repetitive strain injury, headaches and eye strain from VDUs, risk of accidents caused by tripping over loose wires	The Health and Safety Officer should ensure that the work area is free from all avoidable hazards, for example all cables should be in ducts and should not run across an office floor. Careful ergonomic design of workstations should help to reduce the risk of repetitive strain injury. Anti-glare screens will reduce eye strain.

SELF-TEST QUESTIONS

The Data Protection Act 1998

1   What is personal data? (1.1)

2   What prohibitions are imposed on the transfer of data? (1.4)

The Computer Misuse Act 1990

3   What were the new crimes created by this Act? (2.3)

Copyright law and software contracts

4   In what way is the Copyright, Designs and Patents Act of 1988 relevant to computer software? (3)

Physical threats

5   What are the main physical threats to computer systems? (6.1)

Countering physical threats

6   How can an organisation protect its computer systems and data against fraud? (7.6)

Passwords

7   What are the inherent problems associated with the use of passwords? (9.1)

A logical access system

8   What is a logical access system? (10.1)

Hacking

9   What controls may be implemented to prevent hacking? (11.2)

Encryption

10   What is encryption? (12)

Computer viruses

11   What is a computer virus? (13.1)

FOULKS LYNCH
PUBLICATIONS

Data security

(a)   An organisation may hold sensitive data on computer. A logical access system is essential to protect such data. What is a logical access system, and how does it work?

(8 marks)

(b)   Explain the meaning of the following terms when relating to data security:

(i)   encryption   **(4 marks)**

(ii)   hacking   **(4 marks)**

(iii)   computer viruses   **(4 marks)**

(Total: 20 marks)

Security factors and the Computer Misuse Act

(a)   You are an outside consultant specialising in computer security brought in by an organisation to advise on the security aspects relating to a new computer centre.

(i)   What potential physical threats would you make your client aware of; what precautionary measures would you suggest; and what techniques would you propose should be implemented to control access to the computer centre?

(6 marks)

(ii)   You also feel that a contingency plan is an essential aspect of the new computing facility.

Explain to the client the purpose of such a plan, how it might be developed, and the standby options that are available.   **(8 marks)**

(b)   The *Computer Misuse Act* came into force in August 1990. What are the three offences that the Act defines and the penalties for each?   **(6 marks)**

(Total: 20 marks)

Data protection principles

The Car Drivers Society (CADS) is an organisation funded by members' subscriptions, providing services to members. These services include supplying handbooks, road maps, a monthly magazine and preferential rates for insurance and continental ferries.

Currently there are approximately seven million members each paying an annual subscription. Some members pay by direct debit, others by standing order, but most receive an annual invoice on the first day of the month in which they first joined.

The membership masters file is maintained on a computer file at Head Office from where all invoices and reminders are issued.

You are required, as a consultant employed by CADS, to prepare a report for the chief executive describing the implications of the Data Protection Act 1998 on the maintenance of the database and the proposed use of the data by other organisations for direct mailing. You should report on:

(a)   The requirements of the *Data Protection Act*.   **(4 marks)**

(b)   The data protection principles described in the Act.   **(8 marks)**

(c)   Conclusions and recommendations related to direct mailing.   **(8 marks)**

(Total: 20 marks)

For answers to these questions, see the 'Answers' section at the back of the book.

FOULKS LYNCH
PUBLICATIONS

Chapter 15
QUALITY ASSURANCE AND TESTING

The specification and production of software, like all human endeavours, can be affected by errors or incompetence. The costs that can result from errors in software systems can be large in both financial and human terms. Software errors can potentially threaten the financial health of enterprises or the physical health of human beings.

The disciplines of quality assurance and testing are employed to ensure the delivery of software systems of known and reproducible quality.

Objectives

By the time you have finished this chapter you should be able to:

- define the characteristics of a quality software product

- define the terms, quality management, quality assurance and quality control

- describe the V model and its application to quality assurance and testing

- explain the limitations of software testing

- participate in the quality assurance of deliverables in requirement specification using formal static testing methods

- explain the role of standards and, in particular, their application in quality assurance

- briefly describe the task of unit testing in bespoke systems development

- define the scope of systems testing

- distinguish between dynamic and static testing

- use a cause-effect chain (decision table) to develop an appropriate test script for a representative systems test

- explain the scope and importance of performance testing and usability testing

- define the scope and procedures of user acceptance testing

- describe the potential use of automated tools to support systems and user acceptance testing.

1   Quality software

1.1   What is quality software?

The aim of all software developers is to produce high quality software. However, what is meant by quality software may vary from developer to developer or between what the user expects from the software and what the developer is prepared to provide.

Whatever view is taken regarding software quality, the following characteristics will normally apply to it:

Reasonably bug-free. It is difficult, if not impossible, to ensure that complex software written today is 100% bug free. However, there is an expectation that software will perform its main activities accurately without any errors occurring.

Delivered on time. Organisations will rely on delivery dates for software, either because their systems need changing (due to changes in tax laws, for example) or because revised systems are needed to implement specific client service or other objectives. Delivering that software on time will therefore help organisations to meet their obligations and objectives. If software is delivered ahead of schedule, the service will be perceived to be significantly better.

Meets initial specification. Software is written to meet a requirements specification. The purchaser of the software will expect that the specification is adhered to when the final product is delivered. Meeting the specification provides good evidence that the software production has been correctly planned with appropriate focus onto user requirements.

Meets quality control standards. In other words, the software has been written to meet appropriate quality control standards, set by the ISO (International Organisation for Standards) and the IEEE (Institute of Electrical and Electronics Engineers). Meeting these standards provides good evidence that the software will be robust and adhere to the initial specification.

The actual mix of objectives to be met may vary depending on the software being written and the user groups interested in maintaining quality. For example, accountants may require that quality software is written within budget, while users require that quality software is user-friendly, providing an easy-to-understand user interface. Whatever the mix of objectives, the software must do the job expected of it, meeting the software specification originally developed.

1.2   Quality terms

Management has a duty to ensure that all tasks are completed consistently to a standard that meets the needs of the business. To achieve this they need to:

- set clear standards

- plan how to meet those standards

- track the quality achieved

- take action to improve quality where necessary.

2   Quality, quality and more quality

Quality is maintained at three different capacities within an organisation, namely:

- quality management

- quality assurance

- quality control.

2.1   Quality management

Quality management suggests a concern that the organisation's products or services meet their planned level of quality and perform to specifications.

2.2   Management role

Management has a duty to ensure that all tasks are completed consistently to a standard that meets the needs of the business. To achieve this they need to:

- set clear standards
- plan how to meet those standards
- track the quality achieved
- take action to improve quality where necessary.

Setting standards

To manage quality, everyone in the organisation needs to have a clear and shared understanding of the standards required. These standards will be set after taking account of:

- the quality expected by the customers
- the costs and benefits of delivering different degrees of quality
- the impact of different degrees of quality on:
  - the customers and their needs
  - contribution to departmental objectives
  - employee attitude and motivation.

Having decided on the standards these must be communicated to everyone concerned to ensure that the right standards are achieved. Documentation of the standards must be clear, specific, measurable and comprehensive.

Meeting the standards

Having decided on appropriate quality standards management should then:

- agree and document procedures and methods to meet the standards
- agree and document controls to ensure that the standards will be met
- agree and document responsibilities via job descriptions and terms of reference
- prepare and implement training plans for employees to ensure they are familiar with the standards, procedures, controls and their responsibilities.

Tracking the quality

After the process to achieve quality has been set up, an information system to monitor the quality should be set up. This is called quality control.

When a good system to track the quality has been achieved, it can be used constructively to improve quality and work on problem areas.

Employees within the organisation have a huge influence on the quality of their work and to gain their commitment and support the management should:

- publish the quality being achieved
- meet regularly with the staff involved to discuss the quality being achieved as well as the vulnerabilities and priorities as they see them. They should also agree specific issues and action points for them to work on to improve quality
- encourage ideas from the staff about improvements and consider introducing short-term suggestion schemes.

2.3   Quality assurance

Quality assurance is the title given to the more traditional view of quality. It may be defined as the process of:

- establishing standards of quality for a product or service
- establishing procedures or production methods that ought to ensure that these required standards of quality are met in a suitably high proportion of cases
- monitoring actual quality
- taking control action when actual quality falls below standard.

Quality assurance is the term used where a supplier guarantees the quality of goods supplied and allows the customer access while the goods are being manufactured. This is usually done through supplier quality assurance (SQA) officers, who control the specification of the goods supplied.

Some companies follow Japanese practice and use supervisors, workpeople or quality circles to control suppliers' quality. These representatives or the SQA officer may enter suppliers' plant, to verify that production is to the correct specification, working tolerances, material and labour standards. For example, the Ministry of Defence would reserve the right to ensure that defence contractors produce to specification, since defective work could mean the failure of a multi-million pound aircraft, loss of trained pilots and possibly ground crew as well as damage to civilian life and property. Likewise, a weapons system failure could have disastrous consequences.

One great advantage of SQA is that it may render possible reduction of the in-house quality control headcount, since there will be no need to check incoming materials or sub-assemblies or components.

2.4   Quality control

Quality control is concerned with maintaining quality standards. There are usually procedures to check quality of bought-in materials, work-in-progress and finished goods. Sometimes one or all of these functions is the responsibility of the research and development department on the premise that production should not self-regulate its own quality.

Statistical quality control through sampling techniques is commonly used to reduce costs and production interruptions. On some occasions, where quality assurance has been given, customers have the contractual right to visit a manufacturer unannounced and carry out quality checks.

In the past, failure to screen quality successfully has resulted in rejections, re-work and scrap, all of which add to manufacturing costs. Modern trends in industry of competition, mass production and increasing standards of quality requirements have resulted in a thorough reappraisal of the problem and two important points have emerged:

1   It is necessary to single out and remove the causes for poor quality goods before production instead of waiting for the end result. Many companies have instigated 'zero defects' programmes following the Japanese practice of eradicating poor quality as early in the chain as possible and insisting on strict quality adherence at every stage. As Crosby points out in his book Quality is Free, this is cost effective since customer complaints reduce dramatically.

2   The co-ordination of all activities from the preparation of the specification, through to the purchasing and inspection functions and right up to the function of delivery of the finished product, is essential.

It is accepted that it is not possible to achieve perfection in products because of the variations in raw material quality, operating skills, different types of machines used, wear and tear, etc. Quality control attempts to ascertain the amount of variation from perfect that can be expected in any operation. If this variation is acceptable according to engineering requirements, then production must be established within controlled limits and if the variation is too great then corrective action must be taken to bring it within acceptable limits.

2.5   The V model and its place in quality assurance and testing

The V model is illustrated in the figure below. 'V' refers to the two legs of the diagram. System design runs down the left leg of the V and follows testing back up the right leg. You will be familiar with most of the stages in the design and implementation of systems from studies in chapter 7, where the SDLC and different design methodologies were discussed. The V model is particularly relevant to the introduction of quality control within the design of information systems because of the three 'links' that are established between the initial design phase and the implementation of the system.

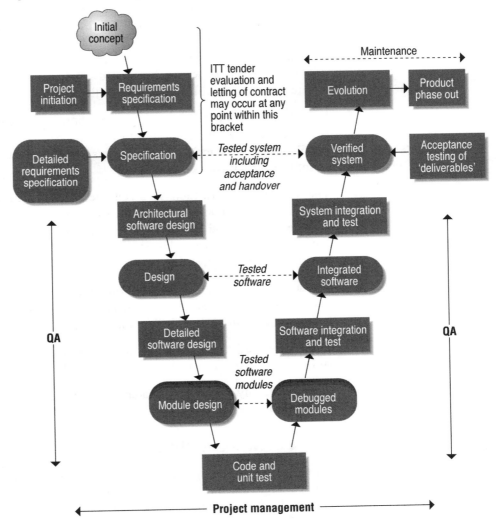

The first quality link is between the *specification* and the *verified systems* sections of the model. The specification provides the detailed requirements of the system, while the verified system includes the final user acceptance testing and final handover of the system. The purpose of acceptance testing at this stage is to ensure that the original requirements have been met. Checking that this is the case provides some assurance regarding the quality of the final product, although the quality underlying software may still be in doubt.

The second quality link is between the *design* and the *integrated software* sections of the model. During the design stage for software, the specific objectives for that software will be stated along with the different software modules that will have to be written. The software is then written and the different modules tested individually and together to ensure that they work correctly. The quality check then occurs when the integrated software is compared to the specification for that software. The tested software should meet the initial design; if this is not the case then amendments to the software will be required.

The third quality link is between the *module design* and the *debugged modules* sections of the model. This check tries to ensure that the individual software modules have been written and tested correctly. The overall design for the software is broken down into the different software modules. Each module is written, tested and debugged and then compared to the actual module design. As with the other quality checks, the module design, and the actual software produced should match with each other. If there are any differences, then the software module will need to be amended.

Following the V model therefore provides three quality checks in the writing of software, which hopefully ensures that the final software package is as error free as possible. One of the main strengths of this model is that it follows the normal hierarchy of software specifications, namely

The functional specification is a precise description of the required behaviour of the software. That is, it describes what the software should do rather than how the software achieves its goals and may also specify constraints on how this may be achieved. This separation is often described by saying that a functional specification defines the functionality of the software.

The design specification, which describes the architecture of a design that implements the functional specification. Components within the software and the relationship between them will be described in this document.

The detailed design specifications, which describe how each component in the software, down to individual units, is to be implemented.

The three quality control checks above correspond to these three levels of specification of software.

3 Software testing

For all bespoke systems, whether written in-house or externally, and for any off-the-shelf packages that have been modified in any way, testing is an integral part of the systems development process. The main standard for software testing is contained in the ANSI/IEEE standard 829-1983 – *Standard for Software Testing Documentation.* Some software testing may also be performed by computer, in which case the abbreviation CAST (computer aided software testing) may be encountered.

Testing broadly follows the structure of the V model, although some testing systems do recognise four distinct stages of testing, as outlined below.

3.1 Stages of testing

Testing can be broken down into four basic stages:

1   Testing the logic of the system and program

The technique of dry running can be used to make sure that the logic that has been set down by the analyst is correct. The programmer or analyst will trace by hand the progress of a number of sets of data through the structure diagrams or program flow charts. If all data produces the results that are expected, the individual programs can be written.

2   Program testing

Each program is thoroughly tested with test data. As explained earlier the test data is carefully selected to make sure that all sections of the program are working correctly. The testing process is carefully documented – with the data being tested, expected results, actual results and any action taken as a result of the test being recorded. The test documentation produced is an important part of the overall system documentation, being especially vital for system maintenance.

3   System testing

Once it has been established that individual programs are working correctly, the system must be tested as a whole. This is an equally important task, and the results should be documented in the same way as those for the testing of programs. It is not only the software that is evaluated during the system testing process, it is also important to test operating procedures, staffing levels, etc.

System testing must be carried out prior to installation (off-line testing) and immediately after implementation (on-line testing). The more off-line testing that is carried out, the lower the risk of failure during implementation. However, off-line testing cannot possibly find all of the problems with a system, as some will only appear during live operation.

4   Acceptance testing

The earlier stages of testing can be carried out by the systems development team. The users of the system must be involved at the last stage to ensure that the system is usable for them. It is just as important to ensure that the users will accept a system as it is to make sure that it performs to its specification. The users operate the system with test data, with their use of the system being monitored closely, and the users reporting on their experiences.

The involvement of users in the development process and the use of prototyping can cut down the problems that may be revealed during acceptance testing.

The producers of software packages also need to assure themselves that their software will be well received by their customers. Pre-production copies are sent to selected companies for their appraisal. Not only does this enable the software house to assess how popular the package is likely to be, it also allows any remaining bugs to be identified and eliminated. This process is often called beta testing.

These four stages of testing also correspond to the software development lifecycle where each phase of software writing is matched by a corresponding phase of testing. These links (again similar to the V diagram) are shown below.

The software development cycle

Feasibility ▪▪▪▪▪▪▪▪▪▪▪▪▪▪▪▪▪▪▪▪▪▪▪▪▶ Acceptance test

      Analysis ▪▪▪▪▪▪▪▪▪▪▪▪▪▪▪▪▪▪▶ System test

           Design ▪▪▪▪▪▪▪▶ Integration test

                 Program
               specification ▪▶ Unit test

                         Coding

3.2 Dynamic and static testing

Software testing can be carried out in a dynamic or static environment.

Dynamic testing is the process of evaluating a system or component of that system based upon its behaviour during execution.

Static testing is the process of evaluating a system or component of that system without executing the program or system.

The difference between the two testing methods is that dynamic testing means the program is actually running, while static testing is carried out by reviewing the program code; that is the program is not running.

There is a place for both types of testing within software development. A static test has the benefit that the program is not being executed, so errors will not affect other programs or the computer equipment. Many logical and code errors can be found by simply reviewing the code prior to running.

However, dynamic testing is essential before any software is implemented. It is only in live testing that the actual results of running the program can be seen and any potential conflicts within the program or between the program and other programs on the same computer be identified. Dynamic testing can last for days, and may involve users running the software to try and isolate as many bugs and errors as possible before the final software release date.

3.3 Overview of testing methods

As noted above, static testing methods mean testing the software, but not actually executing that software. The aim of testing is to ensure that the software is as bug-free as possible, while also meeting the initial design specification.

The design specification to be tested may have up to three different layers of documentation:

- the functional specification, which provides a precise description of what the software should do
- the design specification which explains how the functional specification will actually work
- the detailed design specification, which describes how each part of the software will be implemented.

Each element of the design specification has its own testing level:

- **unit testing** where each part of the software is tested to ensure that the detailed design for that unit has been correctly implemented
- **software integration testing** where individual units of the software are tested together until the whole program is working

DEFINITIONS

Dynamic testing is the process of evaluating a system or component of that system based upon its behaviour during execution.

Static testing is the process of evaluating a system or component of that system without executing the program or system.

- **system testing** the software is integrated into the final product and a check made to ensure that the functionality defined in the functional specification is actually available.

This section of the book focuses on detailed unit testing. Systems testing is covered in more detail later in this chapter.

3.4   Static testing plan

The design of tests for software follows the same basic principles as actually writing the software. Testing will be carried out on the overall strategic objectives of the software, followed by lower-level tests on the detail design specifications being carried out later.

The steps that will normally be carried out in testing software for appropriate quality using static testing methods will normally include:

1.   **Formulate a testing strategy.** This provides a statement of the overall approach to testing, identifying what tests are to be applied and which techniques or tools are to be used. The test strategy itself is normally part of the overall quality plan in producing the software.

2.   **Developing a test plan.** The plan states what items are to be tested and at what level they will be tested. The sequence of testing and the test environment will also be explained. In this situation, the test environment is a review of the documentation, rather than a live test.

3.   **Design the tests to be used.** Using a static testing system, the tests that can be used are relatively limited. One of the main tests will be reviewing the program code for functional and/or logic errors. A functional error means that the program has been written incorrectly (e.g. one command has been used when another is actually required) while a logical error means that errors in processing may occur (e.g. an person's age could be specified as being less than 25 and more than 60 at the same time).

4.   **Carry out the tests**. Each test will be stated as a test procedure, specifying the exact processes to be following in carrying out the tests. This type of detail is required to ensure that the test is valid and repeatable.

5.   **Document results of tests.** Any errors found in reviewing the software will be formally documented. This provides a record of errors as well as a review sheet for programmers to check the completeness of clearing the errors found.

6.   **Re-test.** Finally, the software may need to be re-tested to ensure that the errors found have been remedied.

3.5   Rules for software testing

As software is being tested, it is useful to remember the following rules:

- always test against a specification – testing without a specification implies that there is no need for the test as nothing of value is being tested

- document the testing process

- use different forms of testing techniques such as static and dynamic testing to provide a complete testing plan

- test positively, checking that the software does what it should do, and negatively, that it doesn't do what it shouldn't.

- have the right attitude to testing – it should be a challenge and not a chore.

3.6   Limitations of software testing

Although software is normally tested quite extensively, there are still some limitations in the testing methods and amount of testing that can be performed. Remember that software testing at this stage is concerned with checking the individual software programs. Full systems testing comes later when the individual software modules are integrated.

Limitations in software testing therefore include:

Not testing all possible values

Test data not testing all the possible types or values of data input that may occur within the system. For example, the range of data being tested may include values up to and including £999,999.99; because these appears to be the highest value that will be required in the system. However, in a few years, this value may be exceeded as values of transactions increase and inflation increases the overall price level. A broader range of values should be tested to ensure that the software can process them effectively and allow for future expansion of the system.

Inadequate error messages

Ensuring that all error messages contain adequate explanations of the error occurring. Many error messages are quite understandable to the program writers, but not necessarily to the users of the software. Users must be involved in the software testing to ensure that they can understand error messages and are aware of the appropriate action to take if an error does occur.

Not testing all the functionality of the software

The test plan may not cover all the functionality of the software. This may happen where software has been amended away from the initial specification, but inadequate documentation of those changes has been maintained. If the test plan is based on the initial specification then these changes will be omitted from the testing.

Inadequately documented testing process

The testing process is inadequately documented. This may occur, for example, due to human error or lack of complete documentation to record the tests actually taking place. The main risk is that errors in the software are not correctly recorded, and so those errors are not resolved prior to the software going forward to full system testing.

Inappropriate focus to the testing

Inappropriate focus to the testing. The software can be tested to check that it does what it should do rather than checking to ensure that it doesn't do what it shouldn't. Negative checking is as important as positive checking to ensure that the software responds appropriately to error situations or unusual data. For example, the need to allow for high value items was discussed above; although this is positive testing in that values above zero are expected. The software should also be tested to ensure that values below zero (values that are not expected) or alphabetical characters being entered into that particular field are actually rejected as being incorrect.

The basic rules of software testing noted earlier must be adhered to. Any attempt to rush testing is likely to result in failure, as errors in the software may not be detected.

KEY POINT

Limitations in software testing include:

- not testing all possible values

- inadequate error messages

- not testing all the functionality of the software

- inadequately documented testing process

- inappropriate focus to the testing.

4 The role of standards

4.1 Standards used in software testing

There are various standards that are used concerning the writing and testing of software. Within the UK, the British Standards Institution initially set many standards, although worldwide, other standards are also available developed by the International Standards Organisation (ISO) and the Institute of Electrical and Electronics Engineers (IEEE).

The ISO standards concern quality systems and are assessed by external auditors. They actually apply to many kinds of production and manufacturing organisations, not simply software development. The standard most commonly used by software developers is 9001; this covers documentation, design, development, production, testing, installation, serving and other processes. The standard ISO 9000-3 (not standard 9003) is the guideline used for applying ISO 9000 into software development organisations. ISO certification lasts for three years, after which reassessment is required. Note that ISO 9000 certification does not relate to the quality of software itself, but simply that documented processes are followed.

For reference, the full ISO series affecting software and similar development consists of five individual standards, ISO 9000-9004. Two of them are guideline standards and the others are reference standards.

- ISO 9000 is the *Guide to Selection and Use,* which is the guide to other standards in the series.

- ISO 9001 is the *Specification for Design/Development, Production, Installation and Servicing,* covering organisations concerned with all activities from conceptual design to after-sales service.

- ISO 9002, the *Specification for Production and Installation,* concerning organisations with product and service quality in production and installation only.

- ISO 9003 is the *Specification for Final Inspection and Test.* This is for activities that can only be quality assured at final inspection and test.

- ISO 9004 is the *Guide to Quality Management and Quality System Elements.* This is a guide to good quality management practice.

The IEEE provides similar standards to the ISO, although these standards tend to focus on the actual testing of software, not the initial development. The main standards are:

- IEEE 829 – 1983 *Standard for Software Testing Documentation*

- IEEE 1008 – 1986 *Standard for Software Unit Testing*

- IEEE 1012 – 1986 *Standard for Software Verification Plans*.

The British Standards Institution standards are now included within the ISO standards.

Program testing

- correct functioning of feasibility and validity checks on input data

- correct functioning of branching and looping

Program testing should cover:

- impossible values (e.g. negative stock) which causes confusion

- adequate storage and buffer areas

- proper batch control totals

- checking the interface with other programs and systems work

- the correct form of the output
- any operational problems in running the programs.

The scope of program testing is just the program module.

Systems testing

The systems testing extends beyond program testing to include:

- Interfaces between programs
- suitability of input documents
- any practical input problems
- availability of information when required
- ability to modify data
- procedures to deal with special situations
- audit requirements
- ability to handle seasonal peaks
- viability of hardware
- practicability of operating procedures.

Testing is normally carried out by feeding test data into the system, and then comparing the actual results with the desired results as the following figure illustrates:

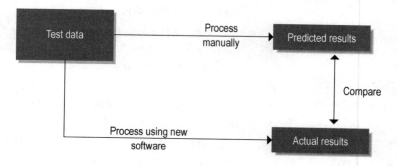

KEY POINT

During testing:

- data should be processed through all stages
- data volume should represent actual transactions
- processing should carried out by the users
- all extremes of data should be used.

DEFINITION

A test script is a list of tests that new software must be attempted on new software prior to that software being accepted as finished.

Test data can be artificial or taken from actual transactions.

It is important the at some time during testing:

- data is processed through all stages
- the data is of sufficient volume to represent actual transactions
- all the processing is carried out by the users, rather then the project team
- all extremes of data are used to test the program suite.

Using test scripts

A test script is a list of tests that new software must be attempted on new software prior to that software being accepted as finished. The script will provide information to the user or programmer, showing precisely the tests to undertake, and how to identify and record error conditions that may arise during the testing.

The actions to take from identifying errors during testing can be explained in the form of a decision table, as shown overleaf:

FOULKS LYNCH
PUBLICATIONS

Module 42 – Payments system																
Value field accepts numbers only	Y	Y	Y	Y	Y	Y	Y	Y	N	N	N	N	N	N	N	N
Value field accepts positive values only	Y	Y	Y	Y	N	N	N	N	Y	Y	Y	Y	N	N	N	N
Value field accepts maximum of 1,000,000	Y	Y	N	N	Y	Y	N	N	Y	Y	N	N	Y	Y	N	N
Value field must be completed during input	Y	N	Y	N	Y	N	Y	N	Y	N	Y	N	Y	N	Y	N
Test passed	X															
Amend exit condition for form		X		X		X		X		X		X		X		X
Amend field properties – maximum value			X	X			X	X			X	X			X	X
Amend field properties – reject negative values					X	X	X	X					X	X	X	X
Amend field properties – accept numeric input only									X	X	X	X	X	X	X	X

The condition stub shows the different attributes of the form that the user must test. This is a system for inputting cheque payments, so those attributes relate to the value of the cheque payments field.

The condition entry shows the normal matrix of Ys and Ns used to determine whether or not the error has occurred.

The action stub shows the action required when different errors are found.

Finally, the action entry shows precisely when each action is required. Note that only when four Ys are obtained can that particular module of the software be accepted.

While this example may be simplistic, it does help to show how decision tables can be used in system testing.

4.2   Performance testing and usability testing

Performance and stress testing

Performance testing evaluates the compliance of a system or component with specified performance requirements.(IEEE).

Performance testing can be extended into **Stress Testing**, which tests the software under increasing workload demands. The initial specification for the software will provide some guidance concerning the numbers of transactions to be placed through that software. However, demands on software tend to increase over time, so it is useful to know exactly how many transactions the software will actually cope with before it 'falls over' or breaks.

In stress testing, the number of transactions is increased until the software effectively breaks. Checking the total number provides a good guide to the limits of the software. This type of testing is frequently used on web sites to try and determine the number of 'hits' that a site can cope with before it breaks. Popular sites must be able to cope with thousands of hits an hour. Stress testing is extremely important in commercial web sites; if the web site becomes unavailable due to volume of hits, then the company cannot make any sales!

Usability testing

Usability testing checks the ease with which users can learn and use a product. Clearly this is subjective, and will depend on the targeted end-user or customer. User interviews, surveys, video recording of user sessions, and other techniques can be used. Programmers and testers are usually not appropriate as usability testers.

User acceptance testing

User Acceptance Testing is an end-to-end test of a system or application, involving the end user, which verifies that the system provides the required business functionality and correctly produces the expected business information. It also allows the user to test the non-functional, or performance, requirements before accepting the system.

User acceptance testing is normally carried out towards the end of the development of the software. Within the V model (see above) user acceptance testing comes after module and systems testing. The main objective of the testing is to ensure that the system specification has been met in the software. Users will have a test script and test data to run against the new software, and note errors or deviations where the output does not meet the original specification.

Where these differences from the specification are found, then difficult decisions may need to be made concerning amending the software, or accepting it 'as is' with an incomplete specification. Amendments at this stage may be difficult, hence the decision to accept with the differences. However, if the V or similar model of systems development has been followed, then situations where the software does not meet the specification should be rare.

5   Use of automation in systems testing

If all testing had to be performed manually, then this would be very time consuming and quite boring (imagine pressing the same key on a keyboard every few seconds for an entire day to run the same program!). Fortunately, a lot of testing can be automated, saving considerable amounts of time, and providing more reliable testing environment. The results of automated testing can also be stored and evaluated statistically to identify trends which could otherwise be missed.

Automated testing means writing a test script in a 4GL which will then automatically run tests such as regression tests on the software that is being developed. Specific activities that the automated testing tool will be able to perform include:

- Record and replay test scripts as required.
- Track, report, and chart all the information about a quality assurance testing p process.
- Detect and repair some of the problems associated software being tested.
- View and edit your test scripts while you are recording.
- Use the same script, without modifications, to test an application on multiple software platforms.

Testing can be carried out by the same organisation that is writing the software; however there are also some specialist software testing organisations that specialise in testing software.

Conclusion

This chapter has explained the importance of testing and checking software to ensure it is as error free as possible, and outlined some of the main techniques that are used to carry out that testing. It is unlikely that you will have practical experience of testing, so ensure that you understand the principles of testing, and can spot weaknesses in any testing system you may find in an examination question.

Quality software

1   What characteristics normally apply to quality software? (1.1)

Quality, quality and more quality

2   What is quality control? (2.4)

Software testing

3   Draw a picture of the lifecycle, linking the testing stages with the development stages. (3.1)

The role of standards

4   Why are standards needed in software testing? (4.1)

QUIP Ltd – Software development

Software in QUIP Ltd is written in-house by a team of five programmers who work in the Software Development Department. The programmers write and maintain existing software programs and extend the range of programs where necessary. Programmers are normally responsible for one or two systems and write, test and install the software onto the organisation's computer systems.

Due to the pressure of work, programmers occasionally take software home on CD/RWs to continue development work on their own computers. As well as extending the working hours, this provides a useful off-site backup for the company's computer programs.

The main computer room is only open during normal office hours, although there are no special control checks on staff visiting this room; the board of QUIP like to promote an open and friendly atmosphere throughout the entire workplace. Programmers do maintain their own password controls over 'their' programs.

Required:

Explain the controls that should be present over the development of programs and access to the system development centre. Your answer should also identify any weaknesses with the software development systems within QUIP Ltd.   **(15 marks)**

Software testing

(a)   Two stages of computer software testing are:
- systems testing
- user acceptance testing.

Briefly describe each of these two stages.   **(10 marks)**

(b)   Certain deliverables in the development life cycle cannot be easily tested because they are in the form of written documentation. This is particularly true of deliverables in the analysis stage, such as data flow diagrams and entity-relationship models (logical data structures).

Explain how the correctness and quality of these deliverables can be checked.

(5 marks)
(Total: 15 marks)

Chapter 16
IMPLEMENTATION METHODS AND ISSUES

This section of the manual discusses the implementation of a new system and the reviews that can take place to determine the success (or otherwise) of implementing that system. The different implementation strategies are discussed, along with the main differences between parallel running and direct changeover. The various reports that can be produced following implementation are also mentioned in this section.

Objectives

By the time you have finished this chapter you should be able to:

- plan for data conversion and creation

- discuss the need for training and suggest different methods of delivering such training

- describe the type of documentation needed to support implementation and comment on ways of effectively organising and presenting this documentation

- distinguish between parallel running and direct changeover and comment on the advantages and disadvantages of each.

1   System implementation strategy

1.1   System implementation strategy

The implementation stage of a computer system can be considered to be a project in its own right. In some very large organisations, some analysts actually specialise in implementation activities. It is the stage when the theoretical design becomes a working, practical system.

It is the user department that carries the major workload here. Without careful planning, the result is always chaotic. This is the most crucial stage in the attainment of a new, successful system and in providing user confidence in it.

It is normal to encounter a variety of problems at the implementation stage of a computer system; the more complex the system, the greater the likely number of problems.

To some extent the problems will be unavoidable. Many, however, can be avoided or lessened by proper planning and control.

The implementation procedures should be designed so that:

- most problems are anticipated and avoided
- the unavoidable problems can be managed.

The prerequisites of implementation are:

- the systems specification must be complete
- programs must be fully tested
- planning must be complete
- the required resources must be available or provided for
- operation techniques must be fully planned
- a fallback system must be fully planned.

1.2   Implementation tasks

The tasks involved in any normal implementation process are given in the diagram below:

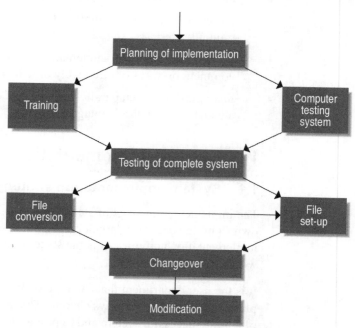

In greater detail, the activities below are linked to the major tasks in the diagram:

- allocating premises
- hardware commissioning
- design/coding/testing or programs
- designing new forms
- staff training
- writing instruction manuals
- production of complete set of systems documentation;
- testing for user acceptance
- changeover planning
- file conversion
- system testing.

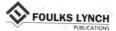

1.3   Staff training and education

People are a vital part of any system. the introduction of a new system must mean changes in roles and relationships and, by their nature, most people resist change.

If the system being introduced is opposed by some or most staff, it is less likely to be successful. A new system may involve the recruitment of new staff, redundancy, or the need for new skills for existing staff.

It is part of the task of the project team to ensure that user staff are involved in the new system from the earliest design stages. Where their jobs change, then the nature of the changes and details of the necessary training should be explained. If redundancies are anticipated, then these should be made clear to staff at an early stage.

The project team should therefore:

- arrange presentations to staff on the use of the new system and the effect this will have on the work. A positive approach is necessary to help alleviate any fears concerning their own employment. Questions should be encouraged

- a training schedule should be prepared and circulated in order that everyone is aware of what is taking place and when

Management's role is to handle the other staff ramifications of the implementation. They should:

- encourage staff to apply for any new jobs created rather then pressurise them into re-training

- provide counselling services to discuss individual fears regarding their future. Re-training in other areas should also be discussed

- ensure staff are re-trained without loss of pay or pressure of work put upon them.

It is useful to send senior staff not directly involved in the operation on computer appreciation courses if they are unfamiliar with such systems. It may also be necessary to recruit specialist staff.

Education complements training: it explains the background to the changes and the reasons for them, providing the foundation for confidence in, and commitment to, the new system. A good deal of educational effort goes into the presentation of seminars to management under such titles as 'What every manager should know about the computer'.

Training is dealt with in more detail later in this chapter.

1.4   Testing

Testing includes both the testing of the individual programs, and the testing of the whole system as an operating entity. Faults not found during testing will reveal themselves more expensively later in the operation. Therefore the testing must be comprehensive. Systems testing was explained in detail in Chapter 11 of this text.

1.5   File conversion

Most commercial systems are file-based, depending on the processing of one or more files. These files must be created before the system is operational. File conversion is the process of moving data from files in the existing system into files in the new system. These files could contain different information, and will be in a different format. File conversion might be from a manual system to a computer system, or from an existing computer system to a new computer system.

Creating the basic data files is an important but often time-consuming task. There are five different scenarios:

1   **The data is available in hard copy.** This data must be collated onto input forms and then entered into the system. This process is likely to be time-consuming and labour intensive and may require the hiring of temporary staff to ensure that data entry is done in a timely manner. If the data entry is on-line, it is often better to use the temporary staff to carry out the ongoing work while the existing staff enter the data. This helps with training and helps test the system.

2   **The data is in hard copy form but some data is missing or incomplete.** If this data is crucial it must be researched or estimated.

3   **The data is fully available on magnetic media from existing applications.** This is the easiest situation to deal with, although it is still important to validate or verify the data after it has been converted.

4   **The data is partially available on magnetic media.** The additional fields should be researched or estimated as in the scenario above.

5   **Part or all of the data is contained in a central database.** The data dictionary must be updated as appropriate.

The main stages are shown in the following figure:

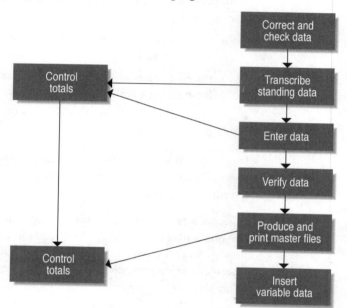

The diagram shows standing (or reference) data being set up first. This produces a skeleton file and can often be done well in advance of the changeover date, as the reference data is static. Only the variable data remains to be dealt with at the changeover date. Skeleton files therefore help to reduce the time pressure of file conversion.

Dead records will be identified and eliminated before conversion. The data must be as 'clean' and as accurate as possible before being printed into the new system.

It is essential that adequate reconciliation details are maintained to agree the old system's control total with that produced by the new system. Control over conversion can be by:

1   **One-for-one checking.** This involves checking each record on the old system to a record on the new system.

2   **Sample checking.** Where numbers are too large for one-for-one checking, statistically monitored samples can be checked.

FOULKS LYNCH
PUBLICATIONS

3   **Control total checking.** This involves checking the total number of records and transaction details from the old to the new system.

4   **Programmed validation.** This involves using a computer program to assist in the conversion, e.g. when converting from a bureau system to an in-house system, a computer program might be used to handle the conversion and reformatting of master files.

When the file conversion is from an existing computer system to a new computer system, program routines will be available (in the case of application software packages) or can be written (in the case of bespoke systems) that will do some of the file conversion automatically.

1.6   Going live

The key moment is when the new system is introduced and goes live.

This moment must be carefully fixed and agreed by all parties involved. It is essential that at this stage:

- all staff training is complete
- all systems are fully tested
- all documents are available for use
- the cut-off procedures on the old system have been properly established.

Accountants will readily appreciate how, unless there is a proper cut-off, transactions could be processed twice, or missed entirely.

It is essential that during the early stages after going live, the new system be carefully monitored to ensure that the data is being properly processed.

There are four approaches to achieving these objectives:

1   **Parallel running.** This involves running the new system in parallel with the old system and making a comparison of the results of both. If the new system performs exactly the same as the old system as far as control details are concerned, then the go-ahead can be given for live running. Despite the theoretical advantages, this is difficult to manage and nowadays is rarely used.

2   **Direct conversion**. This involves the direct conversion from the old to the new system without any parallel running. Direct conversion is often the only practicable approach to conversion although there is clearly the danger that the new system will not work correctly and that the organisation will be in serious trouble. It is essential that the method of control be clearly established.

3   **Phased conversion** is where a complete section of the existing system is run on the new system. This entails a greater degree of safety than a direct changeover with less disruption at any time. The section chosen needs to be a complete section. If that part is successfully run, then other parts of the existing system will be transferred over to be run on the new system, until eventually the whole of the system has been changed over.

For example, if the accounting system were being computerised, first convert the sales ledger. If successful, then convert the stock system and so on.

4   **Pilot operation.** Here, the conversion is carried out department-by-department or branch-by-branch. Thus, if a manual sales ledger is being converted, it might be carried out geographically area-by-area. Each area would be run in parallel until satisfactory, then the manual system dropped and the next area run in parallel.

The actual approach used will depend on the specific application and the existing systems. Direct conversion is simple but can be risky. Other methods are more complex and can sometimes create the problems they are designed to avoid.

1.7 Advantages and disadvantages of some changeover methods

Parallel running

Advantages

Parallel running provides a safer systems changeover environment because a backup system (that is, the old system) is available should the new system fail. Provision of the backup will help to minimise any disruption.

The changeover method is also safer because the output from the new system can be verified as being correct by comparing it to the output from the old system. Direct changeover does not provide this facility as only one system is ever running. Providing this check may mean that initial testing of the system will be less rigorous, as there is the assumption that processing errors will be identified during the parallel run.

Disadvantages

The disadvantages of parallel running revolve around the additional cost and work involved with this changeover method. Additional costs result from having to run two systems in parallel with additional staffing and other resources that this may entail.

There will also be an extra workload imposed on staff. In addition to this costing the organisation more in terms of wages, employees may also become overworked, resulting in errors being made in using the computer system. It may be difficult to identify whether errors actually relate to system weaknesses or human error caused by tiredness.

Direct changeover

Advantages

Direct changeover is one of the quickest methods of systems changeover; basically processing stops on the old system and then immediately starts on the new system. There may be a brief delay while data is transferred between the two systems.

Direct changeover minimises the cost of systems changeover. As there is only one system running at a time, there will be a reduced requirement to pay staff overtime or to hire in temporary staff to help with running two systems at once.

Finally, direct changeover minimises the workload of staff as processing is carried out on one system at a time only. As noted above, the need for overtime working is therefore reduced.

Disadvantages

The main disadvantage with direct changeover is what to do should the system fail. As there will be no backup system in place, the cost of rectification in financial terms as well as loss of business can be extremely high.

However, direct changeover may be the only possible method of changing systems. For example, if systems are not comparable, or to run two separate systems would be confusing, then direct changeover will be used.

2   Training

2.1   The need for training

Training is needed for two reasons:

KEY POINT

Training is needed:

- to ensure staff operate the system correctly

- to ensure staff feel confident to perform their tasks.

- if staff are not adequately trained, they will not operate the system correctly or efficiently

- if staff feel that they are being asked to perform tasks that are outside their capabilities, they may become demoralised and alienated.

Investment in systems will only be worthwhile if the expected benefits that were identified in the feasibility study develop. That is unlikely to happen if training is inadequate and the organisation risks wasting its investment.

Training will be needed when:

- a new system is introduced

- there is a material change to a system

- a new staff member is recruited

- someone's job changes within the organisation

- someone's job changes as part of a general development programme

- reminder or booster courses are needed to keep skills fresh.

2.2   Types and levels of training

KEY POINT

Training is needed at three levels:

- operational

- tactical

- strategic.

You will be familiar with the three levels within organisations: strategic, tactical and operational. The information needs of staff depends on the level at which they are working and their training needs are similarly affected.

Operational staff

Operational staff are mainly responsible for recording transactions. Typically they will be entering amounts into the accounting system, taking telephone orders for sales, etc. Their tasks are routine, repetitive and limited.

Their training will be targeted at the specific skills they need, eg how to enter a sale, or how to answer a customer query about a product.

Tactical level

Staff at this level have some management tasks. Their jobs are more open-ended and their use of computers will have to be more flexible. Typically they will need to know how to operate the management information system. They will probably also need to know how to set up a spreadsheet and simple database.

Their training will be targeted at some specific skills (for the MIS) but also at equipping them with more general skills.

Staff at this level may be in a career structure and some training will equip them for their next jobs in the organisation.

Strategic level

At this level, managers will be using MIS systems, decision support systems and executive information systems. They will need training in how to operate these. It is also likely that they would want some spreadsheet skills.

The types of training outlined above have all been about skills in using computers. However, as managers become more senior they may also need training in how to manage information systems. For example, senior managers should know that it is wise to have a feasibility study before contracting for a new system and that security is an important aspect of any IT system. Therefore, training about managing information systems should form part of a manager's development.

2.3   The training plan

The training plan can be represented by the following diagram:

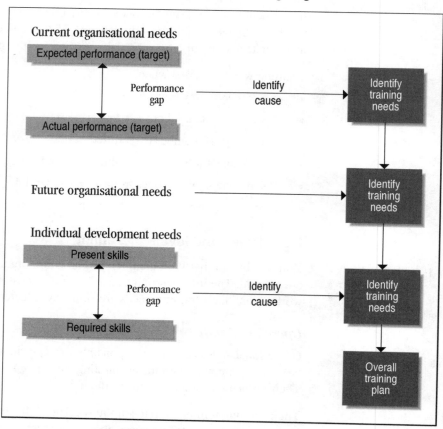

Let's see some examples of training needs:

1   A mail order organisation finds that its level of bad debts is running above budget. It identifies that the principal cause of this is that operators are over-riding the computerised credit limit system.

     The training need is that operators should be told when manual over-ride is permissible. This training could be achieved by a simple memorandum or could be told to the operators during regular staff meetings.

2   An organisation is shortly to introduce a new system. This will require extensive training of all staff who are going to use it. An extensive training program is planned at the offices of the software house who will use case studies to mimic real life scenarios.

3   A young staff member who is on a management trainee scheme will soon be moved to the treasury department. A specific training course is arranged on the operation of the company's cash and foreign exchange management system.

2.4   Methods of delivering training

There are many different methods of delivering training to employees in an organisation. The precise method or methods chosen will depend on various factors including budget, availability of training rooms and simply time available for training at the time of implementation of a new system.

The training methods that can be considered will include the following.

Classroom-based training

Classroom training normally provides use of the real software, but in a training environment. Trainees will be using the real software, but only processing data against dummy or training files specially set up for the course. While the training method tends to be relatively labour-intensive (possibly one trainer to six trainees), it does provide an excellent training environment as trainees can ask the trainer questions and receive an immediate response.

Computer-based training (CBT)

Alternatively, the training course can be produced on a CD; the trainee can then run the course where and when it is convenient for them to do so. While the training method does provide flexibility in terms of location and time, it is expensive and time consuming to produce. The CBT may not use the real software, but rather use prototype screens built into the CBT itself. While this should not be a problem, the functionality of the software will be limited at every stage, limiting the usefulness of the system.

Case studies and exercises

Both classroom tuition and CBT will be supplemented with case studies and exercises based on the processing of the real software. Case studies are essential to the understanding of the software, because they duplicate the processing of actual items in the software. They are usually quite easy to produce and they do help the user understand exactly how the new software will work.

Reference material

Following on from training, some form of reference material will be required so that users can remind themselves of the content of any training course or find more detailed technical information as required. The reference material provided will normally be a mixture of course manual containing the exercises, reference manual explaining how the system works, quick reference card demonstrating shortcuts and commonly used procedures and finally some form of electronic help system. Generally, the more types of material that can be provided the better, because users can then choose their own method of obtaining information about the software.

At desk training

Training can also be provided at the employees' desk as they are using the software. Trainers are employed to 'floor walk', that is, monitor the work of a number of employees for a day and then provide advice and assistance when problems in using the software become apparent.

Alternatively, training can be provided literally at the employees' desk. This gives the benefit of working on the real software, but can be frustrating for the employee and trainer due to distractions from telephones, e-mails and other members of staff wanting to communicate with the employee being trained.

3   Documentation

The word 'documentation' refers to a very wide range of reference materials used in the running and maintenance of computer systems. It takes various forms, ranging from the very technical to the completely non-technical.

The level of documentation will vary according to the situation. Bespoke or internally produced software will require very comprehensive documentation enabling it to be maintained, whereas a package will require only enough documentation to enable the organisation to exploit the package's full capabilities. ISO 9001 requires that that implementation, as with any other quality activity in the analysis and design of a new system, is correctly documented. Similarly, ISO 9000 requires project managers to use those tools and techniques, which they consider appropriate for the situation. So, the scale of implementation may change, and this will result in different standards of documentation being produced; however, that documentation must always be adequate for specific situation.

3.1   Types of documentation

The first category of documentation that must be kept is that which was used in the initial system development process – the feasibility study, system specification, program specification, test data, security precautions, etc.

Details of all changes to the system must be recorded and documented to the same standard as the original system. *All* copies of all documentation must be updated when changes are made. Costly errors too often occur when someone referring to an outdated manual operates the system. Most organisations require changes to be authorised and justified formally.

The second category of documentation is that aimed at helping the users. It includes user manuals, help screens, handy reference cards, CDs and various other references designed to make life easier for the users.

3.2   User manual

During the development of a system it will be necessary to produce documentation to support the system in use, and to aid further development or modification. The user manual is designed to support the training of users, and to provide them with a reference guide in case they experience problems during the operation of the system.

The user manual will be written in non-technical language, and will normally include the following sections.

- system objectives
- system overview
- input stage activities
- processing and storage activities
- output: on screen
- reports
- appendices: a glossary of technical terminology
- input screens, with a completion guide
- sample reports
- error messages, and what to do about them
- fault reporting procedures
- support details and helpdesk contact numbers

3.3   Technical manual

The technical manual is designed to be used by future project teams who may need to fix, modify or upgrade the system. Its language will be far more technical than that of the user manual and its contents will differ.

A typical technical manual might contain the following:

- system objectives
- system overview
- performance specification
- technical specification
- appendices
- data dictionary
- dataflow diagrams, entity models and life histories
- program specifications
- likely upgrades and fixes required in the future
- contact details for the original designers and developers

3.4   Support services

No matter how well trained the users are (see above), the unexpected can still happen, and provision must be made to give the users specialist help as and when they need it.

This specialist help can take various forms. Purchasing staff may be needed to obtain special stationery and supplies. Computer and telecommunications staff may have to deal with hardware problems. Various software specialists may be asked to help users work with the computer operating system, networks and applications software.

Providing users with access to the relevant expertise is an important part of system implementation that is sometimes forgotten. The implementation plan should make sure that whatever support services will be needed are available as soon as the system goes live.

Conclusion

This chapter has explained some of the activities that take place towards the end of a project such as the methods of implementation of a new system and the different reviews that take place. The need for appropriate training was also mentioned with the importance of maintaining appropriate documentation.

Systems implementation strategy

1   What are the main tasks involved in system implementation? (1.2)

2   How can control of system conversion be maintained? (1.5)

3   What are the four main methods of system changeover? (1.6)

Training

4   How is an overall training plan developed? (2)

Documentation

5   What are the normal contents of a user manual? (3.2)

Chapter 17
POST-IMPLEMENTATION ISSUES

This section of the manual discusses the implementation of a new system and the reviews that can take place to determine the success (or otherwise) of implementing that system. The different implementation strategies are discussed, along with the main differences between parallel running and direct changeover. The various reports that can be produced following implementation are also mentioned in this section.

Objectives

By the time you have finished this chapter you should be able to:

- describe the metrics required to measure the success of the system

- discuss the procedures that have to be implemented to effectively collect the agreed metrics

- identify what procedures and personnel should be put in place to support the users of the system

- explain the possible role of software monitors in measuring the success of the system

- describe the purpose and conduct of an end-project review and a post-implementation review

- describe the structure and content of a report from an end-project review and a post-implementation review.

1   System monitoring (system audit or post implementation review)

After the changeover is complete and the new system is running, it should continue to be monitored for a period, to establish whether:

- the advantages claimed for the new system are being obtained in practice

- target dates are being met

- costs are as estimated

- any unforeseen problems have arisen

- redundant work has, in fact, been discontinued

- the outputs of the system (e.g. management reports) are being properly used

- the procedures for detection and correction of errors are working properly

- too many errors are occurring

A company would expect to hold a post implementation audit six months or twelve months after the system has gone live, during which these issues will be examined.

1.1   System evaluation

The main reason for software evaluation is to check that the system requirements agreed at the beginning of any systems project have been met. (See chapter 4 for a more detailed discussion of where system requirements are established.)

Evaluation, or determining the success of the system can be less than straightforward as various aspects of its impact are not quantifiable or easily identifiable. There are, however, some elements, which can provide a useful gauge:

1　**Significant task relevance** considers the effect of using the system. For example, minutes of meetings may be distributed more quickly as a result of introducing electronic mail into the organisation.

2　**Perceived value.** The willingness of user departments to contribute to a specific upgrade may provide a useful indicator as to the value they ascribe to the system.

3　**Systems logs.** In the case of a system which is used on a voluntary basis, systems logs can be used as an indicator as to the value of the system.

4　**User satisfaction.** Asking users for their assessment of the system collects this information. The areas upon which they may be asked to comment could include: quality of output; timeliness; response times; reliability (e.g. a new LAN may be often down with the result that specific applications are not available when urgently needed).

The evaluation process will require careful planning to incorporate a comparison with the previous system. The timing of the evaluation is also important; if the evaluation is undertaken too soon after implementation, the results will be distorted by the effects of introducing any new system ('teething problems'; frustration while users familiarise themselves with something new; the inevitable opposition to change, etc).

1.2　Use of metrics

While it may be tempting to measure 'everything that moves' in a system, it is useful to measure certain key items when checking the success of the particular system. The most appropriate measures for most projects are:

- agreement to original specification
- time
- money
- achievement of financial objectives.

The metrics to be collected will depend on the measures being used to determine the success or otherwise of the system. Where success is measured in terms of achieving the original system specification, then a comparison between that specification and the outcome of the system will provide the appropriate information. No other data collection will be necessary.

However, other objectives such as time and money will require comparisons between the estimated time or budget, and the actual time and money spent. A variance analysis can be produced and reasons for significant variances determined and included in an end-project review.

Other measures concerning the financial success of the project, as outlined above such as payment and NPV or IRR also have specific information that will need to be collected. There may be some element of judgement concerning the appropriate discount rate to use, but otherwise the information should be available.

Other, less quantifiable measures such as *user-satisfaction* or *enhanced customer service* may be more difficult to quantify and measure. However, use of appropriate questionnaires or actually contacting some users directly to assess the impact of any new system or information system can be particularly effective. It is useful to agree the data collection method and metrics to be tested in advance so that there is no dispute later, or an appearance to use the most favourable metrics at the time.

Checking the actual efficiency of a system may take additional work, as outlined in the next section.

2 Efficiency and effectiveness of an information system

The two main objectives of project management are that the process should be effective and efficient. Here, the project to which we refer is the information system.

2.1 Efficiency of an information system project

Efficiency is a measure, or ratio, of the outputs from a process or activity in relation to the resource inputs into that process or activity.

The project can be described as efficient if all stages (development, delivery, installation and implementation):

- are concluded within the constraints identified at the outset, or within the resources specified in terms of manpower, costs and time
- exploit the resources of the members of the project team and the users' time to the full
- avoid unnecessary idle time, delays or wasted time brought about by undertaking unnecessary tasks or activities
- are effective in integrating the activities of the members of the project team, and the interactions and dependencies with other parties outside the project team (users, suppliers, consultants or managers)
- are capable of timely delivery of resources including hardware, software, services and training. Note the use of the word 'timely'; resources must be delivered neither too late nor too early. Resources arriving before they are required may lead to storage problems, deterioration, unexpected fluctuations in planned cash flows and a proportion of the warranty period elapsing before equipment has been used. Much of the benefit of training will be lost if the user is unable to apply the newly acquired skills; therefore delivery of training must be carefully synchronised with the delivery of new equipment or software.

2.2 Effectiveness of an information system project

Effectiveness is a measure of how well or completely a task is performed.

A project can be described as effective if it:

- meets with established objectives including the required needs of the user
- is produced to quality standards that have been specified to satisfy user needs
- can be integrated within existing organisational information systems, structures and processes
- is sufficiently flexible to be capable of responding to changes in the environment in which the system will operate, or to changes in the requirement of the users
- provides appropriate support to decision-makers at all levels – operational, tactical and strategic.

3   Computer-based monitoring

Performance monitoring can be used as an aid in systems evaluation. The main computer-based monitoring methods are hardware monitors, software monitors and systems logs.

3.1   Hardware monitors

The purpose of a hardware monitor is to measure electrical signals in specific circuits of the computer hardware. Based on these electrical signals idle time, the extent of CPU activity or peripheral activity can be measured. The sensors send data to counters, which write to magnetic tape. A program is then used to analyse the data and produce the findings as output. Inefficiencies in performance could be identified in this way.

3.2   Software monitors

The software monitor is a computer program that records data about the application in use. During the monitoring process the application being monitored is interrupted; this results in a decrease in the operating speed of the program. Software monitors might be used to identify excessive delays during the execution of the program.

3.3   Systems logs

Computer systems often produce automatic system logs, the data from which can be useful for analysis of the system. The type of data recorded may be the times a job starts and finishes.

3.4   Evaluating system performance

System performance is the evaluation of all components of an existing system to determine the extent to which existing resources are being utilised and to identify resource deficiencies.

3.5   Measuring and improving systems performance

The main areas an organisation would consider when reviewing the performance of a system are as follows:

1   **Growth** in, for example, transactions processed or the size of files. With this information, trends could be identified, and future growth extrapolated (with caution). These projections could be used to identify any potential problems.

2   **Delays.** Any delays in processing should be identified and the impact of these delays assessed.

3   **Security.** The efficiency of security procedures should be assessed.

4   **Manpower.** The clerical requirements of the system should be assessed, and compared with the estimated requirements.

5   **Error rates.** If these are high, the reason/s should be identified: it may be related to the poor design of input documents, for example.

6   **System amendments.** Are any amendments to the system required?

7   **Output.** An assessment of the uses to which output is put.

8   **System documentation.** Ensuring that the documentation prepared is appropriate and of an acceptable standard.

9   **Feedback from users.** Collating users' views of the system.

10   **Operation running costs.** A close examination of individual processes: the overall costs may be satisfactory, yet costs for individual processes may be excessive.

11   **Review report.** This report should be presented to senior management and should include relevant recommendations.

12   **Unanticipated factors.** Ascertaining whether or not system performance has been affected by any unanticipated external factors.

3.6   Methods of improving systems performance

Outputs of the system

The value of outputs could be improved – with no increase in input resources – if the system was capable of:

- processing more transactions

- producing more management information

- increasing the accessibility of information.

Outputs of little or no value could be eradicated from the system. An example of this might be reports which are distributed too widely, too frequently and which are too lengthy. Input costs should be reduced as a result of this action.

The timeliness and quality of outputs should be reviewed. The information that is available may be out of date or lacking in other ways. The value of the information will often diminish under these circumstances. Access to information could be improved by the use of databases, file enquiry or spreadsheets. The volume of output (e.g. data processing) may be enhanced by altering the equipment used.

Inputs to the system

The systems efficiency could be improved by retaining the same volume of output, but with fewer input resources and at a lower cost. For example:

- operator efficiency can be improved with the introduction of a multi-user system. Unlike a standalone system, the multi-user system facilitates multiple accesses to the same file. Thus, operator effort can be levelled out: an operator with some free time is better placed to help out a colleague with a heavy workload

- upgrading software: a more recent version of a package may provide labour-saving features

- increasing storage capacity of computers: this can help reduce waiting time (e.g. The time taken for a particular file to become available after having been called up)

- the method of input may be changed: shared access to file means data requires inputting only once. This reduces effort and the risk of mistakes.

4   Post-implementation review and end of project reviews

4.1   Post implementation review

A post-implementation review should be carried out a short time after implementation of a new system or a system amendment. Its prime purpose is to establish whether the planned benefits and objectives have been achieved and whether the cost budgets and timetable of the project were met.

If there have been failings, it is important to identify why these have occurred. A knowledge of this will help to prevent similar problems in future projects and may help management to decide what corrective action might be needed now to achieve a satisfactory outcome later.

The typical structure of a post-implementation review report will be:

- executive summary of findings
- a review of system performance and user satisfaction. system performance can be assessed by recording response times, down times, errors. User satisfaction can be assessed by questionnaires
- a cost-benefit analysis comparing actual costs with actual benefits so far identified
- a comparison with the costs and benefits identified at the time of the feasibility study
- recommendations for system modification and for future project management.

4.2   End of project review

An end-of-project (or project closure) review is a meeting held at the end of a project which concludes the project. The objectives of the meeting are to:

- bring the project to an orderly close
- confirm that all planned work has been carried out
- check that all technical exceptions and quality review actions have been closed off
- agree that all the documentation needed to maintain the delivered system is available
- confirm that acceptance letters have been signed off
- review any lessons learnt from the project for future reference.

The review itself is normally attended by the project board, the project assurance team or members of the steering committee and the project manager. A final report on the project will be prepared summarising the key points of the meeting. This report is then presented to the board of directors, or similar controlling group in the organisation, to conclude the project.

An end-of-project review will normally have the following content:

1   **Review of project initiation document**, specifically to note the objectives from the project and check whether or not those objectives have been met.

2   **Performance**. A review of achievements versus original objectives. This review provides a commentary on the way that the objectives were achieved, noting areas such as lack of clarity in objectives or whether information to run the project was made available from project staff.

3   **Productivity**. How efficient the project was in terms of budgets for resources and the actual resources used. Budget comparisons will normally be available for the cost of the project, number of hours spent by the different grades of project staff along with an explanation for significant variances.

4   **Quality** of the product and the process of the project itself. Comments in this section will focus on the appropriateness of the systems used within the project (such as different software packages) and issues of overall project quality caused by lack of documentation or development methods.

Project management review provides a comment on how well the project worked overall, including the effectiveness of the different meetings and other means of communication such as task lists. Any issues regarding staff such as frequent staff changes can also be commented on in this section.

Conclusion

This chapter has explained some of the activities that take place towards the end of a project such as the methods of implementation of a new system and the different reviews that take place. The need for appropriate training was also mentioned with the importance of maintaining appropriate documentation.

SELF-TEST
QUESTIONS

System monitoring

1   What key metrics can be used to measure system performance? (1.2)

Post-implementation review

2   List the contents of a post-implementation review report and an end project review. (4.2)

EXAM-TYPE
QUESTION

Review of implementation

A small chain of four department stores is located in and around a major metropolitan area. The company has recently implemented, in all stores, a point of sale system with linkages to a central computer. Previously, the stores all used conventional cash registers. You have been asked to assess the success of the conversion to the new system.

Produce:

(a)   An evaluation of the various approaches to the system changeover.   **(8 marks)**

(b)   A checklist, in sequence, of the activities likely to be carried out during implementation.   **(4 marks)**

(c)   Suggestions as to how the new system might be evaluated after three months of operational training.   **(8 marks)**

(Total: 20 marks)

Chapter 18

MAINTAINING SYSTEMS

While a lot of the focus on system change is actually designing and implementing a new system, the maintenance of that system and ensuring that the system continues to process correctly are also essential activities. This final section of the book reviews the need for system maintenance as well as reviewing the need to maintain quality throughout the whole project management process.

Objectives

By the time you have finished this chapter you should be able to:

- identify what procedures and personnel should be put in place to support the users of the system
- describe the different types of maintenance that a system may require.
- explain the need for a change control process for dealing with these changes.
- describe a maintenance lifecycle.
- explain the meaning of problems of regression testing.
- discuss the role of user groups and their influence on systems requirements
- describe the relationship between project management and the systems development process
- describe the relationship between the system development process and quality assurance
- explain the time/cost/quality triangle and its implications for information systems projects
- discuss the need for automation to improve the efficiency and effectiveness of information systems management, delivery and quality assurance
- explain the role of the accountant in information systems management, delivery and quality assurance.

1 Systems maintenance

Even after they have been implemented, systems will need to be modified and adapted to make sure that they continue to satisfy user needs. The process of modifying existing systems is termed systems maintenance.

1.1 Systems maintenance

It has been estimated that 70% of software costs are incurred in maintaining existing systems. It is essential, therefore, that maintenance is strictly controlled and effectively carried out. **Maintenance** can be defined as the redoing of certain aspects of the systems development process, which implies that documentation and control procedures should be as carefully carried out as in the initial development of the system.

1.2 Systems redevelopment

Because maintenance costs are such a high proportion of overall software costs, systems analysts will try to build as much flexibility as they can into their systems. This allows changes to be made as easily and cheaply as possible, and helps to ensure that the system can evolve to fit changing needs. Even despite this inbuilt flexibility,

DEFINITION

Maintenance is the redoing of certain aspects of the systems development process..

there will come a time where it is more cost effective to design a completely new system rather than to continue to modify an existing system. This will usually happen when new technology becomes available, or when the old system becomes too unwieldy to run effectively, or when aspects of the system environment (such as the company structure or other computer systems) change drastically.

2 Types of system maintenance

Systems maintenance is often put into four basic categories: corrective maintenance, perfective maintenance, preventative maintenance and adaptive maintenance.

2.1 Corrective maintenance

The elimination of bugs from a system is termed **corrective maintenance**. Although most of the faults in the system should be identified and eliminated during the testing process, problems may be revealed during the operation of the system. In this case the elimination of the errors is likely to be a matter of urgency, since the system will not be fully operational until it has been corrected. Indeed, expensive errors in processing could have been happening for some time.

Corrective maintenance is an expensive process, and an important facet of the design and implementation process is to try to minimise the need for corrective maintenance.

Problems are not solely caused by errors in the programs. Hardware faults can cause damage to files, and faulty procedures or incorrect operation can cause a system to fall down. Suitable back-up procedures may enable the recovery of a system without the need for programmer intervention.

2.2 Perfective maintenance

Perfective maintenance is carried out to improve efficiency or the effectiveness. It may be prompted by the availability of new technology, the development of new techniques, or by a request for system enhancement from the users.

An example of perfective maintenance is the adoption of a graphical user interface (GUI) to make a system more user-friendly.

2.3 Adaptive maintenance

Adaptive maintenance enables a system to adjust to changes in its environment. User information needs may change; organisational structure may be altered; legislative changes may impose new obligations on the software.

2.4 Preventative maintenance

Preventative maintenance is maintenance carried out in advance of a problem occurring, to reduce the risk of that problem. It is the same as having a car regularly serviced in order to reduce the risk of breakdowns. In theory, more preventive maintenance means less corrective maintenance. This is good, because preventive maintenance can be carried out at a time most convenient to the organisation, whereas corrective maintenance always seems to be required during the busiest periods.

2.5 Other forms of maintenance

Sometimes system updates do not fit neatly into the categories that have been defined. The errors caused by incorrect procedures may need perfective maintenance to avoid

KEY POINT

Types of system maintenance:

- corrective
- perfective
- preventative
- adaptive.

KEY POINT

The elimination of bugs from a system is termed **corrective maintenance**.

KEY POINT

Perfective maintenance is carried out to improve efficiency or the effectiveness.

KEY POINT

Adaptive maintenance enables a system to adjust to changes in its environment.

KEY POINT

Preventative maintenance is maintenance carried out in advance of a problem occurring.

FOULKS LYNCH
PUBLICATIONS

recurrence, as well as corrective maintenance to eliminate their effect. The changes required to make a system more user friendly may also need the system to be adapted.

3   The causes of system maintenance

When considering what causes system maintenance, we need to differentiate between the immediate spur to the maintenance activity and the underlying causes. It is important for systems designers to build in mechanisms that identify when maintenance is needed, and to start the process of updating the system.

Both the underlying causes of maintenance and the immediate spurs will vary according to the type of maintenance being undertaken, and each type of maintenance needs to be examined separately.

3.1   The causes of corrective maintenance

The basic underlying cause of corrective maintenance is a system failure of some kind. This may be an error in one of the programs, or it may be that data has become corrupted. Program bugs are likely to be caused by ineffective testing or by the failure to undertake adaptive maintenance when required.

Data problems are caused by:

- human error
- poor documentation
- physical computer faults
- sabotage
- poor training
- inadequate supervision
- sometimes by the unforeseen impact of other computer systems
- malicious damage can be caused to both programs and data.

Whatever the cause, it is vital that problems are identified as early as possible. Gross problems are likely to be obvious to the users who can, as long as suitable reporting procedures have been set up, inform whoever is responsible for maintenance. More subtle errors can have longer-term results because it is more difficult for the users to spot the problems.

One example of an unidentified problem of this kind affected a major international company. One of their systems relied upon a particular file being in strict alphabetical order. Because the system was not adapted to deal with changing conditions, the file had some records that were not in the correct order. The resulting errors were not sufficiently major for the system users to think it worthwhile to report them, but their cumulative effect was very costly.

The problems caused by this incorrect data file could have been nullified by a routine which could validate that it was in the correct format, and in general the best protections against subtle faults are designed into the system when it is first created. The protective measures used may be operating procedures or they may be extra validation programs.

A periodic system audit is another way in which faults can be identified. An analyst will analyse an existing program to make sure that it is still achieving the results that it should do. Although this process can be expensive, it may still be cost-justified.

3.2   The causes of perfective maintenance

Perfective maintenance may be carried out to enable a system to exploit advances in technology, or it may be to make a system more user friendly. IT specialists will need to constantly monitor advances in technology, and their input can be reinforced by including users in the monitoring process. Regular formal and informal user group meetings can be used to help identify when improvements are needed. Questionnaires can be designed to assess user satisfaction with the present system's performance. 'Wish lists' can be compiled.

Perfective maintenance may also be needed when system performance begins to degrade. The system should be constantly monitored against target indices and performance criteria, and action taken when performance declines below pre-set values.

3.3   The causes of adaptive maintenance

There are three basic reasons why adaptive maintenance may be needed:

- user requirements may have changed or have been ill-defined when the system was being designed

- the system environment may have significantly changed

- the system may have grown beyond the limits that were originally envisaged for it.

3.4   Changes in user needs

Changes in user needs may be identified through regular re-assessment of system requirements, or the users may recognise the need for change and request a system upgrade. For example, recent legislation governing financial advisers means that clients' financial details have to be recorded. The need for change may also be predicted in advance, and the integration of IT planning in the general business planning process in an important agent for change

3.5   Changes in the system environment

The system must relate to all aspects of its environment, and any changes must be catered for, whether they are sudden changes or evolutionary development. The application of system theory in the organisation is a useful tool to make sure that these changes are recognised and can be adapted to. For example, the company may have been taken over and data now has to pass to and from head office.

It should be easy to recognise the need to respond to sudden changes such as new legislation, but recognising more gradual changes is more problematic. If the computer system has been defined in systems theory terms, a re-examination of its root definition, boundary and environment will show when adaptive maintenance is needed.

3.6   Adapting to growth

The system will originally have been designed to deal with a maximum number of transactions per day, maximum file sizes, specific code lengths, etc. If these constraints have been properly documented, the system can be modified when required. The problem occurs when documentation is poor, or when no thought is given to system maintenance. The disastrous problem described earlier (of a file not being in alphabetical order) was caused when the need for change was not recognised.

3.7   Management of change

Whatever the reason for the change, full documentation must be kept of any amendment to systems. As well as being required for ISO9000 certification, keeping a record of changes is important for a number of reasons.

To ensure that the systems documentation, both user and technical systems, is updated.

A history of changes made is available, so that the precise date of any change can be found later.

If errors start to occur in another part of the system, these can be traced back to recent changes. Checks can then be made to find out whether the initial system change caused the error.

Authority for each change can be recorded, and the amendment signed off by appropriate personnel.

The record of amendments must also be kept as part of the standard system documentation.

4   The systems maintenance lifecycle

It is important to see maintenance not just as a series of disconnected ad hoc reactions to problems but as a planned, formalised activity that is integrated into the system design process. The actual processes involved in maintenance can be set down as a cycle of activities.

4.1   Planning for maintenance

Good maintenance practice starts within the system design process, and a major objective in planning a new system is to make maintenance as easy as possible.

Flexibility and adaptability are major considerations when building a system. A flexible system can cope with widely varying volumes of transactions and can be adapted to cope with changes in procedures and requirements.

Another major consideration is the recognition of problems when they occur. Validation routines are built into programs to identify when data errors occur and to deal with them where possible. Not only should data be validated as it goes into the system but existing files and data should be checked periodically.

Monitoring the effectiveness and efficiency of a system is an important part of the maintenance process. Each system will have a number of performance indicators that are calculated during each run of the programs and compared with target values. When performance starts to fall below target, investigations can be carried out and remedial action taken if it is needed.

Once an existing problem has been identified, or a possible future problem predicted, action must be taken. Likely problems can be anticipated and contingency plans made during the initial design. Extra storage capacity, for example, can be made available to cope with increasing volumes of data as and when existing capacity is exceeded.

 FOULKS LYNCH
PUBLICATIONS

4.2 The maintenance life cycle

The procedures involved in maintaining software can be presented in the form of a diagram:

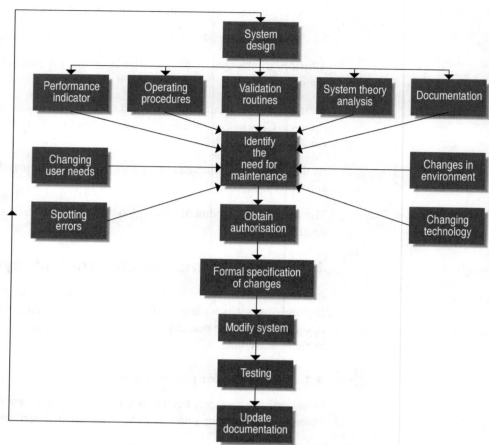

As you can see, the initial design leads into the procedures of actually producing the software along with the performance indicators that will be used to check whether or not the software is actually meeting its requirement. However, the actual need for maintenance can arise from a number of different sources:

Performance indicators show that the software is not running as efficiently as expected. This may be caused by situations such as an increase in the number of transactions being processed or higher volume of network traffic. The reason for the poor performance will need to be identified and methods of improving performance agreed.

Errors may occur, even within the final release of the software! System testing is unlikely to test all possible combinations of use of the different modules of the software, so actual use may still identify some errors.

Changes in the environment may occur, such as different taxation rules making the payroll system obsolete or possibly illegal if the new rules are not followed!

Changing technology may not actually make a system obsolete, but new technology features may be incorporated to make software, faster or provide reports in a more appropriate format.

Operating procedures can change, so making the software obsolete. For example, revised filing systems may make access and amendment of the software difficult. Alternatively, field sizes in the software may be inappropriate and require amendment.

Other issues such as validation routines and systems theory may indicate that the software should be changed to avoid possible error in the future, e.g. possible incompatibility with a new operating system.

Finally, documentation may occasionally result in a change requirement, for example, new forms required by tax authorities may need additional output from the system.

Having identified the need for maintenance, then authorisation will have to be obtained for that change and a formal specification produced. The latter will be needed to help track exactly what changes are being made and so that appropriate testing can be carried out after the change has been made.

After the change has been made and tested, documentation must be updated to ensure that users have full information about any changes made. The whole process can then start again!

5   Regression testing

When software is changed, normally as a result of a problem found during acceptance testing, then in an ideal world, all the tests that have already been performed should be run again; as a result of the change the software is technically a different system. Changes made in one part of a system may have unexpected side effects in other parts of that system. Re-performing tests from the beginning of the testing process helps to ensure that the software has not reverted (or regressed) to a faulty state in any area or section of code. Re-performing of tests is therefore referred to as **regression testing**.

In most situations, regression testing will only be performed on part of the software. Writers of the software are normally able to identify those sections of the software that are most likely to be affected by amendments, and then focus regression testing on those areas specifically. There is obviously the risk that some errors in the software may be missed; however, this risk has to be balanced against the cost of re-running all of the tests on the entire software each time an error is found.

Computer assisted software engineering tools are available to perform some regression testing, and these do help to minimise the risk of missing an error. As noted above, the risk of error cannot be eliminated.

Regression testing is particularly useful where software is developed in modules. Where some modules have already completed their testing phase, regression testing can normally be limited to more recent modules where testing is not complete. As long as all modules pass a final systems test, then additional testing on completed modules is unlikely to be required.

6   User groups and help lines

When users begin to use new software and hardware they will often need help and advice – even if they have had some training. User groups and help lines can provide this.

6.1   User groups

User groups exist for most common packages. The purpose of the groups is to provide help and support to users of the software; they can also act as pressure groups to encourage the software manufacturers to correct or add certain features to their software.

The software company often starts up user groups as they can provide valuable marketing focus for additional products. Membership of these groups is made up of

users from all or most companies that use the package. A committee of users will then normally run the group, rather than the software company itself. Typically, they will organise a series of meetings throughout the year where users can meet each other to discuss the software. Presentations of new software or applications of the software will often be arranged.

Some software companies run users' forums on the Internet or on service providers such as CompuServe. Users can send in queries by e-mail and receive responses from the software house and from other users.

The benefits arising from user groups are that they:

- help to solve technical problems

- aid access to other users who may use the software differently or who may be able to pass on ideas

- increase in enthusiasm and motivation of the software users

- are relatively cheap

- put pressure on manufacturers for new facilities and bug fixes.

6.2   Help lines

Help lines are telephone numbers which users can ring to obtain help and advice on software and hardware. Some software and hardware companies provide help free without time limit, others provide it free for a limited period, and then the user has to take out an annual contract to provide help and backup.

Within an organisation using bespoke software, help line services are likely to be provided in-house, perhaps making use of the company's information centre.

In general, help and advice can be provided in the following ways;

- help screens, ideally context sensitive. Most software now has a help button that allows users to look up an index of topics or search for the occurrence of a term

- tool tips. When the mouse point lingers over a button on the screen, a small sign appears saying what function that button will perform

- wizards – invented by Microsoft, a wizard takes you through a procedure step by step

- help lines (see above)

- documentation

- user groups (see above)

- on-line user forums (see above)

- information centres: in-house expertise that can be called on.

Information centres have increased in importance as personal computers have become more common. Because these computers are relatively cheap, departments are often allowed to look after their own information technology requirements rather than the process being handled centrally through an IT department. This approach, known as end user computing, should give the departments more flexibility to obtain the IT system they need.

However, there are dangers in this approach. The staff in the departments are likely to be relatively unskilled in IT and may make costly mistakes. Two separate departments may duplicate development work. To avoid these dangers, an information centre can be set up by the organisation. This is like an internal IT consultancy and its roles are:

- to provide users with support and training

- to help users develop their own applications

- to advise users on suitable hardware and software

- to co-ordinate the activities of different departments to avoid duplication and to inform other departments of what has been developed

- to ensure that there is as much compatibility between systems as possible

- to advise on security and standards.

Quality assurance in system projects

Quality assurance is the term used where a supplier guarantees the quality of goods supplied and allows the customer access while the goods are being manufactured. In the context of projects, quality assurance can be taken to mean activity checking the system development process at all stages to ensure that appropriate quality control is being exercised.

The organisation may decide to implement some form of quality management system (QMS) to implement and then maintain appropriate quality within the system development process. Adherence to ISO9000 would suggest that this plan is necessary.

After a QMS is established within an organisation, the main method of showing that the system is working is the production of a quality plan for a particular product or project. The quality plan has various direct and indirect benefits including:

- providing a formal definition of how work is to be accomplished

- providing a discipline for the project manager, providing a framework around which issues relating to the project can be considered and address, both before and during the project

- providing a reference point for members of the project team, and

- acting as a bridge between the project team and the board or customer for the project.

There is no agreed format for a quality plan, and so many aspects of it may incorporate into the project plan. However, the plan should fit into the organisation's overall management of quality, and specifically into the quality management system structure, as outlined in the figure overleaf.

Quality management system structure

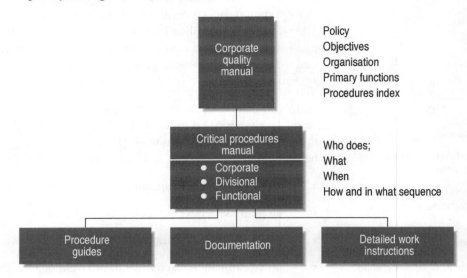

Corporate quality manual — Policy / Objectives / Organisation / Primary functions / Procedures index

Critical procedures manual — Corporate / Divisional / Functional — Who does; / What / When / How and in what sequence

Procedure guides | Documentation | Detailed work instructions

The quality plan will be made available to the client company by the systems analyst as soon as the project starts. The plan then provides quality assurance for the client organisation, as adherence to the plan can be checked as the project progresses. Standard reports back to the client organisation can also comment on the achievement (or otherwise) of quality, and provide suggestions for improvement where necessary.

7 Time, costs and quality triangle

7.1 Project objectives

The objectives of a project must be clearly understood at the outset. Objectives often take three forms, and project management is often a delicate balancing act, as the various objectives normally conflict with one another.

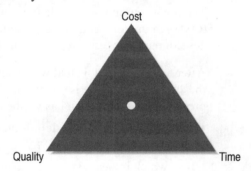

Cost / Quality / Time

The three dimensions of project management objective shown in the above diagram are as follows:

Cost

There are two main aspects to cost that must be considered for any project. In almost all cases there is a budget available for project completion, and the project manager should not exceed the budget without authorisation. This may be very difficult to achieve, as often the budget is set without a clear idea of exactly what is going to be involved in the project. It is not uncommon, as a project manager, to be put in the position of having to make a project solution 'fit' the budget available.

The second aspect to cost is the need, in most projects, to prove that the benefits of the project exceed the costs. This is a major problem because often the costs are all financial or can be stated in financial terms (e.g. the time taken by staff) but the benefits are difficult or impossible to quantify.

FOULKS LYNCH PUBLICATIONS

Quality

Once again, there are two aspects to the quality dimension of a project. Firstly, there are a certain series of tasks or activities to be performed in reaching the project solution. It is important for the project manager to ensure that all the work required is completed; omitting an essential part of the project will have an overall detrimental effect of the quality of the project.

Secondly, each task will have an expected quality level associated with it. It is also important that the tasks are performed well, and that the sponsor's quality expectations are met.

Time

There are also two aspects to the time dimension of a project. Firstly, there is often an overall time constraint on a project (sometimes called a deadline) by when the project must be completed. This may be due to an internal business constraint such as a financial reporting deadline, or an external commercial constraint such as a promise made to a customer.

Secondly, there may be a 'time budget' for the project. This is often expressed in terms of resource availability and measured in person-hours or person-days. This may be due to a resource shortage within the organisation or a constraint placed on a supplier if the project is outsourced to a specialist contractor.

It is essential not only that all the objectives are achieved to the greatest possible extent, but also that a balance is maintained between them (hence the dot in the middle of the triangle).

8   Improving quality assurance

8.1   Automation and quality assurance

While there may not be a specific need for computer assistance in reviewing and monitoring systems, the time and cost savings generated will normally outweigh the initial setting up and running costs of the computer systems. Automation can assist in checking the quality of projects as well as the efficiency and effectiveness of information systems management in various ways.

Providing tools and techniques to assist the project team in the performance of their duties, e.g. project planning software such as Microsoft Project.

Assisting in testing new computer software using computer assisted software testing (CAST) tools. Using these tools will help to improve the quality of the completed software. Computers can perform testing faster and more accurately than humans and so, it is to be hoped, identify more bugs for the same amount of effort!

Monitoring the use of systems and then providing appropriate metrics on those systems. For example, the amount of network traffic can be monitored and displayed reviewed weekly or monthly in a graph or chart. Projections for the amount of traffic will assist in planning for future hardware and software upgrades to systems.

Providing platforms for fourth generation languages to run and the processing power to convert those prototypes into deliverable systems where necessary.

8.2   The role of accountants in information systems management

Even in small businesses, the management will want systems in place to ensure that the information systems within the business are operating efficiently. Part of this assurance can be obtained from the use of appropriate metrics, based on use of the information system, or possibly an analysis of errors produced by the system. Accountants can provide some assistance in checking the information, and specifically, Internal auditors can check whether or not laid down accounting and control procedures are being carried out correctly.

In larger organisations it may be deemed necessary to employ full-time staff to monitor and report on the operations of the company. These accountants are normally called internal auditors. The main differences between internal and external auditors are summarised in the table below:

Internal auditor	External auditor
Responsible to management and is an employee of the organisation.	Independent of the organisation.
Responsibilities are established by management.	Responsibilities are fixed by statute.
Reports to management.	Reports to the members.
Work may be wide-ranging, and determined by management.	Work is undertaken with the primary purpose of enabling him to form an opinion as to whether or not the accounts are true and fair.

9   Maintaining computer systems

When an analyst is designing a new system, he or she must make sure that whatever is set up will work well in practice. All aspects of the system must be considered, not only how the programs link together and data is stored but also the physical security is appropriate. Attention must be paid to avoiding any likely problems and contingency plans made for recovering from any mishaps that occur.

9.1   Recording performance information

The use and performance of a computer system will be monitored. This will help provide information on how well the system is coping with requests from users, as well as identify any systems where additional hardware or software is needed to meet increases in use. For example, an increase in the number of e-mails being sent within the organisation may decrease the response time of the e-mail server. This will in turn delay the forwarding of messages to the intended recipient. Similarly, the sending of large attachments via e-mail to internal or external destinations will increase the amount of work for the e-mail server, and in the case of large attachments, may significantly delay the time taken to send those attachments.

System performance may also deteriorate as additional users are added onto a network. If additional memory and processing power is not made available on the main network servers, then requests from users will take longer to fulfil.

Many computer systems will automatically monitor and record information such as volume of e-mails, number of user requests to a central server etc. Over time, this information provides a picture of past usage, so that future use can be forecast. This information in turn will be turned into plans to increase the memory of certain servers or even purchase new items of computer equipment to cope with the increase in demand. Preventative maintenance is therefore undertaken to ensure that processing can continue.

9.2   Accommodation

Any major new system is likely to need new equipment, which must be suitably housed. Physical safety and security must be designed into the accommodation from the outset, and the analyst must specify these requirements.

Large projects will often require new buildings or major refurbishment of existing premises. Since the lead time on locating sites, drawing up plans, sourcing and getting delivery of equipment and carrying out building work is long, this aspect of project management must be carried out early. It is essential that accommodation is ready when hardware is delivered and installed.

To stress the importance of this aspect of project management, we can examine the disastrous results of neglecting to plan for the physical accommodation of a computer system.

A local government authority had decided to install a major new computer system. This involved the purchase of a new mainframe computer and development of a software system. Unfortunately, when the computer was ready for delivery and the software complete, it was found that no suitable accommodation was available. The preparation of suitable accommodation would take a considerable amount of time and insufficient money was available to fund it. The computer had to be stored and all expenditure was eventually written off at a cost of over a million and a half pounds.

9.3   Security procedures

The design of a new computer system will also involve the specification of operating procedures. These must take into account the need to protect against all of the threats that have been described earlier.

Sentinel programs

Attempts to infiltrate a computer system will often occur at times when the vigilance of the system's operators is relaxed. At these times it is useful to have the computer to watch out for any suspicious activity. Special program routines may be designed to look out for suspicious activity and to alert operational staff when strange transactions are being processed.

Examples of this sort of program are virus detectors, which stay resident in computer memory and suspend activity when something suspicious occurs. Some credit card companies run another example of a sentinel program. An expert system detects when a significant change in a client's spending pattern has happened and warns the credit card company.

9.4   Contingency plans

Contingency planning is an important part of designing and setting up a system. If a physical problem such as a fire would have a potentially disastrous effect, then the organisation must be able to immediately call into effect a contingency plan. The contingency plan chosen may need action to have been taken on an ongoing basis. The use of a computer bureau for back up processing, for example, is likely to require contracts to have been drafted and signed and several other actions to have been taken. Bureau staff may need to have been trained, and a limited amount of processing may be contracted out on a regular basis so that the bureau can take over with the minimum of disruption in the event of a problem occurring.

FOULKS LYNCH
PUBLICATIONS

Conclusion

Systems have to be maintained in order for them to continue working efficiently and effectively. In this chapter, you have learnt the reasons for the different types of maintenance and how appropriate support can be provided to users to help them use the systems correctly. Finally, although they only provide a relatively small input to a project, the work of the accountant and internal auditor was also mentioned.

SELF-TEST
QUESTIONS

Types of systems maintenance

1   What are the main types of system maintenance? (2)

The causes of systems maintenance

2   State the three main reasons that adaptive maintenance may be needed. (3.3)

EXAM-TYPE
QUESTION

Systems maintenance

(a)   (i)   Discuss the need for and the nature of the various types of maintenance.

(6 marks)

(ii)   Explain what is meant by a quality plan.   **(7 marks)**

(b)   From the auditing point of view, explain the need for documentation, and the nature of documentation which should exist for the system.   **(7 marks)**

(Total: 20 marks)

Answers to exam-type questions

CHAPTER 1

EXAM-TYPE QUESTION

IS strategy

There is now a growing recognition amongst organisations of the importance of information as a business resource. It follows, therefore, that the systems manipulating, storing, processing and distributing this resource must not be left to chance.

Information has in the past been collected, stored, processed and dispersed during the course of an organisation's operational activities. However, organisations have seen the introduction of information technology and such systems as management information systems, decision support systems and executive information systems as the means to gain a competitive advantage.

Previously, organisations used computers to perform the mundane tasks and computerised data processing has become a routine function. Generally organisations are now more computer literate and this, together with the low price of hardware and new technology, has made organisations more aware of the competitive advantages to be gained by the correct application of technology and its related systems.

For an organisation to invest in information technology and information systems, it will require some sort of information strategy. The IS/IT strategy would be based upon the corporate strategy, which can be defined by a study of the mission statement.

The mission statement is a statement of purpose by the organisation, and from this the aims and objectives can be ascertained. The aims and objectives state what needs to be achieved and the strategy outlines how to achieve them.

Therefore, before an IS/IT strategy can be drawn up, the corporate strategy must be studied to ensure that they are aligned.

An information strategy will comprise two parts:

1   Organisational – this is the systems management which is concerned with the collecting, processing and distribution of information.

2   Technical – this is concerned with the means by which the information will be collected, processed and distributed.

Strategic planning for IT ensures:

1   Compatibility between the various systems under development and hardware purchased within an organisation.

2   Commitment from the strategic level of management.

3   Resource allocation – the monetary commitment from the organisation.

CHAPTER 2

EXAM-TYPE QUESTION

Centralising IT

REPORT

To: Finance Director

From: A Consultant

Date: 20 April 20X4

Subject: Information Technology Management Structure

Introduction

This report was compiled for Mugen Industrial PLC to recommend a management information structure within the group. It contains an appraisal of the advantages and disadvantages of centralising the management of information technology and includes other relevant, but non-IT factors.

Advantages of centralising the IT structure

The benefits to be derived from a centralised service include:

1   Improved central control with overall co-ordination in the organisation.

2   Company-wide information systems to support and exploit business opportunities, with a common approach to systems development.

3   Centralisation enhances the authority of IT staff and the overall quality of management, establishing company wide technical standards and work procedures.

4   More formalised career paths for IT specialists help attract and retain high quality staff.

5   There may be economy of capital expenditure due to the relatively high cost of computers through having only one computer for use by the group instead of several located in various units.

6   Where one powerful computer is installed, the resultant advantages are increased security, speed of operation, storage capacity and processing capability.

7   Economy in computer operating costs due to centralisation of systems analysts, programmers, operators and other data processing staff as compared with the level of costs that are incurred with each unit in the group having its own computer on a decentralised basis.

8   Centralisation would also facilitate the standardisation of applications but this would depend upon the extent of diversity in the dispersed operations regarding payroll and invoicing structures etc.

9   Centralisation will give greater bargaining power with suppliers of hardware and software. The company may also benefit from a better quality service from suppliers if its purchases are perceived as high value.

Disadvantages of centralising the IT structure

1   It may take longer to get something carried out by a centralised resource over which the user has no direct control.

2   Concentration of resources means that the organisation is more vulnerable to sudden breakdowns than it would be if resource were available in its separate units (which would have enough spare capacity to help one another out in emergencies).

3   Because the centralised staff are taking a broader view, or because they are less attuned to the circumstances of an individual unit, their contribution may be less focused than that of an insider might have been.

4   Users may feel that they lack influence and become unable or unwilling to commit time and resources to developing computer applications.

5   The reduced expertise at local level may result in delays in processing system enhancements.

Non- IT implications for Mugen Industrial PLC

1   The centralised facility can reduce costs and excess capacity, can produce career opportunities for staff, and ensure consistent standards across the organisation. But the decentralised approach may give faster and more relevant service to the users and customers and is less vulnerable to problems involving an equipment failure.

2   Unfortunately, the group is not starting from scratch as far as structure is concerned, because they already have a substantial information system structure in place. This is a decentralised structure where managers are used to taking their own decisions and forming their own IS strategy. It will be expensive and disruptive to change it, especially when the benefits of doing so are uncertain.

3   The organisation needs to assess the criticality of information technology to them. McFarlan's strategic grid could be used to identify their current dependence on information systems. If the subsidiaries' use of information systems is of strategic importance to current or future operations, falling in the strategic or turnaround sectors of the grid, then they are likely to object to centralisation of these aspects of their business. However, if the usage of information technology is in the factory or support section of the grid, then the subsidiaries may not mind the IT operations being taken over by the London headquarters.

4   The existing structure with each subsidiary developing and implementing its own IT strategy to suit the local needs and culture has not been unsuccessful and might be more advantageous in its use of IT to gain local competitive advantage. The trans-border locations of the subsidiaries, with little transfer of goods across national boundaries, would make it difficult to argue for a centralised IT structure with centrally controlled databases of information. Changing the structure of the information technology management, in the hope of reducing costs, would need to be part of the overall IT strategy and its alignment to the structure, taking into consideration the diversity of styles and rate of change throughout the group.

5   A change to centralisation will result in a different management style of objective setting to that of top-down as opposed to bottom up. Mintzberg suggests that the top down objectives and strategies are intended strategy and the bottom up proposals result in emergent strategy. The management's job is to deliver the overall objective required by the organisation in a way that offers the best chance of success – which is that contributed to, supported and believed in by the employees concerned – i.e., bottom up.

CHAPTER 3	EXAM-TYPE QUESTION

National Counties Hotel plc

Memorandum

To: Head Office official

From: Advisor

Date: Today

(a)   The major components in the National organisation appear to be

- each hotel – running the local operation
- head office – co-ordinating and managing hotels; some central bookings.

Within each hotel the sub-systems are:

- the bar – sale of drinks and, perhaps, bar snacks

- the restaurant – sale of food and drink
- room letting – individuals
- room letting – group bookings from tour companies
- the housekeeping department – looks after laundry, cleaning and furnishings in rooms
- conference arrangements – liasing with conference organisers and marketing the hotel's facilities.

All of these areas are closely linked. For example:

- activities in the restaurant will affect bar takings
- lettings and conference arrangements will affect the restaurant and the bar and, for residential conferences, room lettings
- the rooms that can be let to individuals will be sometimes dependent on the rooms that have been let to groups
- housekeeping workload will depend on room lettings.

Each hotel will be linked to head office (many bookings are referred from a central booking department) and will be linked to other hotels in the chain so that onward accommodation can be arranged.

Typically, head office will carry out the functions of accounting, marketing, senior appointments, finance, strategic planning, investment decisions, pricing.

(b)   It is common for guests in hotels to be given a card showing their room number, name and period of residence. Many hotels ask to see this before items can be charged to room accounts.

The card is usually printed as the guest registers and it would be possible to include a bar code on it. This would encode the same information as was printed normally, but could be scanned by a reader each time the guest asked for an item to be charged.

The advantages of this system would be:

- accurate recording of information
- fast recording of information
- valid bar codes can be made difficult to forge
- the card would still be very cheap to produce and could be discarded by the guest after use
- guests should find the system no more awkward to use than conventional cards
- bar code scanners are cheap and can be connected to lightweight, portable recording devices.

If you have any questions regarding the above, please do not hesitate to contact me.

| CHAPTER 4 | EXAM-TYPE QUESTIONS |

Question 1: Cost-benefit analysis

Note: The list of costs and benefits is straightforward. The need to mention factors that could distort the net present value is more complex: think about the problems of calculating NPVs for this type of project.

The costs and benefits associated with a proposed computer system can be divided into two main categories:

1   Installation

These are the costs and benefits involved in the changeover from the existing system to the new one, and will be incurred before the system begins to produce any operational benefit. Costs are likely to include:

- hardware purchase and installation
- software development or purchase
- personnel, including recruitment, training and redundancy
- file conversion
- the use of consultancy or bureau services during the changeover period.

The only benefit to arise at this stage would be the avoidance of renewal or major overhaul costs associated with existing equipment that is being replaced, and the disposal needs of any equipment being sold.

2   Operation

The costs and benefits associated with the operation of the new system will arise from year to year as the system is used. Costs will include:

- any equipment rental, maintenance and depreciation charges
- stationery and other consumables, including magnetic media
- overheads associated with office and computer room accommodation
- recurrent staff costs, such as salaries.

The benefits will consist partly of savings in these costs due to the greater efficiency of the new system, which will be taken into account in arriving at the net operation costs, and partly the information improvement arising from a better system. This benefit is extremely difficult to quantify but without it any analysis is likely to be misleading because it is a major reason for changing processing methods.

The analysis of these costs and benefits using net present value calculations may give an inaccurate result for two main reasons:

- As can be seen from the categories of costs and benefits given above the major costs associated with the changeover are likely to be incurred at the start of the project, while the benefits will arise from the future operation of the system. This means that those benefits will only be experienced if the business has adequate resources to meet the initial costs. Any reduction caused by cash flow problems may make the new system uneconomical.

- The information benefits of the new system are usually very difficult to quantify, and any errors in their estimation may easily distort the results of the analysis, leading to an invalid decision.

Because of this, it is important that businesses should use a range of evaluation techniques and consider all the implications of proposed new systems.

Question 2: Feasibility report

(a)   **Main sections of a feasibility report**

- Objective: what the report sets out to achieve.
- Terms of reference: the limits within which the report has been prepared.
- Method of study: how the study has been conducted.

- Objectives for the system: a statement of the requirements of the company that will be satisfied by the measures contemplated in the report. How the system will work in conjunction with other company systems.

- Alternatives considered: the nature and extent of other systems and methods that were taken into account before the recommended solution was put forward.

- Effect on company operations: the nature, timing and extent of the changes that would occur in procedures, practices and staffing.

- Financial effect: a summary of tangible costs and benefits that would flow from the adoption of the system.

- Achievement of company objectives: a summary of the intangible losses and benefits that would flow from the adoption of the system.

- Conclusion: a recommendation to proceed or otherwise with the system envisaged.

- Appendix 1: Present procedures: anything between a full description and a brief summary and list of working papers that sets out what was learnt about current operations in the course of the study. It is important that volumes and timing constraints are recorded.

- Appendix 2: System as envisaged: behind every feasibility study there has to be a mind's eye system. If that system cannot be implemented for any reason, the feasibility study may be invalidated and this appendix is a record against which any changes can be measured.

(b)   **Financial justification**

Note: In real-life situations, non-accountants with insufficient knowledge of 'true and fair' views often present financial justifications for new systems. In consequence, many are spurious. The title 'financial effect' is used in section (a) above as the word 'justification' assumes that all feasibility reports will make a recommendation to proceed.

There are two aspects to costs: operating costs and development costs. These are the revenue and capital sides of the proposal.

Operating costs: The marginal cost of current operations that would be displaced by the proposal:

- staff costs
- supplies – stationery, etc
- outside services
- space costs
- other

The marginal costs of operations under the envisaged system:

- computer costs
- staff costs
- supplies – stationery, etc
- system maintenance
- other

Development costs

Systems design and development: a cost on a full cost basis from the start of the feasibility study until the system is handed over for maintenance. This heading includes all programming and testing.

Installation costs: preparation costs of the site, delivery charges and other costs arising from any new equipment or computers required.

Capital costs: computers and equipment required for the application.

Launching costs:

- staff training
- file conversions
- systems testing
- parallel running or other change-over costs.

Policy costs: un-recovered costs of incremental capacity increases.

Cost benefits: value of equipment no longer required.

CHAPER 5	EXAM-TYPE QUESTIONS

Question 1: Squiggy

A project normally has a specific purpose, which can be readily defined. The statement from the FD is not specific concerning the systems to be updated or why they actually need updating. Providing this detail is essential to ensure that the project does meet the requirements and a post-implementation review can confirm that the requirements were, in fact, met.

The focus of the project on the Board may be inappropriate. Many projects are *focused on the customer* and customer expectations rather than internal requirements. As information systems area normally designed to provide some form of competitive advantage and provide appropriate customer service, the initial focus must be external. Additional sub-systems to provide Board information can be implemented later.

A project is made up of a *series of activities* that are linked together because they all contribute to the desired result. These activities range from an initial investigation into the existing systems through to implementing a new system. There is no need to stop using the existing system just because a project has started. The project manager will follow a recognised methodology that will allow for an appropriate changeover method, and it is only at this time that some processing ability may be temporarily lost.

Although the project will have clearly defined *time constraints* and a date when the results are required, these are normally suggested by the project manager and then agreed by the Board. To impose a time restriction before the project commences may severely limit the scope of the project as well as providing an information system that may not meet the organisation's needs.

Most projects are *complex* because the work involves people in different departments and even on different sites. Although there is no information about the processing systems within Squiggy, the systems change appears to be quite fundamental and so it will affect many different departments. A project team is likely to be required rather than a single systems analyst.

All projects have *cost constraints* that must be clearly defined and understood to ensure the project remains viable, the FD is therefore correct to start thinking about the cost of the project. However, agreeing a budget before the project is even started may

cause some problems. There is no indication of whether the budget is for analyst costs or to cover replacement hardware/software etc. Setting a budget will normally wait until after a feasibility study; the FD may be wise to obtain a quote for this study first rather than try and constrain the whole project by an unrealistic cost estimate.

While the project will provide opportunities for new working methods, the overall control normally rests with the systems analyst. The analyst will be skilled in the running of projects, and provide a summary report for the Board on progress at agreed times. The Board input will therefore be more strategic in monitoring overall project progress rather than the operational detail.

Question 2: Skills of a project manager

Leadership. Project managers should be able to stimulate action, progress and change.

Technological understanding. Project managers need to have an accurate perception of the technical requirements of the project so that business needs are addressed and satisfied.

Evaluation and decision making. Project managers should have the ability to evaluate alternatives and to make informed decisions.

People management. Project managers should be able to motivate and enthuse their teams and have a constant personal drive towards achieving the project's goals.

Systems design and maintenance. Project managers should be able to demonstrate their individual competence and have a complete working knowledge of the internal administration of their project.

Planning and control. Project managers should be constantly monitoring progress against the plan and taking any necessary corrective action using modern planning and monitoring methods.

Financial awareness. Project managers should be proficient in risk management and have a broad financial knowledge.

Procurement. Project managers should understand the basics of procurement and be able to develop the procurement strategy for their project.

Communication. Project managers should be able to express themselves clearly and unambiguously in speaking and writing and be able to do this in a wide range of situations and with a wide range of people.

Negotiation. Project managers should be skilful in managing their clients and should be able to plan and carry out a negotiation strategy.

Contractual skills. Project managers should be able to understand the contract that defines their project and should be able to manage subcontractors to ensure that the contractual terms are met.

Legal awareness. Project managers should have an awareness of any legal issues that could affect their project.

CHAPTER 6	EXAM-TYPE QUESTIONS

Question 1: Drawing networks

(a)   There are both logical errors and departures from convention.

   Logical errors

   - two start events – 1 and 6
   - dangling activities – H
   - there is a loop joined by activities K, L, M and N.

Conventions broken

- event 7 precedes event 5
- activity J is drawn from right to left.

(b)   There are both logical errors and departures from convention.

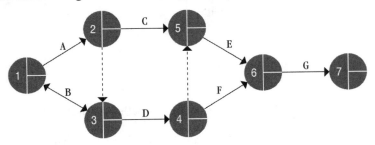

Question 2: Finding the critical path

(a)

Activity	Immediately preceding activity	Start event	End event	Duration (mins)
A	-	1	2	5
B	A	2	3	5
C	B, D	3	5	5
D	-	1	3	15
E	B, D	3	4	10
F	E	4	5	5

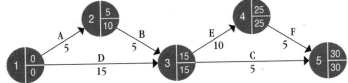

The critical path is DEF, and the duration is 30 mins.

(b)

Activity	Immediately preceding activity	Start event	End event	Duration (mins)
A	-	1	2	4
B	A	2	3	2
C	B	3	5	10
D	A	2	4	2
E	D	4	6	5
F	A	2	7	2
G	F	7	8	4
H	G	8	9	3
J	C	5	10	6
K	C, E	6	10	6
L	H	9	10	3
Dummy		5	6	

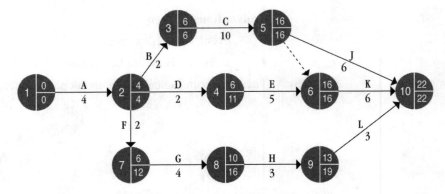

There are two critical paths – ABCJ and ABCK. The total duration is 22 hours.

Question 3: Calculating the float

(a)

Activity	Duration	Manpower	IPA	From	To	Float
A	5	£1000	-	1	2	0
B	2	£200	A	2	3	2
C	2	£400	B	3	4	2
D	4	£1500	C	4	5	2
E	3	£6000	D	5	6	2
F	5	£2000	E	6	7	2
G	5	£1600	E	6	8	2
H	4	£6000	F, G	8	12	2
J	3	£250	A	2	9	3
K	4	£1550	J	9	11	3
L	12	£600	K, M	11	12	0
M	10	£100	A	2	10	0
N	11	£2000	M	12	12	1
Dummy 1	-	-	F	7	8	
Dummy 2	-	-	M	10	11	

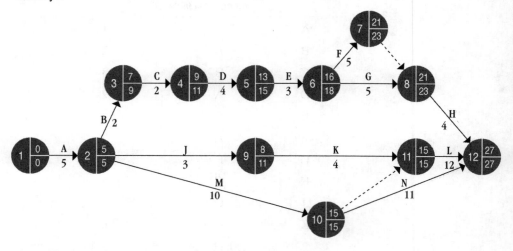

The critical path is AML, the total duration is 27 days.

The total cost is =

£1000 + £200 + £400 + £1500 + £6000 + £2000 + £1600

+ £6000 + £250 + £1550 + £600 + £100 + £2000 + 27 × £1000

= £23200 + £27000

= £50, 200

Increasing D by 2 days will use up the entire float on B, C, D, E, F, G, H but will not increase the total duration.

Decreasing L by 1 day will reduce the total duration by 1 day but will eliminate the float on activity N.

The cost is reduced by £1000.

There are now several critical paths:

A, B, C, D, E, F, H

A, B, C, D, E, G, H

A, M, L

A, M, N

CHAPTER 7
EXAM-TYPE QUESTIONS

WRF Inc

(a + b)   **Report**

To: The Board of WRF Inc

From: Chartered Certified Accountant   Date: 23 May 200X

Subject: Systems development life cycle approach to providing a successful systems changeover

1   Introduction

The systems development life cycle (SDLC) is a disciplined approach to developing information systems. It is a model that is based upon a phased approach. There are many versions of the SDLC, and different terminology may be used, but the basic intent is similar. It covers the following stages:

- requirements and specification
- design
- implementation.

SDLC is the preferred option for the following reasons:

2   The current situation

The systems analyst has prepared the initial proposal; this appears to have been done without following any formal methodology. The systems analyst is on a fixed-term contract that is due to terminate when the system installation is complete. These two factors represent a risk to the successful system changeover: the solution provided may be satisfactory, but is unlikely to be optimal; also the systems analyst's contract may terminate at a critical stage of the development.

Before embarking on the phases of the SDLC, it is worth considering that prior to a new system being designed and built, the existing system needs to be fully understood; therefore, it is important that a study of the current system is undertaken.

3   Requirements and specification

Initially it is important to ascertain the purpose of the new system, what the new system is required to do, and what level of performance is expected etc.

At this stage, business requirements are clearly defined: the inputs, files, processing and outputs of the new system. Resulting from this initial analysis, performance criteria can be set and solutions developed, resulting in appropriate specifications; the specification of a 386 processor running at 20 MHz and 2 Mb RAM running Windows® 3.1 was arrived at because the systems analyst 'thinks the users will require' this.

4   Design

This stage considers both computerised and manual procedures, and how the information flows are used. Computer outputs are normally designed first; inputs, program design, file design, database design, and security are also areas to be addressed.

It will also be necessary to consider operability at this stage i.e., who should have access and capability to do what to which data.

At this stage a detailed specification of the new system is produced. A 386 processor running at 20 MHz may well be considered to be too slow: a 486 processor running at, say, 33 MHz may be necessary to produce the required results.

5   Implementation

This stage may include the building of prototypes and the finalisation of specification requirements e.g., 2 Mb will almost certainly be considered insufficient RAM; 4 or 8 Mb may be deemed more appropriate.

The implementation stage takes the development through from design to operation. This involves acquiring or writing software, program testing, file conversion, acquiring and installation of hardware and training.

When following a formal methodology, implementation and all it embraces should be considered from the initial analysis stage so the likelihood of problems should be substantially diminished.

6   Review and maintenance

This final stage ensures that the project meets with the objectives set, that it is accepted by users, that its performance is satisfactory, and allows for future enhancements and development.

7   Recommendation

It is recommended that the Board of WRF Inc approve the utilisation of SDLC for the systems changeover. Not only does this approach encourage discipline during the development process, communication between the developers and the users, and recognition of the importance of analysis and design, but it also ensures that business needs are met and provides a useful basis for future development.

Signed: Chartered Certified Accountant

CHAPTER 8

EXAM-TYPE QUESTION

Analyst

(a)   The analyst will spend a large proportion of time during the fact-finding stage interviewing users on a one-to one basis. The purpose of the interviews depends upon the level of the person being interviewed:

- If the interviewee is at a senior level, the objectives will be to identify the boundary and constraints governing the study, and to obtain a high level working picture of the current system, and why the changes are needed. Reporting requirements and outputs will be identified.

- If the interviewee is a department or office manager, the information sought will be more to do with inputs and outputs of the department, standards and targets that the system has to meet, and a profile of the main procedures. The manager at this level will also identify the staff that the analyst will need to interview to get a detailed view of the current workings.

- If the interviewee is a 'front-line' worker, i.e. someone who handles the day-to-day transactions, and is involved with dealing directly with the customers (customers of the whole company, or customers of that department's services). This person can describe the detailed procedures to follow, highlight any problems with the way that they are specified or conducted, and give examples of all documentation used.

The interviewer needs to plan the interview programme well. As well as deciding whom to interview, in what order, where and when, s/he must also plan the course of each interview. To help in this task, it is useful to base the questions on Kipling's 'Six Honest Serving Men': What, Why, When, How, Where and Who? These specific questions allow the interviewer to direct very detailed questions, to understand in fine detail procedures, documents, authorities an detailed sets of requirements for the new system.

As well as targeting the information using these specific questions, the analyst must also control the interview by the judicious use of open and closed questions, probing questions, linking and reflective questions.

(b)   If the study involves replacing or enhancing a current system, the analyst needs to use observation to underpin his/her understanding of the system. Formal observation involves the analyst (with the users' knowledge and permission) watching a set of tasks being undertaken, and asking questions about the procedures. Interviewing users at their own site gives an opportunity to observe the working environment informally, looking for signs of bottlenecks, issues relating to ergonomics and local cultural issues.

(c)   If the user population to be interviewed is too large, or split across multiple sites, the analyst can consider the use of questionnaires. Information from questionnaires must be easily analysable, because of the quantity of data that might be collected.

The analyst must pilot the questionnaire before sending it out, to be sure that ambiguities are found first, and loosely worded questions identified and improved. Questionnaires do not always have a high response rate, so if the information is necessary, it is a good idea to have some form of incentive. One reason for low response rates is that the questionnaires can take up too much time for the respondents; it is important, therefore to keep the questions clear

and concise, preferably allowing a multiple choice style, or a 1-5 scale, for speed ease of completion.

(d)   Prototyping means producing a mock-up of the system, perhaps using a tool like Visual Basic to produce screens of the proposed input. This can be used either to design the input screens and user interface, or to confirm the requirements. When a user sees what the computer can do, by means of this mock up, they often think of new requirements. The prototype might consist of a menu screen, with their required functions shown as menu entries.

It is important to manage the users' expectations, as they may assume on seeing the prototype that it is the complete system, and expect to be able to use it straight away. While the response time will be very quick with a single terminal system, if the final system is to be multi-user and multi-terminal, the actual response time may be much slower. The prototype demonstration must take this into account, so that the users are not disappointed with the real working system.

| CHAPTER 9 | EXAM-TYPE QUESTIONS |

Question 1: Process model of a mail order firm

Note: The dataflow diagram drawn below represents the procedures that take place in the existing system. The system represented is the agency system of a mail order firm. The solution offered below is only one solution that might be given. A structured English description would be equally acceptable.

The purpose of an initial dataflow diagram is to illustrate the analyst's understanding of the procedures carried out and to use the same as a means of communication with the user.

(a)

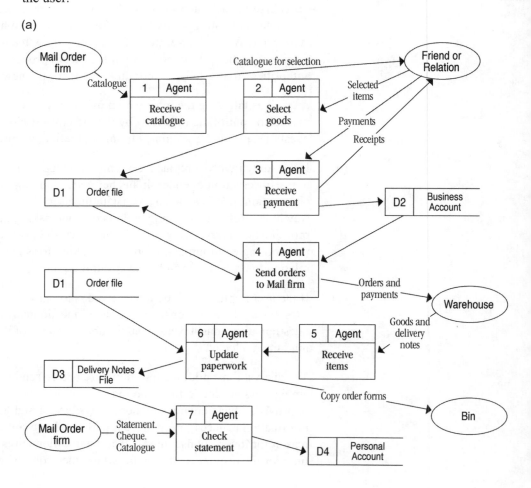

(b)   Two tools that amplify the logic of the processes identified in a dataflow diagram are:

   (i)   decision tables

   (ii)   decision trees.

(i)   **Decision tables**

A decision table is a very simple guide for making decisions in set situations. A decision table is made up of four parts:

1   condition stub

2   condition entry

3   action stub

4   action entry.

The condition stub contains all possible conditions that might occur; the action stub contains all courses of action available. Condition entry specified whether that condition has occurred whilst the action entry marks the action to be taken.

Condition	1	2	3	4
Is it Saturday?	Y	Y	N	N
Is it raining?	Y	N	Y	N
Go downtown	X	X		
Go jogging				X
Study			X	

(ii)   **Decision trees**

A decision tree is an alternative way in which to present the logic of a decision. A decision tree shows courses of action available together with possible outcomes for each course of action.

To describe the various factors influencing a decision two symbols are used, a square to denote a decision point and a circle to denote a 'chance point'.

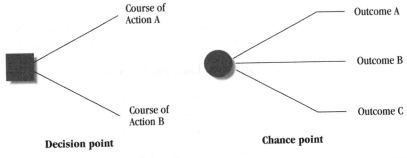

Decision point   Chance point

Note: You could also give the answer to this part of the question in structured English.

Question 2: Limited and extended entry decision tables

Note: This requires modest skill in the use of a decision table. The technique is very easy to learn and the table easy to draw. Again, though, the logic demands intellectual attention. Thankfully, the logic here is straightforward.

(a)   **Discount decision table**

Total order less than £50	Y	N	-	-	-
Account less than 4 weeks in arrears	Y	Y	N	N	Y
Account more than 8 weeks in arrears	N	N	N	Y	N
Bought over £2,000 in 12 months	-	-	-	-	Y
Give 2% discount	X				
Give 5% discount		X			
Pro forma invoice				X	
Add 1 to discount					X

(b)   With limited entry decision tables the entries on the right of the table are always a Y for yes, an N for no or, if necessary, a 'don't care' indication.

With extended entry decision tables the entry to the right may be a value. For example, the entries in an extended entry decision for the example above could have read:

How long has account been overdue?	Less than 4 weeks	4-8 weeks	More than 8 weeks
What is the order value?	Less than £50	£50 or over	

These are entries only, not the logic of a decision table.

(c)   Decision tables help to resolve ambiguities. There is always difficulty in making clear what is to happen if, as in the example, orders are for exactly £50 or arrears are exactly eight weeks. Decision tables make it easy to see that all cases are unambiguously covered.

Decision tables are easy to understand. There is an accepted format for decision tables, so the meaning of the rules can be made clear with fewer words than would be needed in a descriptive solution.

Decision tables can be converted directly into computer programs. There is software available (e.g. Detab) that will accept the rules in decision table format and produce the correct branching structure in the form of a program.

Question 3: Dataflow terms

(a)   An external entity is the instigator, initiator or end user of the systems data. It is a body outside of the system itself, which either provides data for the system or uses data from the system.

(b)   The context level is the very top level of the dataflow diagram. The context level is the starting point. At this level, it is the only process we would expect to see. The context level diagram would therefore contain the process or system being investigated plus the external entities that are the source or destination for the data used by the system.

(c)   Decomposing or exploding is the term used for 'going deeper' into the details of the process. When drawing dataflow diagrams the major functions and processes are looked at first. These are then decomposed into their constituents. Once the context and level 1 diagrams have been drawn, each process within level 1 would be looked at in more detail and a level 2 diagram of each separate process would be produced.

(d)   A top down approach is the term used for starting at the highest level, and working down in a modular format. In other words, a top down approach takes a global view of the system or process and then looks at that system or process in various and increasing degrees of detail. A top down approach has the advantage of enabling rectification and amendments to take place to the dataflow diagram whilst minimising the disruption of the diagram as a whole.

<table>
<tr><td>CHAPTER 10</td><td>EXAM-TYPE QUESTION</td></tr>
</table>

Report layout

(a)   Further standard items might include:

- page numbering convention
- date to which the data in the report refers
- date and time the report was printed
- a standard identifier or code for the report
- distribution list for the report
- source of the data on the report
- standards for spacing between headings and sub-headings, etc.
- standard for denoting the end of the report.

(b)   The usability of the report might be enhanced by:

Re-ordering the columns

One of the main purposes of the report is to compare total stock value with total value at re-order level. It would help if these two columns were next to each other on the report (preferably towards the left-hand side of the layout) as this would facilitate comparison.

Re-ordering the rows

The second main purpose of the report concerns the identification of products that have gone below their re-order level. Products currently fulfilling this criterion appear to be shown by the use of eight asterisks. This is a cumbersome way of highlighting the relevant products. Re-ordering the rows so that all products below their re-order levels are shown at the top of the report would enhance its usability.

Deleting irrelevant totals

The usability of the report is reduced by the production of irrelevant totals such as total cost per unit. This has no logical meaning.

Using spacing and colour

The usability of the report might be improved by using spacing between product groups or (in a re-ordered report) between products that are below their re-order level and those that are not. Colour or emphasised typeface (bold or italic) might also be used to identify the relevant products and to show if the total percentage had exceeded 10%.

Using lines and centring column entries

The usability of the report may be improved by adding lines between the headings and body of the report and adding lines between each column so that the columns are better delimited. Most columns appear to be right justified. It might be more helpful if the column entries were centred.

(c)   A check digit is a letter or number attached to the end of the code to make the code self-checking. The check digit is designed to check for transposition and substitution errors.

Check digit example

(Not necessarily required from the candidate – the question did not specifically ask for an example, but it is useful for revision purposes.)

The code may be 124127 where the last digit (7) is the check digit.

The product code (excluding the check digit) may then be weighted with appropriate weights).

Code	1	2	4	1	2
Weights	5	4	3	2	1
Value	5	8	12	2	2

Total value: (5 + 8 + 12 + 2 + 2) = 29

In the modulus 11 check this weighted total is divided by 11 and the remainder becomes the check digit – in this example: 29/11 = 2 remainder

Locating transposition errors

For example: 121427

Code	1	2	1	1	2
Weights	5	4	3	2	1
Value	5	8	3	8	2

Total value: 26

Check digit: 26/11 = 2 remainder 4. This does not match with the check digit and so the error will be trapped.

Locating substitution errors

For example: 128127

Code	1	2	8	1	2
Weights	5	4	3	2	1
Value	5	8	24	2	2

Total value: 41

Check digit: 41/11 = 3 remainder 8. this does not match with the check digit and so the error will be trapped.

CHAPTER 11   EXAM-TYPE QUESTION

Software packages

(a)   A software package is a generalised software solution usually developed by a software house for sale to an unrestricted business community. Software packages are normally developed for common business applications, such as accounts and payroll, and these are offered for sale to prospective purchasers. The software is not developed against a specific requirement (as in a bespoke solution) but is developed to provide a range of facilities usually required in the business application. It is the responsibility of the buyer to ensure that the functionality of the software fits the specific requirements of their own organisation.

FOULKS LYNCH PUBLICATIONS

A bespoke solution is where a software system has been specifically developed to fulfil a defined business requirement for a specific organisation. In this approach the business develops a functional specification defining the business requirements of the system. Software is then developed from scratch to implement the requirements defined in the functional specification. Bespoke solutions may be developed by a software house or by an in-house information systems department. It is the responsibility of the developer to ensure that the software fulfils the requirements defined in the functional specification.

(b)   **Cost savings**

The software package solution is almost certain to be cheaper than a bespoke solution, particularly at CAET plc where bespoke systems development is performed in-house. This is because the full cost of systems development (specification, programming and testing) has to be completely borne by the organisation commissioning the bespoke solution. In contrast the costs of package development can be spread across a number of customers (or potential customers) so reducing the cost per unit. These cost benefits will also be reflected in reduced maintenance and support costs once the package is operational. This is possible because the cost of providing support and maintenance is shared between all the users of the package. It is also likely that more financing options (such as renting or leasing) will be available from the supplier providing the software package solution. Buying application software packages may also address the year 2000 issue by eliminating year 2000 work on the current systems.

Time savings

The software package is a product ready for implementation. In contrast the bespoke solution has a period of system construction and testing (programming, unit testing and system testing) which will mean that both the effort and elapsed time of a bespoke project is likely to be much greater than that for a software package solution. It is also likely that user requirements will change in the elapsed period of system construction and testing leading to further project problems due to changes (and subsequent implementation delays) in systems requirements. The software package approach will allow the IT department to implement systems quickly, hence exploiting any competitive edge that might exist.

Guaranteed quality

Bespoke systems should undergo unit, system and acceptance testing. However, it is unlikely that all errors will be found in the system prior to software release. It is difficult to ensure that a quality product has been released and consequently the early days of a system's use may be disrupted. This often leads to reduced user confidence in the software and it may prove difficult to restore such confidence. The software package will have also undergone relevant testing but will have been used in other installations and it is likely that most of the errors have already been located and fixed. The users at CAET plc have already complained about the poor quality of bespoke systems and the adoption of the software package approach should address this concern. However, it is worth pointing out that the IT director may be over-stating his case. The packages can seldom guarantee quality!

Prototyping

(a)   **Definition of a prototype**

A prototype is a working system that captures the essential features of a later implementation. It is usually used to verify parts of the system (such as requirements or dialogues) with users, or to prove (or disprove) some concept of idea. A prototype system is intentionally incomplete. It will be subsequently modified, expanded, supplemented or supplanted. Prototypes may be iteratively developed into the final system, so that each prototype represents a stage in the development of the finished product. Alternatively, prototypes may be 'thrown-away' after the objective of the prototype has been achieved.

(b)   **Advantages and disadvantages of a prototype**

Advantages might include

1   **Pleases users**. Users have conventionally had to review paper-based screens and report layouts and sign off requirements and operations that they could not fully visualise. The prototype represents a tangible thing that they can touch and feel and the inputs and outputs of the system are represented in the medium in which they will eventually be used – on a computer screen, not on paper.

2   **Prototyping decreases communication problems.** Training takes place incrementally through the development of the software. Furthermore, excessive documentation is not needed because users gain knowledge of the software through use rather than through reading user manuals.

3   **Reduces marginal functionality.** There is evidence to suggest that prototype systems produce fewer reports and screens programmed to meet the 'I think I need' requirements that often emerge in specified systems. Prototype systems usually contain fewer validations and unnecessary controls.

4   **Prototyping provides tangible progress.** The user can see the progression of the development through a series of usable systems, rather than through abstract diagrams and models.

Possible disadvantages

1   **In most instances the prototype produces a less coherent design** than a system that has been specified. The iteration of the development means that it is difficult to produce an initial design that is likely to be applicable to the final agreed system.

2   **Prototypes can be oversold**. By definition a prototype has limited capabilities and captures only the essential features of the operational system. Sometimes unrealistic user expectations are created by overselling the prototype. This may result in unmet user expectations and disappointment. The system looks ready, but is actually very incomplete.

3   **Prototypes are difficult to manage and control.** Traditional life cycle approaches have specific phases and milestones and deliverables. These are established before project initiation and are used as a basis for project planning and control. Planning and control of prototyping projects are more difficult because the form of the evolving system, the number of revisions to the prototype, and some of the user requirements are unknown at the outset. Lack of explicit planning and control guidelines may bring about a reduction in the discipline needed for proper

management (i.e., documentation and testing activities may be bypassed or superficially performed).

4   **It is difficult to prototype large information systems**. It is not clear how a large system should be divided for the purpose of prototyping or how aspects of the system to be prototyped are identified and boundaries set. In most cases, time and project resource constraints determine the boundaries and scope of the prototyping effort. Moreover, the internal technical arrangements of large information systems prototypes may be haphazard and inefficient and may not perform well in operational environments with large amounts of data or large numbers of users.

(c)   **Useful facilities in a fourth generation language include:**

1   **Integrated screen design tool**. This allows the quick construction of example screens. Many languages allow the developer to construct the screen with the user; it is possible to discuss field positioning, display and validation as they go along. This approach provides effective user involvement and uses the medium (the VDU or PC) that will be used in the final system.

2   **Dialogue design tool**. This will be used for the construction of menus, prompts and error messages. These often change during the development of the prototype and so the language must support flexibility and ease of amendment. To many users the dialogue is the system, and so it must reflect the way users wish to go about their work.

3   **Non-procedural programming code.** Most fourth generation languages have their own development language. This language is usually concise and non-procedural allowing the quick development of programs that might later be discarded. Conventional programming languages are generally verbose and procedural. They are time-consuming to change and hence are not suitable for prototyping.

4   **Object set.** Many fourth generation languages include standard object sets that can be used in the development of the system. Thus a developer does not have to write a printer driver, merely select a printer icon from the object set. The code for printer control is already written in a program attached to this icon. This again allows fast system production.

CHAPTER 13   EXAM-TYPE QUESTION

Disaster Recovery

Disaster Recovery has commissioned a new integrated information system to manage the stock levels, and also to track the whereabouts of volunteer drivers, trucks and aid that is in transit.

Because most of its money is earmarked for disaster relief, the Directors have stipulated a low budget to cover basic functionality, not wanting to divert too much money from the core activity.

You are a consultant working on the specification Write a report for the Directors explaining the technical requirements that the system may need to meet, and explaining why this may demand a higher investment than they wish to make.

DISASTER RECOVERY (DR)

From: IS Consultants Team

To: Directors of Disaster Recovery

Subject: Contingency plans for new information system.

Background

The Directors of DR have proposed a new, integrated information system to monitor and control their stocks of emergency relief supplies. The Terms of Reference stipulate that the cost should be kept as low as possible, in order not to divert DR's funds away from their primary target – disaster relief.

Non-functional requirements

Non-functional requirements are those aspects of the requirements that specify how the system should *perform*. For example, response and throughput times, security and access considerations, availability of systems, usability, ability to handle given volumes of transactions. Because the non-functional requirements involve both design and infrastructure decisions, there may be a cost involved in implementing them.

Response times

The frequency of transactions is not so great in normal times that response times could prove a problem. Most of the routine IS work is concerned with recording supplies and equipment. It is only during the handling of a disaster that the frequency and volumes of traffic increases. Even so, because the work is of a relatively short-lived intensity, there is a case for designing only for the average number and rate of transactions rather than the maximum. This means that a lower specification computer can be acceptable.

Security

The company cannot afford to lose data through mischievous hacking, or infection by viruses, so it should invest in firewall security. Because data entry can take place from remote sites, it must run on a network, either dedicated (expensive) or public (cheaper, but less secure).

The Board must make a decision as to the risk to DR's operations of contamination by a virus, or intrusion by a malicious hacker. If the data held is not personal or financial, the risk of harm is reduced, but as the essence of the organisation is rapid response, there must be a significant investment made to ensure that that response is guaranteed.

Availability

Because the nature of the system means that its use is unpredictable, (i.e. that news of a disaster can occur at any time without warning), it should be available all of the time. This means that if the system should go down for a period, whether through hardware failure or housekeeping procedures, there is a danger that a disaster could be notified during that downtime, and DR be unable to respond until the system is back. All the data regarding equipment and location of equipment would be unavailable, with the possible result of loss of lives. A way to avert this threat would be to have back-up systems working in tandem, so that should one fail, the back-up would be able to take over immediately. This is a very expensive solution, but one that would meet the problem.

The Board must calculate the likelihood of this risk, based upon the number and frequency of disasters that they need to respond to over the course of a year.

Usability

Most of the data input will be performed by dedicated staff in a stable environment, and so usability issues will be relatively minor; however, data will be entered from the field in disaster areas, and so there must be investment in robust equipment that can be taken out to e.g. earthquake zones, and simple data entered quickly and accurately.

Conclusion

Although the Directors wish to spend money only on the core functionality for this system, in order to preserve as much money as possible for the basic activities, they must be prepared to spend money on meeting extra technical requirements to be sure that the system is available when they need it, will be safe from outside attack, and can be operated both from a clean environment at home and a volatile environment in the field.

CHAPTER 14

EXAM-TYPE QUESTIONS

Question 1: Data security

(a)   A logical system involves a system of facilities, developed and maintained for the specific purpose of protecting a database – and in particular the confidential aspects thereof.

Initially it will be necessary to assess the security risks with regard to the computer-based applications: the data may be inaccurate; falsified; disclosed – to unauthorised individuals or to the public at large – or lost.

The next stage will be to classify the data in terms of sensitivity: e.g. public data (giving wide access to read/copy); limited access (e.g. to specific users in the personnel or finance functions); private data (access to identified individuals only).

A logical access system should, therefore, be capable of:

- establishing the user's identity be means of an ID code
- verifying the use, usually by means of a password
- confirming that the user has authorised access to the requested data.

To accomplish this the system should be capable of:

- identifying each user by means of a logical identifier
- matching the identifier with the terminal being used, to ascertain that access is from the authorised location
- controlling access to specified data and resources by users, terminals/computers
- logging accesses and usage of resources, to facilitate auditing.

(b) (i) **Encryption**

Encryption provides a defence to augment physical security measures.

Encryption is the technique of disguising information to preserve its confidentiality; this should occur during transmission and when stored. Encryption derives enciphered text from plain text, thus transforming the latter into an unintelligible form.

The process of encryption and decryption comprises an algorithm and a key; the algorithm is the operation itself, which transforms the data into cipher, and the key controls the algorithm; changing the value of the key can alter the effect of the algorithm so that the conversion for each key value is completely different.

In 1977 a federal standard was established in the US, the *Data Encryption Standards* (DES), which identifies various requirements of a cipher (the results produced should not be distinguishable from random and it should not hold statistical information about the plain text).

Computers, because of their computational power, facilitate sophisticated encryption techniques that would otherwise be unrealistic. The cryptanalyst must devise a system with a cost of decoding which is sufficiently high to deter a potential unauthorised decoder but which has, at the same time, a level of sophistication no higher than necessary as this slows down the processing time – which costs money.

(ii) **Hacking**

Hacking is the deliberate accessing of on-line systems by unauthorised persons. Often this activity is considered by the offender as fun and may often not be done with malicious intent. As modems and micros have become more widespread, the threat of hacking has increased. Many systems now have dial-up facilities due to changing working practices; this facilitates entry into the system by the hacker after the telephone number has been obtained, or by means of an auto dialler. Once a number has been obtained, hackers make them available over the Internet.

A knowledgeable hacker can hide any evidence of their deeds by disabling the journal or console logs of the main CPU.

Once the hacker has gained access to the system there are several damaging options available to him. For example, he/she may:

- gain access to the file that holds all the ID codes, passwords and authorisations
- discover the method used for generating/authorising passwords
- develop a program to appropriate users IDs/passwords
- discover maintenance codes, which would render the system easily accessible
- interfere with the access control system, to provide the hacker with open access to the system
- generate information which is of potential use to a competitor organisation
- provide the basis for fraudulent activity

- cause data corruption by the introduction of unauthorised computer programs and processing onto the system (computer viruses)

- alter or delete files.

(iii) **Computer viruses**

A computer virus is a small program that, having been introduced into the system, proliferates; its purpose is to spread extensively impairing both data and software.

The potential for the damage a virus can cause is restricted only by the creativity of the originator; once a virus has been introduced into a system, the only course of action may be to regenerate it from back up. However, some viruses are written so that they lie dormant for a period, which means that the back-ups become infected before the existence of the virus has been detected; in these instances, restoration of the system becomes impossible.

It is extremely difficult to guard against the introduction of computer viruses. Steps may be taken to control the introduction and spread of viruses, but these will usually only be effective in controlling the spread of viruses by well-meaning individuals. The actions of hackers or malicious employees are less easy to control. Preventative steps may include:

- control on the use of external software (e.g. checked for viruses before use)

- use of only tested, marked discs within the organisation

- restricted access to floppy discs on all PCs and workstations.

Software is written to protect against viruses, but all these may only detect and cure known viruses; they will not restore data or software that has been corrupted by the virus. As new viruses are being detected almost daily, it is virtually impossible for the virus detection software to be effective against all known viruses.

Question 2: Security factors and the Computer Misuse Act

(a) (i) The potential physical threats that an organisation should be aware of are:

Weather. This is a constant threat to buildings; high winds, rain and storms can have a destructive effect on the building which might result in it becoming structurally unsound or be penetrated by water which could cause damage to equipment.

In addition, storms could affect the power supply, by reducing power or by power surges. The company should fit lightening conductors, and anti-surge equipment. Where necessary a back-up generator should also be installed.

Fire. Fire, smoke and excessive heat can all cause damage to sensitive equipment. Data records can also be destroyed by damage causing, at the very least great inconvenience to the company. Precautions should include the use of low-flammable materials and smoke detectors. Water sprinklers may be used in areas where there is no electronic equipment. In addition, back-up copies should be taken regularly and kept at a separate physical location.

Water. This might also be a common threat if the building is situated on low-lying land. Computer rooms should be situated above ground level and flood defences installed.

Environment. High temperatures, dust and static electricity can all affect electronic equipment. Controls should be introduced to minimise the risk from these environmental factors.

Unauthorised access. Entrances and exits to the building should be kept to a minimum. Emergency exits should be alarmed to prevent their use as an illegal back entrance. Guards, receptionists etc, should control public access to the building. Visitors should be issued with special recognition; signature recognition can be used where appropriate as a control measure.

(ii)   Contingency planning is the planning process set up to deal with an unplanned or disastrous event. So far as computing is concerned this usually means the breakdown of the system.

In most businesses very few areas are not computerised or would not be affected by a breakdown in the computing facilities. Organisations now have to cope with unauthorised access to systems and the possible theft of valuable data.

The losses that would be incurred in the breakdown of a computer system would obviously increase with the amount of time it was unavailable; it is therefore important to make plans to keep the computer downtime to an absolute minimum.

Management must fully realise the impact of the loss of computing facilities because any contingency plans will obviously involve considerable expense.

Standby plans to be considered should include:

- the company can set up a distributed support system whereby the work is transferred to another site in the event of computer breakdown

- an arrangement can be made with another company to use their equipment, but this would obviously depend upon their having the capacity available to cope with increased processing

- a spare computer room can be set up in the event of a disaster occurring. This is a very expensive option, but if the computer is vital to the operation of the organisation then this might be the best option

- a portable computer room can be installed on the users site, but there would be a time delay in setting this up.

The key feature to disaster recovery is the regular back up of data and software. Contingency plans must specify the procedures to be taken in the event of computer breakdown, and until normal processing is restored.

The better the contingency plans, the more likely a company will survive a disastrous event.

(b)   **The Computer Misuse Act 1990**

'Hacking' is the term used to describe the unauthorised access to a computer system. Until the *Computer Misuse Act 1990* was enacted, there were no specific laws that adequately dealt with this aspect of computer crime. (The Act received Royal Assent in 1990 and took effect from 29th August 1990.) The act produced three new criminal offences.

The *Computer Misuse Act* now makes it unlawful for anyone to obtain unauthorised access to computer systems. A person is guilty of an offence if he/she 'knowingly' gains unauthorised access into a computer system.

A person found guilty under this offence is liable to a term of imprisonment of up to six months or to a fine, or to both.

If a person gains unauthorised access into a computer system with the intent to commit further offences then the term of imprisonment could reach five years:

- on summary conviction, to imprisonment for a term not exceeding six months or to an equivalent level of fine or to both

- on conviction on indictment, to imprisonment for a term not exceeding five years or to a fine or to both.

In addition, a person is also guilty of an offence if he/she deliberately causes unauthorised modification to computer programs. A person is guilty under this offence if the intention is to prevent or hinder access to any program or data or to compromise the reliability of the data by causing modification of any sort to the computer system.

A person found guilty under this offence is liable to the following:

- on summary conviction, to imprisonment for a term not exceeding six months or to an equivalent level of fine or to both

- on conviction on indictment, to imprisonment for a term not exceeding five years or to a fine or to both.

Any unauthorised act causing actual physical damage to a computer system would also fall under the provisions of the Criminal Damage Act 1971.

Any unauthorised act which causes a computer system to obtain money or property dishonestly would fall under the Theft Act 1968.

Any unauthorised act which intercepts data during its transmission over a public telecommunications system would fall under the Interception of Communications Act 1985.

Question 3: Data protection principles

Note: The format of this answer should be in report style. Fewer marks would be awarded if the answer were to be submitted in essay style.

REPORT

To:

From:

Date: X-X-20XX

Subject:

The following report is in reference to the *Data Protection Act 1998* and its implications to CADS.

Terms of reference

Report requested by the Chief Executive of CADS; to investigate the implications of the *Data Protection Act 1998* on the maintenance of the database and the use of data for direct mailing; investigations undertaken by A. Consultant – conclusions and recommendations called for:

Findings

(a) **Part I – Requirements of the Act**

1　It is required under Schedule 1 of the *Data Protection Act* that all data users who are in control of personal data must register with the Data Protection Commissioner.

2　All registered data users must comply with the data protection principles.

3　It is a criminal offence not to register.

4　Security for personal data is the responsibility of the data user and must only be used within the terms of the agreed registered entry.

(b) **Part II – Data protection principles**

1　The information to be contained in personal data shall be obtained, and personal data shall be processed, fairly and lawfully.

2　Personal data shall be held only for one or more specified and lawful purposes.

3　Personal data held for any purpose shall not be used or disclosed in any manner incompatible with that purpose.

4　Personal data held for any purpose shall be adequate, relevant and not excessive in relation to that purpose.

5　Personal data shall be accurate and, where necessary, kept up to date.

6　Personal data held for any purpose shall not be kept for longer than is necessary for that purpose

7　An individual shall be entitled:

- at reasonable intervals and without undue delay or expense:
  - to be informed by any data user whether he/she holds personal data of which that individual is a subject
  - to have access to any such data held by a data user
- where appropriate, to have such data corrected or erased.

8　Appropriate security measures shall be taken against unauthorised access to, or alteration, disclosure or destruction of, personal data and against accidental loss or destruction of personal data.

(c) **Conclusions**

From the above, it has been concluded that membership lists are excluded from the *Data Protection Act*. This exclusion only applies if the lists contain only names and addresses. However, the data that would be held on the membership database would relate to more than just the name and address of the individual and is, therefore, not exempt from registration.

CADS should be registered as a data user with the Data Protection Commissioner.

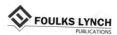

It has also been concluded that it is the legal duty of the user (CADS) to ensure the security and safety of all personal data. Also, the data held should be checked for relevance and accuracy.

All members will need to be notified that their details are being held on a database and that they are at liberty to check those details if they wish.

As far as supplying data to other organisations is concerned, it could only be supplied if it had been originally stated that it was to be obtained for that purpose. This is considered to be unlikely.

Recommendations

CADS should, if it has not already, register under the *Data Protection Act.*

Notification should be sent forthwith to all members asking them whether they object to their names and addresses only being supplied to other organisations and giving them the option to have their name and address deleted from any such mailing list.

Ensure that any mailing list contains no more data than names and addresses.

Signature

CHAPTER 15

EXAM-TYPE QUESTIONS

Question 1: QUIP Ltd – Software development

(a) **Control over development**

At the initial development stage, rules should be established relating to who will be permitted to access, add, change or delete data. The system should be fully tested, and special software is available to assist such testing. It is clearly preferable for both internal and external auditors to be consulted fully at this development stage. This is particularly important as QUIP has software written in-house.

(b) **Division of responsibilities**

The data processing and other administrative staff are likely to have clearly segregated functions. It is important however for adequate supervision in places where administrative staff have access to terminals.

There may be a lack of division of responsibilities within QUIP, especially where programmers write and install their own programmes. Programming errors, fraudulent or otherwise, may not be detected due to the lack of review controls.

(c) **Physical access restrictions**

Terminals should be kept in rooms that are locked when the terminal is not in use. Operators may be issued with a terminal key and unauthorised personnel should have access to the terminal restricted. Controls that are more stringent may be provided at the computer centre through the use of special keys, badges, closed circuit television, etc.

The directors need to strike an appropriate balance between allowing a friendly working atmosphere and promoting appropriate security. Allowing access to any employee may result in programs being copied or amended without appropriate authority being provided.

(d)   **Logical access restrictions**

Logical access to the data can be restricted by the use of passwords. Each operator has his or her own password, which allows the use of certain terminals and allows access only to certain data held on the computer. Different passwords may be used to either read data from a file or write data onto a file. Clearly the distribution of passwords should be carefully controlled and any attempted violations should be recorded by the operating system, reported to management and thoroughly investigated.

It is not clear how effective password controls are within QUIP. Care is needed to ensure that employees do allow other programmers to access program code they are writing to allow appropriate access in case of emergency.

Taking work home may provide a security risk, especially where the programmer is working on confidential information or software. Care will be needed to ensure that home computers have appropriate anti-virus software installed, and that copies of QUIP programs are removed from these computers. Home PC's are likely to have fewer controls over access than office based PCs.

(e)   **Program documentation**

Full documentation of amendments to programs must be maintained. This provides an audit trail to show what amendments have been carried out. Similarly, system documentation should be complete and updated for any amendments that do take place. This will allow other programmers to access the program code and make further amendments as and when necessary, and also to check the code for errors, if the need arises.

(f)   **Back-up facilities**

The usual need to retain security copies of files by regular dumping routines applies in on-line systems. Copies of all programs should then be maintained at a secure off-site location – preferable not a house of one of the programmers.

There may be a good case for having standby terminals and power supplies.

(g)   **Computer log file**

A sophisticated on-line system will maintain a computer log file that is used to produce statistics of all activities in the system. This file can highlight downtime, operator efficiency, unauthorised attempts to gain access to data, and may be a powerful tool for management control, especially where other controls over the system are quite weak.

Question 2: Software testing

(a)   **Systems testing**

Individual programs are usually tested by the programmers who wrote them and by their team leader who has certain testing responsibilities. Once a program has passed, program or unit testing it is passed on for systems testing. Systems' testing is usually undertaken by a systems analyst or project leader.

Systems' testing considers whether the individual units or programs fit together properly. In doing such tests the analysts will wish to verify that the programs interact successfully (passing data from one to the other) and correctly.

Systems testing will also usually consider the error trapping and reporting facilities of the system. Consequently, the tester will enter values that will cause the system to fail or undertake procedures that will lead to sudden or unpredictable failure – such as switching off the machine in mid-process. The systems tester will also need to ensure that the error reporting messages are correct and that appropriate messages are displayed.

The systems tester may also take responsibility for ensuring that the interface is consistent (for example, the same function key is always used to quit the system) and, where appropriate, it conforms with agreed industry conventions and standards.

Finally, systems' testing ensures that the system fulfils its functional requirements (as defined in the systems specification). It is the last chance to do this prior to the release of the system out of the department to its user.

User acceptance testing

After the completion of systems testing the system is passed on for user-acceptance testing. In this stage, users, or their representatives, are asked to formally consider whether the system fulfils their requirements. In theory users should evaluate the system against the formal specification (defined in entity-relationship models, dataflow diagrams etc.) they approved earlier in the project. In practice, it is the time when deviations between the system's operations and user's actual requirements become known.

User acceptance testing will consider the functional characteristics of the system but it is unlikely to replicate the detailed range and format checks undertaken in systems testing. By this stage users should expect error-trapping to work successfully. In contrast, user acceptance testing will focus on the usability of the system, checking that the natural flow of the business process is reflected in the way that the software works.

User acceptance testing may also be concerned with:

- testing and agreeing cyclical activities (such as end of month and end of year routines)

- testing and accepting generalised housekeeping functions (such as back-up and restore)

- testing and accepting documentation.

(b)   **Systems testing**

Systems and user acceptance testing is usually undertaken for physical working deliverables – programs or systems whose behaviour can be executed and documented. For example, a program to calculate the average price of timber can be tested to see if it performs (by not failing during operation) and that it performs the calculation accurately. This procedure is not always possible for deliverables early in the systems development life cycle – such as dataflow diagrams and logical data structures. Consequently these are usually reviewed in structured walkthroughs. A structured walkthrough is a formal meeting where a product is presented and checked for its:

1   **Functional accuracy.** This is usually undertaken by the user representative at the walkthrough. Their role is to confirm that a business process has been properly understood.

2   **Technical accuracy and adherence to standards.** A standards or audit representative is present to ensure that the product meets the quality standards defined in the methodology.

The walkthrough may also be attended by the presenter or author of the product, a chairperson and a scribe. The product will be formally accepted at the meeting or referred back for further work.

Walkthroughs are also appropriate for testing working deliverables such as programs and systems and so they are appropriate in all stages of the systems development life cycle. However, many analysis deliverables can only be checked by walkthrough – execution testing is just not possible.

CHAPTER 17	EXAM-TYPE QUESTION

Review of implementation

(a)   **Essentially, there are four approaches from which to choose:**

Direct changeover

The existing system is abandoned for the new at a given point in time. *Prima facie* this seems an economical approach, but this is balanced by the risk that the new system will not work perfectly. Furthermore, there will be no safety net, in terms of existing procedures and staff, with which to recover the situation. It is not suitable for large systems crucial to the well-being of the organisation. If the new system bears little or no similarity to the old, this may be the only route. In the context of the department store, it should be obvious that this is not a viable option; if the new system collapses, then the store potentially loses all sales until it is remounted.

Parallel running

This involves the running at the same time of both old and new systems, with results being compared. Until the new system is proven, the old system will be relied upon. This is a relatively safe approach, which also allows staff to consolidate training in the new system before live running commences. It is expensive, however, because of the extra resources required to run two systems side by side. Parallel running is necessary where it is vital the new system is proven before operation. In the case of the POS system, this would be the most suitable method of changeover.

Phased changeover

Here the new system is introduced department by department, or location by location. This is less drastic than direct changeover, and less costly than parallel running, although each department may still be parallel run. For the department store group it might well be a sensible approach to introduce the new POS system into just one store, initially, and parallel run at that store first, before switching to phased changeover, and subsequently to implementation at all other stores.

Pilot changeover

This is another compromise approach, involving the running of the new system, or functions/subsystems thereof, on a sample of users, transactions, files, etc. in parallel with the new system. This might be followed by full parallel running, or a switch to phased changeover. Care must be taken with the choice of sample. The nature of the new system here makes it unlikely that this approach could be adopted.

Whichever approach, or combination of approaches, is adopted, good management control, including thorough monitoring, will be essential if the new system is to be successful.

(b)   **Checklist of implementation activities should include:**

- development of a changeover timetable
- involvement of all affected personnel in planning
- advance notification to employees, followed by periodic progress bulletins
- development of training programme
- consider possible needs for external resources
- delivery of POS equipment
- testing of equipment
- installation and testing of software
- completion of documentation
- training for systems operators
- system trials
- changeover period
- acceptance of new system
- operational running.

(c)   **Systems evaluation**

This is a vital and important part of system implementation. Its objective is the systematic assessment of system performance to determine whether the established goals are being achieved.

Several criteria are commonly used to measure the performance of the systems:

Time, i.e. the time required for a particular action to be performed. Response time is the time that elapses before a system responds to a demand placed upon it; for the POS system, this must be measured in seconds. Turnaround time is the length of time required before results are returned; for a POS system, little processing is done, and this may not be significant.

Costs, sometimes the only measure applied, are used to determine whether the various parts of the system are performing to financial expectations, and include labour costs, overheads, variable costs, maintenance costs, training costs, data entry costs, data storage costs, etc. For the POS system, all of these should be considered.

Hardware performance should be measured in terms of speed, reliability, maintenance, operating costs and power requirements. The performance of the POS devices in the various store departments, the central computer servicing the POS system and any networking components must be evaluated.

Software performance should be measured in terms of processing speed, quality and quantity of output, accuracy, reliability, maintenance and update requirements. Again, this is necessary for all software involved in the POS system.

Accuracy is a measure of freedom from errors achieved by the system and can be measured in several ways; but it is important that the type of errors as well as volume is analysed to ensure that serious errors are quickly identified. In the POS system, it is essential, for example, that the prices charged to customers are accurate.

Security means that all records are secure, that equipment is protected and that unauthorised or illegal access is minimised. It is important that the central database containing product prices is not corrupted, for example.

Morale is reflected in the satisfaction and acceptance that employees feel towards their jobs. Absentee rate and employee turnover are two factors that can be used to assess morale of the POS operators in the stores.

Customer reactions are an important factor in the context of the POS system; large numbers of complaints from customers would indicate that the system is not performing satisfactorily.

All the data gathered from the various components of evaluation should be studied to assess the success or otherwise of the system and, if the latter, to help pinpoint the reasons why performance is not reaching expectations.

CHAPTER 18	EXAM-TYPE QUESTION

Systems maintenance

(a)   (i)   The term 'maintenance' is normally used to describe the process of modifying a system after it has been implemented and is in use, i.e., to correct errors and provide new facilities.

Maintenance falls into three categories. These are:

- perfective maintenance, which encompasses changes demanded by the user; 65% of maintenance is perfective

- adaptive maintenance, which is caused by changes to the system environment; 18% of maintenance is adaptive

- corrective maintenance, which is the correction of previously undiscovered errors in the system; 17% of maintenance is corrective.

(ii)   It is impossible to produce a system of any size and complexity which does not need to be maintained. Over its lifetime, its original requirements will be modified to reflect changing needs, and obscure errors will emerge. Because maintenance is unavoidable, systems should be designed and implemented so that maintenance problems are minimised.

In the context of a system which has only been in operation for six months, it is not likely that adaptive maintenance plays a significant part – it is too soon, given no substantial changes in the environment, for this to arise.

If the system has been implemented without sufficient liaison and contact with users, and they were not given the opportunity to finally approve the systems, then it is quite possible that in many ways it does not satisfy their requirements, or they find it difficult to use and they are now demanding changes.

Similarly, if the system has been implemented without adequate testing, then the first six months is the period during which this omission will become clearly apparent, as errors are discovered during operational running.

Three areas need to be examined to discover the cause of poor performance. In terms of hardware, a particular component may well be of crucial importance, and may well act as a bottleneck in a particular system, e.g. the printer in a system requiring a lot of high quality printed output, or the CPU in a system carrying out many complex mathematical calculations. Other typical hardware bottlenecks include the speed of communications links and disk drives.

A second area is that of software performance, which may be affected by the number and complexity of the programs; the amount of memory required, the accuracy and precision of the programs making up the system, and the ease of maintenance of the system.

Finally, the operation and management of the system may have an effect on the performance of the system. Relevant factors here include the way the system is configured, the complexity of the security procedures for the system, and the attitudes and abilities of the computer operations staff.

(b) The nature, size and scope of a system determine the optimum amount and scope of documentation. The following points summarise the case for good system documentation:

- to enable analysis, programmers, users and computer operations to communicate
- to assist in the detection and correction of errors in the system
- to facilitate revision of modifications to the system
- for use in the training of users and operations staff
- to ensure consistent application of maintenance throughout the system
- to assist auditors in the computer audit process.

Documentation can be categorised into:

- systems documentation, which describes the overall function and dataflow in a system
- program documentation, which includes program specifications, program listings and sample input/output
- operations documentation, which relates to the day-to-day running of the system, and provides operators with guidelines on how to run the system
- user documentation that provides users with the information required to interface properly with the system.

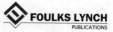

Index

 FOULKS LYNCH PUBLICATIONS

FOULKS LYNCH
PUBLICATIONS

TEXTBOOK REVIEW FORM

Thank you for choosing the Official Text for the ACCA professional qualification. As we are constantly striving to improve our products, we would be grateful if you could provide us with feedback about how useful you found this textbook.

Name: ....

Address: ....

....

Email: ....

Why did you decide to purchase this textbook?

Have used them in the past	☐
Recommended by lecturer	☐
Recommended by friend	☐
Saw advertising	☐
Other (please specify)	☐

Which other Foulks Lynch products have you used?

Examination kit	☐
Distance learning	☐
Lynchpins	☐

How do you study?

At a college	☐
On a distance learning course	☐
Home study	☐
Other	☐

Please specify ....

Overall opinion of this textbook

	Excellent	Adequate	Poor
Introductory pages	☐	☐	☐
Syllabus coverage	☐	☐	☐
Clarity of explanations	☐	☐	☐
Clarity of definitions and key points	☐	☐	☐
Diagrams	☐	☐	☐
Practice questions	☐	☐	☐
Self-test questions	☐	☐	☐
Layout	☐	☐	☐
Index	☐	☐	☐

If you have further comments/suggestions or have spotted any errors, please write them on the next page.

Please return this form to: Veronica Wastell, Publisher, Foulks Lynch, FREEPOST 2254, Feltham TW14 0BR

Other comments/suggestions and errors

ACCA Order Form

4 The Griffin Centre, Staines Road, Feltham, Middlesex, TW14 0HS, UK.
Tel: +44 (0) 20 8831 9990 Fax: + 44 (0) 20 8831 9991
Order online: www.foulkslynch.com Email: sales@ewfl-global.com

Examination Date:
Jun 04 ☐
Dec 04 ☐
(please tick the exam you intend to take)

		Textbooks	Revision Series	Lynchpins	Distance Learning Courses
		£20.95	£11.95	£6.50	£95.00
Part 1					
1.1	Preparing Financial Statements (UK)	☐	☐	☐	☐
1.1	Preparing Financial Statements (International)	☐	☐	☐	☐
1.2	Financial Information for Management	☐	☐	☐	☐
1.3	Managing People	☐	☐	☐	☐
Part 2					
2.1	Information Systems	☐	☐	☐	☐
2.2	Corporate & Business Law	☐	☐	☐	☐
2.2	Corporate & Business Law (Scottish)	☐			
2.3	Business Taxation – FA 2003	☐	☐		☐
2.3	Business Taxation – FA 2003 (Hong Kong)	☐			
2.4	Financial Management & Control	☐	☐	☐	☐
2.5	Financial Reporting (UK)	☐	☐	☐	☐
2.5	Financial Reporting (International)	☐	☐	☐	☐
2.6	Audit & Internal Review (UK)	☐	☐	☐	☐
2.6	Audit & Internal Review (International)	☐	☐	☐	☐
Part 3					
3.1	Audit & Assurance Services (UK)	☐	☐	☐	☐
3.1	Audit & Assurance Services (International)	☐	☐	☐	☐
3.2	Advanced Taxation – FA 2003	☐	☐	☐	
3.2	Advanced Taxation – FA 2003 (Hong Kong)	☐			
3.3	Performance Management	☐	☐	☐	☐
3.4	Business Information Management	☐	☐	☐	☐
3.5	Strategic Business Planning & Development	☐	☐	☐	☐
3.6	Advanced Corporate Reporting (UK)	☐	☐	☐	☐
3.6	Advanced Corporate Reporting (International)	☐	☐	☐	☐
3.7	Strategic Financial Management	☐	☐	☐	☐

Postage, Packing and Delivery:

Textbook & Revision Series	First	Each Extra	Lynchpins	First	Each Extra	Distance Learning (Per subject)	First	Each Extra
UK	£5.00	£2.00		£2.00	£1.00		£6.00	£1.00
Europe (incl ROI and CI)	£7.00	£4.00		£3.00	£2.00		£15.00	£2.00
Rest of World	£22.00	£8.00		£8.00	£5.00		£40.00	£5.00

Postage, Packing and Delivery

Product Sub Total £.............. | Post & Packing £.................... | Order Total £.................... | **(Payment in UK £ Sterling)**

Customer Details
☐ Mr ☐ Mrs ☐ Ms ☐ Miss Other ....
Initials:.................... Surname: ....
Address: ....
....
....
Postcode: ....
Telephone: ....
Fax: ....
Email address: ....

Delivery Address – if different from above
Address: ....
....
Postcode: ....
Telephone: ....

Payment
1 I enclose Cheque/Postal Order/Bankers Draft for £........................
Please make cheques payable to '**Foulks Lynch**'.
2 Charge MasterCard/Visa/Switch card number:

Valid from: | | | | Expiry date: | | | |

Issue no: (Switch only)

Signature: .... Date: ....

Declaration
I agree to pay as indicated on this form and understand that
Foulks Lynch Terms and Conditions apply (available on request).
Signature: .... Date: ....

Notes: Prices are correct at time of going to print but are subject to change

For delivery – please allow:
United Kingdom – 5 working days
Eire & EU Countries – 10 working days
Rest of World – 10 working days

Notes: All orders over 1kg will be fully tracked & insured.
Signature required on receipt of order. Delivery times subject to stock availability. A telephone number or email address is required for orders that are to be delivered to a PO Box number.